Russian Opera and the Symbolist Movement

California Studies in 20th-Century Music

Richard Taruskin, General Editor

Russian Opera and the Symbolist Movement.

SIMON MORRISON, S.A.

University of California Press

BERKELEY   LOS ANGELES   LONDON

University of California Press
Berkeley and Los Angeles, California
University of California Press, Ltd.
London, England
© 2002 by the Regents of the University of California

Library of Congress Cataloging-in-Publication Data

Morrison, Simon Alexander, 1964–
    Russian opera and the symbolist movement / Simon Morrison.
        p.   cm. — (California studies in 20th-century music ; 2)
    Includes bibliographical references.
    ISBN 0–520-22943-6 (alk. paper)
    1. Opera—Russia (Federation)—20th century.   2. Symbolism
(Literary movement)—Russia (Federation)—History—20th century.
I. Title.   II. Series.

ML1737.5 .M67   2001
782.1'092'247—dc21

                                        2001003293

Manufactured in the United States of America

11   10   09   08   07   06   05   04   03   02
10   9   8   7   6   5   4   3   2   1

The paper used in this publication meets the minimum requirements of
ANSI/NISO Z39.48–1992 (R 1997) (Permanence of Paper). ∞

08/02

For Melanie

Contents

Acknowledgments

I am deeply grateful to Carolyn Abbate for her essential guidance in developing and improving the dissertation on which this book is based. I am also indebted to Caryl Emerson, who gave the dissertation a critical reading and directed me to crucial primary and secondary sources. For indulging my obsession with the Russian Symbolists and strengthening my work on them, I could not have asked for more inspiring advisors. My special thanks to Richard Taruskin, who helped edit the dissertation for publication, offered corrections and refinements, identified lacunae in the arguments, and was unwavering in his support. I am also grateful to Marina Frolova-Walker for her recommendations concerning the book's organization and to Angelina Shapoval, Michael Wachtel, and Leonid Yanovsky for their assistance with the Russian-language translations. My thanks, finally, to Mary Francis and Mary Severance of University of California Press for shepherding the manuscript to publication.

The research was conducted in Moscow, St. Petersburg, and London in 1995 and 1996 with the support of a Charlotte Elizabeth Proctor Honorary Fellowship and an American Musicological Society Dissertation Fellowship. I am grateful to the staffs of the Russian State Archive for Literature and Art (especially Elena Gafner), the Glinka Museum of Musical Culture (Irina Medvedeva), the Scriabin Memorial Museum (Olga Tompakova), the Russian National Library, and the Prokofiev Archive at Goldsmiths College, University of London (Noëlle Mann). I am indebted to Marina Rakhmanova and the late Marina Sabinina for their wise counsel on the original dissertation proposal, which I read and defended before a friendly crowd at the Institute for Art Research in Moscow on 14 June 1995. I am also grateful, in various ways, to Victoria Adamenko, Alla Bretanitskaya, Britta Gilmore, David Kasunic, Alice Nash, Galina Zhitina, and especially Victor Peters.

Two sections of this book have appeared previously in print: chapter 3, in an earlier guise, as "Skryabin and the Impossible," *Journal of the American Musicological Society* 51:2 (1998): 283–330; and part of chapter 4 as "The Third Version of *The Fiery Angel*" ["*Ognenniy angel:* tret'ya versiya"], *Muzïkal'naya akademiya* 2 (2000): 221–28. I read a draft portion of chapter 4 on 9 November 1996 at the American Musicological Society annual meeting in Baltimore and on 28 December 1996 at the American Association of Teachers of Slavic and East European Languages annual meeting in Washington, D.C. At the invitation of Boris Gasparov, I also read a draft portion of chapter 2 on 21 November 1997 at the American Association for the Advancement of Slavic Studies annual meeting in Seattle. Finally, I presented a version of chapter 1 in colloquia at University of California–Davis on 27 April, University of California–Berkeley on 28 April, Stanford University on 1 May, and University of North Carolina–Chapel Hill on 27 October 2000. The responses to these talks shaped my thinking on several fronts and find reflection throughout the text.

Note on Dating
and Transliteration

The Julian calendar (marked "O.S." for "Old Style") was used in Russia until 1 February 1918, and remains the calendar of the Russian Orthodox Church. On that date, the Gregorian calendar (marked "N.S." for "New Style") was decreed the official calendar, and 1 February became 14 February 1918. Since the Gregorian calendar had been in use in Europe and America long before 1918, Russians would frequently double-date their letters and diary entries, especially when traveling abroad. To avoid any confusion, in this book dates are specified according to the calendar in use in Russia.

The system of transliteration employed in this book is the system designed by Gerald Abraham for the *New Grove Dictionary of Music and Musicians* (1980), with the alterations introduced by Richard Taruskin in *Musorgsky: Eight Essays and an Epilogue* (1993). The principal benefit of the system is that it allows for the consistent representation of adjectival and noun endings. For example, ии, the genitive singular of the noun ending ия, is denoted by *ii*, while ий, the genitive plural, is denoted by *iy*. The Russian letter ы is represented as *i*.

Following Taruskin's example, in the main text I have chosen to use commonly accepted spellings of Russian names and places (e.g. "Scriabin," not "Skryabin"), the sole intentional exception being the replacement of "Tchaikovsky" with "Chaikovsky," a more accurate transliteration in English. I use the surname suffix -*sky*, as opposed to -*skii* or -*skiy*, and omit soft and hard signs. In the bibliographic citations, where adherence to Cyrillic orthography is most useful, the transliteration follows the Abraham system (e.g. "Prokof'yev," not "Prokofiev"). Here, surname suffixes are represented in full, and soft and hard signs retained.

Finally, the transliteration of the *Preparatory Act* libretto in the appendix reflects current Cyrillic spelling, rather than Scriabin's pre-1918 orthography.

Introduction

This book concerns the efforts of Russian composers to create Symbolist operas, efforts that were evaluated in their own time as successes, as failures, and, perhaps most frequently, as successful failures. The four composers in question occupy different places in the history of Russian Symbolism. The first, Pyotr Chaikovsky, was prescient, anticipating, rather than actually joining, the movement; the second, Nikolai Rimsky-Korsakov, was resistant, conceiving his penultimate opera as a rationalist and realist reaction to Symbolist decadence, yet nonetheless succumbing to it in the end. The third composer, Alexander Scriabin, was obsessive, extending, in his metaoperatic project, the precepts of Symbolism to hazardous extremes. And the fourth composer, Sergey Prokofiev, was parodic: his third completed opera constitutes a modernist response to the atavism and excesses of the Symbolist movement. Despite the pronounced stylistic and technical differences between the composers, their creative activities provide case studies of the amazing potentials and equally amazing pitfalls of the Symbolist enterprise. On one level, their works affirm that music, inasmuch as it defies the barrier of meaning, can invoke the otherworldly; on another level, their works attest to the insurmountable barrier between the representation of the miraculous and its enactment.

Russian (and, for that matter, French) Symbolist opera does not travel lightly: each of the operas featured in this book carries an enormous amount of philosophical and aesthetic freight. For this reason, in the first half of this introduction I will provide a brief overview of the Symbolist movement that will define the musical symbol versus the poetic symbol, evaluate the relationship between Symbolist writers and musicians, and outline the contents of the book. In order to clarify and extend some aesthetic and theoretical observations, in the second half of the introduction I will

1

summarize the solitary and unique effort of a Symbolist poet to create a Symbolist opera, *The Rose and the Cross (Roza i krest)*. The core of this drama might best be described as an impossible song intended to transport its hearers, willingly or unwillingly, into a trance-like state.

THE MUSICAL SYMBOL

The Russian Symbolist movement is often divided into two generations of writers: the first, "decadent" generation includes the poets Konstantin Balmont (1867–1941), Valeriy Bryusov (1873–1924), Zinaida Hippius (1869–1945), and Dmitriy Merezhkovsky (1865–1941); the second, "mystic" generation includes Andrey Belïy (1880–1934), Alexander Blok (1880–1921), and Vyacheslav Ivanov (1866–1949). The list is far from complete, and the division between the generations is inherently artificial, since the "decadents" and "mystics" worked with each other and Symbolism occupied only part of their careers. But one generalization can be made: whereas the first generation found inspiration in French Symbolism, the second found it in German idealist philosophy. Bryusov's activities centered on enhancing the perceived musicality of poetry through the manipulation of sonorous word combinations. He similarly employed ambiguous and suggestive words that, he deduced, referred back to an essence, a universal meaning beyond the power of language itself to express. From the French Symbolists, he determined that there were three interrelated genres of Symbolist poetry. The first genre includes "works that give a complete picture, in which, however, something incompletely drawn, half-stated, is perceptible; as if several essential signs are not shown."[1] Bryusov cites the sonnets of Stéphane Mallarmé (1842–98) as examples. The second genre includes "works which have been given the form of a complete story or even drama, but in which separate scenes have a significance not so much for the development of the action as for a certain impression on the reader or viewer." Bryusov does not furnish an example of this genre, but he likely had in mind the drama *Pélleas et Mélisande* (1892) by Maurice Maeterlinck (1862–1949), which he translated in 1905, and which Claude Debussy had previously turned into the preeminent Symbolist opera. The third genre includes works that "appear to you to be an unrelated grouping of images." Bryusov here cites Maeterlinck's "Hothouse Bloom" ("Serre chaude") the opening poem in *Hothouse Blooms (Serres chaudes*, 1889), Maeterlinck's first collection of poetry. The emphasis in Bryusov's three-part schema is on the Symbolist poet's unique perception of the world and the symbol's capacity to disclose the hidden content or inner essence of reality. By revitalizing conventional verbal syntax (this being confined to outer appearances and rational thought) Bryusov sought to cultivate a poetry of pure suggestion. Within his verses, he made fleeting allusions to ancient legend and ancient history, broke apart lines of verse into discordant and concordant phonemes, and relied upon such irrational adjective-noun pairs as "satin gardens" ("atlasnïye sadï"), "violet hands" ("fioletovïye ruki"), and "chocolate skies" ("shokoladnïye neba").

Like Bryusov, Belïy aspired to liberate art from formalist constraints; unlike the older poet, however, he sought to engage art with religious and political causes. Belïy interpreted the Symbolist movement as a Gnostic journey toward a syncretic, pluralistic existence. He derived his thinking from an eclectic assortment of philosophical sources—some Western European, some Far Eastern, some cultivated in the soil of his own nation. From German classical philosophers, he gleaned that the nature and function of a symbol differed fundamentally from that of an allegory. On this point, he referred to two famous aphorisms by Johann Wolfgang von Goethe (1749–1832): "the allegory transforms the phenomenon into a concept, and the concept into an image, but in such a manner that the concept can only be stated, confirmed or expressed in the image in a way that is always limited and incomplete"; and "the symbol transforms the phenomenon into an idea, and the idea into an image, but does this in such a way that the idea in the image has infinite repercussions, and remains intangible; even when expressed in every language it will always remain unexpressed."[2] From German idealist philosophers, Belïy also gleaned that the symbol had the potential to render the immaterial material. "The aim of [Symbolism]," he declared, "lies not in the harmony of forms, but rather in the visual actualization of the depths of the spirit."[3] The formalist definition of the symbol as a multivalent, multi-interpretable device became entangled in his imagination with religious concepts of transubstantiation, pagan beliefs in magical spells, and medieval occult doctrine. Belïy and his "mystic" Symbolist colleagues fantasized that their activities would precipitate the spiritual transfiguration of the world, although, inevitably, they differed on the actual date of its occurrence. For Belïy, Avril Pyman explains, "art was but one flank, albeit a most important one, of the intellectual army he was mustering for the redemption of all culture." "For Ivanov," she continues, "art was a temple or sacred grove of the spirits to which the poets, a chosen company, should be drawn to celebrate half-forgotten gods—a sanctuary of recollection to which, one day, all people would follow." Finally, "for Blok, art like life itself was a hell which must be traversed in order to emerge—somewhere beyond art—into the unimaginable light of a new Eden, a New life."[4]

The distinction between the "decadent" and "mystic" Symbolists—exemplified in this brief overview by Bryusov and Belïy—thus rests on the distinction between an interpretation of the symbol as a device for suggestion and allusion on the one hand, and, on the other, as a device for disclosure and revelation. According to the first generation poets, symbols stimulated the imagination, invoking ancient times, recalling forgotten experiences, and, as a consequence, temporarily renouncing reality for dream, cognition for intuition. According to the second generation poets, symbols had the capacity to transform reality, to make the familiar unfamiliar (a notion later adopted by the Russian Formalists), and to have a narcotic impact on the psyche. Bryusov considered Symbolism to be magical: the symbol was apparitional and incantational, leading the reader on imaginary journeys to other times and places. Belïy, in marked contrast, considered himself to be magical, a divine creator capable of giving material form to the postulates of knowledge, of summoning different worlds into being. Steven Cassedy notes that Belïy, like the other "mystic" Symbolists, "assigned himself the same power of God in the logology of Eastern Orthodoxy: by pronouncing the Word (Logos), which then becomes incarnate, he (He) is creating a concrete 'world' reality that exists as a hypostatic emanation of his (His) own being."[5] Bryusov, as a "decadent" Symbolist, did not share the spiritual fervor of his young colleagues. However theirs, not his, were the views that garnered attention as the Symbolist movement matured and that eventually captured the imaginations of composers.

Of the various reasons for the collaboration between poets and musicians, the most basic was a shared interest in resurrecting the theatrical practices of the ancient Greeks, practices which, in the poets' opinion, facilitated communal bonding and could, if reconstituted, enable society to regain lost unity. It was a fantasy akin to that which had obsessed Giovanni Bardi (1534–1612) and Jacobo Corsi (1561–1604)—the two members of the Florentine Camerata whom the Russian Symbolists occasionally cited—and that led to the creation of opera at the end of the sixteenth century. In "The Poet and the Mob" ("Poet i chern," 1904), Ivanov argued that the memory of the ancient bond between artists and the masses survived in legends and myths. As the designated custodians of these legends and myths, the "mystic" Symbolists set out to create ritual-based dramas that would resurrect the forgotten heritage. The endeavor became all-important to poets who emerged as a cultural force during a period of political and spiritual crisis in Russia and who sought through their art to bridge the chasm that had opened between the ruling elite and the rural populace, Church and State, adherents of theological doctrine and adherents of bourgeois morality. Although ridiculed by their opponents (one of them being Rimsky-Korsakov), the "mystic" Symbolists clung to the belief that communal art represented a possible solution to the problem of social disintegration. Ivanov, placing his rather dubious hopes for spiritual synthesis on the music drama, embraced the theory of art developed by Nietzsche in *The Birth of Tragedy* (*Die Geburt der Tragödie*, 1872), specifically the idea that artistic creation was regulated by "Apollonian" and "Dionysian" principles, the former comprising "dream," the "plastic energies," the "immediate apprehension of form," and "individualism," the latter comprising "drunkenness," "enchantment," "reconciliation" with nature, and "Primordial Unity."[6] Music, as the most "Dionysian" art, generates a multiplicity of meanings, which lead, ultimately, to an all-encompassing meaning. In "The Hellenic Religion of the Suffering God" ("Ellinskaya religiya stradayushchego boga," 1904), Ivanov speculated that "perhaps once again genuine tragedy will arise from the matrix of music; perhaps the resurrected dithyramb will 'prostrate millions in the dust.'"[7] He implies here that music might one day form the basis of a universal drama.

Though fanciful, these abstract theoretical musings influenced actual operatic composition. It inspired, for example, innovations in the handling of operatic time and space relationships and touched off dreams of expanding stage action to encompass what had previously seemed unencompassable. In Russian Symbolist opera, the past, present, and (even) future intertwine, with each musical, verbal, and visual level pockmarked with allusions to the others. The central images are those of falling and rising: fiery angels descending earthward and the religious faithful ascending heavenward.

The origins of Russian Symbolist opera reside less in mythic Greece and mythic Russia than in the *Festspielhaus* at Bayreuth. Richard Wagner's music dramas were a colossal influence on the "mystic" Symbolists, chiefly for their verbal imagery (the references to omnipotent swords, endless nights, and grail pilgrimages), but also for their "symbolic" leitmotifs. They were venerated as well for their acoustic novelties: those moments in the scores that evidence disdain for secure semantic communication, where meaning becomes unclear, hence evocative of hidden ideas. The best examples of these effects are the unsynchronized horns, the frequent mishearings and misquotations, and the act III *alte Weise* of *Tristan und Isolde* (1859). Wagner's music dramas in large measure inspired Belïy to musicalize his poetry by freeing it from conventional rules of meter (writing lines of varying length and cadence, usually not rhymed) and by experimenting with so-called verbal leitmotifs (unifying his works by repeating, intact or in variation, sonorous word and syllabic groupings). His experiments resulted in four verbal "symphonies": the *1st (Northern and Heroic) Symphony (Severnaya simfoniya: 1-aya geroicheskaya, 1900)*, the *2nd (Dramatic) Symphony (Simfoniya: 2-aya dramaticheskaya, 1902), The Return: 3rd Symphony (Vozvrat: 3-aya simfoniya, 1905)*, and *The Chalice of Blizzards: 4th Symphony (Kubok meteley: 4-aya simfoniya, 1908)*. Referring to Belïy's turn-of-the-century memoirs, Rosamund Bartlett, author of the first comprehensive study of Russian Wagnerism, explains that "with phrases as his material . . . [Belïy] wished 'to proceed as Wagner had done with melody,' using the themes as a 'strong line of rhythm' that would absorb subsidiary themes 'according to the rules of counterpoint.' Elsewhere he declared that the subjects of his first four books had been drawn from 'musical leitmotifs.'"[8] Roger Keys adds that the plots of the "symphonies" tend to be cluttered, as Belïy endeavored to shake the reader's confidence that events would unfold logically. These texts, however, achieve order on another level. In the *1st (Northern and Heroic) Symphony*, for instance, Belïy combines a cluster of "negative" leitmotifs (images of lonely people and barren vistas) with a cluster of "positive" leitmotifs (pious rituals and radiant sunsets). The resulting mixture reflects Belïy's dream that "the confusion and purposelessness of earthly life" would be "resolved in a higher, cosmic or spiritual purpose."[9]

The motivating force behind Belïy was Emiliy Metner (1872–1936), a notoriously anti-Semitic lawyer and music critic obsessed with Wagner's *Der Ring des Nibelungen* (1874).[10] Metner divided his friends and enemies into Wälsungs and Nibelungs, related events in his life to events in Wagner's narrative, and even associated shifts in his mental and physical health with the content of different leitmotifs. Concerning the Wälsung leitmotif, for example, Metner told Belïy: "You know, I once fell ill . . . before I became ill, the Wälsung theme arose involuntarily before me: tam-ta-ta-tam . . . ta-tam-tam."[11] Just as Metner cast himself as the tragic figure of Siegmund, Belïy adopted the heroic guise of Siegfried, plotting to vanquish his artistic foes in defense of his philosophical beliefs. In doing so, he hoped to dissolve the border between art and life, imagination and reality. Such intentionally preposterous role-playing games were typical of the "mystic" Symbolists, who described them as vehicles for changing social alliances. Participating in one another's fantasies, they elevated the experience of being in love into religious ecstasy and their creative journeys into spiritual pilgrimages. Together, they considered themselves to be martyrs in an epic struggle for the future of Russia. The music drama, they declared, could serve as the vehicle for religious and political change. Pyman notes that during the 1905 St. Petersburg performance of *Der Ring des Nibelungen,* "Wotan was clearly identified with the old regime, Siegfried, the smith's apprentice, with the people, and Brünnhilde—at least to Blok, Bely, and Lyubov [Mendeleyeva], who attended the theatre together—with the World Soul, more specifically the soul of Russia about to be awakened from an enchanted sleep."[12]

With regard to the overall structure of Wagner's scores, the Symbolists dwelled on the deployment of the leitmotif as a mnemonic device and the depiction of events on multiple dramatic planes. Following a January 1901 concert of highlights from *Parsifal* (1882), for example, Blok composed an untitled poem concerning the manner in which Wagner used music to recall images from the distant past. Quoting the poem, Bartlett notes that while "Blok 'never understood before / The art of holy music,' hearing excerpts from *Parsifal* provoked a surge of involuntary memory, 'So that all former beauty / Came back from oblivion in a wave.'"[13] Ivanov likewise posited that the leitmotif was a device of remembrance that established bridges between the objective and subjective, the conscious and unconscious, the world of objects and the world of essences. He asserted that the characters in the music dramas behaved like figures in a dream, the orchestral music emanating from beneath their feet, disclosing both their thoughts and the nameless forces that determined their destinies. Like Blok, he was short on specifics, and when he declared that all of the leitmotifs in *Der Ring des Nibelungen* were symbolic, referring to unknowable entities, he was rebuked by a rival, who countered that they were most often allegorical, associated with concrete objects and ideas. Though they might seem to be ambiguous, they actually display a fixed logic in their repetition.[14]

One searches in vain for detailed discussions of music by the Russian Symbolist poets. They regarded composers as wizards, figures like Morgan La Fee, King Arthur's sister, who in order to baffle enemies created castles in the air substantial enough to stimulate desire yet dissolving under close scrutiny. For its sheer absence of technical information, perhaps the most intriguing Symbolist examination of music is Belïy's essay "On Theurgy" ("O teurgii"), published in 1903 in the short-lived religious-philosophical journal *New Path (Novïy put').* This essay attests to Belïy's fervent belief in the theurgic nature of musical and poetic symbols, their capacity to modify our perception of reality. Theurgy, a term coined by the third-century philosopher Iamblichus, is most often defined as incantation by the gods. In Belïy's usage, however, it refers to the god-like capabilities of the Symbolists, their ability to transform artistic creation into religious creation. The symbol—whether musical or poetic—not only asserts the existence of the objects that it connotes, it actually has the power to summon new objects into being. From a purely literary perspective, Belïy sought the formation of a syntax in which words assume the same ontological status as their referents. His source for this concept was Mallarmé, who in his 1897 essay "The Crisis of Poetry" ("Crise de vers") recalled a mythological time when language could actually produce objects by fusing sound and sensation. From a purely musical perspective, Belïy sought the formation of a syntax in which sounds were divorced from their cultural referents and prevented from assuming a concrete semantic identity. By constantly shifting their expressive value, they would compel the listener to contemplate their various possible implications, their various possible sources in experience. Drawing on Schopenhauer, Belïy hypothesized that, through music, the listener perceives the deepest forces that regulate the cosmos: the concentrated energies that constitute the noumenal Will. Unlike poetry, which concerns the material traces of objects, music concerns their immaterial essences. Thus, whereas the "mystic" Symbolist poets, as theurgists, were forced to confine their activities to this world, Symbolist composers could gain direct access to the other world.

Yet the theoretical apparatus that frames Belïy's discussion of specific compositions is much more sophisticated than the discussion itself. In "On Theurgy," he focuses his "analysis" on *8 Stimmungsbilder* (opus 1, 1897) by Nikolai Metner (1880–1951), Emiliy's younger brother. Against these slight works, which are evocative of Robert Schumann in their use of programmatic titles and Johannes Brahms in rhythmic inventiveness, Belïy juxtaposes the first stanza of an untitled 1843 lyric by Mikhaíl Lermontov (1814–41), the intention being to demonstrate the expressive superiority of the music over the text:

> The first number *[Prolog]* of the collection *[Stimmungsbilder]*
> expresses exactly that feeling which inspired Lermontov to write
> his famous lines:
>
> > Lone I walk upon the road;
> > The stony path gleams through the mist;
> > The night is still. Wilderness heeds God,
> > And star speaks with star.
> >
> > [Vïkhozhu odin ya na dorogu;
> > Skvoz' tuman kremnistïy put' blestit;

Noch' tikha. Pustïnya vnemlet bogu,
I zvezda s zvezdoyu govorit.]

But this division between nature, solemnly peaceful in the embraces of
night's dark blue ether, and the soul, poised above the crevices, is felt
somewhere deep inside when one hears the chords flowing, as though
soaring to heaven. . . . In subsequent passages. . . where Lermontov
either broke off or, surrounded by chaos, prognosticated, Metner, inspired by love, aspires to make his way through the mist. Like any
profound, active, and actual (rather than apparent) aspiration to light—
only a prayer, but in any case strengthened by the power of prayer—
Metner's endeavor, like his compositions, is *theurgic*.[15]

There are no programmatic suggestions in the music; the alignment of
Metner with Lermontov is purely hypothetical, reflecting what Belïy considers to be the common subjective implications of their works. Belïy implies that translating musical discourse into verbal discourse is a futile
exercise, since music evades and eludes rationalization. The result will either be passionate exaggeration or empty contemplation. While modestly
trained in music—he had lessons in piano and composition from his
mother—the poet avoided discussing compositional syntax and technique,
asserting that the analysis of melody and harmony impedes surrender to
musical rapture.

The "mystic" Symbolists' musical musings only touched ground, paradoxically, when they proposed definite measures for distorting the surface
clarity of compositions, for transferring the listening experience from the
realm of the intellect to the realm of the senses. In their theoretical writings, they expressed impatience with the longstanding debate concerning
the semantic content of music, asserting that music does not express anything beyond itself, that is to say, anything that can be translated into images and words. This does not mean that, to the poets, "music in itself" was
meaningless, a dark void; rather, it bore endless meanings, offered thousands of shades of emotions, and provided "release from everyday perception" through the revelation of "countless possibilities of being."[16] The
poets conceded, however, that not all compositions were symbolic. The invocation of the ineffable could not be achieved through fixed compositional
systems, for such systems assign "grammar" and "syntax" to music, labels
and terms that conceal its indefinable content with a definable, "extra-
musical" cover. Recognizing that the issue of musical meaning—how so-
natas and symphonies had been interpreted in different historical eras, and
how such interpretations change as styles and genres undergo transformation and dissolution—had been addressed by numerous historians and

theorists, the "mystic" Symbolists contended that attempts to provide scientific descriptions of the experience of music decreased its mystery, hence its value.

In a 1907 article for the Symbolist journal *The Golden Fleece (Zolotoye runo)* entitled "Music, As One of the Highest Mystical Experiences" ("Muzïka, kak odno iz vïsshikh misticheskikh perezhivaniy"), K. Eiges claimed that music was the most "symbolic" of the forms of art. After quoting the usual philosophical suspects, he concluded that "music is super-empirical. It combines within itself both 'subject' and 'object,' 'I' and 'not I,' representation and the will. In ontological terms it is the will to sounds. This point alone is sufficient to indicate that music exists beyond the limits of scientific inquiry."[17] Speaking ex cathedra for his poet colleagues, Eiges suggests that "mystic" Symbolist composition requires the composer to encode his thought processes into the actual structure of the material. The results of this procedure, he implies, are compositions in which harmonic and melodic relationships of cause and effect are supplanted by a free play of sounds in which the borders of musical grammar and syntax are continuously pushed back. Through the fusion of what later aestheticians called "experience" and "practice," the composer creates a link between "secondary truths of life" and "first principles."[18] Finding that traditional forms of composition placed limits on musical discourse, discourse that should be infinite, the Symbolists insisted on loosening formal constraints and embellishing musical syntax. They became the first advocates of "open" compositions, which would allow for what might be called the "flight" or even "escape" of the musical signifier.

The composer most enamored with "mystic" Symbolism was of course Scriabin, whose creative path seems to have followed the "dialectical progression" that, according to the poets, separated their activities from those of other artists. In a seminal 1910 essay, "The Behests of Symbolism" ("Zavetï simvolizma"), Ivanov, Scriabin's friend and Symbolist tutor, charted this "dialectical progression" as follows. During the first phase, the "thesis," the artist determines that "the world is not narrow, flat, or poor, it is not desolate or predetermined, for there is much in it that yesterday's wise men [the realists] did not dream of, there are passages and openings into its secret from the labyrinth of man's soul." The artist thereafter seeks to give expression to the fleeting correspondences between this world and the other world using symbols. There ensues the second phase, the "antithesis," in which the artist endures a period of moral and spiritual turmoil, the successful outcome being the commitment of his life and work to "the worldview of mystical realism." At this point, Ivanov claims, the artist has moved from viewing art as an object of worship to viewing himself as an object of worship. Finally, in the third phase, the "synthesis," the artist is brought "face to face with his true and ultimate goals": the enactment, rather than the representation, of transcendence. The creative act now becomes "vital and significant." It allows for a "commemorative secret sight of correlations with higher essences." Moreover, it transforms itself "into a sacred secret action of love" that overcomes "the division of forms" to become a "theurgic, transfiguring *Fiat.*"[19] Surveying Scriabin's career, one can locate the "thesis" phase in the composer's Symphony No. 1 in E major (opus 26, 1900), whose choral finale praises the power of music, the "antithesis" phase in *Prometheus: The Poem of Fire* (opus 60, 1910), whose "program" refers to the composer as a divine agent, and the "synthesis" phase in the inchoate *Mysterium (Misteriya)*, a vision of cosmic dissolution. In a 1919 speech that introduced a piano recital in Scriabin's memory, Ivanov provided a slightly more refined summary of the composer's career, declaring that Scriabin's aesthetic platform reflected "a threefold idea, a threefold emotion, [and] a threefold vision." He claimed that the "thesis" phase consisted of a "vision of surmounting the boundaries of the personal, the individual." The "antithesis" phase, in turn, consisted of a "vision of the universal . . . , communal mingling of all humanity." The "synthesis" phase, finally, comprised a "vision of a stormy breakthrough into the expanse of a different, free plane of being—universal transformation."[20] Through benefit of hindsight, one realizes that Scriabin's creative activities evolved—more accurately, devolved—from the realizable to the potentially realizable to the unrealizable.

Beyond accepting Symbolism as a philosophical worldview, Scriabin absorbed concrete compositional ideas from the poets. Like Rimsky-Korsakov, he was interested in the concept of synaesthesia, more precisely, "color hearing"; unlike Rimsky-Korsakov, however, Scriabin acquired his knowledge of "color hearing" from the writings of Belïy and Ivanov, which in turn stemmed from Goethe's pseudo-scientific treatise *Toward a Theory of Color (Zur Farbenlehre, 1810).* In Belïy's extremely late Symbolist publication *Masks (Maski, 1932),* characters and settings are denoted by colors and sounds, the intention, according to John Elsworth, being "to express that which lies beyond the customary domain of descriptive language."[21] On one level, Belïy sought to assign color and sound semantic content; on another, he sought to illustrate the semantic limitations of descriptive language. Elsworth also remarks that, for Belïy and the other "mystic" Symbolists, rational perception constituted only one element of essential perception, which was regulated not by the mind but by the five senses.

Cognitive or rational perception places a veil over essential reality, which exists at the extreme fringes of consciousness and can only be intuited. In *Prometheus: The Poem of Fire*, Scriabin proposed to represent, rather than to enact, synaesthesia using a projector called *tastiera per luce* ("keyboard for light"), which splayed different colored beams, each calibrated to a specific pitch and specific tonality. For example, according to Scriabin's "Musico-Chromo-Logo Schema," the chart of color-sound relationships that Bulat Galeyev devised to the composer's specifications, the pitch F and the tonality of F major were analogous to red, which stood for "Diversification of Will"; the pitch G♭ and the tonality of G-flat major were analogous to blue or violet, which stood for "Creativity"; and the pitch G and the tonality of G major were analogous to orange, which stood for "creative play."[22] Unfortunately, the *tastiera per luce* did not function properly, and Scriabin acknowledged that, even had it done so, the result would have only advertised, rather than achieved, the transference of reality from the domain of the intellect to the intuition, a process that the composer hoped would occur spontaneously in the experiences of his listeners. He fantasized that, during the performance of his compositions, the visual and aural senses would be mutually stimulated. Sight would be divorced from its usual causal stimuli and would be "causally" associated with hearing.

Though Scriabin is often, perhaps too often, regarded as the "mystic" Symbolist poster child, at least three other composers, working in familiar operatic contexts, also exploited the hallucinatory potential of the musical symbol. Chaikovsky, Rimsky-Korsakov, and Prokofiev all incorporated symbolic passages into their mature operas, passages that infuse the vocal and instrumental lines with nostalgia and foreboding, euphoria and depression, and that serve to oscillate between external and internal, material and spiritual worlds. The stage characters are portrayed in extremely fragile emotional states, straddling the border between conscious and unconscious impulses. The music that marks their entrances and exits attests to the numinous heterogeneity of the dramatic events, the occult relationships between overlaid semantic spaces. As a transmediating device, the musical symbol not only aligns scenes and events within the confines of single scores, it also aligns scenes and events within different scores. It operates, in short, to concatenate the ideas and thoughts of composers of disparate times and places. In this regard, it underscores the Symbolist aspiration to create works with potentially unlimited meanings. More than is usual in opera, hearing these works entails tracing both the teleological unfolding of the narrative (the diachronic enchaining of events) and the layers of allusions that supplement this unfolding (the synchronic enchaining of events).

Yet the poetic symbol is translated into musical terms in much less tangible ways. Stefan Jarocinski observes, for example, that Debussy sought

> to speak directly through bird-song, the sound of the sea, the rocking of a boat by the waves, the movement of clouds in the sky, or drifting mists, to lead our thoughts to the origin of things and cause them to dwell on the ultimate questions in life. His music does not answer any questions, create any myths, or suggest any solutions, but for that very reason acts all the more forcefully on our minds, and forces us to follow in its wake.[23]

Jarocinski reports that a musical symbol can be as simple and direct as a framed measure of silence (like measure 6 of Debussy's *Prélude à L'après-midi d'un faune* [1894]) or as complex and indirect as a harmonic pattern distributed over several acoustic registers and distorted by unusual instrumentation. A melodic sequence might be dismantled into seemingly random fragments; a cadence or structural point of repose might be made apparitional, blurred by chromatic ornamentation or obliterated by tremolos and glissandi. The fusing of tonal and nontonal melodic sequences can be symbolic, as can the ascribing of tonal functionality to dissonant or nontriadic harmonies. Structural pitches can succumb to unusual harmonizations and thus be relegated to the status of epiphenomena. Perhaps the most familiar examples of musical symbols are inconstant bell and bell-like sounds, which lead the listener's imagination back through multiple spatial and temporal tiers. Their oscillation and reverberation point to those attributes of musical experience that structural and functional hearing overshadows. These sounds are not selected for their ability to represent dramatic events but for their polymorphousness, their inability to remain interpretively still. Acoustically deracinated and desemanticized, they at once impede and precede cognition. They characterize not only Debussy's French Symbolist operas (*Pélleas et Mélisande* and the unfinished *Fall of the House of Usher* [*La chute de la maison Usher,* 1917]), but also the four Russian Symbolist operas discussed in this book.

Chapter 1 concerns the Russian *fin-de-siècle* and the founding of the World of Art (Mir iskusstva) artists' circle. I contend that Chaikovsky's *Queen of Spades* (*Pikovaya dama,* opus 68, 1890), composed on the cusp of the Symbolist movement, is at once a fantasy about the operatic potential of the movement and—paradoxically—its finest operatic exemplar. Within it, Chaikovsky manufactures a hallucinatory atmosphere by offset-

ting musical forms and styles dating from both the eighteenth and nineteenth centuries. The text in part concerns gambling addiction; the music
progresses accordingly from logic to illogic to active chance. Herman, the
chrysomaniacal anti-hero, is represented as a "Romantic" character trapped
in a "Classical" world, a madman who possesses the future.

To compensate for the brevity of the source novella, during the compositional process Chaikovsky and his librettist brother expanded the opera
by including within it a Mozartean divertissement and scenes of aristocratic music-making. Taking the rich symbolic possibilities of these interpolations into account—their potential to transform the stage events by
offering different subjective interpretations of them—the Chaikovsky
brothers decided to transpose the setting of the opera from the epoch of
Alexander I back to the epoch of Catherine the Great. In doing so, they
made several of the literary and musical borrowings anachronistic. As a
consequence, some of the characters "recall" events not from their pasts
but from their presents or—even more surrealistically—their futures.
These aberrances do more than undercut the verisimilitude of stage events;
they facilitate the juxtaposition of different dramatic levels, the presentation, in other words, of different times and places at right angles to each
other.

In the chapter, I develop this last point by interpreting the principal musical motifs of the opera as gateways not only between the eighteenth and
nineteenth centuries but also between natural and supernatural worlds.
The motifs anticipate and demonstrate the characters' subjugation to the
power of malevolent fate. I also contend that the opera addresses the decline
of Imperial Russia, the sense—prevalent in the Symbolist movement—
that the nation was undergoing a transition. The atmosphere of foreboding
that suffuses the stage events intimates that, ultimately, *The Queen of
Spades* less concerns "Classical" or "Romantic" Russia than "Modern"
Russia. The opera articulates the conditions of the *fin-de-siècle* in its pre-
carious relationship to *inoy svet*—the other world.

Chapter 2 evaluates Rimsky-Korsakov's *Legend of the Invisible City
of Kitezh and the Maiden Fevroniya* (*Skazaniye o nevidimom grade Kitezhe
i deve Fevronii*, 1905) through the prism of the ecumenical religious philosophy of Vladimir Solovyov (1853–1900), which influenced the "mystic" Symbolists and Theosophists alike. The most important of the opera's
various source texts, the 1223 Kitezh chronicle, is concerned with syncretism: the process by which components of one religion are assimilated
into another religion as an expression of spiritual communion. The opera's
title character was derived in part from the sixteenth-century hagiography

of St. Fevroniya of Murom but also from writings about another religious figure known as the Divine Sophia, a symbol in Symbolist literature of the Eternal Feminine. Significantly, Rimsky-Korsakov conceived the *Legend of Kitezh* not as a Symbolist opera but as a pageant of patriotic nationalism. His librettist, Vladimir Belsky, had a vastly different conception of the work, however, and incorporated references to Symbolist literature into the libretto. Since the two of them were unable to see eye to eye, the result of their collaboration is a somewhat contradictory score that conflates realistic and fantastic scenes. From the theater audience's perspective, it combines events in a material (urban) sphere (acts II and III, scene 1) and events in an immaterial (forest) sphere (acts I and IV, scene 1). From the pious stage characters' perspective, it blends events in an unreal but visible world (the profane city of Lesser Kitezh) and a real but invisible world (the sacred city of Greater Kitezh). The chapter is separated into an overview of the genesis of the libretto, cast in part in the style of seventeenth-century religious prose, and an overview of the genesis of the music, cast in part in the style of pre-Petrine Orthodox chant. Near the end of the chapter, I contend that, although Rimsky-Korsakov often described himself as an atheist, his opera has a profound spiritualist message. His depiction of synaesthesia, his "syncretic" admixture of "forest" and "urban" sounds, and his emphasis on bell and bell-like sounds all serve to demonstrate that paradise emerges through extrasensory perception.

Chapter 3 concerns the "mystic" Symbolist concepts of collective creation and theurgy. In 1904, Scriabin, influenced by Wagner as interpreted by Ivanov, conceived a composition that would realize the Symbolist ideal of spiritual emancipation. In 1913, he determined that this composition, the *Mysterium*, could not be completed, since his uncertainties about his dual roles as author and participant had led him to a dead end. In its place he decided to compose an introductory, invocational work called the *Preparatory Act (Predvaritel'noye deystviye)*. Before his sudden death in 1915, he had completed only a draft libretto and fifty-five partial pages of musical sketches for it. Analysis of the extant material reveals the paradoxes of attempting to create communal drama. It also relates a Symbolist tragedy: how one composer's philosophical speculations resulted in creative silence and personal trauma. To fill a significant gap in the English-language literature on Scriabin, the appendix to this book offers a complete translation of the *Preparatory Act* libretto.

Scriabin conceived of the musical symbol as a wholly original chord or motif. While the most illustrious of these is the "mystic" (Symbolist) chord, other sonorities, often analyzed as subsets of whole-tone and octatonic scales, can also be called symbolic. Related by tritone, major second, or minor second, these sonorities are deployed in single or multiple registers and interact in homophonic and polyphonic contexts. Clifton Callender, in an analysis of prominent whole-tone, "mystic," acoustic (aligned with the harmonic series), and octatonic collections in Scriabin's mature piano works, contends that these sonorities occupy a "relational network of split relations," a "relational network," in short, in which certain pitches are separated into upper and lower neighbor notes, the upper neighbor belonging to one referential collection, the lower neighbor belonging to another.[24] Interacting in a closed system of chromatic associations, these sonorities attest to the absence of functional harmonic patterns—the absence of teleological unfolding—in Scriabin's compositions. Given that the composer interpreted functional harmonic relations as representations of the creative consciousness, their attenuation in his mature piano works appear to be aimed at narrating the dissolution of the individual Will. It might also be argued that Scriabin's efforts to simulate (or stimulate) states of stasis and timelessness serve to evoke spiritual ascension from the physical to the astral plane—an ascension described in the Theosophical doctrine of Helene Blavatsky (1831–91), a seminal influence on the "mystic" Symbolists. Through his phantasmagoria, Scriabin substituted symbolic portrayal for symbolic absorption. Having cast himself as a demiurge, a creator of spiritual gateways from one plane of reality to another, Scriabin sought to engulf listeners in his compositional system, to allow them to realize the potential of music to elevate the consciousness to a transcendental nexus.

Chapter 4 centers on the imitation of life in art and its "mystic" Symbolist antithesis, the imitation of art in life, otherwise known as life creation *(zhiznetvorchestvo)*. It was aversion to this concept, among other things, that spurred Bryusov to write his infamous 1908 *roman-à-clef The Fiery Angel (Ognenniy angel)*, this being the source of Prokofiev's infamous opera of the same name. In the chapter, I argue that the opera is a parody of a parody, an amplification, in short, of the stylistic and thematic transgressions of the *roman-à-clef*. Bryusov subverted one of the theoretical premises of "mystic" Symbolism: the idea that a symbol was a device that oscillated not simply between perception registers within the confines of a text but also between internal and external reality. (For example, Gretchen, the heroine of part one of Goethe's *Faust* [1808], was viewed by the "mystic" Symbolists as a symbol of the Eternal Feminine and, as such, a figure whose fate warranted emulation in reality.) Bryusov also cast a jaundiced eye on the "mystic" Symbolist aspiration to transform earthly love into heavenly love. Prokofiev, in his turn, broadly mocked the themes that Bryusov had subtly critiqued. In his opera, the outwardly self-assured hero Ruprecht stumbles from confusion to confusion, the occult practitioner Agrippa of Nettesheim is exposed as a pretender, and the heroine Renata waits in vain for a superhuman entity to liberate her from the confines of a subhuman reality. From a "mystic" Symbolist standpoint, the score heretically eradicates states of transcendence. Renata's vocal lines are locked into elaborate ostinato passages that, on one hand, serve to mimic the broken sequences, obsessive litanies, and repetitive rhythms of *fin-de-siècle* poetry (as well as Igor Stravinsky's neoprimitivist music) but, on the other, confine her to a pattern of recurring nightmares from which no escape is possible. Near the score's cataclysmic climax, her voice, like the other characters' voices, dissolves in the cognitive noise of the chaotic orchestra.

The Fiery Angel was not staged in Prokofiev's lifetime, the principal reason being the paucity of visual action, a consequence of his conscious decision to confine the central conflict between angelic and demonic forces to the music. Seeking a producer, in 1927 he completed a revision of the original 1923 score and in 1930 composed an English-language scenario, two pages of stage instructions, and seven fragmentary pages of musical sketches for a new version. The chapter traces Prokofiev's creative process, focusing on his shifting views about the relationship of natural and supernatural events in the opera, while also isolating those passages that can be called symbolic. The final paragraphs are speculative, a meditation on the manner in which the cultural mythology of the Symbolist era informed that of the Soviet era. These paragraphs also reflect the various gaps in the scholarly record about the years immediately predating and postdating Prokofiev's decision to return from Western to Eastern Europe.[25]

In view of the novelty of the subject matter, I have attempted as much to chronicle the genesis as to analyze and interpret the content of the scores under discussion. Each chapter is heavily documented, with multiple prose and poetry citations, the intention being to situate the musical artifacts of the Symbolist movement in an appropriate historical context. The theoretical apparatus of the book stems from contemporaneous sources, though where it serves to elucidate or elaborate I also refer to the work of post-Symbolist scholars, notably Boris Asafyev and Yuriy Lotman. My overall purpose is to illustrate how attempts to create Russian Symbolist operas pushed dramatic technique to an extreme. Unifying the four chapters is the concept that a musical symbol oscillates between temporal and narrative layers: the past and present (and future), the natural and supernatural, the internal and external, the real *(realia)* and more real *(realiora)*. This concept is intertwined with several vexing questions: How does one translate euphonious (musical) literature into music? How does one convey timelessness in music, a temporal art? Lastly, and most problematically, How does one represent the unrepresentable, the realm beyond sensory awareness, on stage? To the poets, it seemed sufficient to pose the questions. Composers who searched for the answers found themselves unable to resolve the contradiction between the materials and metaphysics of composition, and thus unable to transform theatrical representation into enactment. Other composers, sensing the futility of this pursuit, confined Symbolism to the opera house. The latter group adhered to the dictates of Nietzsche's Apollo, wherein music heightens perception, rather than the dictates of Nietzsche's Dionysus, wherein music actually transforms reality.

THE ROSE AND THE CROSS

Alexander Blok's 1913 drama *The Rose and the Cross* was a thwarted attempt to realize the enigmatic musical ideals of his time and place. It constitutes the most elaborate product of a short-lived endeavor among the "mystic" Symbolist poets to write opera libretti, song texts, and plays calling for incidental music.

The basic theme of this drama is the heterogeneity of human existence, the idea that there exist two realities, one cognitively graspable by the mind, the other intuitively graspable. The plot brings together dissimilar characters, settings, images, and events: a grief-stricken lady and a dejected knight, a dilapidated castle and a windswept beach, the bells of a sunken city and a ghost in a dungeon, a peasant dance around a decorated tree and a song contest in a flowering dale. The spring that sets the plot in motion is a song so provocative that it haunts the *dramatis personae* for years after they hear it performed by an itinerant troubadour. The troubadour reappears at the drama's end for an encore performance. Extracted by Blok from Breton poetry, the song's pastoral text identifies joy and suffering as equivalent emotional states. Its music was intended to mesmerize its listeners—both those on and off the stage.

Here Blok faced a familiar problem: Could a composer actually write a song for *The Rose and the Cross* that would have this effect? Could the poet actually find someone to compose music that emanated (or appeared to emanate) from another level of reality, a fourth dimension amid the three? The climax of the drama suggests that the task is utterly beyond completion, the song impossible. Having idealized the troubadour and his song in memory, the lady is disappointed when she hears him perform again: the actual music cannot match the transcendent music in her memory. This turn of events does not mean that Blok was thwarted in his poetic aspirations, or that his drama does not contain passages in which dream and legend supplant reality and history. Rather, it foregrounds the special challenges that he and his colleagues presented to their composer counterparts: to create music that opens windows into other levels of perception and to elevate opera into something beyond itself. In a journal entry, Blok commented that, "for a play," *The Rose and the Cross* "was too much of a mosaic" and that in the figure of the downtrodden knight "there was something that had outgrown opera."[26]

Blok conceived *The Rose and the Cross* while melancholic. His journal entries for 1912 and 1913 contain gloomy thoughts about his marriage, his fragile health, and his creative work. The resulting drama in part expresses his yearning to escape a dull present into a bright past. Blok juxtaposes passages of historical narration and personal reflection, comic and tragic events, philosophical fulmination and anecdotal digression. The narrative is disjointed; instead of falling into two matched parts, the pattern of scenes suggests an unsolved geometry problem. For purposes of cohesion, Blok makes repeated references to the practices of Rosicrucianism, an esoteric faith that, like Theosophy and Cabalism, was revived during his lifetime: astral projection, aura reading, hypnotism, meditation. He also suffuses the narrative with references to music—both music as a poetic *topos* (the alchemy of rhythms and rhymes, consonants and vowels endemic to French and Russian Symbolist literature) and as actual vocal and instrumental sounds possessing rhythm, melody, and harmony. In this regard, his drama helps define the nature and function of the musical as distinct from the poetic symbol. Quotations from the troubadour's song are interwoven, inevitably, with quotations from Wagner's music dramas, the supreme influence not only on Blok but on all the "mystic" Symbolists.

The drama is set at the start of the eighteenth century, though the poetic imagery dates from the outset of the thirteenth. The eighteenth-century locale is the unruly castle of Archimbaut at Languedoc; the thirteenth-century locale is the unpopulated seaside of Brittany during the Albigensian crusade. References to the legends and myths of the earlier historical period infuse the real-time action, transporting the reader back and forth between them as though by metempsychosis.

The conflation of historical past and present is reflected on a small scale in the conflation of the experiential past and present in the mind of Izora, the young wife of the crotchety Count Archimbaut.[27] Upon hearing a song about endless struggle sung by the handsome troubadour Gaetan, she falls sick with melancholy. The count summons the castle doctor, who advises that her ailment can only be treated by bloodletting, in accordance with the ancient prescriptions of Galen and Hippocrates. The plot then shifts to the castle chaplain, who declares his love for Izora's chatelaine Alisa. Alisa shuns him because she yearns for the castle page Aliksan, who pines in turn for the self-centered Izora. Frustrated and jealous, the chaplain takes revenge on Alisa by suggesting to the count that Izora has been unfaithful to him. The count imprisons Izora and Alisa in the "Tower of the Inconsolable Widow." The tower is the residence of the "Knight of Misfortune" Bertran, who is devoted to Izora but shunned repeatedly by her. When the count dispatches him to the north of France on military business, she beseeches him to find the troubadour who caused her malaise. Meanwhile Aliksan, recognizing that Izora will not return his affections, sends Alisa a pastry containing a love letter.

The climax of the drama takes place at the May festival. Maidens encircle a decorated tree, jugglers and acrobats entertain the crowd of knights and ladies. The song contest begins. The first minstrel sings "I love the breath of the beautiful spring," which Blok described as a "free translation of three strophes (I, II and IV) from the famous *sirventes* by Bertram de Born"; the second minstrel sings "Through the dense forest at springtime," a "free adaptation of a song by a Picardie trouvère of the XIIIth century."[28] Gaetan reluctantly appears to sing his renowned song. Finding him old and undesirable, Izora loses interest in the performance and directs her attention to Aliksan, who has attended the festival out of boredom. Earthly love conquers unearthly dream: the lady invites the page to her chamber. At this moment the watchman appears to announce that the castle has been attacked by the army of Count Raymond, a Toulouse nobleman fighting on behalf of the Albigensians. Bertran defeats Raymond in a duel but is gravely wounded. Ignoring his condition, Izora orders him to stand guard beneath her chamber window to guarantee her own and her lover's privacy. Meanwhile, Alisa, upset at Aliksan's transgression, finally decides to reciprocate the amorous entreaties of the chaplain. Bertran keeps lonely vigil through the night and dies at sunrise. The clatter of his sword hitting the flagstones has unspoken significance, attesting to the splintering of reality in the drama as a whole.

Blok modeled the "Knight of Misfortune," the central character in *The Rose and the Cross*, in part on himself. Izora was modeled on the actress Lyubov Mendeleyeva (1881–1939), with whom he fell in love in 1898, and who inspired him to write about the possibility of achieving goodness and harmony in the world. Blok's first collection of poetry, *Verses about the Most Beautiful Lady* (*Stikhi o Prekrasnoy Dame*, 1905), attests to his state of romantic bliss but suggests that the feeling may not last. *The Rose and the Cross*, in contrast, fully acknowledges the loss of the dream. Bertran's sadness at Izora's infidelities mirrors Blok's sadness at those of his beloved Lyubov. The intrigues and jealousies between the residents of the castle, moreover, reflect those between Blok and his artistic rivals. Like Blok, Bertran fondly recalls his youth, but confesses that his memories of it have soured. Blok's tendency toward depression, lastly, is figured in the knight's frequent visits to a barren beach.

Donald Rayfield comments that Izora symbolizes Mendeleyeva but also the "eternal feminine, spiritually responsive to the song that haunts her, but physically responsive only to the page boy."[29] She also brings to mind two Wagnerian heroines: Isolde and Kundry. Blok's knowledge of Wagner was sparse, confined to his interest in German idealist philosophy, but he was active in editing and translating Wagner's prose and poetry. Rayfield observes that, together with *Die Kunst und die Revolution* (1849), Blok "had to edit *Der Ring*, and produce a new version of *Tristan*. Substantial sketches exist for a dramatic 'tableau' of *Tristan und Isolde*."[30] Izora has three characteristics in common with Isolde: her obsession with Gaetan and his song recalls Isolde's longing for Tristan; her suffering in her husband's castle recalls Isolde's fear of marriage to King Marke; and her reliance on her chatelaine Alisa recalls Isolde's dependence on her maidservant Brangaene. She resembles Kundry, however, in her insomnia and her futile efforts to achieve spiritual redemption with the assistance of a virtuous hero. The relationship between Izora and Bertran differs markedly from that between Tristan and Isolde, but as another Slavicist, Robert Hughes, remarks, "the three stages of Bertran's death and transfiguration (wherein Joy and Sorrow—[the knight's] physical suffering—do indeed become one) are very much like the long dying of Tristan as he awaits the arrival of Isolde." Tristan's death, moreover, is "accomplished in three stages of reminiscence and a final transfiguration in which the joy of understanding becomes at one with his suffering."[31] Verbal allusions to Isolde's "Liebestod" are intertwined with incipits from authentic Provençal romances and Celtic legends.

Gaetan has no counterpart in Wagner's music dramas: he is a character from Rosicrucian legend, a Medieval emissary seeking to found a society devoted to the secret sciences. And yet the contest scene in which he performs his song was obviously based on the equivalent scene in *Die Meister-*

singer von Nürnberg (1868), which Blok heard on 15 January 1913, in the midst of work on the final pages of *The Rose and the Cross.*[32] Bartlett states that, although the general moods of *The Rose and the Cross* and *Die Meistersinger* are entirely different and there is little similarity between Gaetan and Hans Sachs, "the coincidence between the significance of Gaetan's song . . . and Walther von Stolzing's 'Prize Song' is indeed striking."[33] Bartlett supplies no details, but the relationships between the two numbers are worth outlining. Just as the leitmotif aligned with Izora's passion for Gaetan evolves into Gaetan's festival song in act IV, scene 3 of *The Rose and the Cross,* so too does the leitmotif of Walther's passion for Eva (appearing at measure 97 of the act I overture of *Die Meistersinger von Nürnberg*) evolve into Walther's prize song in act III, scene 5. Moreover, the poetic imagery of Gaetan's song appears to negate that of Walther's song. Gaetan laments his endless search for an unattainable ideal; Walther describes finding and tracing the path to paradise. Referring back to *Tristan und Isolde,* it is worth noting that the scene in which Bertran meets Gaetan is replete with wind and storm imagery reminiscent of the sailor's song that begins act I of Wagner's score. The troubadour describes himself as an orphan raised in captivity by a fairy near the seashore. Before he ventured out into the world, the fairy instructed him to "heed the songs of the ocean" and "observe the crimson dawns" and prophesied that he would always wander the world.[34] Thereafter in the drama, the troubadour and his song symbolize eternal struggle.

In act I, scene 3, before the May festival has taken place, Izora unwittingly finds herself humming the first and second stanzas of the number under her breath: "'The snow swirls . . . / The fleeting age rushes . . . / The blessed shore is dreamed.'" Turning to her chatelaine, she declares: "I can't recall any more a . . . strange song! 'Joy-and-Suffering . . . law immutable to the heart. . . .' Help me remember it, Alisa!" Bemused, Alisa replies: "How can I help you, my lady, if even the doctor can't help[?]"[35] Her inexplicable anamnesis causes the outlines of the castle to fade, to cede to an idyllic recollection of the world, the world as it perhaps existed in her youth. On the surface, the symbolic function of the song, imprinted in fragments in Izora's mind, is the stirring of memory. But the nature imagery, the references to the "fleeting age" and "blessed shore," appear to probe deeper, provoking not only individual memory but communal memory. The song recalls prelapsarian bliss and mourns its loss.

Bertran believes that Gaetan has brought coded messages to the castle denizens and hears in his recital vestiges of ancient legends, the incantations of forgotten balladeers. He hears echoes of his own love and longing in the love and longing that Gaetan expresses; he observes that, within the song's text, motifs of chivalric devotion and repressed desire blend with motifs of enchantment and sorcery. In act IV, scene 5, as he guards Izora's bedchamber, suffering from the wounds that he sustained in his sword fight with Count Raymond (comparable to the wounds that Tristan sustained in his sword fight with Melot), Bertran remembers the pain and sorrow in Gaetan's voice:

> How beautiful the night!
> Hark, into the solemn voice of trumpets
> Bursts rustling . . .
> No, again quiet . . .
> Nothing more disturbs the peace.
> God, your thunderous silence
> Your poor slave
> Hears clearly!
> The wound opened,
> My powers wane . . .
> Burn, rose!
> Death, you make the heart wiser . . .
> I understood, understood, Izora:
> "Law immutable to the heart—
> Joy-and-Suffering is one . . .
> Joy, oh, Joy-and-Suffering—
> The pain of unheard-of wounds! . . ."

> [Kak noch' prekrasna!
> Chu, v torzhestvennïy golos trub
> Vrïvayetsya shelest . . .
> Net, opyat' tishina . . .
> Bol'she nichem ne narushen pokoy.
> Bozhe, tvoyu tishinu gromovuyu
> Yavstvenno slïshit
> Bednïy tvoy rab!
> Rana otkrïlas',
> Silï slabeyut moi . . .
> Roza, gori!
> Smert', umudryayesh' tï serdtse . . .
> Ya ponyal, ponyal, Izora:
> "Serdtsu zakon neprelozhnïy—
> Radost'-Stradan'ye odno . . .
> Radost', o, Radost'-Stradan'ye—
> Bol' neizvedannïkh ran! . . ."][36]

These lines concern the relationship between reality and dream, physical and spiritual values. Separated, the rose and the cross stand for love and honor; intertwined, they stand for each human's ability to evolve toward God. In accord with the "Law immutable to the heart," Bertran must sacrifice his love, strength, and life to regain honor. Gaetan's song informs him of the "mystery of self-crucifying love" and recapitulates the ancient idea that love brings about salvation.[37] The song is no mere allegory, a lesson about forsaking personal desire to attain spiritual grace, but a symbol, a facilitator of supersensory experience. It is an integral element of the thing that it represents. The music's effect on the knight and lady cannot be translated into prose since, as Blok insists, to do so would be to set up a crimping equivalence between acoustic and verbal gestures.

Considering the immense importance he ascribed to the music, it is not surprising that Blok wavered about how to use it in *The Rose and the Cross*. The story of the music is in fact a story of diminishing expectations. Blok conceived the drama in January 1912 as a scenario for a ballet about the lives of the Provençal troubadours. He asked Alexander Glazunov to compose the score, but Glazunov's heavy teaching schedule and heavy drinking prevented him from complying. That May Blok abruptly changed the ballet scenario into an opera scenario. His journal entries for the month contain psychological profiles of each of the characters except Gaetan. His doubts about the genre of the work resurfaced in June, and he informed his mother that "it once seemed to me that it would not turn out as an opera, but as a play, but all the same it will become an opera: I was deluded by one of the dramatic figures—the unfortunate Bertran—whose character is more dramatic than musical."[38] On finishing the first draft of the text in September, however, he decided that the subject warranted realistic treatment in dramatic rather than operatic form. The second draft was finished at the end of October 1912, but the play was only accepted for stage production in November 1915 at the Moscow Art Theatre. A letter of 22 October 1916 from the theater director Vladimir Nemirovich-Danchenko to Blok provides information about plans to incorporate music in *The Rose and the Cross*: "At this time it is still not determined who will write it. The fact is, to this end I contacted [Sergey] Rachmaninoff, as it would be ideal if he himself did it. But he is very busy and won't reply." The reason for Rachmaninoff's apparent disinterest is made clear a few lines later, when Nemirovich-Danchenko remarks that he had instructed Rachmaninoff to compose music with a "Scriabinesque tone" and to allow Gaetan's song "to recede further and further into the distance on some kind of violin note."[39] Any good will that might have existed between the director and composer would have been undone by these proposals, as Rachmaninoff disliked Scriabin and did not seek inspiration for his compositions from

Symbolist poetry. Blok was left to commission the young "Wagnerian" composer Mikhaíl Gnesin (1883–1957) to write the music. However Gnesin's setting of the song disappointed Blok—"Not Gnesin—at least not his Gaetan," the poet wrote in his journal on 10 March 1916[40]—and the prospective collaboration fell apart. It was a devastating blow to the composer, who had published "Gaetan's Song" as his opus 14, no. 2 in 1915, and had also written music for the chorus of maidens in act IV, scene 3 ("Now it is May, bright May" ["Vot on, may, svetlïy may"], opus 23), and a song for the page Aliksan in act I, scene 3 ("Happy day, blissful hour" ["Den' vesolïy, chas blazhennïy"], opus 14, no. 1). Only the last of these works was ever performed as part of the play, as staged in the winter of 1920 in the provincial town of Kostroma.[41]

In her 1978 memoirs, the Armenian poet Marietta Shaginyan (1888–1982) observed that *The Rose and the Cross* "calls for unusual sound, for 'decadence in music,'" and yet recalled that Blok rejected Gnesin's music "because he wanted to stage [his drama] realistically."[42] Her statement is only partly correct; the rejection reflected Blok's uncertainty about the drama's overall structure. Like the symbol itself, *The Rose and the Cross* had the potential to assume many different forms but turned out as a hybrid work that did not conform to any of them. Blok's ambivalence may also have reflected his realization that, given the philosophical freight he had assigned to it, *any* setting of the song would prove anticlimactic and deficient. More concretely, however, the rejection illustrates Blok's distaste for Gnesin's adherence to the traditional rules of harmony, his penchant for Romantic clichés (distant horn calls, harp glissandi, nature imagery), and his resistance to rhythmic and metric experimentation, the latter being the means by which Symbolist poets endeavored to alter morphemic and phonic relationships. The composer's aspiration to semanticize music—to create aural analogues to words and images—affronted the Symbolist credo that music alone among the arts could serve to express the ineffable. For Gaetan's song, Blok doubtless desired scoring that would supplant logically structured musical signifiers with "pure" sound values.[43]

What, then, is Gnesin's setting of the song like? If we were to describe it using a Symbolist poet's ornate, metaphoric language, we would pass over such immediately obvious points as its loosely ternary (A-B-A') form and its compound duple meter. Rather, we would point out the striking text-representational devices, especially the dazzling if somewhat garish hurricane motifs. Of these, the most prominent is a harp figure aligned with allusions to the windswept Breton beach, the swift passage of time, and the meteorological events described in the text. First heard in measure 4, it takes shape as an ascending and descending scalar figure in the outer sections and an arpeggiated figure in the middle. Its rhythmic values range from sixteenth notes to thirty-second notes to various mixed groupings. The harp figure recurs in pairs, a feature of the score that, in the ternary frame, increases the sense of design and destiny. The trumpet-like fanfares in the voice part at measures 15 to 18 and 97 to 100 (accompanying the words "The fleeting age rushes, / The blessed shore is dreamed!") are clearly word-painting devices, as are the undulating neighbor-note configurations in the strings at measures 25 and 26 (accompanying the words "The spinning wheel hums and sings"). The relatively narrow range of the two- and four-measure vocal phrases enhances the sense of dispirited monotony.

The song unfolds in a series of lyrical waves, each stanza demarcated by changes in tempo (*moderato* to *andantino* to *lento*, each gradation including a *ritardando* and an *a tempo*) and dynamic (*piano* to *forte* to *mezzo-forte* to *fortissimo*, each gradation including a *crescendo*). Gnesin disguises the ternary structure somewhat by overlapping the conclusion of the B section music and the outset of the A′ section at measure 84, and by emphasizing a single tonality, A minor, throughout. There is a brief modulation to the relative major at measure 57, the exact center of the song, just before the phrase describing the relationship between joy and suffering, an event that serves to magnify a detail of the song while presenting a view of the whole. The harmony tends to meander. The outset of the A′ section (measures 85–88), for example, is marked by a recurring, vacillating progression describing a tritone. Although the chord rooted on E is often embellished by a seventh, it is never deployed as a functional dominant. Gnesin robustly accentuates the line "With the sign of the cross!" (measures 82–84) with ascending *fortissimo* C major, D major, and E minor triads, but only delicately underscores the central revelation that "Joy-and-Suffering is One!" (measures 64–65) with a cadential figure in the voice and a scalar flourish in the first violins.

It is evident that Gnesin tried to find musical equivalents for Blok's words, while the poet wanted precisely to avoid such alignments.[44] The composer worked with what Jarocinski has in a French Symbolist context called a "system of musical metaphors" and a "musical topography" that offers analogies to the other arts.[45] The music for the song is semantically stable, when in fact the text calls for blurring and obfuscating rhythmic patterns and destabilizing and combining harmonies—a gradually estranged syntax, in short, that would accord with gradually estranged verbal imagery. Such traits are routinely identified in the mature scores of

Example 1.   Gaetan's Song *(continues)*

Example 1. *(continues)*

Example 1. *(continues)*

Example 1.   (continues)

Example 1. *(continues)*

Example 1.   *(continues)*

Example 1. *(continues)*

Example 1. *(continues)*

Example 1. *(continues)*

Example 1.   *(continues)*

Example 1. *(continued)*

Debussy. In a 1908 lecture, the philosopher T. E. Clark hypothesized that "Debussy uses chords like Mallarmé uses words, as mirrors which concentrate the light from a hundred different angles upon the exact meaning, while remaining symbols of that meaning and not the meaning itself. These strange harmonies . . . are not the end, but the point of departure of the composer's intentions; they are the loom upon which the imagination must weave its own fantasies."[46]

In the appendix to *The Rose and the Cross*—an alternate ending titled "Bertran's notes, written by him a few hours before his death" ("Zapiski Bertrana, napisannïye im za neskol'ko chasov do smerti")—Bertran describes the impact that Gaetan's song had on him: "The melody about Joy-and-Suffering, which [Gaetan] often repeated, particularly troubled me. At times his words and songs, which had some secret meaning that I could not at all grasp, horrified me, for it began to seem that it was not a person before me, but only a voice, calling me to the unknown."[47] The "voice" was to be accompanied by the real-or-imagined chiming of bells. Like other Symbolists who embroidered their works with archaic references, Blok provided an annotation to the chiming effect in his drama. The sound, he contended, would provide a subliminal point of equilibrium between disparate times and places, bridging the 1,300-year span between the real-time action of *The Rose and the Cross* and the fifth-century legend about the underwater city of Ker-is (the Breton equivalent to the thirteenth-century Slavic legend about the underwater city of Kitezh). According to most versions of the legend, Ker-is stood near the sea but was protected from it by a large pond that prevented flooding at high tide. The pious King Graalon ruled Ker-is and kept the key to the dyke separating the city and the pond on a chain around his neck. One night, his duplicitous daughter Dagyu, having mistaken the voice of the sea for the voice of her lover, stole the key and unlocked a secret door to the dyke. Water poured in and the city sank. "To this day," Blok surmised, "fisherman see the remnants of the wall towers jutting out of the water at low tide, and in a storm they hear the ringing of bells on the seabed."[48]

Bertran hears the ringing, a traditional symbol of Russian Orthodox faith that, owing to distortion and muffling, loses its connection to any one fixed point of origin. It instead becomes an eternal sound, an image of suspended time, the essence of the phenomena to which the name "bells" is assigned. Whereas the common function of bells is to mark the passage of time, in Blok's drama they lose this property and instead mark the cessation of time. Hearing them, the knight perceives an ebbing affinity between his diminutive stature in the present and the larger-than-life heroes of the past. The reverberation is elegantly described in his dialogue with Gaetan in act II, scene 3.

Gaetan:
Now—the underwater city is not far away.
Do you hear the bells ringing?

Bertran:
I hear
How the roaring sea sings.

Gaetan:
And do you see
That Gwenole's gray chasuble drifts
Over the sea?

Bertran:
I see how the gray fog
Is parting.

Gaetan:
Now do you see
How the roses play on the waves?

Bertran:
Yes. It is the sun rising behind the fog.

[*Gaetan:*
Teper'—podvodnïy gorod nedaleko.
Tï slïshish' zvon kolokolov?

Bertran:
Ya slïshu,
Kak more shumnoye poyot.

Gaetan:
A vidish',
Sedaya riza Gvennole nesyotsya
Nad morem?

Bertran:
Vizhu, kak sedoy tuman
Raskhoditsya.

Gaetan:
Teper' tï vidish',
Kak rozï zaigrali na volnakh?

Bertran:
Da. Eto solntse vskhodit za tumanom.][49]

Bertran does not associate the bell chiming with the underwater city. The mysterious ringing is transformed in his imagination into natural sounds: swelling waves crashing against rocks, gusting winds parting fog. The deluded mishearing has direct Wagnerian antecedents. Friedrich Kittler remarks, for example, that act II of *Tristan und Isolde* "opens with a whirring and ambiguous orchestral sound that Isolde's maidservant Brangaene hears only too correctly as King Mark's horn signal. On the other hand, the 'wildness' of Isolde's 'desire' for Tristan brings her 'to interpret as' she 'pleases'—the definition of an acoustic hallucination. Her maidservant answers Isolde: 'No noise of horns sounds so sweet; the spring, with soft purling of waters runs so gaily along.'"[50] In *Tristan und Isolde*, the "acoustic hallucination" is achieved by supplanting musical signifiers with "pure" sound values that express otherwise inexpressible rapture. The "acoustic hallucination" in *The Rose and the Cross* is achieved by similar means, but accomplishes a liquidation of the relationship between internal and external reality. Blok seeks to convey the ebb and flow between the self and the world, to establish what Charles Baudelaire called "correspondences"[51] between the world in which we live and the world of spirit.

In the scene, Blok provides an explicit definition of a musical symbol. (Unlike Belïy and Ivanov, his "mystic" Symbolist colleagues, Blok did not possess any technical knowledge of music; however, like them, he speculated about music's supremacy over the other arts, including his own.[52]) It is a resonant device that, in a dramatic work, mediates between temporal and spatial levels and traverses perceptual registers. In *The Rose and the Cross*, it takes the form of a sound that fades in, catches the ear, and fades out. Its retreat from audibility opens up a contemplative space, protected by its evanescence from the sound's phenomenal associations. It invites the listener to ponder what lies beyond sensory capacities, the essence that, by virtue of its immateriality, has no definable content. For Bertran, the symbolic chiming becomes increasingly multi-layered and dissonant—in terms of both sound and meaning. It *seems*—an all-important verb for the Symbolists—to have no beginning and no ending. Rather, it throws a bridge across time and space, supplanting the temporal motion of the world—what the French intuitivist philosopher Henri Bergson called *durée*, or time as experienced by consciousness[53]—with an assemblage of indefinite associations. These associations envelop an essential truth or, to invoke the phraseology of Gaetan's song, a "Law immutable to the heart."

This description might well seem to cloak a simple concept in pretentious language. One could argue, for example, that a musical symbol resembles a leitmotif, a group of pitches that, on repetition, invites the listener to draw connections between different events in a drama. In *The Rose and the Cross*, however, musical symbols are defined locally, within the framework of a set piece, a constrained and idiosyncratic duration. In placing so much emphasis on Gaetan's song, Blok implies that an intensely subjective sensorial experience of a composition can serve as a portal to the beyond. Some passages in the song become so familiar to the characters that they demand transformation or elaboration in their apprehending consciousnesses. To Izora and Bertran, a familiar (nonsymbolic) sound on the way to becoming an unfamiliar (symbolic) sound must pass through the corridor of the too-familiar-to-bear. By doing so, it induces a cerebral condition removed from conscious activity, withdrawn from social and historical imbrication.

Owing to its many Wagnerian allusions, Rayfield calls *The Rose and the Cross* "Russia's first and last Wagnerian opera."[54] However, in one crucial respect, the drama opposes Wagnerian aesthetics. Rather than a *Gesamtkunstwerk*, a synthesis of the forms of art, Blok created a fragmented and dichotomous work. The "Knight of Misfortune" Bertran, the troubadour Gaetan, and the page Aliksan can all be interpreted as reflections of his personality. Blok did not seek to erase his elocutionary presence in the drama but, on the contrary, sought to give voices to these different parts of himself. The inherent solipsism of *The Rose and the Cross* serves to explain why the poet vacillated between writing a ballet, an opera, or a play. Having conceived it in a private, idealized fantasy world, he found it difficult to cede control of the project to directors and actors. Just as Izora's adolescent memory of the troubadour's song was spoiled when she heard it performed at the festival, Blok could not accept the substitution of actual music for the fleeting music in his imagination. He acknowledged an irreconcilable conflict between the envisaged song and its merely auditory effect. Like Blok's other prospective musical collaborators, Gnesin faced a perplexing task: to write the music for the scenes of spiritual uplift in the poet's drama, which, given the drama's basis in reality, meant writing the music for the scenes of spiritual uplift in the poet's life.

Blok's difficulty in finding a composer for *The Rose and the Cross* need not imply that he was preaching to deaf ears when he conceived his symbolic sounds. Coming late in the history of Russian Symbolism, the drama illuminates the idiosyncratic preoccupations of the movement: research into ancient myths, revival of pagan rituals, advocacy of social and political upheaval, and the fusion of art and life. Blok's inclusion of actual music in his drama was the inevitable outcome of an attempt by the poets to inscribe what they considered to be the ineffable qualities of music into their creations. Besides stressing the intonations and rhythms of language over its syntactic formation, they relied on syllabic echo effects and reverberations and sought to splinter grammatical phrases into differentiated acoustic moments. They conceived the central images of their texts as verbal icons: as replications of previous images and "knowable" embodiments of "unknowable" faiths. The Symbolists determined that, just as a viewer perceives a religious icon in a different way from other images, so too does the reader apprehend the verbal symbol in a different way from the verbal sign. In *The Rose and the Cross*, Blok succeeded in demonstrating that a musical symbol requires a different mode of hearing, the replacement of what the Russo-French philosopher Vladimir Jankélévitch termed "the illusion of discursive hearing" with the contemplation of "the intangible and unattainable center of musical reality."[55] By actually collaborating with a composer, Blok imagined he might probe the metaphysical space that words alone could not probe. His disappointment prefigured Scriabin's creative catastrophe.

NOTES

1. This and the next two quotations in the paragraph are taken from V[aleriy] Bryusov, "A Reply" ("Otvet," 1894), in *The Russian Symbolists: An Anthology of Critical and Theoretical Writings*, ed. and trans. Ronald E. Peterson (Ann Arbor: Ardis, 1986), 23.

2. Johann Wolfgang von Goethe, *Sprüche in Prosa: Sämtliche Maximen und Reflexionen über Natur und Wissenschaft*, 1887, quoted in Stefan Jarocinski, *Debussy: Impressionism and Symbolism*, trans. Rollo Myers (London: Ernst Eulenburg, 1976), 23.

3. Andrey Bely [Belïy], "Symbolism as a World View" ("Simvolizm kak miroponimaniye," 1904), in *Selected Essays of Andrey Bely*, ed. and trans. Steven Cassedy (Berkeley: University of California Press, 1985), 79.

4. Avril Pyman, *A History of Russian Symbolism* (Cambridge: Cambridge University Press, 1994), 197–98.

5. Steven Cassedy, introduction to *Selected Essays of Andrey Bely*, 18.

6. Friedrich Nietzsche, *The Birth of Tragedy [from the Spirit of Music]*, trans. Clifton P. Fadiman (New York: Dover, 1995), 2–4.

7. Vyacheslav Ivanov, "Ellinskaya religiya stradayushchego boga," *Novïy put'* 3 (March 1904): 51. The phrase "prostrate millions in the dust" comes from the choral finale of Beethoven's Symphony No. 9 (opus 125, 1824), which Ivanov characterized as the "dithyramb of the new world."

8. Rosamund Bartlett, *Wagner and Russia* (Cambridge: Cambridge University Press, 1995), 144.

9. Roger Keys, introduction to *The Dramatic Symphony*, trans. Roger and Angela Keys (Edinburgh: Polygon, 1986), 10.

10. On Metner's politics and psychology, see Magnus Ljunggren, *The Russian Mephisto: A Study in the Life and Work of Emilii Medtner* (Stockholm: Almqvist and Wiksell, 1994).

11. Belïy, "Nachalo veka. Vospominaniya. Tom Tretiy, Berlinskaya redaktsiya (1922–23)," quoted in Bartlett, *Wagner and Russia*, 148.

12. Pyman, *A History of Russian Symbolism*, 268–69.

13. Bartlett, *Wagner and Russia*, 200.

14. See ibid., 126–30.

15. Belïy, "O teurgii," *Novïy put'* 9 (September 1903): 116–17.
16. Ivanov, "Skryabin," 1919, in *A. N. Skryabin: chelovek, khudozhnik. mïs-litel'*, ed. O[l'ga] M[ikhaílovna] Tompakova (Moscow: Gosudarstvennïy memorial'nïy muzey A. N. Skryabina, 1994), 115.
17. K. Eiges, "Muzïka, kak odno iz vïsshikh misticheskikh perezhivaniy," *Zolotoye runo* 6 (1907): 55.
18. Comte de Lautréamont, *Maldoror and Poems*, 1978, quoted in Julia Kristeva, *Revolution in Poetic Language*, trans. Margaret Waller, introd. Leon S. Roudiez (New York: Columbia University Press, 1984), 217.
19. Ivanov, "Zavetï simvolizma," in *Rodnoye i vselenskoye*, ed. V. M. Tolmachev (Moscow: Respublika, 1994), 187–89.
20. Ivanov, "Skryabin," 116. For an assessment of the implications of Ivanov's commentary for the analysis of Scriabin's music, see Richard Taruskin, *Defining Russia Musically* (Princeton: Princeton University Press, 1997), 320–29.
21. John Elsworth, "*Moscow* and *Masks*," in *Andrey Bely: Spirit of Symbolism*, ed. John E. Malmstad (Ithaca: Cornell University Press, 1987), 212.
22. Faubion Bowers, foreword to Alexander Scriabin, *"Poem of Ecstasy" and "Prometheus: Poem of Fire" in Full Score* (New York: Dover, 1995), 114.
23. Jarocinski, *Debussy: Impressionism and Symbolism*, 150.
24. Clifton Callender, "Voice-Leading Parsimony in the Music of Alexander Scriabin," *Journal of Music Theory* 43:2 (1999): 219–33, esp. 228–29.
25. Completing the record must await the release of documents from the Russian State Archive for Literature and Art. Just after Prokofiev died, Tikhon Khrennikov (b. 1913), the general secretary of the Union of Soviet Composers, headed a committee that prohibited access to certain letters, telegrams, and other autobiographical materials for a period of fifty years owing to their sensitive political content. Despite the collapse of the Soviet Union, the decision to close the archives has not been overturned, which means that archival work cannot commence until 5 March 2003, fifty years to the day after Prokofiev's premature passing. For an overview of the state of Prokofiev research, see Noëlle Mann and Elena Pol'dyayeva, "O Prokof'yeve yeshcho mozhno uznat' mnogo novogo . . . ," *Muzïkal'naya akademiya* 2 (2000): 241–52.
26. Aleksandr Blok, "Dnevnik 1912 goda," in *Sobraniye sochineniy*, ed. V[ladimir] N[ikolayevich] Orlov et al., 8 vols. (Moscow: Gosudarstvennoye izdatel'stvo khudozhestvennoy literaturï, 1960–63), 7: 154 (26 June 1912).
27. The ensuing summary of the plot and structure of *The Rose and the Cross* follows that in Konstantin Mochulsky, *Aleksandr Blok*, trans. Doris V. Johnson (Detroit: Wayne State University Press, 1983), 328–42.
28. Blok, "Primechaniya k drame 'Roza i Krest,'" in *Sobraniye sochineniy*, 4: 519–20.
29. Donald Rayfield, "Celtic, Wagner and Blok," in *Symbolism and After*, ed. Arnold McMillin (London: Bristol Classical Press, 1992), 27.
30. Ibid., 21.
31. R[obert] P. Hughes, "Nothung, the Cassia Flower and a 'Spirit of Music' in the Poetry of Aleksandr Blok," *California Slavic Studies* 6 (1971): 53–54.
32. The next day, Blok wrote in his diary: "To the melodies of Wagner I versified the last scene" ("Dnevnik 1913 goda," in *Sobraniye sochineniy*, 7: 208).
33. Bartlett, *Wagner and Russia*, 214.
34. Blok, "Roza i Krest," in *Sobraniye sochineniy*, 4: 203.
35. Ibid., 173–74.
36. Ibid., 245.
37. Mochulsky, *Aleksandr Blok*, 340.

38. Letter of 27 June 1912, in *Pis'ma Aleksandra Bloka k rodnïm*, ed. M. A. Beketova, 2 vols. (Moscow: Academia, 1932), 2: 207.

39. Russian State Archive of Literature and Art (Rossiyskiy gosudarstvennïy arkhiv literaturï i iskusstva, henceforth RGALI), fund 55, list 1, item 314. In suggesting that the "violin note" should "recede further and further into the distance," Nemirovich-Danchenko invokes a favorite Symbolist fantasy about sound dissolving into silence in the material world but continuing to resonate in the beyond.

40. Blok, *Zapiski knizhki 1901–20*, ed. V. N. Orlov et al. (Moscow: Khudozhestvennaya literatura, 1965), 287.

41. Unhappy with Gnesin, in June 1916 Blok turned to B. K. Yanovsky to compose songs and incidental music for *The Rose and the Cross*. The planned staging of the play with his music at the Moscow Art Theater was interrupted by the Russian Revolution. Blok thereafter lost interest in staging it. Together with Gnesin's lone contribution, the 1920 production in Kostroma featured music by B. A. Fyodorov. This music, along with the music composed by Yanovsky, has been lost.

42. Marietta Shaginyan, "Chelovek i vremya," *Novïy mir* 9 (September 1978): 178.

43. The phrase "pure" sound values—referring to musical motifs that, in their ambiguity and imprecision, cannot be interpreted as narrative metaphors—is used by Jarocinski throughout *Debussy: Impressionism and Symbolism*.

44. Gnesin discusses his approach to setting Blok's poetry in an unpublished 1920 essay entitled "Aleksandr Blok i muzïka" (RGALI, fund 2954, list 1, item 135). Within it, he discusses those poems which have ternary structures and those which have metric schemes typical of popular songs and dances. Needless to say, his attempt to classify Blok's poetry in this manner runs counter to the precepts of Symbolism.

45. Jarocinski, *Debussy: Impressionism and Symbolism*, 51.

46. Ibid., 58–59.

47. Blok, "Zapiski Bertrana, napisannïye im za neskol'ko chasov do smerti," in *Sobraniye sochineniy*, 4: 525.

48. Blok, "Primechaniya k drame 'Roza i Krest,'" 514–15. The Breton legend about Ker-is, or ville d'Ys, is the subject of Edouard Lalo's three-act opera *The King of Ys* (*Le roi d'Ys*, 1888) and, tangentially, Debussy's tenth *Prélude*, Book 1 ("La cathedrale engloutie," 1910).

49. Blok, "Roza i Krest," 205–6.

50. Friedrich Kittler, "World Breath: On Wagner's Media Technology," in *Opera Through Other Eyes*, ed. David J. Levin (Stanford: Stanford University Press, 1994), 225. The quoted words are from the libretto of *Tristan und Isolde*, as translated by Kittler in collaboration with Levin.

51. In his 1857 sonnet "Correspondence," Baudelaire (1821–67) advocates enhancing subjective expression in art to the extent that color suggests sound, sound suggests color, and both color and sound suggest ideas.

52. Blok's critical writings on music—and his frequent allusions to music in verse—are documented and annotated by Boris Asafyev in his pseudonymous 1922 essay "Videniye mira v dukhe muzïki," reprinted in *Blok i muzïka*, ed. M. Elik (Moscow: Sovetskiy kompozitor, 1972), 8–57.

53. See Henri Bergson, *Matter and Memory*, trans. Nancy Margaret Paul and W. Scott Palmer (1911; reprint, London: Allen and Unwin, 1950), 191–200.

54. Rayfield, "Celtic, Wagner and Blok," 29.

55. Vladimir Jankélévitch, *La musique et l'ineffable* (Paris: Éditions du Seuil, 1983), 126–27.

Chapter 1   Chaikovsky and Decadence

On 24 March 1905, the impresario Sergey Diaghilev (1872–1929) was honored at a Moscow banquet by his patron Ilya Ostroukhov. It was a celebration of Diaghilev's service as editor of the Russian Symbolist journal *The World of Art*, which had ceased publication a year before, and of his lavish exhibition of Russian portrait and landscape paintings at the Tauride Palace in St. Petersburg. The speech he gave in return signaled his intention to leave Russia for Western Europe and shift his sphere of activity from the visual to the performing arts. Entitled "At the Hour of Reckoning" ("V chas itogov"), it was at once a farewell to his homeland and a manifesto about the future development of art. He spoke with a tone of foreboding, alluding to two unsettling political events: the disastrous Russian-Japanese War and the tsarist government's violent reprisal on 9 January 1905 against a group of loyal petitioners (an event eulogized by Soviet historians as "Bloody Sunday" and a harbinger of the 1917 Revolution). Diaghilev apprised the assembled guests of his journeys in rural Russia collecting portraits from "gloomy estates, frightening in their dead splendor":

> Here people do not live out their days, a way of life does. This is why I have become entirely convinced that we are living at a frightening time of crisis. We are condemned to die so as to give rise to a new culture, one that will take from us all that remains of our exhausted wisdom. History decrees it and aesthetics confirms it. Having plunged into the depth of the history of artistic portraits and having thus been made invulnerable to the charge of extreme artistic radicalism, I can boldly and certifiably say that I am not mistaken in my conviction. We are witnesses to a great moment of historical summation in the name of a new and unknown culture which will be created by us but which will sweep us away.[1]

Without benefit of hindsight, Diaghilev describes the twilight of the Silver Age[2] and Symbolist movement and, almost uncannily, reveals an awareness of his own place in history. He had come to believe that the growing opposition to the aristocracy and growing unrest in the nation were but a prelude to the end of autocratic rule. The old social order would be supplanted by an undefined new order. Unwilling to subscribe to the fantasy of rebirth through catharsis, Diaghilev intimated that the Symbolists, in advocating revolutionary upheaval, had in effect wished themselves out of existence.

His perception that there was a depressing quality to the palaces and estates of *fin-de-siècle* Russia had been anticipated both in the publications of the Symbolist era and the years preceding it. Signs of decadence, the social malaise that presaged the tumults of the modern era, appear in such prose works as *Nevsky Prospect* (1835) by Nikolai Gogol (1809–52) and *The Bronze Horseman* (*Mednïy vsadnik*, 1833) by Alexander Pushkin (1799–1837). These tales portray St. Petersburg as being suspended between natural and supernatural worlds, but also between the recent and distant past, an eclectic museum of church cupolas and palace columns. The painter Konstantin Somov (1869–1939), a founding member of the World of Art circle, framed Russian aristocratic society in black, filling his canvases with decaying landscapes, lethargic noblemen, and "an almost demonic atmosphere of deathly sportiveness, automatised eroticism."[3] The Symbolists interpreted the clockwork regularity of imperial life in two interrelated ways. First, it suggested to them that the state's subjects were like automatons, moribund beings whose lives were devoid of movement and variation, clinging to outmoded customs and routines. Secondly, and far more fancifully, it suggested that forces beyond the control of human will oversaw historical events. Life seemed increasingly fragmented and unsettled, subject to chance-based operations or supernatural incursions. On this point, the Symbolist dramatist and novelist Fyodor Sologub (1863–1927) asserted that humans were merely pawns in "a demonic game, fate's amusement with its marionettes."[4] Recently developing this concept, the cultural semiotician Yuriy Lotman noted that the dialectical relationship between life as dictated by fixed rules and by random elements is reflected in such social activities as card games.[5]

The only composer at the time to give voice to the growing sense of unease in Russian society, Pyotr Chaikovsky, posthumously acquired cult status among the Symbolists. Surprising and unfamiliar as it may be to those accustomed to thinking of him as a conservative artist, the author of fairy-tale ballets, sentimental operas, and mawkish symphonies, he was revered in his time as a modernist seer. If we characterize his works as emblems of kitsch sensibility, of course, it is easier to reduce them to the level of neurotic effusions or essentialize them as homoerotic fantasies whose values are less ethical than aesthetic, less profound than beautiful. But Chaikovsky was never merely a composer of kitsch. He embraced the spiritual ideals of the nascent Symbolist era, reading the writings of Vladimir Solovyov and setting romances by the young Dmitriy Merezhkovsky. His last opera, *Iolanthe* (*Iolanta*, opus 69, 1891), embodied what Arkadii Klimovitsky calls the Symbolist precepts "of the 'not spoken,' the 'intimated,' the 'penumbral,' and at the same time of an ecstasy and a religious/pantheistic Utopia."[6] In perhaps an oblique reference to that opera's gestural, topical Wagnerisms, a critic for the Moscow-based Symbolist journal *Libra (Vesï)* went so far as to label Chaikovsky the prodigious herald of "the music of the future":

> One could say that the VIth Symphony [in B minor, opus 74, 1893] was insufficient to elucidate conclusively the fundamental motif of Chaikovsky's creative work. It is as though he placed within it the cards of sorrow and joy, love and hate, all of life . . . and the card of death.
> Entering the world with words of Joy (Chaikovsky's examination cantata on [Friedrich von] Schiller's [1786] text "To Joy"), the poet from his first steps became a priest of the minor mode, a poet of Grief. Raised in a moment of inspiration to the starry heights, his immortal soul contemplated Beauty. Incarnated on earth, he looked sadly at earth, at man, and yearned with passionate thirst for Heaven to illuminate man with Beauty's rays. Love and empathy for the helplessness and finitude of man took an upper hand over the titanic might of the poet-demigod. Humanity won. And in the swan song: grief for an Ideal and fear for man![7]

Despite his claim that Chaikovsky's music was less innovative than Wagner's, the author, N. Suvorovsky, posits that both composers combined opposing creative principles in their compositions: the Apollonian and Dionysian. Paraphrasing Nietzsche's *The Birth of Tragedy* out of cultural and national context, Suvorovsky adds that Chaikovsky's music, in its disavowal of Apollonian restraint and control for Dionysian passion and irrationality, sought not to narrate or to represent phenomenal reality but to express the eternal life beyond phenomena, the noumenal essence that precedes all things. Chaikovsky, in his estimation, sought to balance "harmony" and "discord," or, as Nietzsche put it, Apollonian "dream" and Dionysian "drunkenness." On the one hand, his music masked the tragic suffering and "finitude of man" with images of "Beauty"; on the other, it celebrated man's "passionate thirst for heaven" and the eternal Will by revealing the celestial "Ideal." Suvorovsky's comments obviously have less to do with musical technique than with musical metaphysics. This interpretive leap was natural for the Symbolists, who attempted to liberate music from genre and style, function and technique, and associate it with primal drives and celestial energies. Listening to Chaikovsky's compositions, Suvorovsky perceived (or at least wanted to perceive), the presence of eternal harmony.

To ascertain why he revered Chaikovsky (along with or instead of Wagner) as the avatar of "the music of the future," we must examine the remarks about cards in the quoted passage. Although they were made in reference to Chaikovsky's Symphony No. 6—and to the composer's enthusiasm for card-playing—the remarks also bring to mind his penultimate opera, *The Queen of Spades* (*Pikovaya dama*, opus 68, 1890), which is based on Pushkin's terse, thirty-three-page novella of the same name. Much more than Chaikovsky's instrumental works, this opera fascinated the Symbolists, for it played out all of their creative obsessions: the relationship between fortune and fate, dream and reality, societal death and societal rebirth. It also fell under the rubric of what the polyglot Hungarian critic Max Nordau (real surname Südfeldt, 1849–1923) called *fin-de-siècle* "degeneracy," a term taken from forensic studies that stood as a code word for modernism.[8] Significantly, *The Queen of Spades* also helped convert the founders of the World of Art circle from literature and painting to opera and ballet. In 1912, an unidentified critic for the journal *Theater* (*Teatr*) reported that, shortly after the 7 December 1890 premiere at the Mariyinsky Theater in St. Petersburg, Chaikovsky bumped into Diaghilev, the artist and art historian Alexander Benois (1870–1960), and the writer Dmitriy Filosofov (1872–1940) on the street. The three of them immediately began to praise the opera, singing the opening duet of act I, scene 2 to the composer and recalling their enthusiastic impressions of the whole. This delighted Chaikovsky, who had worried that *The Queen of Spades* had disappointed the Mariyinsky audience. Thenceforth, the critic added, Chaikovsky maintained close ties with the World of Art circle.[9]

The anecdote might seem farfetched, but Benois corroborated it in his memoirs. The artist reported that the opera's distorted depiction of St. Petersburg tempered his perspective on its bridges and canals and revived his appreciation of his pied-à-terre. Chaikovsky's transposition of the plot of Pushkin's novella from the era of Tsar Alexander I (specifically 1833) to the era of Catherine the Great (who reigned 1762–96) sparked Benois's interest in that "cult of the past" which was "later reflected in all of the artistic activity of our community—in our periodical publications, in *The World of Art,* in *Artistic Treasures of Russia [Khudozhestvennïye sokrovishcha Rossii]* and, later on, in *Past Years [Starïye godi].* It was reflected in our books—in Diaghilev's monograph on [the painter Dmitriy] Levitsky [1735–1822], and in my monograph on Tsarskoye Selo." Benois concluded that if Pushkin's novella "could be viewed as 'Hoffmannism in a Russian manner,' this 'Hoffmannism in a Russian manner' (in a 'Petersburg manner') could to a much greater degree be viewed in [Chaikovsky's] setting of it."[10]

Benois here alludes to the macabre elements of *The Queen of Spades,* but also acknowledges his fascination with Chaikovsky's ballet *The Nutcracker (Shchelkunchik,* opus 71, 1892), based on an 1816 tale by E. T. A. Hoffmann (1776–1822). Though nowadays trivialized as a holiday diversion for children, the original version, sharing a double bill with *Iolanthe,* explored a concept of considerable significance to the productions of the Ballets Russes (notably Benois's and Stravinsky's scenario for the ballet *Petrushka* [1911]): the malleable relationship between puppet and human domains.[11] It likewise informed the grotesque and scandalous narratives of modernist *commedia dell'arte* works. Benois believed that *The Nutcracker* combined Dionysian and Apollonian devices: discordant, asymmetrical fissures pockmarked otherwise harmonious and symmetrical dances; unconventional instrumental combinations replaced conventional ones; leitmotifs recurred in radically altered forms. Though he admitted that the ballet addressed childhood themes, he asserted that it had to do less with childhood bliss than with the contradictory impressions to which a child is exposed. It offset the perspectives of young and old. In the roughly contemporaneous *Queen of Spades,* one detects this shifting and crossing of perspectives in the interpenetration of dramatic layers, the inclusion of the play-within-the-play in act II, scene 1, and the portrayal of a spectral incarnation in act III, scene 1—metatheatrical effects that anticipate the self-reflexive elements of much later operas.

Outside the World of Art circle, the opera became a source of inspiration for the leading Symbolist poets. In a cryptic letter to Pyotr Pertsov (1868–1947), the editor of the newspaper *Word (Slovo),* Alexander Blok proclaimed Chaikovsky the champion of an artistic polemic with Pushkin. Blok wrote the letter in order to correct a quotation in his 1906 article "A Pedant on a Poet" ("Pedant o poete," 1906). In proofreading the article for inclusion in *Word,* Pertsov had ascribed the quotation to the drama *Masquerade (Maskarad,* 1835) by Lermontov, but, as Blok clarifies, it actually came from the first stanza of Tomsky's ballad in *The Queen of Spades,* act I, scene 1:

"Count Saint-Germain and the Moscow Venus" are not Lermontov's [words]. I evidently wrote so foggily here because for me most of it was self-evident. It is *The Queen of Spades,* and not even Pushkin's, but Chaikovsky's (libretto by Modest Chaikovsky [1850–1916]):

> Once in Versailles at the "jeu de la Reine"
> The Moscow Venus had lost her last *sou* . . .
> Among the Guests was Count Saint-Germain.
> Following the game . . .
> He whispered to her:
> Words, sweeter than Mozart's sounds . . .
> (Three cards, three cards, three cards) . . .
>
> [Odnazhdï v Versale "au jeu de la Reine"
> Venus Moscovite proigralas' dotla . . .
> V chisle priglashennïkh bïl Graf Sen-Zhermen.
> Sledya za igroy . . .
> I yey prosheptal:
> Slova, slashche zvukov Motsarta . . .
> (Tri kartï, tri kartï, tri kartï) . . .]

And so on. This is the place of the "masquerade" (Lermontov's *Masquerade*), the fantastic place where "Pushkin and Lermontov" are no longer the "two founders of the Petersburg era." The "Apollonian" Pushkin tumbled into the abyss, where the hand of Chaikovsky, a magician and musician, pushed him.[12]

Masquerade takes up themes of societal alienation and deprivation. The protagonist Arbenin, like the protagonist Herman of *The Queen of Spades,* is contemptuous of others and demonically destructive. The two works are also related in their ball scenes, where pairs of lovers appear in costume, and where a feeling of unalterable destiny and inevitable tragedy is extolled. They likewise conclude with a peroration on the vanity and frailty of human existence. The relationship that Blok established in his article between the play and the opera illustrates that Chaikovsky, like Lermontov, was one of a select group of older artists whom the Symbolists hailed as central influences on their writing.

Of course, the notion that Chaikovsky was somehow prescient clashes noisily with his conservative contemporary image, which was created long after the Symbolist era by Soviet scholars who could not or would not countenance his penchant for innovation.[13] That Chaikovsky disappeared into "the abyss." The composer was instead regarded as an antagonist of the artistic trends his music actually presaged. A survey of the critical press indicates that *The Queen of Spades* was considered a flawed score, an exception in Chaikovsky's *oeuvre,* created against his and his brother's will at the behest of Ivan Vsevolozhsky, the Intendant of the Bolshoy Theater in Moscow, who had commissioned it. Pyotr was admonished for his musical borrowings and instrumental *diablerie*, Modest for his recasting and expansion of the Pushkin source text. Their intentions were even called into question by the theater director Vsevolod Meyerhold (1874–1940), who had been involved with the Symbolists in his early career, but who produced an anti-Symbolist, re-Pushkinized version of *The Queen of Spades* at the Malïy Opera Theater in Leningrad in 1935. The novelties of the staging resided in the acting, which arose contrapuntally from the music, and the stage décor, which represented the estates of St. Petersburg with a "muddied" tone and strove for a "spherical perspective" on the action through the interaction of color, space, and light.[14] Though the dismal cultural climate of the 1930s ensured that the production would be relatively short-lived (ninety-one performances in two and a half seasons), it supported the official Soviet assessment of *The Queen of Spades* as an aberration in Chaikovsky's otherwise unadventurous operatic career.

In response, I will attempt in this chapter to situate the opera in proper cultural and historical context: the Silver Age. I will argue that Chaikovsky, like the World of Art painters, foreshadowed the Russian Symbolist movement. I will discuss three scenes from the opera in detail, concentrating on their generic and stylistic abnormalities and on the manner in which they project a sense of historical fate, a sense of the decline of aristocratic existence. A central premise of my reading will be that Herman, the protagonist, inhabits the operatic equivalent of a picture gallery, one that includes images of the past, present, and future. The scenes are staged in such a way as to present the other characters less as living beings than as the subjects of these images. The Countess, for example, seems to be enshrined in a somber and wistful portrait of eighteenth-century St. Petersburg, one of those portraits that Diaghilev put on display in his landmark exhibition.

THE PUSHKIN CENTENNIAL ISSUE OF *THE WORLD OF ART*

The *World of Art* journal, a gathering of photo spreads, essays, poems, and reviews, concerned itself with the preservation and interpretation of the Russian cultural heritage. On the literary side, separate issues were devoted to Fyodor Dostoyevsky (1821–81), Lev Tolstoy (1828–1910), and Pushkin. The Pushkin centennial issue of July 1899 featured a series of highly subjective articles by the founding members of the Symbolist movement.[15] The contributors lauded the poet's insights into the subtleties of the Slavic psyche and the workings of Slavic society. They deemed him the inspiration for the artistic directions of their time because he relied, in both his poetry and prose, on words that were more suggestive than explanatory. Central to *The Queen of Spades*, for example, are the traditional symbols of day and night, sun and cloud, which, divorced from their conventional emotional connotations, come to denote madness and the irrational. The most prominent symbol, of course, is the queen of spades playing card, whose meaning shifts from gambling and loss to vengeance and death. Above and beyond the syntax, however, it is clear that the novella's characters are also symbolic. In an elegant interpretation of the novella—one of several that use Vladimir Propp's *Morphology of the Folk Tale* (*Morfologiya skazki*, 1958) as an analytical tool—Natalie Foshko contends that the Countess occupies the ambiguous status of "magic grantor" and "villainous donor," at once providing the hero with "secret information" and harshly punishing him for exploiting it. Liza's status is also ambiguous: depending on the context, she acts as either a "helper" or "mediator."[16] To jump the gun a little, it should be noted that, owing to its malleability, Pushkin's language offered superb text-setting opportunities for Chaikovsky. In the vocal ensembles of his opera, in which each character projects contrasting thoughts and feelings, the same word could project contrasting meanings. The act I, scene 1 and act III, scene 3 choruses provide a useful example. Within them, the secondary characters claim that the queen of spades holds no great significance, whereas the main character asserts that it possesses the galvanism of the supernatural sphere. Yet whereas the ambiguities of Pushkin's language are preserved in Chaikovsky's opera, the ambiguities in the poet's characterizations are not: Chaikovsky assigns his cast members fixed dramatic functions. Herman, the one figure who attempts to change his role—to alter, in a sense, his fate—perishes.

Significant also to the Symbolists was the idea that *The Queen of Spades* was an imaginative reinterpretation of an actual event. Though the poets acknowledged Pushkin's rational, clinical style, they drew attention to the fact that, in *The Queen of Spades*, he had made himself his own creative subject. While this mimetic reflex was nothing new (it is typical of, for example, German Romanticism), Pushkin, according to the Symbolists, did not simply mirror reality according to the conventions of literary realism. Rather, he used symbols to express his subjective perception of life, "to clothe inner reality in outer form." And whereas his realist colleagues sought to depict "life outside themselves," Pushkin trained his focus inward. His writing was not only a creative act but a means to higher perception.[17] Though provocative, the Symbolist assessment of the novella's origin is inaccurate. Neil Cornwell reports that the novella actually has three (fictional and nonfictional) sources: first, Pushkin's "own earlier abandoned prose fragments"; second, an "actual society anecdote involving the then still living (and aged ninety-two) Princess Golitsïna who had allegedly, many years before in Paris, received the advice of Saint-Germain and subsequently therewith enabled her grandson to regain a loss by playing a certain three cards"; and finally, "a supposedly autobiographical episode of an amorous nature."[18] Referring to the novella's prose-poetry admixture, another Pushkin scholar, John Bayley, adds that it "grew up from abandoned story-projects and the characters in them, was grafted on to an anecdote from real life, and given a colouring of fashionably literary *diablerie*."[19] *The Queen of Spades*, in short, is only partially grounded in Pushkin's biography.

The plot of the novella is set in 1833. Chapter 1 opens with a card game at the St. Petersburg residence of Narumov, an officer of the tsar's mounted regiment. The players include two other military men: Herman, an engineer, and Count Tomsky, the grandson of Countess Anna Fyodotovna. Near the end of the game, Tomsky recounts how the Countess once gambled excessively, but ceased after incurring heavy losses at a salon in Paris. The occult practitioner Saint-Germain rescued her from bankruptcy by providing her with the names of three winning cards. She swore never to gamble again and shared the secret of the cards only with her recently deceased husband. Desperate to obtain the winning formula, in chapter 2 Herman asks Liza, the Countess's adolescent ward, for access to the Countess's estate. Liza misinterprets his advances as an attempt to win her affections. In chapter 3, Herman, abetted by Liza, breaks into the Countess's chamber and awaits her return from a society ball. Upon her arrival, he confronts her, demanding to know the winning formula; when she claims ignorance, he loses his temper, brandishing a pistol and calling her "an old witch." Frightened, the Countess suffers a fatal stroke. In chapter 4, Herman confesses his unintended crime to a shocked Liza, who condemns him as a "monster." In chapter 5, Herman attends the Countess's funeral; as he passes by the casket, he thinks that he sees the corpse "mockingly winking" at him. Following an evening of excessive drinking, he retires to his barracks room, only to be roused by a visit from an old woman closely resembling the deceased Countess. The real-or-hallucinated intruder informs him that he can win at faro[20] by playing the three, seven, and ace cards, but cautions that he can play the series only once, in order, at a rate of one card per night. In chapter 6, Herman visits the local gambling salon. He wins on the first night with the three card and on the second night with the seven card, but loses on the third night when the card he plays turns out not to be the ace but the queen of spades. In the brief epilogue, we learn that Herman "lost his mind" after the loss, and that Liza, his forsaken love, subsequently married the rich son of the Countess's steward.[21]

Noting the novella's dramatic potential, in 1886 Vsevolozhsky proposed it to the novice composer Nikolai Klenovsky (1857–1915) as the subject of an opera. He accepted the proposal and enlisted Vasiliy Kandaurov (1830–88) as the librettist. Klenovsky procrastinated on the music, however; eventually, Kandaurov became impatient with him and resigned. Vsevolozhsky, eager to stage a Pushkin-based opera, then enlisted Modest Chaikovsky as the librettist. Modest scripted the first three scenes but then learned that Klenovsky had altogether abandoned the project. He did not write again until the fall of 1889, when Vsevolozhsky convinced Chaikovsky (always his preferred choice as the composer) to write the music. Modest recalled that his brother

> read through what I had done and, being satisfied, immediately decided to compose an opera on my libretto. In the middle of December a meeting took place in the office of the Imperial Theatres' director attended by designers, office heads, V. Pogozhev, and Domershchikov of the administration department, in which I read through my scenario and in which it was decided to transfer the action from the time of Alexander I, where I had set it for Klenovsky, to the end of the reign of Catherine II. To accord with this the scenario of the third scene—the ball—was completely changed, and the scene by the Winter Canal, which had been no part of my plan, was added. Thus in the scenario of the complete libretto these two scenes belong as much to me as to all the other persons attending this meeting. In addition, I. A. Vsevolozhsky recommended many changes of detail to me for the remaining scenes.[22]

Enthused, the composer agreed to prepare a vocal score for rehearsal the following May. Needing an escape from Moscow and St. Petersburg after a grueling series of concert engagements (and after the sudden reappearance in his life of Antonina Milyukova [1848–1917], a former conservatory student whom he had hastily married on 6 July 1877, and from whom he just as hastily sought a separation), he decided to settle in Florence to work on *The Queen of Spades.*

His diaries show that he worked quickly, which was proof of his powers of invention and a reflection of the extremely tight deadline. Chaikovsky first addressed his brother's draft libretto for act I. In ten days he had "laboriously worked through" the short score for scene 1; a week later, he had finished scene 2. Before undertaking act II, scene 1, he moved ahead to act II, scene 2, Herman's portentous encounter with the Countess, which he considered to be the crux of the drama. It was drafted by 23 February. That same day, he turned to act II, scene 1, specifically the middle section, an allegorical pastoral drama performed *within* the opera by Liza, her girlfriend Polina, and Tomsky. "The beginning came with difficulty," he wrote, "but then it went well. . . . At times it seems that I am living in the eighteenth century, and that nothing has occurred since Mozart." He "finished and played through" the entire scene on 2 March.[23] Remarkably, upon receiving the remainder of the libretto from Modest, his compositional pace increased. Act III, scene 1, depicting Herman's real-or-hallucinated meeting with the Countess's spirit in his barracks room, took only three days; scene 2, depicting Herman and Liza's farewell assignation on the banks of a canal, just four more. On 8 March, he began work on the overture and act III, scene 3, completing the former on 14 March and the latter, excluding Herman's final monologue, on 15 March. Minor revisions and the preparation of the vocal score absorbed three additional weeks. On 5 April, just ahead of the rehearsal deadline for the autumn season at the Mariyinsky Theater, he sent the vocal score to Vsevolozhsky. Chaikovsky then took the train to Rome, where he began the orchestration. The first act was finished by 15 April. Though the orchestration of acts II and III was delayed by his journey back to St. Petersburg, with the exception of incidental details, it was completed by 8 June.

Four facets of the creative process illuminate the proto-Symbolist content of the opera: Chaikovsky's conception of the protagonist, the embellishment of the aura of uncertainty concerning the relationship of the natural and supernatural, the symmetrical arrangement of the set pieces, and the transposition of the time of the action. Concerning the first point, it is often noted that Chaikovsky claimed empathy for most of the characters and events in the opera. On 5 August 1890, shortly after finishing *The Queen of Spades*, he informed a friend, Grand Duke Konstantin Romanov, that he had worked on it with "unbelievable ardor and enthusiasm, and actually felt and experienced everything occurring in it (to the point that I once even feared the appearance of the specter of 'the Queen of Spades') and hope that all of my authorial anxiety, agitation, and passion will echo in the hearts of responsive listeners."[24] Of the finale, Chaikovsky recalled that he "wept terribly when [Herman] took his last breath, the result of fatigue, or perhaps because [the opera] is truly good."[25] To Modest he added:

> [I] pitied Herman so much that I suddenly began to weep uncontrollably. This weeping continued for a terribly long time and turned into mild hysteria of a welcome sort: in other words, it was really pleasant to cry. Then I pondered why (for there has never been another time

when I grieved for my hero's fate, and I tried to understand why I so wanted to cry). It seems that Herman was not just a subject for me to write this or that music, but at all times a real, living person, with whom I strongly sympathized.[26]

These comments appear embarrassingly, even improbably personal, but they may be only a projection. For his letter readers—indeed, even for his prospective diary readers—Chaikovsky often adopted the persona of a tormented and persecuted artist, finding within it a rich source for his music. In a 27 June 1888 diary entry, he made a statement about his letter-writing habits that critics ignore at their peril:

> It seems to me that letters can never be completely sincere. I make this judgement at least about myself. To whomever and for whatever reason I write, I always worry about the impression that the letter will make, not only on the correspondent, but on any chance reader. Thus I pose. Sometimes I *endeavor to make* the tone of a letter simple and sincere, that is, to make it *seem* so. Excluding letters written in a fit of *passion*, I am never myself in my letters. But then these latter letters are always a source of remorse and sorrow, and sometimes even great torment. When I read the letters of famous people, published after their deaths, a vague sensation of falseness and deceit always grates on me.[27]

Written two years before the composition of *The Queen of Spades*, this is a warning against taking Chaikovsky's identification with Herman too seriously. For like other nineteenth-century artists, he fictionalized his life, interpreting certain literary works as programs for his own behavior—an activity that Lotman, among others, has dubbed "everyday Byronism."[28] Thus, when the composer expressed a dire emotional situation, he was fabricating a general, rather than personal, feature of human experience. His musical conception of Herman, like his epistolary self-conception, was precipitated more from external than internal conditions.

To identify—or pretend to identify—with a fictional character more akin to a German Romantic literary hero than a Russian one (as his very name—"Gherman" in Russian—attests[29]), Chaikovsky mimicked his lifestyle, attending Florence's casinos, gambling and (doubtless unintentionally) losing, and drinking to excess. Accordingly, among the *dramatis personae* of *The Queen of Spades*, only Herman is portrayed as a full-blooded, three-dimensional figure; compared to him, Liza, the Countess, and Tomsky resemble two-dimensional playing cards. One could even argue that Chaikovsky designed the opera to foreground the idea that humans, from birth to death, are pawns in a universal, cosmic game. The rules of faro become a metaphor for the rules of society, which determine individual fates. Several stages of life, with their attendant rituals and rules of decorum, are represented in the score: infants in arms, adolescents engaged in guiltless caprice, middle-agers pursuing profit, pensioners taking stock. The customs of different strata of society are also depicted: aristocratic amusement, diplomatic business, military routine, religious ceremony. Herman sees these from the outside, standing in the stage wings during the outdoor crowd scenes and wandering alienated through the ball scenes.

While he was sensitive to the intricate system of symbols governing the source novella (the term "symbol" here defined in narrow, formalist terms as a multivalent entity that allows for different interpretations, rather than in broader, mystical terms as an entity that contains, in condensed form, the essence of incomprehensible phenomena), Chaikovsky exhorted his brother to write the libretto as succinctly as possible.[30] The composer sought to represent the intricacies of the novella as far as possible through music alone. Significantly, the two passages of the libretto in which Pushkin's narrative is largely retained—the act II, scene 2 meeting between Herman and the Countess and act III, scene 1 meeting between him and the Countess's ghost—are precisely those in which the border separating the rational and irrational is traversed. The oscillation between the two realms defined the novella for subsequent writers as an example of the literary fantastic, a term applied to texts in which the relationship between the hallucinated and enacted, dreamed and lived, is uncertain.[31] To maintain this uncertainty, Pushkin used the ambiguous verb "to seem" ["pokazat'sya"] to describe such incidents as the Countess's cadaver grinning at Herman as he passes by her coffin . . . it only *seemed* to occur. The dual-world structure of the text is evident not only in the relationship between Herman and the Countess, but also in his relationship to the secondary characters: his plotting to acquire wealth goes unnoticed until the final scene in the gambling salon, when the laws of their world are briefly threatened (Herman wins on his first two wagers, and it seems that he might win the third as well) but then reaffirmed when he loses.

The texts of the paranormal scenes, extracted from Pushkin, provide an additional definition for the metaphor of the card game. Together with rule-bound social order, faro stands for lawless social disorder, the tug-of-war between rational and irrational drives in human affairs. Games of chance stand for the instabilities of history, the historical and political vacillations that affect not only parvenus like Herman, but all humans. Lotman contends that, within Pushkin's novella, "the 'probability' picture of the world, the conception of life as being ruled by Chance, opens before the individual opportunities of unlimited success, and sharply divides people into the passive slaves of convention and the 'men of Fate,' whose appearance in European culture in the first half of the nineteenth century is invariably associated with the figure of Napoleon." The writer clarifies that Herman, depicted by Pushkin as a Romantic hero, "strives amid the turmoil of surrounding life to achieve an aim which he has set himself." However, as his experience in the gambling salon illustrates, he simultaneously manipulates and is manipulated by events. The "power" of the game can "be seen as an infernal force which mocks the Napoleonic hero and plays with him." [32]

The Chaikovsky brothers departed from Pushkin's novella by suffusing the entire opera (not just the second half) with a fantastic aura, suggesting that the characters are combating unknown and irrational elements—both the inflexible laws of the external order and the power of malignant fate. Of the early scenes, the act II, scene 1 *intermède*, which Modest cobbled together from verses by the poet Pyotr Karabanov (1764–1829),[33] first raises the possibility that events are illusory. Entitled *The Sincerity of the Shepherdess (Iskrennost' pastushki)*, it features stylized rustics romping in the outdoors. Their idyllic landscape is governed by mythological gods who descend from the heavens to ensure that the rules of their world—the game that is their existence—are being heeded. By including the opera's "real" characters as participants in the pastoral play, Modest intimates that they too might be subject to manipulation by other forces. The linkage between the inner and outer plots is at first lightly ironic but becomes increasingly macabre as events unfold.

Besides Pushkin, who might Modest's literary source, his libretto-inspiring Saint-Germain, have been? One must turn to other, earlier stage versions of Pushkin's novella to answer this question. In 1836, the comic dramatist Prince Alexander Shakhovskoy (1777–1846) wrote a one-act epilogue-vaudeville based on *The Queen of Spades* entitled *Chrysomania, or The Passion for Money (Krestnitsï, ili Polyubovnaya sdelka)*. Fourteen years later, Jacques Halévy (1799–1862) and Eugène Scribe (1791–1861) composed an opera entitled *La dame de pique*, based on the translation of Pushkin's novella by Prosper Mérimée (1803–70) for the July 1849 issue of *Revue des deux mondes*. Though Halévy and Scribe retained the basic structure of Pushkin's novella in *La dame de pique*, they significantly altered the physical appearances and personalities of the *dramatis personae*. The Countess becomes the wealthy but infirm Princess Polowska, who manages a crew of unruly salt miners at her estate. Herman is transformed from a discontented engineer into the equally discontented miner Roskow. Lizaveta Ivanovna becomes Lisanka, Polowska's daughter, who is prevented from marrying below her station. It is not Roskow who desires the secret card formula but the villain Zizianow, who was once romantically involved with the Princess. The plot is complicated by the insertion of two other characters: Herman Klarenburg, a German banker involved in a business relationship with the tsar, and the virtuous Constantin, who endeavors to repay his father's debts to Zizianow. Carolyn Roberts, to whom this general summary and the upcoming libretto examples are indebted, observes that Scribe's most striking departure from Pushkin's original concerned the infusion of the supernatural:

> What is only suggested in the Pushkin becomes explicit in the Scribe. Responding to the hint that St.-Germain was a magician dabbling in the Black Arts, Scribe has taken his *Pique dame* into the realm of *grand opéra à la* [Meyerbeer's] *Robert le diable* and has written a libretto on the theme of selling one's soul to the devil. Thus, approximately ten years before the opera which was to prove the most popular version of the idea—the Barbier-Carré and Gounod *Faust* (1859)—and several years before any of the other major musical treatments such as Schumann's *Manfred* (1853) or Boito's *Mefistofele* (1868), Scribe had already found the theme which was to have almost archetypal significance for the nineteenth century: he had transformed "Pikovaja dama" into a Faust opera.[34]

It is unclear how well the Chaikovsky brothers knew Scribe and Halévy's opera, but they were certainly familiar with Mérimée, whose 1845 short story *Carmen* inspired Georges Bizet's 1875 *Carmen*, an opera they adored. Roberts points out that the children's mock military chorus in act I, scene 1 of *The Queen of Spades* is based on that in act I of Bizet's opera. "By paying tribute to *Carmen*," she writes, the Chaikovsky brothers paid tribute to Mérimée, the person "responsible for introducing [Pushkin's novella] to the opera in the first place."[35] The influence of Scribe would seem to reside in the eclecticism of Modest's libretto. Whereas the earlier librettist embellished Pushkin's plot with near-quotations from Victor Hugo, Goethe's *Faust*, and other French comic and grand operas, the later one embellished it with a plethora of references to eighteenth- and nineteenth-century Russian playwrights and essayists. Contra Pushkin, Scribe and Modest both stressed—rather than hinted—that the Countess dabbles in the black arts and that the secret card formula is diabolical. The added details allow for special musical and visual effects. The non-Pushkin insertions in *La dame de pique* tend to be incidental, however, while those in Chaikovsky's opera serve to evoke a mystical locale: the shrouded, illusory geography and hydrography of *fin-de-siècle* St. Petersburg.

The other possible hidden source for Modest's libretto is Dostoyevsky's 1866 novel *The Gambler* (*Igrok*), a psychological retelling of *The Queen of Spades* that later served as the basis of Prokofiev's first completed opera. Roberts, quoting a footnote in a 1971 article by the Soviet music critic D. Daragan, observes that there are direct verbal parallels between the two texts.[36] Alongside these parallels, however, are straightforward references to Dostoyevsky's characters. To Liza, the moral center of the opera, Modest assigned a prosperous fiancé, Prince Eletsky, who has no counterpart in Pushkin's *The Queen of Spades* but resembles the French Marquis in *The Gambler*. Moreover, just as Modest's Liza prefers the impoverished Herman to Eletsky (despite being prohibited from wedding beneath her class), Dostoyevsky's Polina prefers the impoverished Alexey to the French Marquis. In fact, the very presence of a romantic subplot in Modest's libretto shows Dostoyevsky's influence. Pushkin chose to leave the relationship between Liza and Herman undeveloped; the engineer merely uses her to gain access to the Countess's chamber. Both Dostoyevsky and Modest, however, portray their lead couples' love as troubled but authentic. Whereas in the novella Herman learns the Countess's card secret before encountering Liza and exploiting her generosity, in the two subsequent texts the sequence is reversed: the heroes fall for the heroines unprompted by external circumstances.

Less tangible—but more striking—are the thematic connections between Modest's libretto and Dostoyevsky's novel. Using the casino as metaphor, Dostoyevsky sustains a dream-like aura throughout *The Gambler*. The card players are represented only externally, like cardboard cutouts, and their destinies are subjected to blind chance. Modest incorporated these ideas into his final scene, highlighting in particular the notion that the casino is a kind of twilight zone. As in the source novella, the narrative of the ghostly visitation is ambiguous in content (it is unclear whether it is an actual event or vision, and whether the card formula is given to Herman or intuited by him), but other scenes indicate that the characters actually acquire knowledge by means other than rational cognition.

The most obvious of these is the first scene, specifically, Tomsky's ballad about the "Moscow Venus's" occult indoctrination in Paris in her youth, which effectively halts the temporal flow of the opera. The surrounding characters do not sense time passing during his performance. Unlike the source novella, in which Tomsky's narrative is interrupted by questions from his audience and his lighting of a pipe, in the opera it unfolds against a static backdrop. The revelation of mystical knowledge (that is, knowledge of which neither Herman nor any other character is cognitively aware) is marked by the alteration or elimination of normal time and space relations in the score. The ballad marks a shift from an animate to an inanimate discursive register, its extra-temporal qualities evinced by the simple fact that Tomsky's audience neither discusses nor disputes its contents with him but disperses, leaving Herman alone on stage to sum up the proceedings. The ballad appears to be intended for his ears alone, its message sinking into his imagination in later scenes. As if affirming Foshko's thesis that Herman belongs to "the fairy-tale world," while the other characters belong to "the real world,"[37] its significance changes for him from something that he initially dismisses as a "fairy tale" (and the other characters consider to be "a mere fluke") into a cabalistic imperative. The broader influence of Silver Age aesthetics on the libretto is evident in those places where the primary and secondary characters express a desire to escape the present into the past. Modest depicts Russia's ruling class as unsteady and enfeebled, groping for shortcuts to lost certainties. In Pushkin's novella, such gentrified atavism—foreshadowing the theory and practice of Symbolism—is expressed solely by the Countess, who identifies herself with an extinct social elite and who seeks in vain to regain the beauty of her youth. Pushkin's narrator notes that her thoughts are fixed on the past, but also notes (at the conclusion of chapter 3) that her attention is scattered and that she does not seem to hear Herman when he quizzes her about the card formula. The details of her establishment, lifestyle, and tastes are recounted in a detached and dispassionate manner. At the start of chapter 2, for example, we are told that "the Countess had not the least claims to the beauty which had long ago faded, but she still kept up all the habits of her youth, closely followed the fashions of the seventies and devoted as much time and care to her dress as she had sixty years before."[38]

In the corresponding scene in the opera, Modest assigns the Countess a long soliloquy in which she laments the inexorable march of time. Narrative reticence is abandoned: she passionately and imaginatively recalls her scandal-tinged Parisian years, disclosing in turn her idiosyncrasies and vulnerabilities. Her mournful nostalgia is presaged by the opening chorus of act I, scene 1, in which pedestrians in the summer garden grumble that the spring was warmer, the days sunnier, and life gentler during the reign of Empress Elizabeth:

Old Women:
We lived better in the past,
And days like these

Each year came early in the spring!
But now it's rare
To have sunshine from the morning.
It's become worse, it's true,
It's time to die!
In the past it was truly better,
Life was happier,
And for us it was not a miracle
To see the sun shining.

Old Men:
For many years we have not seen days like these,
But we used to see them often.
In the days of Elizabeth, a wondrous time,
Summer, fall, and spring were better![. . .]
Ah, in the past life was better, happier,
It's been a long time
Since we had such clear spring days.

[*Starukhi:*
Prezhde luchshe zhili,
I takiye dni
Kazhdïy god bïvali ranneyu vesnoy!
A teper' im v redkost'
Solnïshko s utra.
Khuzhe stalo, pravo,
Umirat' pora!
Prezhde pravo bïlo luchshe,
Bïlo veseleye zhit',
Nam i solnïshko na nebe
Ne bïlo v dikovinku.

Stariki:
Mnogo let ne vidim mï takikh den'kov,
A, bïvalo, chasto mï vidali ikh.
V dni Elizavetï, chudnaya pora,
Luchshe bïli leto, osen' i vesna![. . .]
Akh, v starinu zhilosya luchshe, veseley,
Takikh vesennikh, yasnïkh dney
Davno uzh ne bïvalo.]

The choristers describe a depressing present where even nature is uncooperative: Herman's sudden entrance coincides with a thunderstorm that interrupts the holiday promenade. A stranger in their midst, he shares neither their nihilism nor their melancholia. In the opera's climactic scene he addresses the question of the meaning of life, even though the aristocrats around him have long since concluded that it has none.

Before amplifying each of these issues through specific musical examples, an additional point should be made about the structure and organization of the libretto. Owing to its allusions to Scribe and Dostoyevsky as well as its citations and borrowings from other eighteenth- and nineteenth-century poets and writers, the libretto forms a stylistic bridge of sorts between the psychological characterizations and sequential narratives endemic to much realist prose and the mosaic structure endemic to much Symbolist prose. To Klenovsky, the original recipient of the *Queen of Spades* commission, Modest's embellishment of the source novella using borrowed materials evinced disrespect for Pushkin. Two of the quotations are discussed by Modest in an 1887 letter to his brother concerning the organization of act I, scene 2. He also expresses his oft-repeated desire for Pyotr to take over the project from Klenovsky: "I finished the second scene. I am most satisfied with its general appearance. . . . The two important numbers there are on words by [Konstantin] Batyushkov [1787–1855], 'Dear friends' ['Podrugi milïye,' 1810], and [Vasiliy] Zhukovsky [1783–1852], 'Tis evening' ['Uzh vecher,' 1806]. Lord! If you would write music for them, with what tenfold diligence would I scribble my verses!"[39] The intertextual resonances in the libretto encapsulate the interpenetration of phenomena from different levels of reality that pervades the opera. Taking the hallucinatory possibilities of the interpolations into account—their capacity to reinterpret the stage events by providing different perspectives on them—the librettist and composer jointly made two bold decisions. The first was to organize musical events in the opera in a symmetrical pattern, a grid with both vertical and horizontal dimensions, whose planes overlap and crisscross. For this task, Chaikovsky's adherence to the traditional number format proved advantageous, as it allowed him to structure the score as a series of building blocks with demarcated time spans. The following details will clarify this point. First, the overall structure of the opera—three acts, seven scenes, one score—replicates the winning card formula: three, seven, ace. Second, the four-part format of the *intermède* of the third scene—chorus, dance, duet, finale—refers in compressed form to the most significant events of the greater score: the opening chorus, the ball, the final duet between Liza and Herman, and the tragedy in the gambling salon. As testament to the symmetry of the score, it must also be noted that the first, fourth, and seventh scenes commence with choruses, while the third and fifth are prefaced by entr'actes. Moreover, the second scene begins with a duet, while the sixth ends with one. And the two numbers ("phenomenal" numbers, in Carolyn Abbate's terminology[40]) that are sung by Tomsky to the surrounding stage personnel occur toward the start of the first and seventh scenes. Lastly, and as explained in detail below, the romance performed by Polina in the middle of the second scene presages the arioso sung by Liza in the middle of the sixth scene.

The second bold decision made by the librettist and composer was to shift the setting of *The Queen of Spades* from the era of Alexander I back to the era of Catherine II. In doing so, they made most of the verbal borrowings anachronistic. For example, Liza and Polina supposedly remember the quoted Batyushkov and Zhukovsky texts from their childhood, which, if the plot is set during Alexander I's reign, is a nineteenth-century childhood. But as two eighteenth-century characters, Liza and Polina cannot possibly know the texts they "recall." One could well argue—as post-Symbolist critics did—that the anachronisms were mistakes left uncorrected in the frenzied creative process, oversights that could be excused owing to the stylistic similarities between Batyushkov and Zhukovsky and poets of previous generations. However, the composer and librettist explicitly acknowledged the anachronisms during the creative process and signaled that they were meant to be heard, to call attention to themselves. In a self-deprecating foreword to the 1890 edition of the libretto, Modest claimed that he had included borrowed material because "he regard[ed] with distrust his own ability to control poetic language" and "searched, where possible, for an opportunity to substitute verses of his own invention with verses of actual poets who, *though later, wrote several things in the spirit of the time.*" [41] Voiced by a writer with knowledge of the poetic styles of the eighteenth and nineteenth centuries, this comment cannot be taken at face value. Rather, Modest seems to be preempting attacks from unimaginative critics who would fail to understand the thematic significance of his temporal distortions, these being the first signals in *The Queen of Spades* that time is imaginary and appearances misleading. They afford a unique perspective on plot events, a child's world seen as if through adult eyes or, conversely, an adult world seen through a child's. Like the *intermède* of act II, scene 1 and the Countess's act II, scene 2 arietta, the Batyushkov and Zhukovsky texts are blissful delusions, less real than remembered. They reflect the mentality of a declining class. Even were the anachronisms devoid of these implications, they would still reflect the decadence of the incipient Symbolist movement, which expressed "nostalgia" for the past, Catherine the Great's era, but also "nostalgia" for the future, the events on the horizon.

THE PLAY-WITHIN-THE-PLAY

What of those writers whom Liza and Polina so fondly recall? They are "characters" in the plot of *The Queen of Spades* without a physical appearance. The performance of their poems not only amplifies the wistfulness of the opera's first scene, it introduces images of societal and individual malaise. In 1801, Zhukovsky, a disciple and translator of English and German pre-Romantic literature, founded the Moscow Literary Friendship Society (Druzheskoye literaturnoye obshchestvo), which venerated the sentimentalist literary tradition and defended the language reforms of Nikolai Karamzin (1766–1826). According to the standard biographies, the greatest crisis of Zhukovsky's life was the prohibition of his planned marriage to the daughter of his half-sister, an event that cast a shadow over his work. "'Tis evening," adapted by Modest Chaikovsky from the sixth and eight stanzas of Zhukovsky's 1806 elegy "Evening," captures the central features of the poet's style: descriptions of nature—these being a pretext for the contemplation of the inner world—and feelings of despair and melancholia. Batyushkov, likewise a poet of the sentimental tradition (and therefore antagonistic toward the influence of Church Slavonic and the ecclesiastical languages on Russian writing), devoted himself to translating and imitating Baroque Romance-language poets. In his early career, he professed to be an advocate of carefree pleasure and idle activity. After 1820, however, he began to suffer from depression, an affliction that prompted him to shift his creative focus from literary satire to elegies. His two Silver Age imitators, Afanasiy Fet (1820–92) and Apollon Maykov (1821–97), viewed him as a cult figure, a writer whose lighthearted early works contrast markedly with his funereal later ones. Modest doubtless included the Zhukovsky poem in act I, scene 2 of *The Queen of Spades* for its bucolic simplicity, and the Batyushkov poem for its tragic undertones. To quote D. S. Mirsky, the "strange beauty and haunting emotional intensity" of "Dear friends"—like that of Batyushkov's other elegies—is a "rare instance of the creative influence of mental illness on poetry." [42] The complete text is provided below, with Modest's two alterations shown in square brackets:

Inscription on the Grave of a Shepherdess

Dear friends! In playful lightheartedness
In dance and song you caper in the fields.
And I, like you, lived in happy Arcadia,
And I, in the morning of life, in those groves and meadows [fields]
Tasted momentary joy:

In golden dreams love promised me happiness;
But what did I gain from such wonderful places?
A grave[, a grave, a grave!]

[Nadpis' na grobe pastushki

Podrugi milïye! V bespechnosti igrivoy
Pod plyasovoy napev vï rezvites' v lugakh.
I ya, kak vï, zhila v Arkadii schastlivoy,
I ya, na utre dney, v sikh roshchakh i lugakh [polyakh]
Minutï radosti vkusila:
Lyubov' v mechtakh zlatïkh mne schast'ye sulila;
No shto zh dostalos' mne v prekrasnïkh sikh mestakh?
Mogila[, mogila, mogila!]⁴³

Polina sings these unsettling lines following her act I, scene 2 duet with
Liza (a setting of the Zhukovsky poem). With them, she unwittingly sub-
dues the festive spirit of an evening get-together of her friends in Liza's
parlor. She briefly revives the party with a "clapping" song based on an er-
satz folk tune, but the jovial mood seems to be lost and Liza's hoary Gov-
erness, finding it inappropriate for members of the French-educated aristocracy to perform folk music, complains about the racket. Though it is
Polina who actually sings the Batyushkov romance, it comments on Liza's
state of mind. The opera's heroine is despondent, unable to love her dash-
ing fiancé, Eletsky, and unsure of her feelings for Herman, the military
man who has begun to pay court to her. The other characters do not align
the romance with Liza (they do, however, appear deflated when the performance concludes), nor do they perceive the unsettling refrain of the romance—"a grave, a grave, a grave"—as a harbinger of Liza's act III, scene 2
suicide.

Polina's bemusement at her performance highlights the central distinction in the opera between conscious deeds and unconscious impulses, between those characters who act on their own volition and those who are
mediums for messages from *inoy svet*—the other world. Upon finishing
the romance, Polina emerges from a trance-like state and appears to discern
that she is a performer, someone following a script, without control over
her own utterances. She asks her girlfriends: "I wonder what made me
sing such a melancholy song?" ("Vot vzdumala ya pesnyu spet', slyoz-
zlivuyu takuyu?") The passage is an example of dramatic estrangement
or—to use the Formalist theorist Victor Shklovsky's famous term—*ostra-
neniye* ("making strange"), the disclosure of the artifice of theatrical
conventions.⁴⁴ Polina views herself as though from the outside. Instead
of unconsciously enacting events, she consciously experiences them. Well

ahead of twentieth-century experiments in theatrical realism (notably the innovations of Konstantin Stanislavsky in his stagings of the plays of Chekhov and Gorky at the Moscow Arts Theater), the borderline between the actor, as signifier, and character, as signified, seems to dissolve. Through her sense of estrangement, Polina discerns the automatism of her activities, activities that are obviously confined to aristocratic circles. By default, one could argue that the view of reality that results from her deautomatized perception is one of moribund and sclerotic routines. This same view of reality is provided to the audience in the theater. Chaikovsky incorporates a variety of musical allusions and references into his score that symbolically point back and forth in time, enabling the audience to view the unfolding events with heightened awareness. In the warped story space, the citizens of St. Petersburg appear as animate subjects of inanimate *tableaux.*

From a proto-Symbolist viewpoint, the scene serves to render the outer appearance of stage life artificial and, as a consequence, to reveal the dark underlining of the drama. At the outset of act I, scene 2, Liza's reality appears joyful and protected; there is no forewarning in "'Tis Evening" that her entanglement with Herman will lead to her martyrdom. But Polina's lament imbues the scene with unease. This unease does not fade but lingers like a struck note through the rest of the opera, calling into question the verisimilitude of all that follows and presaging the disaster of the last act. In the transition between the Zhukovsky and Batyushkov settings, the tragic infuses the commonplace and the grotesque the sentimental. The harshness of the shift in mood is underscored by the harshness of the modulation between the G major (3/4) duet and the E-flat minor (4/4) romance. It occurs in the three measures preceding the romance by means of a common-tone transition from the third-inversion dominant seventh chord of E major to the second-inversion tonic chord of E-flat minor. The unsettling effect of the diachronic clash between the two text settings has a synchronic equivalent. During Polina's performance, a trapdoor opens between different dramatic levels in the opera. A melodic motif from her number— identified by Richard Taruskin[45] and labeled X in musical example 2— sounds throughout the opera.[46] (My choice of "X" and, later, "Z" as labels in the score is not fortuitous. Alexander Poznansky reports that, in Chaikovsky's Kamenska diary, the composer coded the emotions—the highs and the lows—that he experienced playing cards as "X" and "Z." "Outside the context of card play," Poznansky notes, "neither Z nor X is ever found" in the diary.[47]) Skeletally comprising an ascending and descending perfect fourth and minor third, motif X appears in the accompaniment to the romance and then in Herman's vocal part during his amorous overtures to

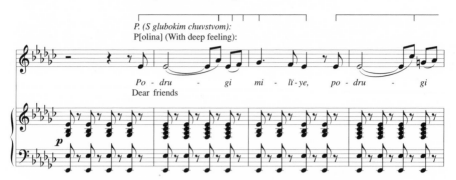

Example 2.   Motif *X* in Polina's act I, scene 2 romance

Liza at the end of act I, scene 2. It also appears in muted violins before Herman's turbulent assignation with the Countess toward the end of act II. In both cases, music once played and sung on stage, as part of the opera's surface, penetrates the orchestral substratum. The sublimation of the motif parallels the sublimation of plot events, the recession from semblances to essences or—to use the phraseology of the German Romantics—the "Clarity of the Day" to the "Night of the Soul."[48] By the conclusion of the opera, however, it comes to symbolize dematerialization, providing the melodic contour for the line "Good and evil are only dreams!" ("Dobro i zlo odni mechtï!") in Herman's famous final monologue. Though the motif is in this last instance presented in the major, with the minor third inflected to a major third on the second syllable of the Russian word for dreams (mech*tï*), it is clearly and pointedly recognizable.

Thus, with the Batyushkov romance, the opera shifts from realism into surrealism or, more precisely, from Naturalism into Symbolism, the two competing artistic tendencies of the Silver Age. Naturalist poetics, characterized by "verisimilitude, temporal and spatial perspective, and unambiguous, metonymic use of language," is superseded by Symbolist poetics, characterized by "metaphoric, ambiguous, and surrealistic" use of language.[49] In *The Queen of Spades*, the former is set off from the latter through the juxtaposition of scenes that evaluate human activity from a rational perspective and those that do so through memory, imagination, and the unconscious. Aurally, the passage featuring Liza and Polina singing together illustrates this juxtaposition; visually, the contrast between the resplendent ballroom and the claustrophobic dimness of the Countess's chamber and Herman's barracks room illustrates it. The rococo *intermède*

Example 3. Motif *X* at the end of act I, scene 2

of the ball scene, in turn, shows Chaikovsky's ability to transform familiar, "unambiguous" musical forms into unfamiliar "ambiguous" ones. As in the preceding parlor scene, the customs of aristocratic music-making, representing domestic reality, are transformed, exposing another reality behind it. The *intermède* literally interrupts Herman's conniving to learn the secret card formula and thus indicates his inability to control the events around him. In this respect, he takes on features of a Naturalist hero who has been encased in a Symbolist work, an inversion of the situation of the source novella, in which Herman—according to Foshko's analysis—is a "fairy-tale" hero encased in the "real world."

The *intermède*, Chaikovsky's most elaborate and most deceptive operatic tribute to his "beloved Mozart,"[50] is an abbreviated variant of the aforementioned Karabanov pastoral play *The Sincerity of the Shepherdess*, itself an abbreviated variant of the third-century Daphnis and Chloë myth. It intermingles two love stories: one between a boy and a girl, the other

Example 4. Motif *X* at the beginning of act II, scene 2

Example 5. Motif *X* in Herman's act III, scene 3 monologue

between all of humanity and nature. Chaikovsky arranged it in four set pieces:

A) Chorus of Shepherds and Shepherdesses
B) Sarabande (in 4/4 time)
C) Duet of Prilepa and Milozvor
D) Choral Finale, a Polonaise (marked *Tempo di minuetto*)

According to David Brown, Chaikovsky's Mozart debt is most evident in the opening chorus and orchestral dances of act II, scene 1, which recall the peasant chorus of act II of *Don Giovanni* (K. 527, 1787), and in the "Duet of Prilepa and Milozvor" from the *intermède*, whose *larghetto* opening theme "sounds much like the second main ritornello theme"—though greatly slowed down—"from the opening movement of Mozart's C major Piano Concerto [No. 25 in C (K. 503, 1786)], extended by a portion of the second subject from the C minor Wind Serenade [K. 388, 1787]." Moreover, the "Choral Finale is identical (though with changed meter)" to a polonaise in the *opéra comique Le fils-rival* (1787) by Dmitriy Bortnyansky (1751–1825).[51] Though Brown does not identify an eighteenth-century source for the sarabande, it too shows fidelity to that century's musical repertoire and styles. Brown seeks in traditional philological fashion to identify Chaikovsky's Mozart citations, but assesses neither the manner in which Chaikovsky transforms these citations—how he makes them his own—nor their overall dramatic purpose.[52] Most obviously, the citations provide a frame for act II, scene 2, reminding the audience and the performers that the stage world is invented, with events arranged in a precise sequence that imparts a sense of destiny. Discerning that the *intermède* comprises borrowed music, one appreciates less the natural splendor of the scene than its aesthetic elegance, less its authenticity than its artifice. The scene is controlled by invisible hands based on a predetermined progression; so too are the lives of the characters. Sometimes the progression appears dictated by the regulations of aristocratic society, and sometimes by the characters themselves. However Chaikovsky, the omniscient master arranger, ensures that they recognize the limitations of their capacity for self-determination.

The *intermède* is performed by Liza (Prilepa, or Chloë), Polina (Milozvor, or Daphnis), and Tomsky (Zlatogor, or Pluto), with the most attractive men and women at the ball taking the roles of shepherds and shepherdesses. After the "Chorus of Shepherds and Shepherdesses," a conventional paean to nature, the lonely and penniless Milozvor appears to declare his long-concealed love for Prilepa, who responds in kind. Their love duet is interrupted by the sudden arrival of Zlatogor and his retinue. He offers Prilepa gold and silver for her favors; she, however, chooses to remain with Milozvor, who has only offered her affection. Zlatogor is dispatched, cueing Amor and Hymen to descend from the heavens to bestow nuptial flower wreaths on the happy couple.

The *intermède* plot, depicting the triumph of love over wealth, is a miniature riposte to the opera's grander scheme, where virtue is sacrificed to greed. Chaikovsky's contemporaries dismissed it as an unmotivated trifle that did not adhere to the style it purported to emulate. But these deviations are actually critical to the opera, not accidental, not incompetent. Chaikovsky was fully capable of accurate emulations of rococo genres, as we know from *Swan Lake* (*Lebedinoye ozero*, opus 20, 1876) and *Sleeping Beauty* (*Spyashchaya krasavitsa*, opus 66, 1889).[53] His critics, then, were deaf to a significant inflection in the *intermède*: the idea that the music was intended to bear the imprint of Chaikovsky's, rather than Mozart's, compositional personality. In G. Mikhailova's words, the "copy" of rococo style was intended to seem more authentic than the "original."[54] It is not "neutral" or "blank," and thus does not have the defining qualities of pastiche. Like a pastiche, however, it is "speech in a dead language."[55]

Chief among the detractors of the *intermède* was Chaikovsky's friend Nikolai Kashkin (1839–1920), a professor at the Moscow Conservatory, who remarked that the opening chorus lacked emotion and that the meter of the sarabande was out of kilter:

> In Florence I visited several times. Once several people from the conservatory were invited to hear the just-completed *Queen of Spades*. . . . After a short break, during which time the author told me that he was extremely satisfied with his tribute to Mozart in the *intermède* of the next act, the performance continued. The *intermède* was truly masterful, but I was taken aback by the opening mood, which somehow came out cold, and also noticed that the number titled sarabande had neither the rhythm nor the character of that dance; the title immediately lost meaning.[56]

While the meter of the sarabande—common instead of triple time—most puzzled Kashkin, if he had developed his analysis further he would likely have found the musical syntax too ornate. The sarabandes of François Couperin (1668–1733) and Marin Marais (1656–1728), prototypical examples of the genre, have a harmonic rhythm of one chord per measure, only use nondiatonic harmonies to facilitate modulations from the home tonality to the dominant or relative major tonality, and (needless to say) leave passing tones and appoggiaturas unharmonized. Chaikovsky "ignores" these norms in his sarabande, enriching alternating pairs of measures with chords that, if not exactly aimless, presume a previously settled tonality and rhythm. Measures 3 and 4, for example, feature the following progression: I 5/3 of D major, iii 6/3, vii 7/5 of V, ii 6/3, v7/5 of vi, IV5/3, vii 6/3, vi 6/4, vii 6/3, V7/5 of vi and vi5/3. The passage, in sum, enacts a brief modulation from D major to the relative minor of B, a tonality aligned with the macabre events in the opera, indicating, perhaps, that forces of disintegration lurk even in the halcyon Arcadian landscape of the *intermède*. The sarabande also has overly sensitive dynamics: *piano* lower woodwinds against *pianissimo* lower strings (the former allotted agitated thirty-second-note turn figures, the latter *pizzicato* scalar eighths), with downbeats in the contrasting middle section marked *sforzando*.

In labeling the opening chorus "cold," Kashkin was doubtless alluding to its formal concision and the insistent repetition of the tonic and dominant pitches in the vocal lines. Prilepa and Milozvor's duet is even more unnatural, however, for it envelops five other dramatic and musical events: Zlatogor's entrance, his aria, his dance, his duet with Milozvor, and Prilepa's arioso. While each subsection of the duet is through-composed, the transitions between them are ragged, denoted by rapid changes of meter (2/4 to 6/8 to 4/4 time) and tempo (72 to 100 to 120 pulses per measure). This compression of musical events also typifies the finale, notably the *allegro vivo* section, in which a brass fanfare, unison mixed chorus, and antiphonal exchange between male and female voices occur in the span of a minute. One senses that vocal and instrumental *topoi* endemic to the rococo style are being isolated, run past at ruinous speeds, as though speed itself was intended to compensate for their disintegration and loss, the fact that they are irrevocably "of the past." The effect is aggravated by the unidiomatic orchestration: Prilepa's cheery line "I'm happy to live with my love in a hut in the fields!" ("Ya s milïm sred' poley i v khizhine zhit' rada!"), sung just prior to the *allegro vivo* section, is tainted by chromatic thirty-second-note trill figures in the clarinets and flutes, which unsteadily ascend by step on off-beats. The *allegro vivo* section itself juxtaposes *fortissimo* oboes and *pianissimo* strings, an example of dynamic inversion or, in Rimsky-Korsakov's derisive words, "topsy-turvy"[57] orchestration that reflects a central feature of the dramaturgy: the portrayal of objective reality from a skewed perspective—the very same feature that the Symbolist poets detected (or wanted to detect) in Pushkin's novella. At the end of *The Sincerity of the Shepherdess,* the dramatic focus turns back to Herman. James Parakilas observes that "by slipping us from the world of artistic performance in which [H]erman plays no part [the "sung" *intermède*] to the world of Gothic fantasy in which he is trapped ["spoken" reality], [C]haikovsky lets us feel how connected all the seemingly incompatible worlds of the mind are: the worlds of social discourse and song, the present and the remembered, the real and hallucinatory."[58]

Whereas the melodic and harmonic writing in the *intermède* invokes the spirit or, more accurately, the haunting specter of Mozart (a lesson for other neoclassicists about digging up the past?), the alchemy of instrumental sounds has several provocative visual arts analogues. In creating the scenery for the premiere production of *The Queen of Spades,* Vsevolozhsky observed that the music had inspired him to present the players in the *intermède* as a set of "antique Sevres porcelain figurines; for this he commissioned the talented sculptor Pavel Kamensky [1858–?], who then managed the prop workshop of the Directorate, to construct porcelain-like pedestals of white with blue and gold."[59] Besides the Atelier de Sèvres, however, the music recalls *Les bergers d'Arcadie* (1638) by the French classical painter Nicolas Poussin (1594–1665). The image, an impersonal, detached meditation on mortality, depicts three shepherds and a mysterious female figure gathered around a tomb bearing the Latin phrase "Et in Arcadia ego" ("Even in Arcady [there] am I [death]") from Virgil's *Ecloga IV.* Two of the shepherds appear to be lost in thought. The tomb is surrounded not by lush vegetation but by parched shrubs and barren rocks, a direct allusion to the transience of life. Another symbolic correspondence can be made between the music and the enigmatic and haunting canvases of a later French classicist, Antoine Watteau (1684–1721), a powerful influence on Somov and other members of the World of Art. Watteau's most lauded work, *L'embarquement pour l'Ile de Cythère* (1717), portraying *haute bourgeoisie* of both sexes descending a steep hill to a lake, and his *Comédien italiens* (1715), portraying melancholy *commedia dell'arte* actors, inspired separate iconographic trends in Russian and French *fin-de-siècle* art. Often denigrated—like Chaikovsky's familiar ballets—as examples of kitsch, Watteau's images allegorize such issues as unfulfilled desire and the triumph of madness over reason. The subject matter is often less relevant than the emotion and mood related to the viewer. *L'embarquement pour l'Ile de Cythère,* one of Watteau's three studies of a mythic locale for which lovers depart but do not arrive, reveals the principal traits of his mature style. In it, aristocratic life adopts a theatrical quality: it is difficult to ascertain whether the figures belong to the stage world or the real world. Analyses of the canvas as a social chronicle tend to reveal formal incongruities and anomalies. Some costume experts have commented, for example, that the dress worn by the figures is pure fantasy.[60] In addition, the painter appears to be relatively unconcerned or ambivalent about accuracy in the spatial relationships: the alignment of poses in the portrait is irrational. The figures in the foreground listen to their companions' words without making eye contact with them; instead, they cast a glance over their shoulders, sensing, perhaps, the lingering presence of something left behind. The *intermède* of *The Queen of Spades* bears comparable traits. Radically accelerated, the finale becomes evanescent, alluding to the transient nature of images and impressions; radically decelerated, the sarabande becomes lugubrious, alluding to lost pleasures. The varied acoustic aberrances—the inverted dynamics, the unusual instrumental groups, and unnatural registers—transform the four movements from utopian into dystopian musical landscapes.

To be sure, the opera's supernatural scenes are marked by additional examples of orchestral distortion. As Taruskin notes in the *New Grove Dictionary of Opera,*

> the prefatory entr'acte [of act III, scene 1] is a weirdly feverish montage of church music (the Countess's burial service) and barracks music. It juxtaposes divided violas and cellos in the pit, *pianissimo,* against snare drum and trumpet offstage, *fortissimo,* producing a sound balanced as to volume but, like Hermann's mind, grossly unbalanced in perspective. (Later the burial music is resumed by an offstage chorus singing in the wind's voice, an indistinct, distant *fortissimo.*) Even the less obviously illustrative music constantly features outré combinations of timbre seemingly at odds with expression—for example, English horn calling lyrically to bass clarinet over an accompaniment of staccato bassoons, as Hermann recalls his crimes with remorse.[61]

These remarks attest to the new conception of sound space developed by Chaikovsky in the opera. In act III, scene 1, the stereophonic juxtaposition of offstage and onstage instruments effectively extends the acoustic range of the orchestra, forging the illusion that the music is emanating from another sphere; the muted wordless chorus, moreover, provides the impression of death in sound. Through these effects, Chaikovsky anticipated the acoustic experiments of Debussy in *Pelléas et Mélisande* (1902). The latter composer obfuscated harmonies by assigning their pitches to different instrumental groups in different spatial registers; moreover, he eroded and dissolved the connections between harmonies using agogic accents, disproportionate dynamic levels, and conflicting articulations. In certain passages, familiar blocks of sound recur in unfamiliar guises. Stefan Jarocinski points out, for example, that in the act II fountain scene, the orchestra, which "had been playing *forte,* is suddenly silent, then re-appears, as if coming out of the shadows, *ppp,* to accompany Pelléas's impassioned recitative."[62] The spatial interchange, he contends, reflects a central conceit of Symbolist drama: the simultaneous projection of events on "two [or more] different planes at the same time: one external, consisting of the words and gestures of the actors, and the other internal, where the real action takes place which conditions the action on the stage."[63] Jarocinski rather uncritically accepts Debussy's claim in his letters and articles that he had manipulated the musical syntax of his opera to a wholly unprecedented degree. For although the subject matter of the two scores is unrelated, it would appear that *The Queen of Spades* anticipated several of the acoustic novelties in *Pelléas et Mélisande.*

One of the few contemporary critics to laud Chaikovsky's innovations was Herman Laroche (1845–1904), Chaikovsky's St. Petersburg Conservatory classmate and staunch advocate. Laroche divined that Chaikovsky had not tried for verisimilitude in the *intermède* but had willfully translated rococo style in the manner of the World of Art movement.[64] It was, he implied, a subjective restoration of the past, whose distortions serve to affront courtliness, to denote the forces of disintegration at play in tsarist society. Ironically, owing to their rejection of the decadent trends of the Silver Age, this interpretation eluded Soviet critics of the opera. On this point, J. Douglas Clayton notes that "Lenin's predilection for naturalist writing was an expression of his philosophical conservatism; his polemics split progressive culture into good (naturalism) and bad (symbolism), and in the long run led to the imposition of socialist realism as the only 'progressive' form of creative activity." The author clarifies that "during the revolutionary period Lenin's voice was far from the only one heard and that symbolist culture, especially the *commedia dell'arte* [revival], was by and large politically progressive (although the political content was usually expressed metaphorically in the rejection of 'bourgeois' aesthetic values) and, in the larger sense, truly revolutionary."[65] The *commedia dell'arte* revival was the product of an attempt by Russian modernists to create drama that would reflect the distortions and instabilities in their world. Yet even the advocates of the revival, arguably the most imaginative artists working in Russia in the 1920s and early 1930s, did not detect the stylistic anomalies in *The Queen of Spades*, especially those of the *intermède*, which, as has been demonstrated, turns rococo conventions inside-out. To Meyerhold, the play-within-the-play was merely superficial theatrical decoration. In a supplementary essay to his re-Pushkinized 1935 production of *The Queen of Spades*, the director charged that the decision to augment the opera with the *intermède* was made not by the Chaikovsky brothers but by Vsevolozhsky, to whom, in his estimation, Pyotr and Modest were obliged to "kowtow." Meyerhold, himself unwilling to kowtow to the conservative dictates of Soviet ideologues—to abandon, in essence, his pre-Revolutionary theatrical methods—contended that the ball scene had been made to order. "Vsevolozhsky," he wrote, "could not imagine an opera theatre that might not be able to afford his obligatory luxurious splendor and that might be bold enough to make do without hundreds of actors, milling about on the stage and interfering with the action."[66]

As a low-budget replacement for the *intermède*, Meyerhold conceived a *commedia dell'arte* play entitled *The Love Note* (*Lyubovnaya zapiska*). It was to provide the correlate to the main plot that he felt was missing from the 1890 score. The play's scenario was drafted by Vladimir Solovyov (not the Symbolist philosopher of the same name), a student of the *commedia dell'arte* who assisted Meyerhold in staging Blok's *The Unknown Woman* (*Neznakomka*, 1907) and *The Puppet Theater Booth* (*Balaganchik*, 1908). The scenario reads as follows:

> 3 *dramatis personae*. One woman (the housemaid Smeraldina) and two men (the old man and servant *Zanni*). The old man can perhaps be replaced by the mask of Tartaglia (stutterer, a Latin *Zanni*). The traditional costume of Tartaglia, it seems to me, is visually more interesting than the stock costume of Pantalone and the D[octor]. Tartaglia's costume is shown on the inaugural cover of *Oranges*. This is the rough plan of the scenario:
>
> Entrance 1: A screen is brought onto the proscenium by two servants.
>
> Entrance 2: Tartaglia in an amorous state.
>
> Appearance from the right (from the viewer) of Tartaglia from behind the screen. He is in love. Comic *lazzi* with spectacles and a sword. He is in a state of extreme agitation.
>
> Entrance 3: Supported by two [illegible] arms, Smeraldina crashes through the screen. Concealing a smirk, she passes a letter to Tartaglia and quickly runs off.
>
> Entrance 4: Tartaglia in spectacles reading with intense delight (letter pressed up to the spectacles). At this moment Smeraldina and Brighella appear from behind the screen. They pause at the screen. Having noticed the love-struck old man, they laugh. The laughter at the old man can perhaps be embellished with the entrance of new characters, associated with the two servants, for ex[ample], the grotesque Capitano with his long sword, and [others]. When Tartaglia walks up to the screen/ wall in amorous bliss, hoping there to find his beautiful beloved, the servants inconspicuously sneak up on him, throw a cloak over him, and carry him from the stage writhing in the cloak. The servants carry the screen from the proscenium.[67]

To these details Meyerhold added the following comment:

> When the pantomime is performed, we will introduce the following scene. On the proscenium is the Countess, near her, Liza. The plot of

the pantomime, performed in the manner of [the Baroque *commedia dell'arte* printmaker Jacques] Callot, revolves around a note, passed from Smeraldina to Tartaglia. At the same time we see Herman, sitting behind Liza, placing a note in Liza's hand.

In the pantomime the female figure (Smeraldina) passes a note to the male (Tartaglia); in the group of guests Herman passes a note to Liza. The one episode reflects the other, as in a mirror.[68]

The use of *commedia dell'arte* masked figures (inspired by and derived from Callot's etchings) is a consistent feature of Meyerhold's stage productions—both before and after the consolidation of Soviet authority in Russia. In *The Queen of Spades* they provide a distorted reflection of the larger drama, forming a grotesque analogy between Herman's tragic persona and Tartaglia's comic persona. More broadly, however, they serve to erode theatrical verisimilitude. The masked figures are actors as well as spectators. They both provide and comment on the action, exposing the illusoriness and ephemerality of everything that unfolds on stage. As a facetious inversion of the larger plot, *The Love Note* would at first glance appear to be an ingenious substitute for Chaikovsky's pastorale, fully in tune with the composer's proto-Symbolist aspirations. Like the original *intermède*, the new *intermède* calls into question the relationship between "performed" and "experienced" events. But there is a crucial difference between them. Whereas Chaikovsky involved his principal characters as participants in *The Sincerity of the Shepherdess*, Meyerhold omitted them from *The Love Note*. He did not cast them as self-conscious performers unwittingly betraying the conventions of a synthetic reality. In this respect, the re-Pushkinized version of the opera excludes one of its central precepts: the notion that Liza and Herman live in the twilight years of the aristocratic era, a period of entropy, malaise, and "automatised eroticism." Meyerhold erased, in short, the unsettling link that Chaikovsky had forged between the principal image of the text sung by Paulina in act I, scene 2 (the solitary "grave of a shepherdess") and the principal image of the *intermède* (frolicking shepherds and shepherdesses).

In its original conception, the *intermède* offers a deceptively cheerful antidote to the somber reality of *The Queen of Spades*, but in the tense atmosphere of the ballroom it acquires a surreal quality, manifest in the incorrect orchestration and incorrect meters—common rather than triple time for the sarabande, *tempo di minuetto* for the polonaise—which sully an otherwise plausible eighteenth-century pastiche. Chaikovsky put childhood things away after the *intermède* (there are no other evocations of fairy-tale landscapes), but he took care to connect its music to the next

Example 6.   The opening of the sarabande from the act II, scene 1 *interméde*

example of self-conscious performance in the score: the Countess's act II, scene 2 arietta.[69] The sarabande and arietta are both small ternary forms whose opening phrases are nearly identical in intervallic content and range (stepwise motion in the range of a perfect fourth and fifth). In addition, Marina Raku notes that the two numbers have comparable dynamic levels (*piano* versus *pianissimo*), tempo markings (quarter note = 72 versus quarter note = 76), tonalities (D major and its relative minor), and accompaniment scoring (solo woodwind lines, *tutti* upper strings, *pizzicato* lower strings).

The sarabande and the arietta—as well as the orchestral introduction to the arietta—share something else: a descending scalar motif that outlines a minor sixth. Heard in several rhythmic and phrasal guises, but usually descending from the submediant to the tonic or dominant to the mediant, this motif (shown as motif *Y* in music examples 16 and 17) is the most prominent, yet at the same time most elusive, motif in the opera. It does

Example 7. The opening of the Countess's act II, scene 2 arietta

not underline the plot or provide the orchestral music with thematic conti-
nuity but changes in significance based on the dramatic context. Owing to
its flexibility and mutability, it acquires the status of a musical symbol: an
acoustic gesture with no single meaning but several possible meanings,
a complex set of potentialities that may or may not be actualized in a listener's imagination. By itself the motif implies nothing; heard as an "intonation" *(intonatsiya)* with links to another Chaikovsky opera and the entire spectrum of Russian nineteenth-century "domestic" *(bïtovïye)* songs,
it takes on a wealth of implications.[70] Just as a symbol arises in reality or—
according to the Symbolist poets—"folk" memory, motif Y arises in *The
Queen of Spades* in scenes of actual music-making. It then devolves, infil-
trating the orchestral substratum. Based on the overall sentiment of those
scenes in which it occurs, one can identify three separate incarnations of
the motif. It accrues, in other words, three layers of meaning, three possible
denotations—a reflection of the mystery and superstition accorded to the
number three in the opera overall. In this inherently subjective—inherently Symbolist—interpretation of the score, the motif's first incarnation
is aligned with allusions to different dream states, the second with allusions

to the decline of the aristocracy, and the third with fate, with malevolent predestination. The first incarnation arises in the ninth and tenth measures of the sarabande and the second at the beginning of the soliloquy that precedes the Countess's arioso. In the sarabande, motif Y descends by step in dotted sixteenth and thirty-second notes from b^2 to $d\sharp^2$ in D (!) major; in the arietta, it descends *ad libitum* from $d\flat^2$ to f^1 in B-flat minor.[71]

In the ballroom scene, this first incarnation of motif Y is part of a passage that, with its fairytale aura, suggests a dream of the ending of childhood, while in the Countess's antiquated chamber, it is part of a passage that, with its ghostly nostalgia, suggests a dream of the ending of human life (the motif is sung to the words "Oh, I hate the world today!" ["Akh, postïl mne etot svet!"]). The ultimate dream, of course, is the dream of the end of the world, which is expressed in Herman's last monologue, which marks both his existential triumph over the force of malignant destiny and his destruction by it. There, however, motif X, rather than motif Y, leaves its mark.

THE TSARIST MORTUARY

The extant records of the composition of *The Queen of Spades* show that Chaikovsky conceived motif Y for act II, scene 2, and then distributed it backward and forward across the pages of the score. Its most unusual occurrences are those in the introduction and middle of the Countess's arietta because, famously, the arietta is not original music but a wholesale quotation of "Je crains de lui parler la nuit" from the first act of the *opéra comique Richard Coeur-de-lion* (1784) by André Grétry (1741–1813), a French domestic romance with stylistic similarities to its Russian counterparts.

Like the duet sung by Liza and Polina to words by Zhukovsky and the romance sung by Polina to words by Batyushkov, the arietta represents a jarring anachronism. *Richard Coeur-de-lion* dates from roughly the same year in which the plot of *The Queen of Spades* is set: it could not be recalled by the Countess from her youth, despite her claim to the contrary. She performs it after being escorted to her chamber by her coterie of retainers. The introduction consists of her describing the dancers and singers at the evening's pageant as "hoydens" ("devchonki") and demanding solace. Her protests subside, her vision clouds, and her thoughts drift back to the *fêtes galantes* she attended as a young and beautiful society figure.

Her performance of the anachronistic arietta can be fruitfully (if equally anachronistically) interpreted using Bergson's theory of *durée*. The theory posits that rational thought is related to phenomena and the indirect perception of time while intuitive perception is related to noumena and the direct perception of time. Whereas the intellect grasps reality in minutes and seconds—as time broken up into isolated segments—the intuition grasps it as a fluid, seamless process of unfolding. Bergson claimed that at moments of intuitive perception conscious states become intertwined and unmeasured. The past and present cannot be separated, since both are formed by intuition in the present. He also asserted that impeded forms of rational thought and disturbances of memory such as hallucinations and nightmares served to emancipate the senses.[72] Applying these thoughts to *The Queen of Spades*, one could argue that the musical anachronisms supplant the rational (objective) passage of time with an irrational (subjective) one. Due to the incommensurable links between the set pieces, the score fluctuates between what Bergson labeled "matter" and "memory," "virtual" and "actual" time. The score not only maintains chronological time, a sustained present into which the listener is absorbed, but also a stratified time which transports the listener through different worlds simultaneously.

The decision to have the Countess recall a song from her youth was made by Modest Chaikovsky, whose draft of the preceding monologue ends with the line, "Once, I remember, at Chantilly, at the Prince of Condé's, the king heard me! I see it all as if it were today." ("Raz, pomnyu, v Chantilly, u Prince de Condé, korol' menya slïkhal! Ya kak teper' vsyo vizhu.")[73] His brother then chose the arietta from one of the seven representative French and Italian eighteenth-century opera scores that he had brought with him from St. Petersburg to Florence: *Rinaldo d'Asti* (1796) by Gennaro Astartita (1745/9–1803), *Didone abbandonata* (1752) by Baldassare Galuppi (1706–85), *Les deux avares* (1770) and *Richard Coeur-de-lion* by Grétry, *Le déserteur* (1769) by Pierre Monsigny (1729–1817), *La fiera di Venezia* (1772) by Antonio Salieri (1750–1825), and *Il burbero di buon cuore* (1796) by Vicente Martín y Soler (1754–1806). Of the six composers, only Martín y Soler had a professional connection to Russia: he was named Kapellmeister to Catherine the Great in 1788 and composed a comic opera to a libretto by the empress herself in 1789. For this reason, he would have been a logical composer to quote in an opera set during Catherine's reign, but Chaikovsky evidently held Grétry in higher esteem. His Florence diary contains two provocative references to the composer: "January 18. . . . Sat in various cafés. . . . Read through Grétry's *Rich[ard] Coeur-de-lion*. In the depths of my soul terrible boredom and cheerlessness [. . . .] February 3. . . . All-Night Vigil in a Russian chapel. Various cafés and cabarets. *La fiera*. Mandolin and charming accompaniment. Studied the Salieri and Grétry scores at home."[74] On 3 March 1890, the day he finished the draft score of the opera, he wrote to Modest: "Modya! I completely forgot to send you the words of the Grétry arietta the Countess sings in the fourth scene. They have to be included in the published libretto."[75]

Since as *Swan Lake* and *Sleeping Beauty* confirm, Chaikovsky had virtuoso skill at the art of Classical stylization (and as act II, scene 1 confirms, virtuoso skill at the art of Classical destylization), he had no technical need to borrow from Grétry. Rather, he was motivated to incorporate the arietta into act II, scene 2 for its French monarchist sentiments, distantly evocative of the ballrooms and courts of the Countess's past, and its Gothic ambience (*Richard Coeur-de-lion* is set in 1193 in Linz). In Grétry's score, the arietta is sung by Laurette (soprano), who is in love with Florestan (baritone), the governor of the castle where Richard the Lion-Hearted has been incarcerated since his return from the Third Crusade. The narrative centers on his rescue by the troubadour and squire Blondel (tenor), who captures Florestan and mobilizes a small battalion to breach the castle walls.

The text of the arietta is replete with images of adolescent love and bashful naiveté. Chaikovsky quoted the first stanza intact:

> I'm afraid to speak to him at night,
> I hear too well everything he says . . .
> He tells me: I love you,
> And despite myself,
> I feel my heart beating, beating . . .
> I do not know why . . .
>
> [Je crains de lui parler la nuit,
> J'écoute trop tout ce qu'il dit . . .
> Il me dit: je vous aime,
> Et je sens malgré moi,
> Je sens mon coeur qui bat, qui bat . . .
> Je ne sais pas pourquoi . . .]

In setting these words, Chaikovsky preserved Grétry's harmony and orchestration (the lone exception being his omission of a part for transverse flute), and only slightly adjusted the tempo (from *andante spirito* to *andantino*). The one significant alteration concerned the tonality: Chaikovsky transposed the arietta from F to B minor.

In the reception history of *The Queen of Spades*, it is this import, this foreign object by another composer, that has sometimes been seen—paradoxically, perhaps—as the most uncanny element of the score. Benois called the arietta the most haunting music of the entire opera. He commented that "nothing so much presages the horror of all of the next scene [in which Herman is haunted by the image of the Countess in her coffin winking at him and in which her ghost appears to give him the secret of the three cards] as this tender, ingratiating arietta, almost dance-like in rhythm, in which, however, one hears something funereal—something more akin to a mourner's laments."[76] His Soviet colleague, the musicologist and composer Boris Asafyev, agreed:

> With the words "But in those days[:] who danced[?]" the synod of tsarist mortuaries is discerned. The corresponding timbres are chosen: a muted French horn supports a psalm tone; under it deafly thread the ribbons of clarinet trills, violins rustle *tremolo ppp*, and *pizzicato* cellos (doubled at the octave with the bass clarinet) support the rhythm. The memoirs (eerily authentic memoirs of the eighteenth century, *first disseminated in the music*) reach a description of the success of the heroine herself; a cold wind (violins with mutes) passes over the crypt. . . . This is one of the most intuitively brilliant moments in the opera and a characteristic example of dramatization through instrumental coloring. Everything stiffens, and Grétry's sentimental arietta sounds as a terrifying voice from that world.[77]

The performance of the arietta foregrounds three components of Chaikovsky's operatic symbolism: alterations in dramatic perspective, audible expressions of inaudible thoughts, and shifts between time and place. The gesture that makes this possible is exceedingly simple: Chaikovsky's transposition of the arietta downward by tritone. Grétry's opening, an F minor tonic chord in the violins, is supplanted by the pitches d^1 and $f\sharp^1$ in the flutes (see measures 2 and 3 of music example 7). The new opening, a barely recognizable paraphrase of the old one, deceives the listener into thinking that the arietta will commence in D major. However, the subsequent introduction of the pitch B in the string basses confirms that it will commence in B minor—a shift in tonal center without the external attributes of a modulation. The shift marks a fault line in *The Queen of Spades* between the Apollonian realm of finishing school, powdered wigs, and polished manners and the Dionysian realm of fleeting shadows, alcoholic abuse, and aberrant psychology. Paraphrasing Maksimilian Voloshin, Lyudmila Karagichova terms the modulation a "crack in the crystal ball"— a rupture that separates two of the opera's three worlds.[78]

Why *three* worlds? Caryl Emerson, commenting on a 1995 production of *The Queen of Spades* at the Metropolitan Opera in New York, observes that the opera is set in three concurrent times. The first is the "historical backdrop" to the main action, "the time of Chaikovsky's setting of the story," namely, the reign of Catherine the Great. The second is the "Romantic era," emblematized by the "bulky, unpredictable," and "Napoleonic [or Byronic]" figure of Herman. The third time, introduced in act III, scene 1, is the Modern era, namely, "the time of Chaikovsky's composing of the opera, forty-four feverish days in Florence in the early spring of 1890, on the brink of Russian Symbolism." Emerson alludes to the moment when the Countess bursts through the floorboards of Herman's barracks room and twice whispers the names of the cards into his intoxicated face. She appears not as a haggard crone but as an attractive young woman, the siren of her Paris adolescence. The passage, Emerson adds, bears the outlines "of a Symbolist aesthetics: the Dionysian that is also demonic; the presentation of primary sexuality as guarantor of knowledge; the genuinely transfigurative experience of dreams; and, mostly, a simultaneous multiplicity of times."[79]

Each of these points warrants amplification. From a musical standpoint, the opera's first stratum, the "Classical" era of Catherine the Great, is represented by the enigmatic Grétry arietta and the Mozartean set pieces. The second stratum, the "Romantic" era, is marked not only by the visual image of Herman in acts I and II but by a subtle allusion in act II to Schumann, specifically, the accompaniment to "Die alten, bösen lieder," the final *lied* in his autobiographical cycle *Dichterliebe* (opus 48, 1840). Boris Kats remarks that measures 4–5 and 11–12 of the piano accompaniment of the *lied* serve as the basis of the twelve-measure orchestral introduction to the chorus sung by the Countess's retainers in act II, scene 2. Both excerpts are aligned in "tonality, certain harmonies, rhythmic structure, salient melodic details, and also the accentuation of the pickups."[80] Moreover, emphasis is placed on neighbor-note relations, upper in "Die alten, bösen lieder" (e^2-f♯^{2}-e^2, c♯^{2}-d♯^{2}-c♯^{2}, b♯^{1}-c♯^{2}-b♯^{1}) and lower in the chorus (c♯^{1}-b♯-c♯^{1}, e^1-d♯^{1}-e^1, g♯^{1}-fx^1-g♯^{1}). The harmonic writing is similarly comparable: while Schumann uses second-inversion tonic chords and first-inversion applied diminished seventh chords (g♯-c♯^{1}-e^1 and a♯-c♯^{1}-e^1-fx^1) in the *lied*'s piano accompaniment, Chaikovsky uses first-inversion tonic chords and second-inversion German sixth chords (e-g♯-c♯^{2} and e-fx-a-c♯^{2}) in the chorus's orchestral accompaniment. Finally, both excerpts feature rhythms of sustained eighth notes in common time.

One could argue that the similarity between the excerpts is merely coincidental, or that Schumann was an unconscious point of reference for Chaikovsky, but this was probably not the case: Chaikovsky made a habit of quoting Schumann, having detected in his scores "echoes of the secretive, profound processes of our spiritual life, of those doubts, despairs, and surges toward the ideal that overwhelm the heart of contemporary man."[81] "Die alten, bösen lieder" and the Countess's arietta (which follows on the heels of the chorus) bear comparable sentiments. Both concern the entombment of past loves, the desire to bury sorrow and grief, and both end with the disintegration of rhythm and accompaniment. The arietta concludes as the Countess begins to forget Grétry's words and fall asleep (before being rudely roused by Herman); "Die alten, bösen lieder" concludes with a meditative piano solo. This postlude acts as an agent of reconciliation, for it repeats the cadential music of the twelfth *lied* of *Dichterliebe*, "Am leuchtenden Sommermorgen," in which nature delivers a loving scold on the head of the singer-protagonist for being despondent. The vocal line of the *lied* is unheard in the postlude, but owing to the iteration of the accompaniment, posited. According to Slavoj Žižek, who has written what amounts to a poststructuralist review of Charles Rosen's *The Romantic Generation* (1995), the "presence" of this "absence" constitutes the "'unreal' dimension of [Schumann's] music (the unrealizable sonority, etc.) which, before it, belonged to the 'empirical' gray zone of liminal confusion and limitation of our perception." [82] Since it is aligned with the singing subject, the disappearance of the melody intimates a loss of identity, a recession into a dematerialized, dream-like environment. [83] In *The Queen of Spades*, the distant, arguably symbolic allusion to "Die alten, bösen lieder" marks an atmospheric transition from the "Clarity of the Day" (act II, scene 1) to the "Night of the Soul" (act II, scene 2). It presages the Countess's performance of the Grétry arietta, during which she repeatedly loses herself in reverie. In contrast to the Schumann lied, in which the singer pauses but the accompaniment continues, in the Grétry arietta, the singer and accompaniment operate in tandem, starting off strong, winding down, and then restarting. Though the scene begins with a ticking ostinato, the appropriate metaphor to describe it is not a watch but a film loop. The Countess threads the music through her mental projector, recreating the past in the present. However, since the arietta is anachronistic—dating, again, from the time of the opera's action—she is actually recreating the present in the present. The "presence" of what she considers to be an "absence" constitutes the "'unreal' dimension" of the scene.

Together with "Am leuchtenden Sommermorgen," there is another intertextual allusion in "Die alten, bösen lieder": it mimes the ending of Clara Wieck's 1840 *lied* "Der Mond kommt still gegangen." Schumann transposes the concluding measures of "Die alten, bösen lieder" from C-sharp minor to D-flat major and B-flat minor, these being the tonalities of the concluding measures of "Der Mond kommt still gegangen." In doing so, he establishes a semantic bridge of sorts between the fictional love affair of the "groom" and "bride" in *Dichterliebe* and his own true-life love affair with Wieck. "Die alten, bösen lieder" recedes through three temporal layers: the present (the immediate unfolding of the *lied*), the recent past (the recollection of "Am leuchtenden Sommermorgen"), and the distant past (the recollection of "Der Mond kommt still gegangen"). In *The Queen of Spades*, the Countess's thoughts also recede through three temporal layers: she ruminates about her exhaustion following the evening's ball, then about the inferior dancing at the ball, and then about the superior dancing at the balls of her youth.

The chain of allusions—intentionally to Grétry's arietta, and perhaps fortuitously to Schumann's *lied* cycle and Wieck's *lied*—conveys more than gloom in act II, scene 2. Here more emphatically than in the other scenes, the intertwining of references and the manner in which they are revealed to the ear suggests dematerialization. The simultaneous conflation of verbal and musical gestures from different points in music history, images that enhance the power of the plot, affirms that what we witness on stage is chimerical and that a force operating outside of time and place governs the character's lives—a force that Pushkin, in the epigraph to his novella, called the "secret malevolence" of "the queen of spades."[84]

THE GAME TAKES ITS COURSE

The Countess's "Classical" arietta and Polina's "Romantic" romance denote two of the three temporal strata in the opera. The third stratum—the "Modern" or, given the Russian Symbolists' interest in paranormal agencies, what might be called the "occult" stratum—is not represented by borrowed music. Syntactically, it is represented by whole-tone passages, specifically, passages in which the whole-tone scale is assigned functional equivalency to major and minor scales. The trapdoor that leads into this stratum, however, is a tonal number that quotes from other operas: Tomsky's act I, scene 1 ballad. This number is the source of all the trouble in the plot, for it is here that Herman hears the legend of the three cards and is indoctrinated into the occult.[85]

Chaikovsky modeled Tomsky's ballad on French comic operatic ballads of the 1830s, which introduce a riddle into the action that demands resolution by the concluding act. It is cast in four strophes in E minor. The opening strophe contains five two-measure phrases, the fifth decorating a deceptive cadence from the dominant B to the submediant C-sharp. There follows a two-measure declaimed phrase that progresses from a tonic minor seventh chord to the subdominant, and a four-measure chromatic phrase rising from A-sharp to e. In this last phrase, Chaikovsky referred directly to a French opera prototype: the chromatic line of the ballad sung by

Peki about a flying magic horse in act I of *Le cheval de bronze* (1835) by Daniel Auber (1782–1871). Moreover, he derived the structure of the un-accompanied concluding line of the strophe—the refrain "three cards, three cards, three cards!" ("tri kartï, tri kartï, tri kartï!")—from that of the refrain of the ballad sung by Zerlino in act I of Auber's *Fra Diavolo, ou L'hôtellerie de Terracine* (1830): "Diavolo, Diavolo, Diavolo!" The repeated descending major seconds and ascending perfect fourths in the accompaniment to measures 37–39 of Tomsky's ballad are also related to the melody of Zerlino's refrain.[86] The linkages do not imply specific plot relationships between Chaikovsky's and Auber's operas. Rather, it appears that Chaikovsky sought to imbue Tomsky's ballad with the spirit of Auber's classicism:

> There was something special in him, reminiscent of the *petits maîtres* and marquises of the past century. The coat of armor of aristocratic impartiality and skepticism protected Auber from romantic fantasies and dreamy sentimentality, which was fashionable in his youth and had such a powerful influence on artists with a different sensibility, like Berlioz.[87]

Through Tomsky's ballad (and through his allusions to Auber), Chaikovsky recreates a realm of sparkling tinsel and elegant ballrooms. Yet, unlike his French forerunner, he did not so much seek to preserve the rococo epoch as to eulogize its passing. Before the ballad's performance, Chaikovsky depicts the *haute bourgeoisie* in full splendor; afterward, all of the positive symbols are inverted: the bright sky darkens and the holiday crowd departs. Herman remains alone on stage. The refrain of the ballad, redolent of that of the ballad in *Fra Diavolo, ou L'hôtellerie de Terracine*, indicates early on in the opera that a pall hangs over the inhabitants of the Imperial City.

Within the refrain is a scalar pattern that descends a major sixth, on its final presentation, from $f\sharp^1$ to a (the submediant to the tonic) in mixed rhythmic values. It is the second incarnation of motif *Y*, the falling scalar pattern whose meaning shifts according to the dramatic mood, and which assumes different rhythmic, phrasal, and tonal guises. Along with the cadential line in the ballad of Auber's *Fra Diavolo, ou L'hôtellerie de Terracine* (shown in music example 9), it resonates with the melodic line in the Kozlovsky polonaise that Chaikovsky paraphrases in the concluding measures of act II, scene 1 to mark the brief stage entrance of Catherine the Great.

The polonaise line, falling a minor third (f-e-d, g-f-e, and so forth) in the dotted figuration that defines that dance, is extended to descend a minor sixth ($d\flat^1$-c^1-b$\flat$-a$\flat$-g$\flat$-f) on its next appearance in the opera, the

Example 8. The refrain of Tomsky's ballad in act I, scene 1

Countess's chamber scene, where it becomes a melancholy solo played by bass clarinet. The score at this point is pitted out (the iterations of the motif are framed by hollow octave trills and thirty-second-note figures in the string basses). In its first appearance in the scene, the solo line, succeeding an agitated string ostinato that Asafyev aptly dubbed a "funereal scherzo," [88] accompanies the Countess's words: "What times! People have no idea how to enjoy themselves anymore. What manners! What tone! Better not to look at them. . . . They don't know how to dance and sing!" ("Nu, vremena!

Example 9.   The refrain of Zerlino's ballad in act I of Auber's *Fra Diavolo, ou l'Hôtellerie de Terracine*

Poveselit'sya tolkom ne umeyut. Shto za manerï! Shto za ton! I ne glyadela bï. . . . Ni tantsevat', ni pet' ne znayut!") On its next appearance (transposed a semitone higher) it bridges repetitions of the first verse of Grétry's arietta. This second incarnation of motif Y could be imaginatively described as an acoustic trace of distant footfalls from an eighteenth-century ballroom. However, because it is so conspicuously prefigured in the Kozlovsky polonaise, the number that concluded a lavish ball scene, it seems to touch on something more provocative, something from the opera's "future" rather than its "past": the decline of the Catherine epoch and, by extension, the decline of aristocratic life. This interpretation finds support in the change in the stage décor (in the original and many subsequent productions) between act II, scenes 1 and 2: a pastel-paneled ballroom with gold and silver trim (the attributes, in effect, of rococo style) is supplanted by a heavily draped, reddish chamber that provides no sense of depth. Bright illumination fades to a single spotlight. The walls of the stage, like the sides of a house of cards, implode.

As musical symbols, the motifs in *The Queen of Spades* are multivalent allegories that forge ties between scenes and make the familiar unfamiliar. The collusion of references reflects not only the discontinuities in Herman's psyche but also the discontinuities in the dramatic spheres. To an extent, the vagaries in the handling of the motifs reflect Chaikovsky's rapid compositional process. In the letters that he wrote to his brother during his forty-four days in Florence, he expressed wonder at his own powers of invention and indicated that he wanted to experience something of his protagonist's dreams and obsessions. His swift writing pace lent spontaneity to the score. While he clearly mapped out the opera in detail, organizing the score around the scene in the Countess's chamber, he treated the principal motifs less as rigid molds than fluid configurations.

To clarify these points, let us take up an additional example: what Brown and others call the "card" motif, but which will here simply be tagged motif Z. It consists of a major or minor second and a diminished, perfect, or augmented fourth, a pattern that, as noted, is also found in the ballad in *Fra Diavolo, ou L'hôtellerie de Terracine.* Unlike Auber, however, Chaikovsky presents the motif in both horizontal (melodic) and vertical (harmonic) guises. The former consists of a three-note melodic cell that is sounded up to three times; the latter consists of a three-note chord that is sounded up to three times. The horizontal version sometimes appears alone, but the vertical version (heard in act I, scene 1, act II, scene 1, and act II, scene 2), always appears in conjunction with the horizontal one. Brown reports that repetitions of the horizontal version can occur "either at the same [pitch] level [i.e., in the same tonality] or, more often, as a rising sequence [i.e., each repetition transposed upward by a major second]."[89] Chaikovsky does not repeat the vertical version of the motif at the same pitch level but always transposes it by a major second. Combined, the three-by-three patterns of the horizontal and vertical versions produce a whole-tone cluster that underscores two central features of the dramaturgy. In accord with the tradition of Russian nineteenth-century opera, it suggests the paranormal, sounding during those passages in which Herman confronts the Countess.

In accord with the modernist sense of malaise that permeates the score, the whole-tone cluster suggests a condition of immobility and stagnation. In either case, Chaikovsky exploits the invariance of the whole-tone scale, the fact that it replicates itself when transposed by any of its constituent intervals.

The horizontal three-by-three pattern appears in act I, scene 1 to herald the Countess's stage entrance and to facilitate a modulation from G to F-sharp minor.[90] It is then heard in the orchestral introduction to Tomsky's ballad, in the vocal line of the ballad (the opening phrase of each strophe features the pitch combinations f♯-e-a and g-f♯-b), and in the orchestral accompaniment to the ballad (as Tomsky quotes Saint-Germain's statement "Countess, in exchange for one 'rendezvous,' I am able, if you wish, to name you the three cards" ["Grafinya, tsenoy odnogo 'rendezvous,' khotite, pozhaluy, ya vam nazovu tri kartï"]). The distinctions between the versions are both tonal and rhythmic. Motif Z is repeated at the same pitch level in the ballad's introduction, but transposed upward by a major second on each repetition in the vocal and accompanimental lines of the ballad itself. It is progressively lengthened from two sixteenth notes and an eighth note in the introduction to two eighth notes and a quarter note in the vocal line to two quarter notes and a half note in the accompaniment. Comparable treatments of motif Z color Herman's interaction with Liza and the Countess's rebuke of her in act I, scene 2. While it is unnecessary to document all of the motif's appearances in the opera, its final iterations warrant scrutiny. In act II, scene 2, as Herman steels himself to confront the Countess in her chamber, the first, fourth, and seventh pitches of the three-by-three pattern yield the whole-tone scale fragment F, G, and A; two measures later, the three-by-three pattern recurs, with the first, fourth, and seventh pitches yielding the whole-tone scale fragment B, c♯, e♭. The result is a complete whole-tone scale, with parallel whole-tone scales generated by the second, fifth, and eighth as well as the third, sixth, and ninth pitches of the two sequences—one a major second below the original, another a minor third above. Primacy in the passage is assigned to the first scale of the group, whose pitches occur on strong beats, rather than to the second and third scales, whose pitches occur on agogic accents. (The third whole-tone scale is, however, the complement to the first one; together, they exhaust the twelve pitches of the chromatic scale.) The chords built on the six degrees of the first whole-tone scale are all vertical incarnations of motif Z: F-G-B, G-A-c♯, A-B-d♯, B-c♯-e♯, c♯-d♯-fx, e♭-f-a, f-g-b. Heard at the beginning of the final episode of act II, scene 2—after the orchestral texture flattens into a single staff—these chords constitute what Jarocinski would likely term (based on his analysis of comparable clusters in Debussy's *Pelléas et Mélisande*) "irrational" and "pure" sound values that enable the composer to dispense with a priori principles of formal-functional harmony and "to build up new structures formed on different principles."[91] In effect, Chaikovsky's combination of the horizontal and vertical guises of motif Z generates a spectral apparition. By rendering harmonic and melodic patterns equivalent, capable of exchanging registers, he provides a tidy encapsulation of the overall structure of the opera, in which dramatic events unfold both diachronically (through time) and synchronically (through the overlaying of temporal strata).

The whole-tone chords precede a spectral apparition of another sort, the real-or-hallucinated appearance of the ghost in act III, scene 1. Orchestral sound floods the stage, which, from Herman's perspective, represents an incursion of "supernatural" noise into "natural" space. The horizontal three-by-three pattern of motif Z sounds in G minor in measures 3–4 (shown in music example 14), 10–11, 19–20, and 23–24 of the orchestral prelude to the scene. It recurs in rhythmic augmentation in measures 53–58 as the ghost intones the fateful formula: G-F-B♭, A-G-c, B♭-A-d♭. Her message reaches Herman's ears through a verbal code, three words that he will decode further on: "three, seven, ace." It reaches our ears through a musical code: three melodic groups, two with an intervallic content of a descending major second and ascending perfect fourth, a third with an intervallic content of a descending minor second and ascending diminished fourth. The chromatic alteration of the third iteration is tonally enigmatic, incorporating a pitch—d♭—distinct from the surrounding F major orchestral music.

Motif Z sounds four additional times in the climactic scene in the gambling salon, first as one of the players, Chekalinsky, comments on Herman's atrocious appearance: "Couldn't look worse! Are you not well?" ("Strashneye bït' nel'zya! Da tï zdorov li?"). The two subsequent occurrences herald Herman's winning bids on the three and seven cards. In these passages, the horizontal three-by-three pattern contains a descending major second and an ascending perfect fourth. Just before Herman's losing bid on the ace, the motif sounds a final time, in rhythmic augmentation, employing a raised fourth that derails the harmonic sequence: f-e♭-a. In sum: before his bid, the harmony progresses from a G minor chord to v 4/2 of C minor; as he bids, it progresses from an E-flat major chord to V 4/2 of E major; finally, when he learns that he has lost, it shifts from a G-sharp diminished seventh chord to an A-major tonic chord. Brown declares—albeit with a few too many generalizations—that Chaikovsky's handling of the motif is a

Example 10.   Motif Z in the orchestral introduction to Tomsky's act I, scene 1 ballad

Example 11.   Motif Z in the vocal line of the ballad

"brilliantly planned and executed *coup de grâce* in an opera whose thematic processes have shown impressive range, skill, insight, and organic power."[92] He overlooks, however, the composer's sleight-of-hand in the manipulation of the motif. In the ghost scene, Chaikovsky lowered the interval of the fourth from perfect to diminished in an omen of Herman's loss at the faro table; however, in the gambling scene, he raised it from perfect to augmented just before that loss actually happened.

For Motif Z is not here to narrate Herman's downfall. Instead it articulates a more significant event: the fusing of dramatic planes. To insist that the whole-tone music denotes a fantastic plane while the tonal music denotes a real one is to overlook the fact that Chaikovsky uses motif Z as a means to unite these two realms. It generates both whole-tone and tonal passages, outlining a whole-tone scale in act II, scene 2 and enacting a modulation from G minor to A major in act III, scene 3. Appropriately enough,

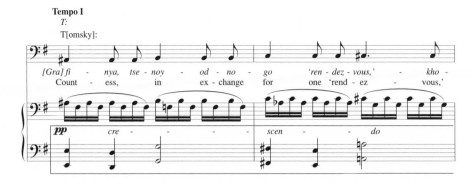

Example 12.   Motif Z in the orchestral accompaniment to the ballad

motif Z, which oscillates between musical spheres, is aligned principally with the Countess, a transitory figure who possesses both mortal and immortal guises and who serves to transmit knowledge between dramatic levels. The whole-tone music that accompanies her fateful disclosure to Herman brings to mind a number of Russian Romantic operas with supernatural happenings (Mikhaíl Glinka's *Ruslan and Lyudmila* [*Ruslan i Lyudmila*, 1842], Alexander Dargomïzhsky's *The Stone Guest* [*Kamennïy gost'*, 1872], Rimsky-Korsakov's *The Snow Maiden* [*Snegoruchka*, 1882]). This music is made contemporary, however, by virtue of its hybridization with major and minor tonality passages. The border between the fantastic and real, blurred at the start of the final scene, dissolves at the finish. Herman loses his mind and dies clutching the queen of spades, whose grim paper face, reminiscent of the Countess's, seems to mock him.

The other gesture that imparts a sense of unavoidable disaster in the opera is what Brown labels the "fate" motif: a descending scalar pattern that outlines a minor (and, within his analysis, major) sixth.[93] It is another instantation of motif Y, which, as noted, accrues meanings as the opera un-

Example 13.   The three-by-three version in act II, scene 2

Example 14.   Motif Z in measures 3 and 4 of the orchestral prelude to act III, scene 1

folds. Instead of tracing all the possible connotations of the motif, Brown isolates only those which, based on the dramatic atmosphere, intimate that a negative energy influences Herman's and Liza's lives. This third incarnation of motif *Y* first sounds in the string basses in measures 2 and 3 of the overture (shown in example 16)—immediately following the appearance of a 12/8 rhythmic pattern that has a symbolic trajectory of its own within the opera.[94] It falls from the mediant to the dominant (d^1 to f♯) in B minor. Subsequent appearances include Herman's act I, scene 1 cavatina, where it

Example 15.   Motif Z in act III, scene 3 (Herman's losing bid on the ace)

underlines his statement "and I do not want to know [her name]!" ("i ne khochu znat'!"), and at the high point of the act I, scene 2 love duet, where it ironizes the words, "You revealed the dawn of happiness to me" ("Ti mne zaryu raskrïla schast'ya"). It likewise appears when the Countess interrupts the love duet, marking Herman's obviously prescient words, "death, I do not want you!" ("smert', ya ne khochu tebya," shown in example 17),

Example 16.   Motif *Y* in the orchestral introduction to act I, scene 1

Example 17.   Motif *Y* (when the Countess interrupts the love duet)

and in act III, scene 2, at the beginning of the final love duet between Herman and Liza, marking her words, "No more of tears, torments, and doubts! You are mine again, and I am yours!" ("Proch' slyozï, muki i somneniya! Tï moy opyat', i ya tvoya!") Its last two appearances in the opera are the most ornate. Following Herman's catastrophic loss in the gambling salon, his thoughts turn to the deceased Liza, and he sings the motif to the words, "How I love you, my angel!" ("Kak ya lyublyu tebya moy angel!"). There follows a modulation from F major to D-flat major, and another occurrence of the motif in the orchestra, albeit expanded with chromatic interpolations: f^1, eb^1, db^1, c^1, cb, bb, bbb, ab. Excluding the brief chorus of sorrow, motif Y is the last music heard in the opera, and by virtue of its liquidation in a chromatic plunge, it denotes Herman's death, his expiration in orchestral noise. As this short litany affirms, motif Y originates as nonverbal sound, infuses the vocal parts, and expires as nonverbal sound. Like a portent, it infiltrates the psyches of its recipients, obliging them to fulfill its terms and leading them to a predetermined end. By internalizing it, Herman and Liza submit to an agency operating beyond the limits of cognition.

Most significant about the evolution of motif Y is thus neither its ability to signal the intentions of the characters nor to comment on the action but its tangential relationship to the action. Its repetitions are not exact but obscured: the scalar descent is filled in, the minor sixth changed into a major sixth, the rhythmic values mixed. Some analysts of the opera have tried to decipher the score, to assign concrete meanings to recurring vocal and instrumental gestures. But this analytical orientation ignores its unstable qualities. The musical language is neither logically limited nor internally static; rather, it shifts in meaning to convey the ambiguous significance of the characters, settings, and events. This is not to say that Chaikovsky avoided musical illustration. In the last scene, for example, he represented his protagonist's descent into madness by combining motifs X, Y, and Z. As in the source novella, Herman

> ends up in the same position as Liza, that of someone who does not know what game the world is playing with him. The fantastic element here is not a "thing" (which is evidence of an author's naïve belief in the direct intervention of supernatural forces in reality), but a sign, whose meaning may be any force. Such a force may be historical, economic, psychological or mystical, but always seems irrational from the point of view of "planning, moderation and hard work" as a program for the behavior of an individual personality.[95]

Lotman here suggests that, for Pushkin, the game of faro stood for the historical process, which is ungovernable, beyond human control. For Chaikovsky, it also stood for the dark ocean of knowledge beyond sensible awareness. In a departure from the norms of Russian opera, the "fantastic element" in the score is not confined to the whole-tone music (which would represent a "naïve" expression of the "intervention of supernatural forces in reality") but embraces the whole network of generic distortions, the pastiche of allusions.

As a symbol of end-of-century, or end-of-life-as-we-know-it malaise, Herman strives to transcend the prohibitions of his social order but dies the victim of the logic he had contested. His psychological deterioration touches on a specific feature of Symbolist poetics: the expression of the disappearance of reason and of the subject's journey from sanity to madness. Herman's and Liza's prefigured deaths, symptomatic of a social crisis, do not affect the surrounding characters. Like the source novella, the opera concludes by affirming the mechanical routine of life. In Pushkin's famous words: "the game took its course" ("igra poshla svoim cheredom").[96]

THE PROBLEM OF MEANING

Since Modest Chaikovsky simultaneously updated and backdated the Pushkin story from the Golden Age to a Silver Age version of Catherine the Great's time, taking vast liberties with it in forging his libretto, no interpretation of the story's content can suffice to elucidate the opera's content. The interpretation of the score as divided into real and unreal, natural and supernatural realms is insufficient to explain the multivalence of the musical motifs, the manner in which they are placed in interlocking spatial and temporal patterns.

The intersection of musical styles corresponds to the intersection of Emerson's three temporal strata: the "Classical," "Romantic," and "Modern." In concluding her commentary on the 1995 production, she refers to Lotman, specifically his assertion that, in certain modernist literary works, "objective reality" is supplanted by "a large number of [subjective] interpretations."[97] Chaikovsky's reworking of musical motifs not only achieves such a conflation of points of view, it serves to create bridges (or, in the Russian Symbolists' parlance, *fortochki*, "little windows"[98]) between perceptual registers.

Somewhat more fancifully, one could argue that the collusion of the first ("Classical") and second ("Romantic") strata of the opera actually discloses the "Modern" stratum. This third, "occult" stratum is independent of the other two and emblematizes Herman's attainment of heightened consciousness, his perception of events beyond the limits of material reality. Andrey Belïy called this attainment of heightened consciousness "symbolization." In a manifesto with an excessively detailed title, *Why I Became a Symbolist and Why I Never Ceased Being One in All the Phases of My Intellectual and Artistic Development* (*Pochemu ya stal simvolistom i pochemu ya ne perestal im bït' vo vsekh fazakh moyego ideynogo i khudozhestvennogo razvitiya*, 1928), the poet defined "symbolization" as a process by which the finite "spatial" and "temporal" properties of phenomena are combined with their "eternal" properties. To explain this concept, Belïy recalled (or invented) an anecdote from his childhood. Hoping to apprehend "the essence of a state of consciousness (fear)," he placed a crimson cardboard box top in the shadows, so that he could see only its color. Each time he passed by it, he noted to himself "something purple." The word "something" represented his fearful reaction to the object (his encounter with the unfamiliar), while the word "purple" represented its actual appearance (obscured by shadow). "Symbolization," Belïy claimed, is a process whereby the experience and the appearance of an object is transformed "into something that is neither *this* nor *that*, but a *third*. A symbol is this *third*. In constructing it I transcend the two worlds (the chaotic state of fear and the object given from the external world). Neither of these worlds is real. But the *third* world exists." [99] Belïy aligned his theory of "symbolization" with Kant's and Schopenhauer's theories of perception, especially their discussions of the relationship between cognitive perception, the means by which knowledge conditions experience, and their discussions of intuitive perception, the immediate apprehension of time and space. He defined symbols per se as entities that mediate between people, who under normal circumstances are unable to access the transcendent, and the otherworldly. The prefecture of symbolism, consequently, "is artistic cognition, which is to say, cognition through revelation, which is to say, religious cognition." [100] This point would appear to be illustrated in act III, scene 1 of *The Queen of Spades*, in which the Countess's ghost enters Herman's barracks room and, illuminated in a red (or green) light, reveals secret knowledge to him. The "occult" moments of the score are those in which there is a slippage between stylistic and temporal layers, in which the admixture of the Classical and Romantic discloses the Modern. The first and second worlds prove to be unreal, "but the *third* world [the composer's proto-Symbolist world] exists."

I hope to have established here that Chaikovsky stratified different times and different places within his opera. His musical motifs, like his musical quotations, are overlaid, tucked inside one another. In this regard, they resemble a set of *matryoshki*, or Russian nesting dolls. The end result is an operatic picture gallery, a music-historical exhibition that comments on the passing of an aristocratic age. Disappointing as this may be to his biographers, the aura of fate derives from anything *but* the composer's own life. Although he grieved for Herman when he finished the score, he did not share that character's sense of existential alienation. Isolation in a realm of subjective idealism was not a feature of his personality. As Taruskin has convincingly argued, Chaikovsky held fast to the view that artistic creation should enhance social discourse and that music should be broadly accessible. For this reason, the sensual and decorative aspects of *The Queen of Spades*—harshly critiqued though they have been by those who would have preferred a more explicit preoccupation with philosophical and spiritual issues, a greater preponderance of "Romantic" over "Classical" values— remain its major source of power. To expand on a statement made by a leading historian of the Silver Age, "Just as the Symbolists had reacted to the Revolutionary turbulence of the years 1904–6 by trying to find adequate expression for it in their works," Chaikovsky reacted to the pre-Revolutionary inertia and decay in his society by composing an opera leavened by "recall and foreboding."[101]

As noted at the outset, Soviet aesthetics could not countenance the mysticism and neurosis of *The Queen of Spades*. The official artistic doctrine of Socialist Realism (drawn up in 1936 following the establishment of Communist Party-led arts unions and the centralization and regimentation of creative activity) demanded allegiance to Glinka-esque operative conventions and a concomitant hostility to subsequent "decadent" trends. For the musicologist Ivan Sollertinsky, oftentimes a proponent of operative innovation, the principal problem with *The Queen of Spades* resided in its anachronisms.[102] The opera suffered from a hesitation between the normal and abnormal, realism and surrealism, portraiture and caricature.

Sollertinsky's was one voice in a chorus of literal-minded detractors who rebuked the Chaikovsky brothers for altering the setting of the opera's action and tampering with the source novella. The Pushkin jubilee celebrations, the impetus behind Meyerhold's re-Pushkinization of *The Queen of Spades*, occurred after Socialist Realist doctrine had been put into practice, though Meyerhold's geometrical stage décor and biomechanical acting method obviously ran counter to the doctrine's tenets. Pushkin and (during his own jubilee) Chaikovsky were subsequently rehabilitated by Soviet historians as "classics." Following Meyerhold's 1935 production, Sollertinsky lauded the director for raising the opera to the status it had initially, inexplicably failed to achieve.[103] He had sound reason to do so, since, along with the director Samuíl Samosud, he had participated in the score's "correction." His comments set the tone for other reviewers; all but one of his colleagues affirmed them. The lone exception was Alexander Fevralsky (1901–84), who in a 22 February 1935 review for the *Literary Gazette* (*Literaturnaya gazeta*) subtly disparaged Meyerhold's decision to eliminate the "gloomy coloration," "pessimism," and "mysticism" of Chaikovsky's 1890 version:

Only now that Meyerhold has returned the true spirit and plot details of Pushkin's novella to *The Queen of Spades* (in place of the Summer Garden "they played cards at cavalry officer Narumov's"; revision of Herman's relationship to Liza; Liza does not die; Herman ends up in an insane asylum; and so on), do we see that this opera is actually "highly original overall."

For Meyerhold brought to this opera his attitude. And it is expressed not only in those features of Herman's stage persona that help to elucidate his social essence. Herman's philosophy, expressed in the aria "What is our life? A game," approximates the fatalistic worldview of Chaikovsky himself. Meyerhold very tactfully discloses this philosophy by theatrical means. He shows how, combined with extreme individualism, it leads to the destruction of Herman's personality.

Now to *The Queen of Spades*'s mysticism. Meyerhold leaves the ghost on stage but enfeebles its mystical component (to eliminate it entirely is impossible because it is rooted in the music). The ghost is as simple and real as the living Countess. Depicted realistically, this fantastic character lacks "supernaturalism"; it is just a conventional theatrical figure.[104]

Meyerhold, though resistant to the conservative dictates of the Stalinist cultural establishment (the dogma of rigid materialism), excised the Dionysian elements from *The Queen of Spades* and embellished its Apollonian elements. Blok's conception of the opera as representing the triumph of Chaikovsky over Pushkin was turned inside out: "the ['Dionysian' Chaikovsky] tumbled into the abyss, where the hand of [Pushkin], the magician and musician, pushed him." The chaotic, discordant, and nocturnal features of the score became logical, harmonious, and diurnal. The Countess, providing otherworldly knowledge in the 1890 staging (assuming, in other words, the guise of a Symbolist poet) was reduced to a cantankerous crone in the 1935 production. The pastorale *intermède*, whose distortions augmented the opera's uncanny aura, was replaced by a *commedia dell'arte* play that placed a mirror between the audience and *dramatis personae*. In "correcting" the stylistic anachronisms of the score, Meyerhold perpetrated one of his own: he transplanted the opera from the "Symbolist" era to the "Classical" or, more accurately, "Neoclassical" era—back, in other words, to the future. He also undermined his own theory of the grotesque, excising that assemblage of features in the score that "synthesizes opposites, creates a picture of the incredible, and invites the spectator to solve the riddle of the inscrutable."[105] Though his editorial tinkering was in its own way grotesque—or, to refer back to Nordau, "degenerate"—it had less to do with compositional process than with historiography.

Since the generic and stylistic abnormalities in *The Queen of Spades* were intentional, one could argue that Chaikovsky actually anticipated his opera's misperception. To borrow an inspired phrase by the film critic Stefan Mattesich, the opera is "the allegory of its own reception."[106] Heard in context, it embodies the maelstrom of contradictions that engulfed the intelligentsia in the Silver Age. To them, reality seemed artificial, a caricature. The alterations that Chaikovsky saw in his world—the metamorphosis of the aristocratic iconography of St. Petersburg into strange bric-a-brac—motivated him to compose an opera that, to quote Mattesich again, drew the audience "from the side of the real into a fiction" and then provided it with "the fiction of the real."[107] Like his stage characters, Chaikovsky anticipated the future as if recalling the past, creating *the* masterpiece of Russian Symbolist opera. In view of the representations of gambling in *The Queen of Spades*, it is an unsettling irony that the later efforts of Rimsky-Korsakov, Scriabin, and even Prokofiev to create Symbolist operas were risky ventures as much governed by chance as by fate.

POSTSCRIPT

The post-Soviet rehabilitation of *The Queen of Spades* was accomplished by Valery Gergiev, the indefatigable conductor of the Mariyinsky Theater, who believes that Russian opera mirrors Russian history, that theatrical politics recapitulates traumatic national upheavals. In his production, the characters are boxed in, the sets a series of picture frames. Besides his production, perhaps the most beguiling re-envisioning of the opera is the 1999 film *Of Freaks and People (Pro urodov i lyudey)* directed by Alexey Balabanov. As of the year 2000, it had not yet been screened in the United States, but it received two awards at the 1999 Cannes film festival. Set in *fin-de-siècle* St. Petersburg, it concerns the activities of Johann, a Mephistopheles-like figure who operates a photography studio in the basement of an upscale apartment block. Though he appears to be engaged in family portraiture, the viewer soon discovers that he deals in pornography. His salacious wares initially elicit giggles from his puritanical clients— who include the teenager Liza, her suitor Herman, her bad-tempered grandmother, a pair of Siamese twins, a blind piano teacher, and an impresario— but they are all eventually lured into the trade. The film begins and ends with a scratchy phonograph recording of the Countess's arietta of act II, scene 2. The opening shot is a freeze-frame of a childhood photograph of Liza, the closing shot a freeze-frame of Johann standing in the center of a frozen Neva River. The citizens of the city have all fled, suspecting that there will be tumult in the spring.

NOTES

1. Sergey Dyagilev, "V chas itogov," *Vesï* 2: 4 (April 1905): 45–46. A section of this passage is translated—and its mood of foreboding assessed—by Pyman in *A History of Russian Symbolism*, 270, and Taruskin in *Defining Russia Musically*, 307.

2. The term "Silver Age" is routinely used to describe developments in Russian culture in the last twenty-five years of tsarist rule. Arkadii Klimovitsky ("Tchaikovsky and the Russian 'Silver Age,'" in *Tchaikovsky and His World*, ed. Leslie Kearney [Princeton: Princeton University Press, 1998], 321) notes that Nikolai Berdyayev (1874–1948), the editor of *New Path*, Razumnik Ivanov-Razumnik (1878–1946), a historian, and Nikolai Otsup (1894–1958), a literary critic, have all been credited with inventing the term. It owes its popularization, however, to the poet Anna Akhmatova (real surname Gorenko, 1888–1966), who immortalized it in *Poem without a Hero* (*Poema bez geroya*, 1940–62).

3. Mikhaíl Kuzmin, *K. A. Somov*, 1916, as cited in Pyman, *A History of Russian Symbolism*, 95.

4. Fyodor Sologub, "The Theatre of One Will" ["Teatr odnoy voli," 1908], in *The Russian Symbolists: An Anthology of Critical and Theoretical Writings*, trans. and ed. Ronald E. Peterson (Ann Arbor: Ardis, 1986), 115. This essay is a polemic against the theatrical innovations of Vsevolod Meyerhold.

5. Jurij M. Lotman, "Theme and Plot: The Theme of Cards and the Card Game in Russian Literature of the Nineteenth Century," *PTL: A Journal for Descriptive Poetics and Theory of Literature* 3 (1978): 456–61.

6. Klimovitsky, "Tchaikovsky and the Russian 'Silver Age,'" 324–25. The Merezhkovsky settings are "Go To Sleep!" ("Usni!") and "Death" ("Smert'"), opus 57, nos. 1 and 2 (1883).

7. N. Suvorovskiy, "Chaykovskiy i muzïka budushchego," *Vesï* 1: 8 (August 1904): 14. The article buttresses Klimovitsky's assertion that "when the Russian symbolists confronted Wagner, they leaned heavily on their experience with Tchaikovsky" ("Tchaikovsky and the Russian 'Silver Age,'" 325).

8. Max Nordau, *Degeneration* (published in English in 1895; reprint, with an introduction by George L. Mosse, Lincoln: University of Nebraska Press, 1993). Nordau enumerates the symptoms of degeneracy between pages 15 and 33. These include "atavism," "hysteria," feelings of "imminent perdition and extinction," "moral insanity and emotionalism," "mental weakness and despondency," "queer and senseless ideas," and "mysticism." Nordau likewise attributes the upheavals in European *fin-de-siècle* culture to the "criminal" and "pathological" tendencies of its artists.

9. *Teatr* 1017 (12–13 February 1912), 13. The anecdote is also related by Klimovitsky, "Tchaikovsky and the Russian 'Silver Age,'" 324.

10. Aleksandr Benua [Benois], *Moi vospominaniya v pyati knigakh*, ed. D. S. Likhachev, 2 vols. (Moscow: Nauka, 1980), 1: 652–53. Though "in five books," the memoirs were actually published in two volumes.

11. See Andrew Wachtel, "The Ballet's Libretto," in *Petrushka: Sources and Contexts*, ed. Andrew Wachtel (Evanston: Northwestern University Press, 1998), 30.

12. Aleksandr Blok, *Sobraniye sochineniy,* ed. M. A. Dudin, V. N. Orlov, and A. A. Surkov, 6 vols. (Leningrad: Khudozhestvennaya literatura, 1983), 6: 93–94. The phrases "Pushkin and Lermontov" and "two founders of the Petersburg epoch" are self-quotations from "A Pedant on a Poet."

13. Blame cannot be assigned only to Soviet musicologists. In a recent revisionist essay about Chaikovsky, Taruskin contends that "no composer conformed less to, or more staunchly resisted, the myth of the artist hero—the surrogate or advance guard for the myth of the heroic German nation—that steadily gained in momentum and in prestige as the nineteenth century wore on, and which reached its dubious triumph in the artistically maladapted twentieth century." He further deduces that "Chaikovsky has consistently landed on the wrong side" of the Western "ideological divide" between "an idea of art oriented toward its audience, hence centered on social reception, public meaning, and human intercourse, and an idea of art oriented at once toward its makers—hence centered on private, hidden, or ineffable meanings—and, finally, toward their product, hence centered on idealized or 'absolute' notions of ontology and structure" (*Defining Russia Musically,* 261).

14. G. V. Kopïtova, ed., *Pikovaya dama. Zamïsel. Voploshcheniye. Sud'ba* (St. Petersburg: Kompozitor, 1994), 23–24. The libretto for the "re-Pushkinized" production was written by the translator and critic Valentin Stenich (1898–1938) after a scenario by Meyerhold, while the sets were conceived by Leonid Chupyatov (1890–1941).

15. These are "A Note on Pushkin" ("Zametka o Pushkine") by Vasiliy Rozanov (1856–1919), "The Pushkin Festival" ("Prazdnik Pushkina") by Merezhkovsky, "The Behests of Pushkin" ("Zavetï Pushkina") by Nikolai Vilenkin (1855–1937), and "On the All-Russian Celebration" ("K Vserossiyskomu torzhestvu") by Sologub.

16. Natalie Foshko, "On the Interpretation of 'The Queen of Spades,'" *Elementa* 3:2 (1996): 189.

17. On these points, see Pyman, *A History of Russian Symbolism,* 178–80. The actual quotations are taken from Valeriy Bryusov's 1905 essay "The Holy Sacrifice" ("Svyashchennaya zhertva").

18. Neil Cornwell, *Pushkin's The Queen of Spades* (London: Bristol Classical Press, 1993), 6. In the biographical supplement to the book ("A note on the Count Saint-Germain," 87–90), Cornwell reports that Saint-Germain was an actual historical figure whom Pushkin learned about from reading Casanova's memoirs. Little is known of his birth, though some claim that he "descended from Franz-Leopold, Prince Ragoczy of Transylvania (he sometimes went as 'Graf Tzarogy' or 'Ragotsy'), who died in 1734, having opposed the Austrian Empire." He received his formal education at the University of Siena, thereafter becoming a restless traveler. He worked as a diplomat in the 1750s "in Paris, under Louis XV and Madame de Pompadour," and entered Russian society. Before his death in 1784 or 1785, he spread "bizarre rumors" about his age and talents, at times claiming to be "an accomplished musician, apparently of unlimited but mysterious wealth, an occult scholar, a fanatical chemist, an alchemical adept and a brilliant dyer and mixer of colors (to a secret formula which he refused to divulge)."

19. John Bayley, *Pushkin: A Comparative Commentary,* 1971, as quoted in ibid., 6.

20. In faro, or *banque,* the banker holds one pack of cards and the player a second pack. The player selects a card from his or her pack and places it face down on the table; the banker then places cards face down on the right and left side of the player's card. The three cards are turned over. If the card on the right has the same

value as the player's card, the banker wins; if the card on the left has the same value the player wins.

21. The preceding summary follows Cornwell, *Pushkin's The Queen of Spades,* 3–5.

22. G[rigoriy] Dombayev, *Tvorchestvo Pyotra Il'icha Chaykovskogo v materialakh i dokumentakh,* ed. Gr. Bernandt (Moscow: Gosudarstvennoye muzïkal'noye izdatel'stvo, 1958), 169.

23. This and the other quotations in the paragraph are taken from P[yotr] I[l'ich] Chaykovskiy, *Dnevniki 1873–1891,* ed. S. Chemodanov (1923; reprint St. Petersburg: Ego and Severnïy olen,' 1993), 252–56.

24. Chaykovskiy, *Polnoye sobraniye sochineniy: Literaturnïye proizvedeniya i perepiska,* ed. K. Yu. Davïdova and G. I. Labutina, 17 vols. (Moscow: Muzïka, 1953–81), 15B: 236.

25. Chaykovskiy, *Dnevniki 1873–1891,* 258.

26. Letter of 3 March 1890, in Chaykovskiy, *Polnoye sobraniye sochineniy: Literaturnïye proizvedeniya i perepiska,* 15B: 87. The account is corroborated by Modest's servant Nazar Litrov (?–1900), whom Chaikovsky took with him to Florence. In a 2 March 1890 diary entry, Litrov recalled that the composer "began to tell how he finished Herman's last words and how Herman committed suicide. Pyotr Ilyich said that he had cried all that evening, and his eyes were still red then, and himself suffering terribly. He was tired, and, despite this fatigue, he still wanted to cry, it seems. . . . Spent this evening quietly, as if he had really buried that poor Herman" (*Tchaikovsky Through Others' Eyes,* ed. Alexander Poznansky, trans. Ralph C. Burr, Jr., and Robert Bird [Bloomington: Indiana University Press, 1999], 191).

27. Chaykovskiy, *Dnevniki 1873–1891,* 213–14.

28. Lotman, "The Decembrist in Daily Life," in *The Semiotics of Russian Cultural History,* ed. Alexander D. Nakhimovsky and Alice Stone Nakhimovsky (Ithaca: Cornell University Press, 1985), 111. Chaikovsky's *Manfred* Symphony (opus 58, 1885), based on Lord Byron's 1817 dramatic poem and on a program written by Vladimir Stasov (1824–1906) and Mily Balakirev (1837–1910), deals specifically with the theme of "everyday Byronism." In a letter to Yuliya Spazhinskaya, Chaikovsky remarked that "Manfred is not simply a person. It seems to me that, within him, Byron with amazing power and depth embodied the tragedy of the struggle between our pettiness and our aspiration to grasp the crucial questions of existence" (*P. I. Chaikovskiy o muzïke, o zhizni, o sebe,* ed. A[lexandra] A. Orlova [Leningrad: Muzïka, 1976], 179). Such was likewise the composer's conception of Herman.

29. In Pushkin's novella, the protagonist is named "Hermann" (or more precisely transliterated, "Germann"), the two n's indicating a surname. By removing one "n," Modest Chaikovsky made it a first name.

30. "You wrote [the opening act of] the libretto very well," he declared, "but it has a deficiency, namely its verbosity. Please, be as brief and laconic as possible" (letter of 23 January 1890, in Chaykovskiy, *Polnoye sobraniye sochineniy: Literaturnïye proizvedeniya i perepiska,* 15B: 23).

31. Dostoyevsky, for example, declared that the novella was "the epitome of the art of the fantastic. You believe that Hermann really had a vision, exactly in accordance with his view of the world, and yet, at the end of the tale, that is when you have read it through, you cannot make up your mind: did this vision emanate from Hermann's nature or was he really one of those in contact with another world, one of evil spirits hostile to man? (N.B. Spiritualism and the study thereof.) That's art for you!" (1880 letter quoted in Cornwell, *Pushkin's The Queen of Spades,* 7).

32. Lotman, "Theme and Plot. The Theme of Cards and the Card Game in Russian Literature of the Nineteenth Century," 474.

33. Karabanov also supplied the text for the chorus of act II, scene 1: "In joy and cheer, friends, let us on this day gather 'round!" ("Radostno, veselo, v den' sey sbiraytesya drugi!")

34. Carolyn Roberts, "Puškin's 'Pikovaja dama' and the Opera Libretto," *Canadian Review of Comparative Literature* 6 (Winter 1979): 13. There was one other nineteenth-century operatic treatment of Pushkin's novella: Franz Suppé and T. Treumann's *Die Kartenschlägerin, oder Pique Dame* (1862).

35. Ibid., 11.

36. Ibid., 22. The footnote reads: "This is not the place for detailed analysis, but I will point out a curious 'echo': M. Cajkovskij's perhaps unconscious borrowing in *Pikovaja dama* of phraseology from Dostoevskij's novel. There is an obvious link between Germann's words 'There are piles of gold lying about over there' ['tam grudï zolota lezhat'] and the words of the writer: '. . . our newspapermen tell of piles of gold which are supposedly lying about on the tables' ['. . . nashi fel'etonistï rasskazïvayut o grudakh zolota, kotorïye budto bï lezhat na stolakh']."

37. Foshko, "On the Interpretation of 'The Queen of Spades,'" 182.

38. A[leksandr] S[ergeyevich] Pushkin, "Pikovaya dama," in *Polnoye sobraniye sochineniy v desyati tomakh*, 3rd ed. (Moscow: Nauka, 1962–66), 6: 324.

39. Cited in N. Sin'kovskaya, "Brat'ya Chaykovskiye v rabote nad libretto 'Pikovoy damï,'" in *Chaykovskiy. Voprosï istorii i teorii. Vtoroy sbornik statey* (Moscow: Moskovskaya gosudarstvennaya dvazhdï ordena Lenina konservatoriya im. P. I. Chaykovskogo, 1991), 23.

40. Carolyn Abbate, *Unsung Voices: Opera and Musical Narrative in the Nineteenth Century* (Princeton: Princeton University Press, 1991), 4–10.

41. Cited in Sin'kovskaya, "Brat'ya Chaykovskiye v rabote nad libretto 'Pikovoy damï,'" 25; emphasis added.

42. D. S. Mirsky, *A History of Russian Literature from Its Beginnings to 1900*, ed. Francis J. Whitfield (1926; reprint, New York: Vintage Books, 1958), 80.

43. K[onstantin] N[ikolayevich] Batyushkov, *Sochineniya*, ed. D. D. Blagoy (Moscow: Akademiya, 1934), 147.

44. See Victor Shklovsky, "Art as Technique" ("Iskusstvo kak priyom," 1917), in *Russian Formalist Criticism: Four Essays*, ed. and trans. Lee T. Lemon and Marion J. Reis (Lincoln: University of Nebraska Press, 1965), 3–24.

45. Taruskin, "Another World: Why *The Queen of Spades* Is the Great Symbolist Opera," *Opera News*, 23 December 1995, 12. This article—together with its precursor in *The New Grove Dictionary of Opera*—was the first to evaluate the proto-Symbolist content of Chaikovsky's opera.

46. Yuriy Vasil'yev reports that the music of act I, scene 2 was sketched in Modest's libretto (which Modest sent to Chaikovsky in Florence in sections), in two sketchbooks (No. 3 and No. 13), and in one exercise book (No. 27). Now preserved at the Chaikovsky State Archive and House Museum (Gosudarstvennïy arkhiv doma muzeya P. I. Chaykovskogo) in Klin, these sources reveal that Chaikovsky drafted Polina's romance quite late in the creative process and then recast the surrounding numbers to resonate with its E-flat minor tonality. For example: he drafted the "clapping" song in C major but then transposed it to A major to effect a jarring tritonal contrast with the romance. There is some ambiguity in the sketches for the final arioso of the scene, "But why these tears?" ("Zachem zhe eti slyozï?"). Chaikovsky drafted it in E-flat major and E major but subsequently transposed it to Eb minor, the tonality of Polina's romance. In doing so, he estab-

lished a correspondence of sorts between the shepherdess's fate in Batyushkov's elegy and Liza's fate. But then Chaikovsky again transposed the arioso, this time to C minor, thus removing the tonal link to Polina's romance. He instead decided to have Herman sing a phrase from it during his love duet with Liza ("K rukopisyam 'Pikovoy damï,'" *Sovetskaya muzïka* 7 [1980]: 99–103).

47. Poznansky, *Tchaikovsky: The Quest for the Inner Man* (New York: Schirmer Books, 1991), 438.

48. See Slavoj Žižek, "Robert Schumann: The Romantic Anti-Humanist," in *The Plague of Fantasies* (London: Verso, 1997), 194–97.

49. J. Douglas Clayton, *Pierrot in Petrograd: Commedia dell'Arte / Balagan in Twentieth-Century Russian Theatre and Drama* (Montreal: McGill-Queen's University Press, 1993), 12.

50. Chaykovskiy, *Perepiska s N. F. fon-Mekk*, ed. B. A. Zhdanov and N. T. Zhegin, 3 vols. (Moscow: Akademiya, 1934–36), 2: 546.

51. David Brown, *Tchaikovsky: A Biographical and Critical Study*, 4 vols. (London: Victor Gollancz, 1978–91), 4: 244–45. Seconding a statement by Boris Asafyev, Brown calls it a "mystery" that Chaikovsky knew Bortnyansky's opera, as it was unpublished when he was composing *The Queen of Spades*, "and not among the scores he took to Italy." But the veracity of the attribution cannot be doubted: Bortnyansky composed *Le fils-rival* for the court of Crown Prince Paul I, who became Russian tsar after the death of his mother, Catherine the Great. Chaikovsky's quotation from it in the *intermède* presages the stage appearance of the empress at the conclusion of act II, scene 2. It functions as another portend, an allusion to actual musical activity at the St. Petersburg court, that is to say, musical activity in the "future" of the opera, not the "present."

Taruskin ("Another World: Why *The Queen of Spades* Is the Great Symbolist Opera," 13) notes that the "acclamations" to Catherine toward the end of act II, scene 2 are sung to the melody of another polonaise, "Thunder of victory, resound!" ("Grom pobedï, razdavayasya!"), which was "composed in 1791 by Osip (or Jozef) Kozlovsky, a naturalized Pole who began his career in Russia as a protégé of Prince Potemkin, Catherine's favorite." It should be added here that Modest Chaikovsky replaced Kozlovsky's text with that of an ode by Gavrila Derzhavin (1743–1816) entitled "An account of the celebration on the occasion of the taking of Izmail" ("Opisaniye torzhestva, po sluchayu vzyatiya Izmayla"). The choice of Derzhavin is significant, for he, like Pyotr Chaikovsky, subscribed to the view that art must have a public role in affairs of the state. Moreover, like the Symbolists, he lived during an exceptionally turbulent time in Russian history.

Modest had hoped to include another Derzhavin text ("National tribute to the Vyazemskys" ["Rodstvennoye prazdnestvo Vyazemskikh"]) in act II, scene 1, but was dissuaded by his brother, who felt that the scene had become too long.

52. Brown has nothing positive to say about the *intermède*. He contends, "It is straining credibility to hear in the Milozvor-Prilepa-Zlatogor tale any ironic resonance from the Hermann-Liza-Eletsky drama of the opera itself." He also claims that Chaikovsky's "agreeable fifteen-minute idyll of arcadian rivalry is too otiose; worse still, the music is no more than pastiche" (*Tchaikovsky: A Biographical and Critical Study*, 4: 246). To justify the latter remark, Brown quotes Chaikovsky's seemingly tongue-in-cheek statement that the ballroom choruses were "a slavish imitation of the style of the past century and not *composition* but, as it were, *borrowing*" (*Polnoye sobraniye sochineniy: Literaturnïye proizvedeniya i perepiska*, 15B: 293).

53. The sarabande in act III of *The Sleeping Beauty* is cast in a "correct" triple

meter, though the contrapuntal imitation of the melody in the accompaniment disguises the pulse. The effect adds to the hypnotic aura of the ballet as a whole. Unlike the "Dionysian" *Queen of Spades*, the "Apollonian" *Sleeping Beauty* is not a polystylistic work: Chaikovsky does not musically represent the hundred-year passage of time between acts I and III. This passage is, however, represented in the choreography.

54. G. Mikhailova, "Tipï stilizatsii v muzïke P. I. Chaykovskogo," in *Chaykovskiy. Voprosï istorii i teorii. Vtoroy sbornik statey*, 137–38.

55. Fredric R. Jameson, "Postmodernism and Consumer Society" in Hal Foster, ed., *The Anti-Aesthetic: Essays in Postmodern Culture* (Port Townsend: Bay Press, 1983), 114.

56. N[ikolay] D. Kashkin, *Vospominaniya o P. I. Chaykovskom*, ed. and introd. S. I. Shlifshteyn (Moscow: Gosudarstvennoye muzïkal'noye izdatel'stvo, 1954), 162.

57. Rimsky-Korsakov used this term to describe the orchestration of *Iolanthe*, the shadowy successor to *The Queen of Spades*. See his *Letopis' moyey muzïkal'noy zhizni*, ed. A[ndrey] N[ikolayevich] Rimskiy-Korsakov (Moscow: Gosudarstvennoye izdatel'stvo / muzïkal'nïy sektor, 1926), 318.

58. James Parakilas, "Musical Historicism in *The Queen of Spades*," in *Tchaikovsky and His Contemporaries: A Centennial Symposium*, ed. Alexandar Mihailovic (Westport: Greenwood Press, 1999), 183.

59. Memoir of Vladimir Pogozhev (1851–1935), the manager of the Office of Imperial Theaters, in *Tchaikovsky Through Others' Eyes*, 152. In 1897, Kamensky sculpted Chaikovsky's cemetery monument.

60. See François Moureau and Margaret Grasselli, *Antoine Watteau (1684–1721): le peintre, son temps et sa legende* (Paris: Champion-Slatkine, 1987), 109.

61. Taruskin, "Tchaikovsky, Pyotr Il'yich," in *The New Grove Dictionary of Opera*, ed. Stanley Sadie, 4 vols. (London: Macmillan, 1992), 4: 668–69.

62. Jarocinski, *Debussy: Impressionism and Symbolism*, 134.

63. Ibid., 130.

64. G[erman] A[vgustovich] Larosh, *Izbrannïye stat'i*, ed. A. A. Gozenpud et al., 5 vols. (Leningrad: Muzïka, 1974–78), 2: 248. Laroche nonetheless offered advice to Chaikovsky about the "proper" style for the *intermède*. This the composer ignored. In a 13 February 1890 letter to Modest, Chaikovsky quipped: "Your letter of today includes Laroche's advice, but it is too late, for the *intermède* is already composed." Then he slyly added: "In my view it came out very much in the style of that era, very concisely and interestingly" (*Polnoye sobraniye sochineniy: Literaturnïye proizvedeniya i perepiska*, 15B: 48).

65. Clayton, *Pierrot in Petrograd: Commedia dell'Arte / Balagan in Twentieth-Century Russian Theatre and Drama*, 13.

66. V[sevolod] E[mil'yevich] Meyerkhol'd, "Pushkin i Chaykovskiy," in *Pikovaya dama. Zamïsel. Voploshcheniye. Sud'ba*, 128–29. This essay was first published in a volume dedicated to the 25 January 1935 premiere of the re-Pushkinized version of the opera at the Malïy Opera Theater.

67. V[ladimir] N. Solov'yov, "Pis'mo V. E. Meyerkhol'du," 1934, in *Pikovaya dama. Zamïsel. Voploshcheniye. Sud'ba*, 109. In keeping with seventeenth-century *commedia dell'arte* norms, the scenario features four stock characters—two old men *(vecchi)* and two servants *(zanni)*—who perform stock tricks *(lazzi)*. Tartaglia is a Neapolitan mask who, because he stutters, cannot express himself coherently; Pantalone, sometimes called Magnifico, is an elderly Venetian merchant; the Doctor is a smug pedant; Brighella and Smeraldina are servant figures of Bergamese origins; Capitano is a Spanish conqueror sporting an oversized moustache and

sword. *"Oranges"* is a reference to *Love for Three Oranges* (*Lyubov' k tryom apel'sinam*), a short-lived Petrograd theatrical journal devoted to the Symbolist *commedia dell'arte* revival.

68. Meyerkhol'd, "Pushkin i Chaykovskiy," 129.

69. Chaikovsky actually composed the scenes in reverse order. On 13 February 1890, he told his brother that he had "received. . . the third scene. It came just in time, as I've already finished the fourth. I began immediately with the interlude, as it gave me the most trouble. I've decided on the pastorale" (*Polnoye sobraniye sochineniy: Literaturnïye proizvedeniya i perepiska*, 15B: 48).

70. See Taruskin, *Defining Russia Musically*, 242–43, and "Yevgeny Onegin," in *The New Grove Dictionary of Opera*, 4: 1194. The author reports that, along with *The Queen of Spades*, the motif infuses Chaikovsky's opera *Eugene Onegin* (opus 24, 1878), which, like *The Queen of Spades*, is a Pushkin setting replete with deceptively decorative eighteenth-century set pieces. The motif is heard in Lensky's act II, scene 2 aria, "Whither, ah whither are ye fled" ("Kuda, kuda vï udalilis'"), but also suffuses Tatyana's part.

The term *intonatsiya* comes from Asafyev. For a definition, see B[oris] V[ladimirovich] Asaf'ev, *Musical Form as a Process*, 1947, trans. James Robert Tull, 3 vols. (Ph.D. diss., Ohio State University, 1976), 1: 184–95; 2: 543, 625–33.

71. One can identify a variant of motif Y in the last example of self-conscious performance in the opera, the drinking song performed by Tomsky in act III, scene 3, a setting of Gavrila Derzhavin's "A Facetious Desire" ("Shutochnoye zhelaniye"), which Modest Chaikovsky renamed, "If pretty girls could fly as birds" ("Esli b milïye devitsï tak mogli letat' kak ptitsï"). There the motif descends a major sixth, rather than a minor sixth, from d^1 to f, the submediant to the tonic, in F major.

72. Bergson, *Matter and Memory*, 191–200.

73. Lyudmila Karagichova, "Dva etyuda o 'Pikovoy dame,'" *Sovetskaya muzïka* 6 (1990): 50.

74. Chaykovskiy, *Dnevniki 1873–1891*, 252–53.

75. Chaykovskiy, *Polnoye sobraniye sochineniy: Literaturnïye proizvedeniya i perepiska*, 15B: 86.

76. Benua, *Moi vospominaniya v pyati knigakh*, 2: 652. Benois made the comment in reference to his set designs for the 1934 production of the opera.

77. Asaf'yev, "Pikovaya dama," in *Kriticheskiye stat'i, ocherki i retsenzii*, ed. I. V. Beletskiy (Moscow: Muzïka, 1967), 142–43.

78. Karagichova, "Dva etyuda o 'Pikovoy dame,'" 52. Chaikovsky's choice of B minor for the scene is significant, since this tonality is commonly associated with the supernatural in nineteenth-century opera.

79. Caryl Emerson, "The Three Worlds of Tchaikovsky's 'Pikovaya Dama'" (paper presented at the annual meeting of the American Association for the Advancement of Slavic Studies, Seattle, WA, 21 November 1997), 5–6. My thanks to the author for allowing me to quote from her text.

80. B[oris] Kats, "Vslushivayas' v 'Pikovuyu damu': Analiticheskiye primechaniya k nablyudeniyam B. V. Asaf'yeva," *Sovetskaya muzïka* 7 (1984): 53.

81. Chaykovskiy, "Vtoroy kontsert Russkogo muzïkal'nogo obshchestva.— Russkiy kontsert g. Slavyanskogo," 1871, in *Muzïkal'no-kriticheskiye stat'i*, ed. V. V. Yakovlev (Moscow: Gosudarstvennoye muzïkal'noye izdatel'stvo, 1953), 38. For an overview of Chaikovsky's musical allusions and references to Schumann, see M[arina] Frolova, "Chaykovskiy i Shuman," in *Chaykovskiy. Voprosï istorii i teorii. Vtoroy sbornik statey*, 54–64.

82. Žižek, "Robert Schumann: The Romantic Anti-Humanist," 199. Žižek quotes from Alain Badiou's *L'être et l'événement* (Paris: Éditions du Seuil, 1988).

83. In Žižek's Lacanian phraseology, the "object-voice which coincides with Silence itself is strictly correlative to the 'barred' subject (the Lacanian $ as the Void of self-negating negativity)" (ibid., 200).

84. Pushkin, "Pikovaya dama," 317.

85. If as Emerson notes, the Modern stratum is none other than Chaikovsky's own time, the cusp of the Symbolist era, it could be argued that autobiography informed his stage characterizations. Some commentators have claimed that Chaikovsky's depiction of the Countess incorporates the personality traits of Nadezhda von Meck (1831–94), his patroness (whom he never actually met). For a detailed account of her relationship with the composer, see Poznansky, *Tchaikovsky: The Quest for the Inner Man* (New York: Schirmer Books, 1991), 511–29. For a highly sensitive, albeit stylized account, see Nina Berberova, *Chaykovskiy: Istoriya odinokoy zhizni* (1936; reprint, St. Petersburg: Limbus Press, 1997).

86. On these points, see Lucinde Lauer, "Cajkovskijs *Pikovaja Dama* und die Tradition der französischen Opéra-comique-Ballade," in *Cajkovskij-Studien. Internationales Cajkovskij-Symposium. Tübingen 1993*, ed. Thomas Kohlhase, 2 vols. (Mainz: Schott, 1995), 1: 199–205. Lauer points out that the formal disposition of Tomsky's ballad has much in common with Raimbaut's ballad in act I of *Robert le diable*.

87. Chaykovskiy, "Ital'yanskaya opera.—Kvartetnïye seansï russkogo muzïkal'nogo obshchestva," 1872, in *Muzïkal'no-kriticheskie stat'i*, 69.

88. Asaf'yev, "Pikovaya dama," 142.

89. Brown, *Tchaikovsky: A Biographical and Critical Study*, 4: 256.

90. Brown calls F-sharp minor the "opera's key of fate," though it should be noted that Chaikovsky himself associated another key, F minor, with fate in a letter to von Meck about his Symphony No. 4 in F minor (opus 36, 1878) (ibid.; letter of 17 February 1878, in Chaykovskiy, *Perepiska s N. F. fon-Mekk*, 1: 217). The notion that the composer relied on tonal symbolism in his operas—like the notion that his symphonies bear autobiographical programs—is an interpretive red herring.

91. Jarocinski, *Debussy: Impressionism and Symbolism*, 53. Jarocinski borrows the adjectives "pure" and "irrational" from the music theorist Kurt Westphal.

92. Brown, *Tchaikovsky: A Biographical and Critical Study*, 4: 259.

93. Ibid., 4: 259–62.

94. Taruskin ("Another World: Why *The Queen of Spades* Is the Great Symbolist Opera," 13) comments, "The very first music the audience hears, at the outset of the orchestral introduction, is an adaptation of Tomsky's ballad to the rhythm of the main theme of Tchaikovsky's recently completed Fifth Symphony in E Minor (1888), whose portentous motto theme echoes as well through the E minor orchestral music at the beginning and end of the opera's penultimate scene, at the river embankment, which ends in Lisa's martyrdom." It should be added that the rhythmic and stylistic displacements endemic to the *intermède* occur in Chaikovsky's Third and Sixth Symphonies, and serve similarly to confound listener's expectations: the second movement of the former is a French waltz marked "*alla tedesca*," "in the German manner," while the second movement of the latter is a waltz in 5/4 time.

95. Lotman, "Theme and Plot. The Theme of Cards and the Card Game in Russian Literature of the Nineteenth Century," 477. Lotman does not identify the source of the quoted words.

96. Pushkin, "Pikovaya dama," 355.

97. Emerson, "The Three Worlds of Tchaikovsky's 'Pikovaya Dama,'" 7; Lotman, *The Structure of the Artistic Text*, trans. Ronald Vroon, Michigan Slavic Contributions no. 7 (Ann Arbor: University of Michigan Press, 1977), 39.

98. Pyman, *A History of Russian Symbolism*, 178.

99. Andrey Belïy, "Why I Became a Symbolist and Why I Never Ceased Being One in All the Phases of My Intellectual and Artistic Development," as quoted in Steven Cassedy, *Flight from Eden: The Origin of Modern Criticism and Theory* (Berkeley: University of California Press, 1990), 52–53.

100. Bely, *Selected Essays of Andrey Bely*, 12. The quotation is taken from Cassedy's introduction to the volume, specifically his summary of Belïy's theoretical essay "The Emblematics of Meaning" ("Emblematika smïsla," 1909).

101. Pyman, *A History of Russian Symbolism*, 305.

102. Sollertinsky complained, for example, that "[a] whole series of Chaikovsky's musical details suggests that the composer was subsequently thinking about the nineteenth century. The Old Countess sings an arietta from Grétry's opera *Richard Coeur-de-Lion*, first produced in 1784 or 1785. Clearly, if the action of *The Queen of Spades* is set in Catherine's reign, we are confronted with a historical absurdity. *Richard* was a modish novelty that should have been familiar to Tomsky and Polina. Obviously, the old woman could not sing from her youth a passage from a composition written fifty or sixty years later. Besides, the Countess is depicted musically by the same Grétry air. Another example: in the ballad of the three cards Tomsky sings of 'words, sweeter than Mozart's sounds.' In eighteenth-century terms this is also chronologically inexplicable: to an officer in St. Petersburg, Mozart would have been a misunderstood innovator like Hindemith or Schoenberg" (I[van] Sollertinskiy, "Pikovaya dama," in *Kriticheskiye stat'i* [Leningrad: Gosudarstvennoye muzïkal'noye izdatel'stvo, 1963], 37–38).

103. He did not, however, think that Meyerhold's alterations to the opera solved its assorted problems: "Can we call V. Meyerhold's splendid work a definitive musical-scenic solution for *The Queen of Spades*? Evidently not. Meyerhold's production is an interesting 'special case,' an experiment which with exceptional lavishness has enriched our theoretical conception of music theater. It is a fruitfully debatable production, debatable first and foremost because it in essence combines two very dissimilar works: Stenich's Pushkin-based play with Chaikovsky's musical accompaniment (scenes 1 and 3), and the opera itself ('Liza's bedroom,' 'the Countess's room,' 'the barracks'), Chaikovsky's organic, musical-dramatic composition" (ibid., 42).

104. A[leksandr] Fevral'skiy, "Novaya 'Pikovaya dama,'" in *Pikovaya dama. Zamïsel. Voploshcheniye. Sud'ba*, 272. Despite the initial critical approval of Meyerhold's production, it was banned in the spring of 1937 as part of an ideologically motivated crackdown on theatrical activity in Soviet Russia. An apparent explanation for the banning is found in the notes of a debate held in Moscow at the State Academy of the Arts (Gosudarstvennaya akademiya iskusstvoznaniya) on 30 January 1935. It involved two groups of critics, the first accusing Meyerhold of transforming Pushkin's love story into a parable of existential loneliness, the second supporting the concept of the production. This latter group, which included Dmitriy Shostakovich, lauded the director's innovations, notably his dynamic juxtaposition of visual and musical gestures. The visual action of the opera is not simply a reflection of the music but unfolds contrapuntally from it. Meyerhold himself participated in the debate, becoming increasingly distraught at the way his intentions were misconstrued.

105. Vsevolod Meyerhold, *Meyerhold on Theatre*, ed. and trans. Edward Braun (London: Methuen, 1978), 139. For a clarification, see pages 119–42.

106. Stephan Mattesich, "Grotesque Caricature: Stanley Kubrick's *Eyes Wide Shut* as the Allegory of Its Own Reception," *Postmodern Culture* [Online] 10:2 (January 2000). Available: www.press.jhu.edu/journals/pmc/vo10/10.2.r_mattessich.html. One of the epigraphs to the article is a line from the opening of Charles Baudelaire's "Quelques caricaturistes français" (1857): "Such was the fashion, such the human being; the men were like the paintings of the day; society had taken its form from the mould of art." Besides Kubrick's film, the line also conveys the spirit of Chaikovsky's opera.

107. Mattesich, "Grotesque Caricature: Stanley Kubrick's *Eyes Wide Shut* as the Allegory of Its Own Reception," 7 (15 paragraphs).

Chapter 2 Rimsky-Korsakov and Religious Syncretism

In his 1902 essay "The Forms of Art" ("Formï iskusstva"), Andrey Belïy divided the arts between plastic and organic forms, and classified the immobile art of sculpture as inferior to the mobile art of music. Belïy believed that while sculpture (and painting) directly represented reality, music (and poetry) revealed its hidden content. Citing Schopenhauer, he proclaimed that music discloses both the Cosmic "Will" and "the inner essence of things." [1] To this idea he added that the artist's creative energy is best channeled into those arts that are least bound to material reality. He posited that "each form of art has reality as its point of departure and music, as pure movement, as its destination," [2] and that "music is not concerned with the depiction of forms in space. It is, as it were, outside space." [3] Then, toward the end of the essay, Belïy adopted the persona of a prophet, making the stunning prediction that the arts, through their gravitation to music, would one day unite fallen humanity with God:

> In music we can catch hints of a future perfection. That is why we say that it is about the future. In the Revelation of St. John we have prophetic images that depict the fate of the world. "For the trumpet shall sound, *and the dead shall rise,* and we shall be changed. . . ." The archangel's trumpet—this apocalyptic music—will it not awaken us to a final understanding of the phenomena of the world? [4]

What does this biblical portent mean? On one level, Belïy asserted that the focus of Symbolist artistic creation should shift from poetry to music. He found poetic images inadequate for disclosing the invisible reality underpinning visible reality and so sought to employ techniques of musical composition in his poetry. Inspired by Wagner's theoretical writings, libretti, and leitmotif technique, Belïy aspired to develop a new synthetic art form that would cross over into life and lead to culture's spiritual revival. On another level, however, he was contending that art must in itself *create a new reality*. In accordance with the teachings of the ecumenical religious philosopher Vladimir Solovyov, Belïy concluded that the goal of all artistic activity was *theurgy:* the synthesis of the material and ideal realms and the emancipation of the human spirit. His sprinkled references to the Book of Revelation attest to his preoccupation with imminent apocalypse and the mystery of the soul to succeed it.

Belïy published "The Forms of Art" in *The World of Art*. Upon reading it, his "mystic" Symbolist colleague Alexander Blok complained to him that he had not explained the relationship between his view of music as art and music as a *theurgic* force. Instead of showing how music was to pass into religion, Belïy, in Blok's opinion, chose

> to shout and cry out about boundaries, about limits, that the apocalyptic trumpet is not "the stuff of art" (your page 344). You have not said the last word, and for that reason your last pages are horror and doubt. . . your last words are heard as if from afar, on the quiet, in a thicket, and we no longer see you. You hid your face precisely when it became necessary to say whether or not music really was the ultimate. The main thing is, what sort of music is this anyway? Is it really a "form" of art? [5]

In his response to Blok, Belïy admitted that he could not reconcile his two definitions of music: music as a "form of art" and music as a vehicle for the transubstantiation of the world. (In this he differed from the German and French Romantics, who came to see the bourgeois concert hall as a pantheistic church and such compositions as Beethoven's Symphony No. 9 and Johannes Brahms's *Ein Deutsches Requiem* [opus 45, 1868] as evocative of a secular heaven.) He wrestled with the problem in his four "symphonies" in prose, his euphonious poetry, and, much later, in his novels *The Silver Dove (Serebryaniy golub'*, 1909) and *Petersburg* (1916), the first two books in a planned trilogy about the destiny of Russia after the "Bloody Sunday" uprising of 1905.

Belïy apparently planned but did not undertake another novel, called *Invisible City (Nevidimiy grad)*, which was to be based on the ancient Slavonic chronicle about Kitezh. That task was accomplished by another prominent artist of the Silver Age, the composer Nikolai Rimsky-Korsakov, who was a positivist, not an idealist, and who feuded with his Symbolist colleagues. Moreover, he was an atheist who complained to his friends that institutionalized religion had become corrupt and hypocritical, since, in his estimation, doctrine promoted exclusion. Rimsky-Korsakov's attitude disturbed Lev Tolstoy, who had abandoned art for religion late in life and encouraged the composer to do the same. On 11 January 1898, the two held a casual debate about religious matters at the writer's home. It concluded in an awkward stalemate, and despite Rimsky-Korsakov's profuse apologies, Tolstoy described the evening caustically as a "face-to-face" encounter with "gloom."[6] Irrespective of the composer's anti-religious outlook, however, in his 1905 opera *The Legend of the Invisible City of Kitezh and the Maiden Fevroniya (Skazaniye o nevidimom grade Kitezhe i deve Fevronii)*, he explored themes of spiritual conversion and salvation. The music makes use of melodic formulae *(popevki)* and modes *(glasï)* redolent of pre-Petrine Orthodox chant, while the libretto, compiled by the composer's friend Vladimir Belsky (1866–1946), a statistician and amateur folklorist, is cast in the scriptural prose style of the seventeenth century. The opera's visual events include the miraculous salvation of Greater Kitezh from invading Tatar-Mongols and the postmortem resurrection of the heroic characters in a garden of paradise. Both wonders are wrought by the Christian God in response to prayer, and both are accompanied by the tolling bells of the Greater Kitezh Church of the Assumption.

What compelled Rimsky-Korsakov to take on such an unlikely project? To explain the enigma of the *Legend of Kitezh,* an opera of faith by a skeptic, we must turn to the older of the two source texts: the 1223 Kitezh chronicle. The original written version of the chronicle, based on tales in oral tradition and widely copied between the thirteenth and sixteenth centuries, recounts a series of battles between feudal Russians and Tatar-Mongols on the shores of Lake Svetlïy Yar, a small body of water located in Zavolzh' (literally, "beyond the Volga") province. The Tatar-Mongols seek to occupy the city of Kitezh; dense woods, however, conceal its location from them. In the seventeenth and eighteenth centuries, this version of the chronicle was altered to accord with the religious views of the so-called Old Believers *(Staroobryadtsï)*, the dissenters who had abandoned the Orthodox Church in protest against the pro-Western reforms introduced by Patriarch Nikon in 1652.[7] Their aversion to those reforms extended to musical issues. The Old Believers rejected part-singing in favor of traditional unison chanting and rejected the square notation employed in the official publications of the Holy Synod in favor of traditional neumatic *(znamennïy)* notation. In the Old Believers' version of the chronicle, the struggle between the Russians and the Tatar-Mongols becomes a test of wills between followers of the old and new doctrines, the drama being divided between a sacred (pre-reform) Lesser Kitezh and a secular (post-reform) Greater Kitezh.[8] God punishes Lesser Kitezh by leaving it vulnerable to the Tatar-Mongols but protects Greater Kitezh by rendering it invisible, shrouding it in a golden mist and submerging it.

In the Silver Age, Symbolist poets embraced the Kitezh chronicle as a representation of religious syncretism, a term that refers to the admixture of elements from paganism and Christianity, from folklore and Christianity, and from Eastern and Western religious thought. To some extent, the poets interpreted the Bible as the product of syncretism, the Israelite religion of the Old Testament incorporating elements of Egyptian, Old Babylonian, and Persian religions. Properly, speaking, however, syncretism concerns the reconciliation of diverse faiths, that is to say, the attempt to find common roots between these faiths. Since the Silver Age was a culturally syncretic era, characterized by the revival of occult doctrine, esoteric teaching, and gnostic speculation, it is hardly surprising that the Symbolists venerated the Kitezh chronicle. To them, it expressed the ideal of spiritual communion, or *sobornost'*.[9] It was also venerated by the Russian Theosophical Society, a diverse group of mystics and occultists who studied the doctrine of Helene Blavatsky and philosophy of Solovyov. Together with the Theosophists, members of three spiritual sects founded after the Russian Revolution—the Brotherhood of the Radiant City (Bratstvo svetlogo goroda), the Knights of the Radiant City (Rïtsari svetlogo goroda), and the Northern-Caucasian United States (Severo-kavkazskiye soyedinyonnïye shtatï)—made annual treks to the shores of Lake Svetlïy Yar.[10] There it was thought that on 24 June, St. John's Eve, sectarians of pure heart could see the spires of the sunken city protruding from the waters and hear the tolling bells emanating from the depths.

The necromancy of the Kitezh chronicle greatly appealed to Rimsky-Korsakov. In consultation with Belsky, he made it the basis of an opera promoting pantheism as an alternative to Orthodoxy. The resulting score—a tapestry of sacred and secular ritual, historical and mythical arcana—is syncretic in its own right. The libretto exhibits an affinity with several late nineteenth- and early twentieth-century writings depicting the pilgrimages to Lake Svetlïy Yar, including the 1906 travelogue "Radiant Lake: A Diary" ("Svetloye ozero: dnevnik") by Zinaida Hippius, the elaborate 1881 novel *In the Woods (V lesakh)* by Melnikov-Pechersky (real name Pavel Ivanovich Melnikov, 1818–83), the 1890 essay "In Deserted Places" ("V pustïnnïkh mestakh") by Vladimir Korolenko (1853–1921), and the 1864 dramatic poem "Wanderer" ("Strannik") by Apollon Maykov (1821–97).

The music, moreover, is suffused with references to earlier Russian operas, a feature that has prompted both Dorothea Redepenning and Richard Taruskin to interpret it as a testament to and summation of the nineteenth-century national tradition.[11]

Somewhat more explicit are the many references to Wagner's music dramas, a belated sign of the "cataclysmic [though often denied] effect" that the German composer had on Rimsky-Korsakov after 1889, when he first heard *Der Ring des Nibelungen*.[12] *Siegfried* (1871) was the inspiration for the forest sounds of acts I and IV, while *Das Rheingold* (1854) provided the prototypes (in the guise of Fasolt and Fafner) for Bedyay and Burunday, two Tatar-Mongols who kill each other following the sack of Lesser Kitezh in act II. Most clearly derivative, however, are two unmistakable references to *Parsifal:* the music that accompanies the disappearance of Greater Kitezh into the mist in act III, scene 1 is a near-paraphrase of the "Good Friday Spell," while the act IV, scene 1 wedding chorus that celebrates the postmortem reunion of Fevroniya and Princeling Vsevolod resembles the "Dresden Amen."[13] Moreover, the influence of *Tristan und Isolde* is evident in Prince Yuriy Vsevolodovich's act III, scene 1 lament, which recalls that of King Marke in act II of the music drama.

The concept of syncretism is defined by the experiences of the citizens of Greater Kitezh (the Old Believers), who perceive that spiritual communion with others as well as with nature will allow them to attain a higher state of being. Although the score was not conceived as a work of Symbolism, it bears the type of dual-world dramaturgical structure endemic to much Symbolist prose. From the audience's perspective, the plot blends events in a material (urban) world (acts II and III, scene 1) and events in an immaterial (forest) world (acts I and IV, scene 1). From the pious stage characters' perspective, it blends events in an unreal, but visible world (Lesser Kitezh) and a real, but invisible world (Greater Kitezh). In what follows, I will discuss the genesis and the structure of the opera and contend that Rimsky-Korsakov, despite his professed antipathy to religious doctrine, succeeded in transforming music, as a "form of art," into a form of religion. Amid the mosaic of quoted sounds and poetic allusions— through which the composer and his librettist amalgamated Eastern and Western creative practices—Rimsky-Korsakov explored the Symbolists' musical metaphysics. He made the bells of the invisible city, which create a sound as indecipherable as the mystery of creation, into a symbol of music itself, and (to paraphrase Fevroniya, the opera's title character) the forest surrounding Lake Svetlïy Yar into a grand cathedral of nature.

SOPHIA (OR FEVRONIYA) THE AEON

Although the preceding comments would seem to suggest that Rimsky-Korsakov willingly, even cheerfully embraced Russian Symbolism, it must be emphasized that his relationship to the movement was, on the whole, negative. He denounced the "decadents" and "mystics" and integrated Symbolist elements into the score only as a concession to his librettist. Both in terms of its genesis and structure, the *Legend of Kitezh* is a heterogeneous, even dichotomous work containing both fantastic and realistic scenes. As Abram Gozenpud notes, Belsky unquestionably conceived the former, and Rimsky-Korsakov the latter:

> Creating his libretto, Belsky dreamed about a liturgical opera, a sacred event. Thus in the original draft of the text one is keenly aware of the poet's endeavor to avoid all realistic, domestic details and to create something of a dramatized hagiography of the maiden Fevroniya. Rimsky-Korsakov totally rejected this treatment of the subject. . . . He reconceived Belsky's text; from the librettist's work, extracted from hagiographies, spiritual verses and legendary plays, all stylized in an ancient manner, he created a powerful epic-heroic work about ancient *Rus'*. Rimsky-Korsakov's opera, which is in no small measure an expert stylization, can only be compared with such great works as the [realist] paintings of [Ilya] Repin [1844–1930], [Vasiliy] Surikov [1848–1916], and [Viktor] Vasnetsov [1848–1926].[14]

Developing this point, Kadja Grönke contends that, in 1902, when Belsky

> started to write the libretto of *The Legend of the Invisible City of Kitezh* (plans for which go back to the winter of 1898/9), what he had in mind was not an action-packed stage work but rather a static work of ideas, full of imagery and allusion. He reveled in noble characters and mythical atmosphere and hardly bothered to work out an attractive outward course of events. What he therefore expected from Rimsky-Korsakov's music was above all concentration on the protagonists' states of mind, which were to be portrayed by the orchestra along Wagnerian lines. Rimsky-Korsakov, on the other hand, saw the business in a much more realistic light. In principle, Wagner was not his ideal opera composer and he also took a skeptical view of Bel'sky's fund of eschatological Christian ideas and his naïve, static portrayals. For all his liking of decorative tableaux, he knew an opera lived mainly by its plot; that is the only way it can interest the public in the long run.[15]

Quoting the composer, Grönke adds that Rimsky-Korsakov frequently enjoined Belsky to minimalize the "liturgical" content of the libretto in favor of "a little realism," but that, *pace* Gozenpud, it remained an "edifying religious narrative," a work of internal rather than external drama.

The anthropologist Alexey Parin has recently argued that the six scenes of the *Legend of Kitezh* possess "the attributes of an icon," its essence being "salvation of the righteous in Heavenly Jerusalem." Parin describes the first iconic attribute, corresponding to the first scene, as the "miracle of healing: the maiden Fevroniya, surrounded by the transfigured Trinity [three forest creatures] becomes acquainted with her 'heavenly bridegroom' and enters into a mystical union with him, bandaging and treating his wound." The second iconic attribute is the "miracle of prayer: the maiden Fevroniya, chaste and pure, disgraced by the 'internal' Antichrist (Grishka) and imprisoned by the 'external' Antichrist (the Tatars), prays for the city of Kitezh to become invisible." The third attribute, Parin continues, is the "miracle of transfiguration: heeding Fevroniya, the people pray to the Virgin to extend Protection over Kitezh (and over all of *Rus'*!) by dispatching 'angels to the defense' [Vsevolod's army]." The fourth attribute is the "miracle of the expulsion of the Tatars," and the fifth is the "miracle of [Fevroniya's] resurrection." The sixth and final attribute is "the culmination of the liturgy, the 'prayer of the faithful,' and the 'grand entrance' into the Heavenly City." Wisely, Parin cautions that his comparison of the *Legend of Kitezh* to an icon is merely metaphorical and relates only to the plot line, since from a "theological viewpoint" the opera "does not fulfill the definition of an icon and the principles of icon creation."[16] His commentary nonetheless lends weight to Grönke's claim that Rimsky-Korsakov reluctantly composed the music for an un-*kuchkist*, oratorio-like opera, one that, despite his protestations to the contrary, contains both Symbolist and Wagnerian elements. Though his relationship to religious doctrine, Symbolism, and Wagnerism was largely negative, it was a relationship nonetheless.

The subject matter of the *Legend of Kitezh* is porous; critics and scholars can find anything and everything in it. Essentially, however, it is a Russian opera about Russian opera. The concluding apotheosis shows the indirect influence of Solovyov, whose religious thinking permeated the Silver Age and was expanded in the writings of the "mystic" Symbolists. Surveying Solovyov's work, one gains a sense of the elements of Symbolist poetics that Rimsky-Korsakov begrudgingly accepted and those he rejected.

Rimsky-Korsakov did, for example, express an interest in religious pilgrimages, this being an outgrowth of his long-standing interest in folklore and pagan rituals. On 22 April 1904, he sent Belsky a postcard proposing an excursion to the fabled site of Kitezh, an excursion akin to that undertaken by Solovyov's "mystic" Symbolist disciples: "If Vladimir Ivanovich and [his brother] Rafaíl Ivanovich wish to take a small trip to the Kersh [enskiye] forests near the city of Greater Kitezh, then drop by tomorrow at nine in the evening (Friday)."[17] In a second postcard dated 11 May 1904, he mentioned that "Yastrebtsev [the composer's assistant and memoirist] found it possible to relate the plot of *Kitezh* to the Kupala ritual, because St. Fevroniya's feast day is June 25, that is, the day following Ivan-Kupala's. Reasonable and indisputable. I, however, corrected him, writing that the action takes place on the shore of Svetlïy Yar; this is hardly the Kupala ritual. Beyond a doubt, it would seem."[18] The ritual in question was a pagan summer celebration of the earth. It took place in honor of the lunar goddess, Kupala (literally, "she who bathed"), and involved the gathering of flowers and plants from different meadows (not, as Rimsky-Korsakov points out, from the lakeside), these being made into wreaths that warded off malevolent spirits. In the early Christian era, the celebration was renamed in honor of a male saint: Ivan-Kupala.

There are three references to Solovyov in Yastrebtsev's reminiscences of Rimsky-Korsakov. On 23 April 1900, Yastrebtsev reported that he and the composer "spoke about a witty review of some performance of *Rheingold*, featured in issue 103 of the newspaper *Son of the Fatherland [Sïn otechestva]* (Sunday, 16/29 April 1900), and the article 'A Newly Discovered Fragment from Dante's *Inferno*,' in which Vladimir Solovyov was very harshly ridiculed and consigned to eternal torment 'for hypocrisy.'"[19] The statement is significant both for the reference to Wagner, increasingly a preoccupation of Rimsky-Korsakov, and the reference to the *Inferno*, which, like the spiritual writing of Solovyov, was regarded by the Symbolists as a parable about their nation's evolution. According to Yastrebtsev, on 29 December 1902, he and Rimsky-Korsakov again spoke about Solovyov "and his essays against the Russian decadents, witty and caustic to the highest degree, which were likewise [directed] against [Vasiliy] Rozanov and his 'special celebration of Pushkin.'"[20] This remark affirms that Rimsky-Korsakov sided with Solovyov in his polemic against the "decadent" (first generation) Symbolists. Finally, on 25 April 1905, Yastrebtsev suggests that Solovyov was in the back of Rimsky-Korsakov's mind as he labored on the *Legend of Kitezh*: "I can't exactly remember on what topic—whether about the [act IV] 'paradise' scene of *Kitezh* or something else—but we started talking about the philosopher-poet Vladimir Solovyov and his absolute belief in the resurrection of Christ." Because the "paradise" scene is a postmortem scene, Rimsky-Korsakov felt obliged to assure Yastrebtsev that "'Personally. . . I don't for a minute believe in the possibility of life beyond the grave, just like I don't believe that in all of the universe only our earth is populated.'"[21]

Who, then, was Solovyov? For the "decadent" Symbolists, he was a religious fanatic susceptible to angelic and demonic hallucinations; for the "mystic" Symbolists, he was a "benevolent ancestor to be sanctified, a visionary, a fallen warrior in the struggle for spiritual renewal, misunderstood and despised (just as they saw themselves to be) by a complacent, rationalist society."[22] Belïy, Blok, and Vyacheslav Ivanov regarded him as a larger-than-life figure—part prophet, part priest, part poet—who hoped to disclose the divine world to humanity. Solovyov was also embraced by the St. Petersburg Religious Philosophical Society (Religiozno-filosofskoye obshchestvo). Its members earnestly debated the pros and cons of his particular brand of syncretism: his vision of a Universal Church (to be founded on the common roots of the Eastern and Western faiths) and his vision of a Universal Brotherhood of Mankind (the culmination, in Solovyov's Nietzsche-informed opinion, of the evolutionary process).[23]

Like Rimsky-Korsakov, Solovyov had uncertain feelings about Christianity, and during his brief but prolific career explored atheism, Buddhism, and Theosophy. In the 1880s he wrote several polemical articles about the relationship between the Eastern and Western churches. He argued that there was no logical justification for separating them because their governing principles had been determined by the same seven ecclesiastical councils. He likewise maintained that the churches should not exclude worshippers on the basis of creed and sect. Toward the end of his career he began to promote Russian Orthodoxy as a model for the establishment of a universal theocracy, with religions and nations united under the pope and tsar. Beyond a theocratic ideal, Solovyov maintained that this union would supply the chemistry for the transubstantiation of the world.[24]

The "mystic" Symbolists were drawn first and foremost to Solovyov for his equation of artistic activity with spiritual rebirth.[25] In his 1890 article "The General Meaning of Art" ("Obshchiy smïsl iskusstva"), Solovyov posits that the creative process enables the artist to transcend subjective perception, to experience, in other words, supernatural or supersensible objects, what Kant named "things in themselves." When a painter or writer represents a natural object, the repository of what Solovyov labels "divine content," he or she assumes knowledge of that object that is otherwise inaccessible to empirical observation. Solovyov thereafter contends that artistic activity furthers a process of divination begun in nature and claims that the artist has the ability to influence this process to the benefit of humanity. Art, in short, completes a task that beauty has begun. This task is the incarnation of the ideal, the surmounting, in Nietzschean terminology, of the "all-too-human." Solovyov amplified this point by declaring, "Beauty in nature is a cover placed on sinful life but not a transformation of that life. And so man with his rational consciousness should not only be the goal of a process in nature but a method that enables the ideal principle to apply an inverse, deeper and fuller influence on nature."[26] In seeking to express "divine content," the artist transforms representation, making creative activity as "permanent and immortal as the [divine] idea itself."[27]

In Solovyov's poetry, the merger of aesthetic perception and spiritual devotion, art and religion, is symbolized by the Divine Sophia. Like Jesus Christ, Sophia is an eternal figure imprisoned in flesh, the incarnation of universal wisdom described in such ancient gnostic documents as the Old Testament Proverbs and Hebrew Cabala.[28] Solovyov's autobiographical poem "Three Meetings" ("Tri svidaniya," 1898) portrays Sophia as the ultimate object of the protagonist's desire, a figment of his imagination who becomes a pretext for spiritual incantation. The poem strongly influenced the leading "mystic" Symbolists, who were captivated by its idiosyncratic combination of erotic and sacred imagery. In Blok's *Verses about the Most Beautiful Lady*, for instance, the protagonist experiences an intense love for a figure who bears a distinct likeness to the Divine Sophia. Their fleeting encounters seem to elevate him to a higher level of consciousness.

Solovyov's recourse to nature veneration and erotic spiritualism was a reaction against the rationalism of his generation—in other words, Rimsky-Korsakov's generation—but also a response to Russian and Western social and political turmoil. The "mystic" Symbolists found in his work an antidote to feelings of intellectual isolation stemming from their study of philosophers who were hostile to religious doctrines. Of Solovyov's philosophical tracts, the Symbolists were most influenced by his last, *A Short Tale of the Antichrist* (*Kratkaya povest' ob antikhriste*, 1900), in which he anticipates events at the end of the world, the end of the twentieth century. The narrator, a monk named M. Z., describes the invasion of Russia from the East and the onset of the second Mongol-Tatar occupation, its consequences being the abolition of materialism and collusion of cultures. The Antichrist appears in the West in the guise of a military leader. Supported by the Freemasons, he becomes the emperor of the United States of Europe. During his tumultuous reign he enacts broad political and social changes, transfers the seat of the papacy from Rome to St. Petersburg, reforms Protestantism, and reconciles the Orthodox Church and Old Believers. Hoping to integrate religious doctrines, he convenes an ecumenical conference of prelates and laymen, their task being to redefine Christianity. At the conference, the emperor proves unwilling to declare Jesus Christ the central figure of history. He is exposed as the Antichrist and exiled. The magus Appolonius is named pope, but he likewise turns out to be a corrupt leader, winning the hearts of false Christians but alienating true Christians, who flee to the desert to marshal their resources against him. *A Short Tale of the Antichrist* concludes with a battle between the Christians and Imperial Army. Appolonius perishes in a volcano that erupts from the Red Sea while the surviving faithful and the spirits of those martyred by the Antichrist are united in ecstatic celebration.

This remarkable publication, Solovyov's last, illustrates his philosophical evolution from an unshakable optimist into an inconsolable pessimist. He deduced that world transformation could not be achieved in the near future, since humanity lacked sufficient faith in the Christian ideal to enact large-scale political and cultural change. On this point, the philosopher parted company with the "mystic" Symbolists, who, in his opinion, confused pseudo-theocracy with actual theocracy. Unlike the Symbolists, who were attracted to occult doctrine, he based his eschatological writings on the Scriptures and the pronouncements of church leaders.[29]

THE THEME OF APOCALYPSE

The notion of an "apocalyptic millennium generated by social catastrophe and resurrection by personal anguish"[30] recurs in much Symbolist art. Though Rimsky-Korsakov envisioned the *Legend of Kitezh* as an anti-Symbolist opera, he offered his audiences a concentrated, if aestheticized, dose of some of the themes of Solovyov's writing: the Universal Church, the Divine Sophia, the Antichrist, and the Apocalypse. Unmediated elements of nonaestheticized mysticism found their way into the libretto from its source material, an elaborate assortment of ancient and modern religious prose. As mentioned, Rimsky-Korsakov's expectations for the opera clashed harshly with Belsky's, the result being a score that at times awkwardly combines epic-heroic scenes and hymn-like paeans to nature. In an otherwise affectionate description of the opera, the stage director Vasiliy Shkafer (1867–1937) confessed that he found it "strange" that Rimsky-Korsakov had "musically burdened [Fevroniya's] role by writing it for a dramatic soprano, for a large voice, whereas the figure of Fevroniya was actually conceived in the colors of a Nesterov painting—light, ethereal, and disembodied."[31] By referring to Mikhaíl Nesterov (1862–1942), a devout artist whose paintings adopted the elongated forms and delicate postures of late Byzantine and Medieval Russian art, Shkafer neatly characterizes the difference between Fevroniya's visual appearance in the opera and her sonorous presence. Although she is seen to enter the heavenly realm in the last act, musically she remains on earth. Shkafer does not mention it, but this dramatic contradiction stemmed directly from the artistic contradiction between Belsky's eudemonic vision of the score and Rimsky-Korsakov's pragmatic one.

In his chronology of the opera's composition, Rimsky-Korsakov's son Andrey acknowledges that "we do not know the separate stages of the composer's and librettist's shared work, nor is it clear which of them developed the motifs suggested and those not suggested by the material in the legends."[32] Besides the thirteenth-century Kitezh chronicle, the "legends" on which Rimsky-Korsakov and Belsky drew included the sixteenth-century *Tale of Peter and Fevroniya* (*Povest' o Petre i Fevronii*), the seventeenth-century epic *Woe-Misfortune* (*Gore-zloschast'ye*), the divine *Logos* (*Slovo*) of Saint Serapion (a fourth-century collection of eucharistic verses consecrating the sacramental elements of bread and wine), the seventeenth-century *Tale of Yulianiya Lazarevskaya* (*Povest' o Yulianii Lazarevskoy*, the chronicle of a villager who reduced herself to poverty by performing selfless acts of charity), wedding and calendar songs, epic ballads, and spiritual verses. The first and second texts furnished the opera's heroine and villain, respectively. By most accounts, Rimsky-Korsakov exhorted Belsky to include them in the libretto so as to avoid the dullness of the two previous settings of the Kitezh chronicle: a 1900 opera and 1902 cantata by Sergey Vasilenko (1872–1954). Yastrebtsev reports that on 6 March 1903, he and the composer "spoke about the Orthodox *City of Kitezh* by [Vasiliy] Safonov [the librettist] and Vasilenko. In Nikolai Andreyevich's opinion, it is less an opera than a cantata (they later made a cantata); moreover, the beginning is good, but the second half is much weaker."[33] Belsky, for his part, preferred to tout his incorporation of the other, more arcane texts in the libretto than those vetted by Rimsky-Korsakov. In his preface to the first published edition of the opera, he claimed, "The *Legend* is based on the so-called Kitezh chronicle, which was reported by Meledin and published in [Pyotr] Bessonov's supplementary notes to the IVth edition of [the early nineteenth-century ethnographer Pyotr] Kireyevsky's collection of songs; second, on different oral traditions about the invisible city of Kitezh, taken in part from the same source; and, finally, on one episode from the legend [tale] of Fevroniya of Murom."[34] Ceding to Rimsky-Korsakov's point of view on the matter, Belsky inserted that such arcane texts had proven to be "insufficient" on their own to propel a large-scale dramatic work.

The author of the *Tale of Peter and Fevroniya* has been identified as

Ermolai Erazm, a monk who labored in the Kremlin cathedrals under the supervision of Metropolitan Macarius.[35] It is presumed to have been written shortly after Fevroniya's canonization in 1547. Most archetypes center on the Tristan-and-Iseult-like love affair between Fevroniya and either Prince Peter or Prince David—the latter an actual historical figure who ruled the city of Murom from 1203 to 1228. The tale has a hagiographical introduction, which provides insight into the allegorical meaning of the central narrative. In Priscilla Hunt's words,

> The archetypes of the introduction. . . . tell us that the tale is about Peter's and Fevroniya's contribution to the "completion" of God's redemptive work. [The archetypes] imply that by repaying their debt to Christ and taking on the way of the cross, Peter and Fevroniya will become God's partners. They will mirror his kingship, revealing his grace through the action of their will. Their mystical marriage with the Creator will reveal the wisdom of God, the providence in the creation.[36]

In the first section of the tale, Peter, the ruler of Murom, slays a serpent that has assumed the likeness of his brother Paul and seduced Paul's wife. The slaying comes with a price: Peter is poisoned with the snake's blood, which causes him to break out in a grotesque rash. (Serge Zenkovsky, the editor of the English-language version of the tale, observes that the motif of the malevolent effect of human contact with serpent blood occurs in the *Nibelungenlied*[37]—another subtle point of correspondence between the source texts of Rimsky-Korsakov's and Wagner's music dramas.) Seeking a remedy, Peter and his retinue call on Fevroniya, a villager purported to have wondrous healing powers. She pledges to tend to the prince's convalescence on the condition that he marries her. Though she is of low birth, Peter accepts the proposition. These events unfold in the second section of the tale. In the third, the self-serving boyars of Murom, unwilling to accept the rule of a queen of common origins, scheme to create strife between Peter and Fevroniya. They succeed in having Fevroniya banished from the city. Peter, desperate without her, voluntarily relinquishes power to reside with her in an outlying forest. In their absence, Murom declines into anarchy. The boyars, reaping the rewards of their treachery, send an emissary into the forest to enjoin the couple to return to Murom. Peter and Fevroniya graciously consent and triumphantly reclaim their thrones. They reign according to the laws of the Church, providing shelter for spiritual pilgrims, tending to the sick, and clothing and feeding the poor. Toward the end of their venerable lives, they arrange to be buried together. However, the backward-looking populace, finding it inappropriate for a man and a woman who have taken monastic vows to share a grave, inter their bodies on opposite sides of the city walls. Years later their bodies are miraculously discovered lying together in a stone tomb on the grounds of the Cathedral of the Holy Virgin.

From this slight account, it becomes clear that the "episode" of the *Tale of Peter and Fevroniya* that interested both Belsky and Rimsky-Korsakov and eventually found its way into the libretto of the *Legend of Kitezh* was the conflict between the boyars of Murom and Fevroniya. There are two obvious parallels between the texts. First, the opening of the second section of the tale closely resembles the close of act II of the libretto, in which Vsevolod and Fevroniya's wedding in Lesser Kitezh is interrupted by the attack of the Tatar-Mongols and Fevroniya's abduction from the city. Second, the start of the third section of the legend closely resembles the end of act IV, scene 1, in which the forest outside Greater Kitezh is transformed into a garden of paradise. It likewise resembles the beginning of act IV, scene 2, in which Fevroniya and Vsevolod are posthumously reunited in the heavenly city and their previously interrupted marriage ceremony concluded. In exchanging vows, they wed not only each other but also their peoples. Their candlelit, bird-filled kingdom is implicitly likened to a Universal Church.

Belsky began writing the libretto in 1901, found the process of gathering and examining material cumbersome, and only finished the draft scenario in 1903. The delay exasperated Rimsky-Korsakov. In a 31 May 1901 letter to Belsky, the composer quipped:

> I have looked over my contrivances for the *City of Kitezh* and I am satisfied with most of them, though these are all insignificant fragments. I have a great desire to start work on them. I began *Navzikaya* [*Nausica*, a planned cantata based on an episode from *The Odyssey*, eventually called "From Homer"] only because you are not giving me anything. Do not think about *Navzikaya*—send me something for *Kitezh*, and likewise the scenario.[38]

Eighteen months later, however, he had only received a handful of textual incipits, and so on 27 September 1902, Rimsky-Korsakov again wrote to Belsky, including in the letter a quatrain from a satirical poem by the fictitious wordsmith Kozma Prutkov, "Junker Schmidt Wants To Shoot Himself with a Pistol" ("Yunker Shmidt iz pistoleta khochet zastrelit'sya"), which he altered in jest to read: "The leaf withers / Summer passes / Wet snow falls / For want of a libretto / I could shoot myself" ("Vyanet list / Prokhodit leto / Mokrïy sneg valitsya / Ot neymeniya libretto / Mozhno zastrelit'sya").[39] Rimsky-Korsakov received the draft scenario of the *Legend of Kitezh* on 13 July 1903, shortly after completing the orchestration of another opera, *Pan Voevoda*.

Several factors, notably difficulties with the characterizations and with the opera's overall dramaturgical shape, impeded Belsky's work. A survey of his drafts indicates that his concern in devising the libretto was less prose narration than poetic symbolism. He commenced work by assembling a diverse set of characters who stood for contrasting ethical and spiritual values. Fevroniya (the heroine), Grishka Kuterma (the anti-hero), Vsevolodovich (the kind-hearted ruler of Greater Kitezh), Vsevolod (Vsevolodovich's son and Fevroniya's true love), Fyodor Poyarok (a citizen of Lesser Kitezh who is blinded by the Tatar-Mongols), Bedyay and Burunday (the buffoonish Tatar-Mongols who abduct Fevroniya), and Alkonost and Sirin (the mythical Slavonic birds of joy and sorrow)—all embody such stock oppositions as the sacred and profane, virtue and vice, good and evil, honey and ashes. Belsky situated these characters in the religious and social context of eighth-century *Rus'*, where thought was based on the icon and symbol, and made the course of their interactions circular, bounded by Fevroniya's joyous prophecy at rehearsal number 42 of act I:

> And something unheard-of will occur: everything will be adorned with beauty. Like a miraculous garden the earth will flourish, and heavenly flowers will blossom. Wondrous birds will fly here, birds of joy, birds of mercy, who will sing in the trees with an angelic voice; and from the holy heavens there will be a mellow chime, and from behind the clouds there will be an ineffable light.
>
> [A, i sbudetsya nebïvaloye: krasotoyu vsyo razukrasitsya. Slovno divnïy sad, protsvetyot zemlya, i raspustyatsya krinï rayskiye, priletyat syuda ptitsï chudnïye, ptitsï radosti, ptitsï milosti, vospoyut v drevakh glasom angel'skim; a s nebes svyatïkh zvon malinovïy, iz-za oblakov neskazannïy svet.]

With its circular structure, the opera libretto reflects the circular structure of the Slavonic chronicles. Indeed, Belsky, in his preface to the first edition of the score, contended that he wanted to retain at least some of the original prose of the *Tale of Peter and Fevroniya* in Fevroniya's ariosos.

Since the Russian government prohibited the depiction of saints on stage, St. Fevroniya of Murom was renamed "Alyonushka" and "Olyonushka" in the first draft of the libretto. On completing his revisions, however, Belsky restored the original name. Andrey Rimsky-Korsakov, writing in a Soviet context, comments:

> Fevroniya is the name of an Orthodox saint having a legendary hagiography celebrated by the church (June 25th; her date of death is reck-

oned to be 1228). True, the saint was not a virgin, but the wife of Prince Peter of Murom. But in another respect, her hagiography served as inspirational material for the *Legend*, which means that the retention of her name (without the Alyonushka mask) for the operatic heroine can only be attributed to censorship issues. Seemingly, the proto-revolutionary period came to the rescue. The publication of the *Legend* took place during a time of limited "liberalization" in censorship (at least concerning church observances). Evidently, after inquiring with the official responsible for publication matters, a decision was made to reveal the pseudonym of the *Legend's* heroine, and a Russian saint entered through the scaffolding of the opera stage.[40]

Belsky wrote the "Alyonushka" version of the libretto in the "half-scriptural folk language" of "spiritual poetry by wandering blind men" and "ancient Christian legends,"[41] a reflection of his affinity for the eschatological writings of the Russian Medieval. Rimsky-Korsakov, however, found the prose style rather unmusical and requested that the text be recast in a modern idiom. The changes were required, he told Belsky, "because otherwise there will be no means of developing the music, and the scenic action will be reduced to pantomime, which I really don't like. . . . I know how much you hate this," he added, "but, truly, it's quite necessary."[42] Conceding this round in their ongoing artistic dispute, in the "Fevroniya" version of the libretto Belsky replaced the intonations of sixteenth-century Church Slavonic with those of nineteenth-century Russian. He evened out the line lengths and cadence patterns of the source text, but nevertheless took care to preserve its semantic content, as shown in the following example:

Fevroniya, Act I Prologue, Original Version:

O loving mother-wilderness,
I press myself to your breast now;
Your nipples are sweeter than honey to a child
Give me the blessed joy of tasting them.
You, oak grove, verdant kingdom,
Where lies and perfidy are unknown.
Who of you here is host, I do not know,
But I set hope upon his kindness

[Ti, lyubeznaya mat' pustïnya,
Pripadayu k grudi tvoyey nïne;
Slashche myodu sostsï tvoi chadu
Day vkusit' ikh blaguyu otradu.
Ti, dubrava, zelyonoye tsarstvo,
Gde ne vedayut lzhi i kovarstva.

Kto u vas zdes' khozyain, ne znayu,
No na milost' yego upovayu.[43]]

Final Version:

Ah, you forest, my forest, beautiful wilderness,
You sweet oak grove, verdant kingdom,
Like my own loving mother,
You raised and nurtured me from childhood,
Did you not amuse your child,
Did you not comfort your foolish child,
In daytime playing gentle songs,
At night whispering wondrous tales?

[Akh tï les, moy les, pustïnya prekrasnaya,
Tï dubravushka—tsarstvo zelyonoye,
Shto, rodimaya mat' lyubeznaya,
Menya s detstva rastila i pestovala,
Tï li chado svoyo ne zabavila,
Nerazumnoye tï li ne teshila,
Dnyom umil'nïye pesni igrayuchi,
Skazki chudnïye noch'yu nasheptïvaya?]

Belsky was self-consciously innovative in altering the passage, retaining the textual repetitions (the iterated "you" and "your," "tï" and "tvoyey") of the original, but enhancing its symbolism. He combined the depiction of maternal, nurturing nature with an allusion to prophetic, magical stories, but also with an allusion to song, an intervention that must have been motivated by Rimsky-Korsakov, as it reflects a desire to elicit a musical *topos* from the literary source.

In the final version of the libretto, Grishka's macabre portends counterbalance Fevroniya's radiant visions. Grishka is a paradoxical figure, at once pathetic and scheming, blind (faithless) and all-seeing (theomaniacal). Though Fevroniya's heavenly prophecy is realized for the citizens of Greater Kitezh—their shared faith makes the invisible city visible to them—for Grishka and the Tatar-Mongols, who lack such faith, it remains unrealized: the city casts a reflection on the waters of Lake Svetlïy Yar, but its golden spires do not appear through the mist. Grishka's defeat is marked by the ominous tolling of the Church of the Assumption bells, a mnemonic and revelatory sound that eventually drives him to madness. In the "realist" portion of the otherwise "mystical" act IV, scene 1, Fevroniya, the divine maiden, absolves Grishka, the fallen angel, but his ultimate salvation is left in doubt, testament to the fact that there was little holy in Belsky's conception of the holy fool (*yurodivïy*). (The conclusion of the opera is nonetheless much more optimistic than that of *Boris Godunov,* in which a holy fool, presented by Musorgsky as a positive figure, intimates that the social and political turmoil associated with Boris's rule and the rise of a Pretender to the throne will not be resolved.)

Belsky modeled Grishka in part on figures from Dostoyevsky's *The Idiot* (1868)—notably Ferdïshchenko—and *The Brothers Karamazov* (*Brat'ya Karamazovï,* 1880). He was also inspired by Maykov's dramatic poem "Wanderer," which relies heavily on Dostoyevskian imagery and features an adolescent character named "Grisha." (The poem might loosely be described as a literary fantasy based on the religious writings of the schismatics. It concerns an Old Believer community whose members must surrender their worldly possessions, social ties, and family relationships in order to live "as Christ.") Belsky's primary source for Grishka, however, was the aforementioned *Woe-Misfortune,* a Faustian tale that relates the travels and travails of a valiant young merchant and his guardian devil— the figure for whom the work is named. The prose style of this allegorical text closely resembles that of the *Tale of Peter and Fevroniya.* However, while Belsky preserved the wise and charitable image of Fevroniya found in the *Tale of Peter and Fevroniya,* he radically transformed the wise and charitable image of the protagonist of *Woe-Misfortune* to create Grishka. In Gozenpud's words, "The composer and librettist altered the social standing of the hero, who is a fine fellow in the epic, the son of wealthy parents. [Grishka] Kuterma is a vagrant, a destitute individual, a representative of degeneration."[44] While the protagonist of the epic manages to escape Woe-Misfortune to live out his days in a monastery, the traditional sanctuary of the Russian sinner, in the *Legend of Kitezh* Grishka falls under evil's sway, leading himself and others to calamity.

The adjustment to his personality came about gradually in the libretto-writing process. A 1903 draft version of the act I libretto portrays Grishka as a member of a corrupt, wealthy elite that dismisses religious observers as ignorant of the demands of real life. He crudely ridicules Fevroniya and Vsevolod and mercilessly taunts the members of their wedding procession. As a result, the heroine suffers a ghastly nightmare: a flock of ravens descends from the skies to torment the citizens of Greater Kitezh, tearing at their eyes, hair, and limbs and taking the innocent maiden, "neither living nor dead," their captive.[45] When, on Rimsky-Korsakov's behest, Belsky reworked the passage, rendering Fevroniya's negative prophecy positive, he changed Grishka from a wealthy merchant with a heart of stone into a tragic victim of moral and social deprivation. Rimsky-Korsakov sought to contrast the ephemeral and unrealistic heroine with a substantive and realistic adversary and thus to incorporate an element of psychological realism into the opera. Grishka became the actual incarnation of woe and misfortune. Of all the poetry borrowed from the libretto's multiple sources, his lines are the blackest in their humor, the bleakest in their sorrow:

Woe-Misfortune:

Ah, woe, woe-sufferer!
To live in woe[ful circumstances], yet not to grieve,
To walk naked is no shame,
And money doesn't bow to money,
There's always a copper for a rainy day.

[Ay i gorya, gore-gorevan'itsa!
A v gore zhit'—nekruchinnu bïť,
Nagomu khodiť—ne stïditisya,
A i deneg netu—pered den'gami,
Poyavilas' grivna—pered zlïmi dni.][46]

Legend of Kitezh, act II [two measures before rehearsal number 96]:

It [drunkenness] has commanded us to
live in woe[ful circumstances], yet not to grieve.
Money, they say, doesn't bow to money,
A half-penny is hanging around for a rainy day.
Squander it all on drink to your last stitch:
It's no great shame to walk naked.

[V gore zhiť velel da ne kruchinnu bïť.
Deneg net, mol, pered den'gami,
Zavelas' polushka pered zlïmi dni.
Propivay zhe vsyo do nitochki:
Ne velik [po]zorom nagu khodiť.]

Through these and other alterations, Belsky and Rimsky-Korsakov struck an imperfect balance between two Old Russian characters who represent divergent destinies. Fevroniya became a proponent of blind faith; Grishka (like the composer himself) an ardent religious skeptic. Though Rimsky-Korsakov and his librettist tinkered with the libretto right up to the date of the opera's premiere performance, this basic binary remained intact throughout. Indeed, at a certain point in the libretto-writing process, it was actually enhanced: Fevroniya assumed features of Solovyov's Divine Sophia; Grishka assumed features of his Antichrist. The transformation is made explicit at rehearsal number 231 of act III, scene 2, when Fevroniya asks her adversary: "Grisha, could you be the Antichrist?" ("Grisha, tï uzh ne Antikhrist li?")

Belsky and Rimsky-Korsakov encoded the opposition between Fevroniya and Grishka into the opera's dramatic structure. The score traces the heroine's pursuit of good and the villain's pursuit of evil. (Their musical paths cross only in act IV, scene 1. At rehearsal number 262, Fevroniya convinces Grishka to join her in prayer, a prayer not to God, but to Mother Earth. He initially repeats her stepwise, modal vocal lines verbatim, but soon loses focus and, by rehearsal number 264, begins to hallucinate, singing increasingly chromatic and disjointed vocal lines.) Their opposition is reflected in the opposition between the scenes in Lesser and Greater Kitezh, city and forest, earth and heaven. Despite its apparent logic, the opera's dramatic structure presents interpretive problems. The musicologist Lyubov Serebryakova comments that it is not certain why the *Legend of Kitezh* has a fourth act, when the main dramatic events—Grishka's betrayal, the Tatar-Mongol invasion, Fevroniya's kidnapping—are basically resolved by the conclusion of act III, scene 2. She also contests Belsky and Rimsky-Korsakov's decision to have the populace of Lesser Kitezh surrender to the invaders without a fight, a detail of the plot that contradicts historical chronicles of the Tatar-Mongol yoke.[47] The explanation for the score's expansion does not reside in the legends, stories, and verses that, in Serebryakova's assessment, constitute the "mythological poetics" of the score. Rather, she believes that the model for the opera was the Book of Revelation itself, the narrative of John the Theologian, which is organized as a series of binary oppositions. Through an exhaustive analysis of the "echoes, allusions, and even citations" in the libretto "from the last book of the Bible," she ascertains that Revelation is one of the opera's primary sources. The Tatar-Mongol assault on Lesser Kitezh recalls John's prophecy of world conflagration; the transformation of Greater Kitezh recalls John's description of a New Jerusalem. Act IV, moreover, depicts "the mystery of death— of new birth and transfiguration, reenacted in the fate of Fevroniya—as a celebration of the blessed Assumption and Resurrection."[48]

Plausible as the straight biblical reading of the opera may be, it overlooks two facts: first, references to Revelation are scattered throughout Solovyov's and Belïy's works, this suggesting that the theme of apocalypse may have come from them. Besides this, the libretto contains allusions to several "decadent" Symbolist writings that describe the Kitezh cult and the Lake Svetlïy Yar pilgrimages. These works, concerned with syncretism and *sobornost'*, likely superseded the Bible as a libretto source by giving the opera its mystical ambience. Indeed, Serebryakova mentions the probable influence of Dostoyevsky—especially *The Brothers Karamazov*—on Belsky and Rimsky-Korsakov, and suggests that, through the novelist, they became familiar with Symbolist philosophy:

> Dostoyevsky is readily evident in the opera—as great as he is evident in Russian spiritual and artistic culture between the centuries. . . . When at the beginning of the twentieth century new idealistic and religious trends arose in Russia, breaking with the positive and materialist philosophical tradition of the radical Russian intelligentsia, they did so under the Dostoyevsky banner. V. Rozanov, D. Merezhkovsky, *New Path*, the neo-Christian S[ergey] Bulgakov [1891–1940], the neo-idealists L[ev] Shestov [1866–1938], A. Belïy, V. Ivanov—all were connected to Dostoyevsky, all conceived themselves in his spirit, and all concerned themselves with his themes.[49]

With this remark, Serebryakova intimates that the discord between Belsky's idealistic and Rimsky-Korsakov's realistic visions of the opera, resulting in a score that offsets utopian and dystopian events, embodied the fundamental discord of Silver Age culture: that between the Symbolists' harmonious, translucent dreams and their fragmented, dissipated realities.

One of the best indications of the incompatibility of the librettist's and composer's aesthetic outlooks is the letter that Belsky wrote to Rimsky-Korsakov in July 1903, before the formal structure of the *Legend of Kitezh* had been finalized. Toward the end, he launched into a discussion of the section that most interested him: the apotheosis. Belsky tactfully made a case for extending act IV, scene 2, thereby shifting the dramatic focus of the opera away from *kuchkist* realism (the defeat of the Tatar-Mongols) and toward Symbolist mysticism (Fevroniya's spiritual transfiguration):

> By the way, I wish to make an argument for an extension of the concluding scene of Kitezh's transformation. A tranquil, spiritual joy dominates it, but breathless enthusiasm appears only at the opening, because in the preceding scene all the glorious wonders, in essence, are only a bright vision amid suffering before death, the shadow of which imperceptibly lingers until Fevroniya's departure with the heavenly bridegroom. Thus, excessive brevity in contrasting the "apotheosis" (as you deign to defame the last scene) perhaps risks as poor an impression as the brevity of the finale of *Kashchey*.[50]

Another indication of Rimsky-Korsakov's and Belsky's contrasting views on the Symbolists comes in the form of a postcard the composer sent to the librettist on 24 January 1904, after finalizing the opera's formal structure. The postcard features a watercolor painting of an unknown female model. At the top of the image Rimsky-Korsakov penciled, "An Exhibition of the *World of Art* N. R.-K."; at the bottom he jotted "'A contemporary Fevroniya'—from a contemporary decadent brush."[51] Vladimir Rimsky-Korsakov, another of the composer's sons (he had four), offers the following explanation of the annotation:

> N. A. Rimsky-Korsakov regarded decadent art of all types very negatively, especially the compositions of many artists in the World of Art group. V. I. Belsky, in contrast, noticeably gravitated toward this innovative direction in painting and literature. Nonetheless, the humorous dispatch to Vladimir Ivanovich of a postcard featuring the "decadent" figure of a fashionable woman, as if taken from an exhibition by the World of Art, cannot be interpreted as a "snide" remark at Belsky's expense.[52]

In fact, the annotation can be interpreted as Rimsky-Korsakov's reluctant acceptance of Belsky's interest in those literary works that anticipated and introduced Symbolism.

The Symbolist references appear to have been no less central to the libretto than the Medieval sources proudly catalogued by Belsky in his preface to the published score. They inform Fevroniya's description of the New Jerusalem of the Book of Revelation. More importantly, the references, as foreign matter, create a secondary narrative level in the libretto. Beyond rendering the language multivalent, they highlight the different time and space relationships in the opera. The two narrative personalities of the libretto—one epic, another contemporary—preserve a conventional pattern of open and closed set pieces, marking the progression of historical, or "chronological" time for acts II and III, while a much more subtle pattern of repeats and echoes imparts a sensation of motionless, or "eternal" time to acts I and IV.

Belsky penned several passages that portray the forest around Lake Svetliy Yar as a sacred shrine. Teeming with life, the forest is a collective body, its many creatures engaged in dialogue with the religious faithful. At rehearsal number 33 of act I, Fevroniya, upon encountering Vsevolod in the forest, asks the following rhetorical question: "Is God not everywhere? You must think: 'this is a deserted place.' But it is not: there is a great big church here" ("Ved' Bog-to ne vezde li? Tï vot mïslish': zdes' pustoye mesto; an zhe net: velikaya zdes' tserkov'"). At rehearsal number 35, she exudes: "Day and night we have tender singing, like jubilation in all voices: birds, beasts, everything that breathes, all celebrate God's beautiful world" ("Den' i noch' u nas pen'ye umil'noye, shto na vse golosa likovaniye, ptitsï, zveri, dïkhaniye vsyakoye vospevayut prekrasen gospoden' svet"). Subsequent lines associate bird song with angelic voices, an indirect expression of Solovyov's theory about the divine content of nature. What is only described in the text of act I is enacted in the visual effects of act IV, scene 2. The path to Greater Kitezh is transformed into an idyllic landscape, a garden of paradise—in other words, into nature as Fevroniya perceives it— and we begin to hear as Fevroniya does. At rehearsal number 328, the birds of paradise, Alkonost and Sirin, appear as Fevroniya jubilantly exclaims: "What wondrous birds, they sing with angelic voices!" ("Shto za ptitsï raschudesnïye, golosami poyut angel'skimi!")

The inspiration for these lines—and the inspiration for the appearance of Alkonost and Sirin—likely came from Melnikov-Pechersky's novel *In the Forests*, a lavishly detailed exploration and celebration of the thought and teaching of the Old Believers. The author's expertise in this subject came from his service in 1845 as the editor of a newspaper in Nizhniy Novgorod and, in 1847, his appointment by the governor to document the activities of the Old Believer communities in the surrounding countryside. His findings resulted in the imprisonment and forced conversion to Orthodoxy of dozens of people and the destruction of their places of worship. Cognizant of the heinous results of his labors, in the late 1850s Melnikov-Pechersky suffered a crisis of conscience. Having once condemned the Old Believers as heretics, he now accused their persecutors, the ordained clergymen of Nizhniy Novgorod, of corruption. His change of heart is manifest in the essays about the schism that he wrote between 1857 and 1862. *In the Forests* (and its companion work *In the Hills* [*Na gorakh*, 1881]) explores the day-to-day life, economic circumstances, and moral fabric of Old Believer society. The prose style is diffuse and opaque, shifting between scientific descriptions of the landscape and populace of the Trans-Volga region and anecdotal digressions about local customs and beliefs. Although the characters are fictional, Melnikov-Pechersky strives for verisimilitude in his representation of local speech. He exceeds narrative convention, however, by fusing "past" and "present" events, "reality" and "myth," "objective" and "subjective" reportage.[53] He also combines stereotyped and cliché-ridden descriptions of his characters' appearances with idiosyncratic descriptions of their psychologies. To illustrate the Old Believers' bond with nature, Melnikov-Pechersky adopts a flamboyant prose style that synthesizes sound, color, and scent. The most detailed passages of this kind are those that describe the sounds of the forest and the church bells, the very sounds that assume such an important role in the *Legend of Kitezh:*

> Forest voices are always heard. In the tall sun grass grasshoppers and locusts chatter without pause, beetles and other small insects circle over the flowers, gray- and green-necked wood pigeons and red-breasted robins pilfer. Black crows issue their call, woodpeckers knock on trees, hazel grouses cheep, yellow-colored orioles dolefully call to one another (or screech like cats), jays chatter, cuckoos mournfully cuckoo, and in various voices waxwings, robins, wood larks and other gentle little birds happily chatter. . . . And all of these sounds blend into one harmonious rustle, contented and full of life.[54]

> They [the town priests] struck the cathedral bell. Its hollow, harmonious rumble spread through the immense space. . . . Another is struck. . . . And another—and all at once fifty town bells were sounding every scale and interval. In the high-ranking merchant villages upland and on the Volga's left bank they joyfully took up the church bell ringing, and the loud rumble carried along the mountain heights, the steep inclines, the descents, the broad water ravine, and the vast, meadow-lined shore. Along the densely populated embankment and on the boats and barges everyone took off their hat and made the sign of the cross, and everyone caught a glimpse of the cathedral on the marvelous majestic mountains.[55]

The first of these two quotations from *In the Forests* is comparable in content and tone to the lines accompanying the "Forest Murmurs" scene in Wagner's *Siegfried*. Along with Wagner himself, Melnikov-Pechersky may conceivably have provided the inspiration for Rimsky-Korsakov's explicit musical reference to the "Forest Murmurs" at the start of the *Legend of Kitezh*.

The scenes of communal bliss in acts III and IV of the libretto recall other contemporaneous texts, some published shortly before the libretto's completion, others shortly after. One example of the former is Korolenko's short story "In Deserted Places." Here a meditation on the natural wonders of the Russian interior, delivered by an itinerant ethnographer, is supplemented by philosophical observations on the high moral stature of its inhabitants. Korolenko underscores the historical plight of the Old Believers and the myths and legends that it has spawned. He describes Lesser Kitezh as a Sodom abandoned by God to the Tatar-Mongols. Greater Kitezh, in contrast, is a sacred shrine whose golden spires can sometimes be glimpsed submerged in the waters of Lake Svetlïy Yar:

So to this day stands the city of Kitezh near small Lake Svetlïy Yar, which is as pure as tears. . . . And it seems from our sinful, unenlightened perspective that there is only the forest, lake, hills, and marshes. But this is merely the deception of our sinful nature. In actual fact, "in reality," splendid steeples and gilded palaces and monasteries stand here in all their beauty. . . . For those who can peer part-way through the veil of deceit, lights from religious processions and tall golden banners shimmer in the lake depths. And a sweet chime carries over the mirror surface of the illusory waters. And then it all subsides, and only the forest grove murmurs.

Thus, above Lake Svetlïy Yar stand two worlds: one real, but invisible, another visible, but unreal. They merge, covering and penetrating each other. The unreal, phantasmagoric world is more manifest than the real world. The latter only rarely flickers through the watery shroud and, at a devout glance, disappears. It reverberates and falls silent. Again the harsh cloud of corporeal sensation settles.[56]

The passage reads like a dream narrative: "lights from religious processions" submerge; the steeples of Greater Kitezh rise from the water's depths like will-o'-the-wisps. The believer, confronting the spectral image, is transformed from within. Korolenko repeats and overlays nouns, verbs, and adjectives. The forest noises and bell peals merge in murky cacophony, far from life, but still within reach of human perception.

A closely related text, Hippius's 1906 travelogue "Radiant Lake: A Diary," reflects the Symbolist preoccupation with the Second Coming, the Christian Apocalypse, and (even) the union of heaven and earth. The author's writing is "musical" insofar as it evinces subtle gradations of color and emotion. Certain sections recall psalm texts. Narrating her pilgrimage to Lake Svetlïy Yar, Hippius discusses the differences between Christian and pagan faiths. Describing her first night at the lakeside, she stresses the compatibility between her own reverent sentiments and those of the local populace:

Then we again began talking about the coming apocalypse . . . and we read the Revelation: "The Holy Spirit and Virgin speak: come. . . ." The conversation was wonderful. We all came in close and formed a circle. There was a calm breeze, and in the flickering belt of the fire the lake lay calm, shadowy, and radiant—like a black diamond. It seemed as though we all heard together, as one person, the quiet chimes of the steeples of the holy city reverberating upon the water. There, where the light from the candles fell on the waters, in the thick mirror of the lake, we no longer saw black hills, but the barely perceptible reflection of golden copulas. The people speaking with us, though utterly unlike us, became our nearest and dearest. We sat together on common ground, dissimilar in all respects: in custom, legend, history, dress, language, and life—but nobody noticed the differences. We had only one being, at once ours and theirs.[57]

Following the reading from Revelation, Hippius summons a fantastic vision of something invisible: the crosses and the steeples of the Church of the Assumption. She clearly believes that spiritual faith—at least the kind of spiritual faith practiced by the rural populace of Russia, seemingly insulated from the skepticism and cynicism of the urban populace—overcomes differences of race and creed. She also suggests that the intelligentsia's selfless devotion to the people would restore ancient bonds. The same sentiment—and the same image of a lakeside séance—pervades the climactic scene of Belsky's libretto. Act III, scene 2, for example, bears this heading: "The first rays of dawn illuminate the surface of the lake and the reflection of the capital city in the lake, although the shore is empty. Little by little a festive peal is heard" ("Pervïye luchi zari osveshchayut poverkhnost' ozera i otrazheniye stol'nogo goroda v ozere pod pustïm beregom. Nesetsya prazdnichnïy zvon, malo-pomalo"). For Belsky, as for Rimsky-Korsakov, seeing the bright vision of the invisible city (matched by hearing the rhythmically uncoordinated clanging of the church bells) became a metaphor for the cessation of chronological time and the beginning of ecclesiastical time. It was a metaphor that they shared with the "decadent" Symbolists, as Korolenko's and Hippius's writings on the Kitezh pilgrimages confirm.

In Belsky's libretto, the image of a Universal Church and pagan-Christian syncretism is enriched with details taken from prose texts that highlight the relationship between theology-centered worship and nature-based worship. All sources converge in the perception that the essence of religiosity resides in the bosom of nature, the amatory garden. Familiarity with this concept evidently allowed Rimsky-Korsakov to reconcile himself with religious doctrine in his later years. The *Legend of Kitezh* cannot be regarded merely as an aesthetic treatment of spiritual matters. Rather, it attests to the consolidation of the composer's pantheistic worldview. Indeed, when the music critic and Rimsky-Korsakov's would-be librettist Yevgeny Petrovsky (1873–1919) asked the composer whether the *Legend of Kitezh* could be called a "liturgical" opera (a genre that Petrovsky vaguely defined as the "exultant and majestic narration of events great and small"), he was informed that the drama alternated between scenes of historical conflict and theological clarification:

In my operas I am not too far from the archetype you recall. I submit that in several scenes in the *Legend of the Invisible City* etc. I will be even closer to this archetype, though somewhat deviating from it toward realism, as I think should always be the case. They [these scenes] will give life and diversity to the liturgical form. Without them the form might easily descend into the monotony and stiffness of the church liturgy.[58]

The "liturgical form" described by Rimsky-Korsakov fuses Christian and folk ritual, the individual worship of the deity and communal worship of the land. The text's syncretic features were inscribed into the music, which juxtaposes stylized liturgical chant and stylized folk song, stylized urban soundscapes and rural ones. Occasionally the composer appears to have lost track of the distinction between these categories: certain musical motifs appear in both the real and unreal, earthly and heavenly episodes. At these points, the score becomes a symbol, facilitating communication between otherwise discrete dramatic realms.

THE ANXIETY OF INFLUENCE

The music critics associated with the Symbolist journals *Apollo (Apollon)*, *The Golden Fleece*, *New Path*, *Libra*, and the *World of Art*, evaluated the *Legend of Kitezh* on the basis of its expression of idealist philosophical ideas as well as on its assimilation of modernist compositional techniques. Their reviews focus on the opera's allusions to Wagner and propose that these allusions somehow articulate the boundary between the "ancient world" of the opera's source chronicle and "future world" of symbolic incarnation. In a three-part review of the 9 February 1907 premiere performance, Petrovsky, a Wagner devotee, compared Fevroniya's search for the invisible city with Parsifal's search for the Holy Grail. In part one, he notes that Rimsky-Korsakov's allusions to *Parsifal* supply the *Legend of Kitezh* with an "epic tone" that approaches "the ideal of [the Holy Grail city of] Monsalvat" and points out that "in the [act IV] 'procession to the invisible city of Kitezh' it is hard not to notice the similarity of certain rhythmic and melodic details with those elements from which the [act I] 'procession to the hall of the Holy Grail' was created."[59] In part two, he posits that the unmistakable reference to the "Good Friday Spell" in the cello and bass ostinato of the act III transformation scene serves to articulate the "acuity of the *experienced* moment . . . in *Plusquamperfectum*."[60] Despite the elegance of his language, it is difficult to ascertain precisely what Petrovsky means here. On one hand, he appears to be making the claim that the gradual dissolve of vocal sound into orchestral sound, stage music into offstage music, expresses the revelation of the otherworldly. On the other, he implies that the introduction of the ostinato pattern inaugurates a shift from chronological time to ecclesiastical time and, in turn, the transfiguration of the narrative into sacrament. This does not render the scene "mystical" by Petrovsky's standards, since he believes that Rimsky-Korsakov evinces only an external interest in liturgical practice. Part three of his review highlights this point: Petrovsky asserts that the story line of the *Legend of Kitezh*, concerned with conversion and salvation, is derivative of *Parsifal* but that, ultimately, the imitation is flawed. To justify the assertion, he broadens his discussion to consider Rimsky-Korsakov's and Wagner's entire oeuvres. Beyond the *Legend of Kitezh* and *Parsifal*, he compares *Sadko* and *Tannhäuser, Kashchey the Deathless* and *Tristan und Isolde*. He concludes that Wagner sought to merge his consciousness with those of his protagonists and to engage directly the emotions and sympathies of the listener. In turning his creative focus inward, in devoting his entire being to his subject matter, he revealed something of the essential nature of human experience.[61] Rimsky-Korsakov, in contrast, portrayed life outside of himself, a process that affected his audiences very differently from the way that Wagner's did. This is not to say that Rimsky-Korsakov froze out his audiences. His portrayals of pagan rituals and customs suggest that he thought that they bore an immortality and immutability that was not present in everyday activity and, as such, could be ennobling and instructive, a facilitator of heightened awareness.

In another review of the premiere performance of the *Legend of Kitezh*, Vyacheslav Karatïgin, an advocate of modernist music, supplemented these very same points. Writing for *The Golden Fleece* (a Moscow-based Symbolist journal that, like the St. Petersburg-based *World of Art*, was conceived as a total artwork), Karatïgin argued that, while Rimsky-Korsakov and Wagner both included "mystical" passages in their operas, the former differed from the latter by rejecting idealist philosophy. He referred to the *Legend of Kitezh* as "an opera of meditation, 'inspiration, pleasant sounds and prayers.' There is little action, and the music is intentionally motionless, devoid of force and bright lyricism."[62] The paucity of visual drama stems from the diffuse content of the libretto, "the language of which does not correspond to the speech of the eighth century, the actual time of the action, but maintains a later mystic-mythic style."[63] While Karatïgin was unwilling on first hearing to pass judgment on the opera's overall quality, he found fault with Rimsky-Korsakov's dramaturgical approach. He asserted that "the sustained expression of lengthy ecstasies, the preeminence of love, pantheistic Christianity, paradisiacal bliss, of these fundamental 'ideas' of an opera-mysterium—are hardly achievable in music." [64] He was likewise unmoved by the two-sided depiction of Grishka as a victim and villain and displeased that the narrative, in its fragmentariness, leaves open the possibility of Grishka's ultimate redemption. Though himself partial to Wagner, he took pains to attribute the opera's "mysticism" not to its Wagner citations but to its "epic" and "liturgical" features.[65] In fact, Karatïgin claimed that Rimsky-Korsakov "neutralizes" these citations by filtering them through Russian folk music.[66]

It is well known that, despite his invocations of *Das Rheingold, Parsifal, Siegfried,* and *Tristan und Isolde* in *Sadko, Kashchey the Deathless,* the *Legend of Kitezh,* and other operas, Rimsky-Korsakov bristled at comparisons to Wagner. In his undated essay "Wagner and Dargomïzhsky" ("Vagner i Dargomïzhsky"), an essay that devotes only a single page to Dargomïzhsky, Rimsky-Korsakov wrote that Wagner "did not build an edifice whose staircases lead to various luxuriant corridors and chambers, but one comprised only of a staircase, leading from the entrance to the exit." [67] Once, when Belsky remarked to Rimsky-Korsakov about the similarities between the *Legend of Kitezh* and *Parsifal,* he received a scolding: "In Wagner's prolixities I can say that I find only his divine conceit, and that I don't perceive other qualities. I appreciate compositions with artistic form, but Wagner has no form, and if he does, then it is inartistic. Don't wish this upon my work." [68] Belsky decided to back down: "You accuse me of desiring some element of Wagnerism from you. God save me! I reveled too much this summer in *Meistersingers* and *Parsifal.* Their formlessness, weight, and extreme artifice bring me undue grief." [69] Despite the retraction, Belsky was well aware that Rimsky-Korsakov's remarks could not be taken at face value, as they were in large measure cathartic, indicative of an increasing fascination with the German composer.[70] Rimsky-Korsakov's fulminations were much less a reflection of the anxiety of influence than of the aesthetics and politics of the New Russian School, the *kuchkist* composers of yore. The academic and publicist Vladimir Stasov (1824–1906), the group's ideological arbiter, argued in a series of militant articles that Wagner posed a threat to the Russian musical heritage and attempted to trivialize his innovations as chimerical and insubstantial, achieved primarily through the manipulation of instrumentation. Moreover, he referred to leitmotivic technique as abstract and inflexible, a practice that limited, rather than expanded, the semantic content of music drama. Rimsky-Korsakov's opinions of Wagner resemble Stasov's but also reflect his distaste for those trends in *fin-de-siècle* composition that countered his own positivist and materialist methods: asymmetrical phrasing, linear motion without formal endpoint, metric obfuscation, and suspended harmony. He likewise found Wagner's reliance on secondary rather than primary literary sources for his scenarios inartistic, irrespective of the fact that Belsky had relied on such sources as well.

Besides Stasov, Rimsky-Korsakov shared his feelings about Wagner with his "mystic" Symbolist antipode Belïy, for whom Wagner's phantasmagoria represented "good and evil," just as the "Apocalyptic trumpet signified both joy and horror."[71] Despite this common aversion, however, both Rimsky-Korsakov and Belïy attempted in their late works to replicate what Petrovsky and Karatïgin regarded as Wagner's principal achievement: the elucidation, through the continuous transformation of orchestral sound, of the inner life of his protagonists' minds. Grönke reports that this same process typifies the *Legend of Kitezh:*

> [the] vocal numbers cannot be isolated, and Rimsky's work takes on a strongly symphonic character throughout as a result of the close interweaving of voices and instruments, as encountered in Wagner. This makes it possible for the numerous orchestral tableaux also to be tied firmly into the opera's basic concept and thus to make tone-painting inseparable from the dramatic structure of the opera. As Belsky originally wished, the orchestra does indeed interpret "inward actions" in the prelude to the first act, in the transformation of the city of Kitezh in the third act, and in the fourth-act interlude.[72]

From a Symbolist perspective, Rimsky-Korsakov's concentration on "inward actions," coupled with his encyclopedic compilation of musical references, led to the creation of an opera that, allegorically, constituted a dramatic synthesis of the various elements that defined his culture and the revelation of its origins, that is to say, the revelation of its spiritual essence.

He wrote the music in fits and starts between 1900 and 1904. Unsurprisingly, the earliest sketches indicate that he considered it of paramount importance to differentiate Fevroniya's and Grishka's vocal styles. To the former he assigned hymn-like ariosos, to the latter bawdy drinking tunes. Rimsky-Korsakov also fashioned distinct musical identities for Lesser and Greater Kitezh. Gozenpud, in a general overview of the sketches, concluded that they have less scholarly value than those for the composer's other operas. "Together with the significant and essential themes for the musical-dramatic conception of the composition (the introduction to act I, the development of the song on the Tatar captivity, the scene on the square of Little Kitezh, and so on), the sketches include variants of less significant episodes and discarded recitatives, but exclude the central, focal characters and strong points of musical action."[73] This summary is basically accurate, though it should be stressed that the sketches attest to the composer's emphasis on the depiction of nature, the verdant temple, and divine rapture.

Of the literally hundreds of pages of material, the following warrant comment. On page 88 of sketchbook no. 5, dated February 1900, the composer drafted the ascending diminished seventh arpeggio (D-F-A♭-B) and chromatically descending sequence of major thirds ($f\sharp^2$-d^2, e^2-c^2, $d\sharp^2$-b^1, d^2-$b\flat^1$, $c\sharp^2$-a^1, c^2-$a\flat^1$, b^1-g^1, $b\flat^1$-$g\flat^1$, a^1-f^1) found in Grishka's act III "mad" scene. On the next eight pages, he drafted different versions of the orchestral introduction to act II. The last of these is noteworthy because it appears beneath the penciled annotation "Solovyov bibliography," a reference not to Vladimir Solovyov (the bulk of whose writings remained unpublished until 1914) but to his father Sergey (1820–79), author of the twenty-nine–volume series, *The History of Russia from Ancient Times* (*Istoriya Rossii c drevneyshikh vremen*, 1851–79). The squib hints that whereas the opera's eschatological content came from the junior Solovyov, its historical content came from the senior. Belsky absorbed the influence of one generation, and Rimsky-Korsakov that of another. On page 93 of sketchbook no. 6, dated December 1900, the composer worked out the Greater "Kitezh chime" motif as it is heard by Grishka in the "mad" scene: an oscillating minor third triplet pattern (e^1-$c\sharp^1$-e^1, e^1-$c\sharp^1$-e^1) that mutates up and down by minor second. On page 3 of sketchbook no. 7, also dated February 1900, he drafted the descending chromatic sequence that denotes the magical blooming of heavenly flowers in act IV, scene 2. The next page includes four harmonized measures targeted for the enraptured opening phrases of Fevroniya's B minor aria "In Praise of the Wilderness" ("Pokhvala pustïne"). Page 6 includes the oscillating sextuplet figuration assigned to a solo flute and clarinet to represent the cuckoo at rehearsal number 1 of act I (it recurs at rehearsal number 286 of act IV, scene 1); page 8, finally, includes the rising sextuplet chromatic passage assigned to the solo viola to represent a black bear at rehearsal number 2.[74]

Thus, at the first stage of composition, the composer dwelled on the forest murmurs and the Greater Kitezh steeple sounds but also on the scene of Grishka's downfall. In addition, page 89 of sketchbook no. 5, page 98 of sketchbook no. 6, and pages 12–15 of sketchbook no. 7 document the evolution of both the Greater Kitezh fanfare motif and the tone-semitone ("octatonic") music associated with the Tatar-Mongols. Rather than establishing blatant oppositions between Lesser and Greater Kitezh, rural and urban spaces, the thematic complex establishes dialogue between them. The forest murmurs, steeple chimes, and fanfare motif permeate the amorous scenes between Fevroniya and Vsevolod, the violent scenes between Fevroniya and Grishka, and the surrounding processional and ceremonial scenes. The reprise of the act I nature sounds during the act IV assumption and resurrection highlights the central message of pagan-Christian synthesis.

Rimsky-Korsakov specifically represented this synthesis by combining abstracted and stylized "folk" and "liturgical" *topoi*. In a 1978 essay that informed subsequent Soviet writings on the *Legend of Kitezh*, the folklorist K. Korablyova describes the opera as an organic work informed from start to finish by the melodic formulae of *znamenniy* chant. In the opening paragraph, for example, she states:

> *Znamenniy* chant in many respects determines the intonational content of the music of *Kitezh*. . . . Almost everywhere in the opera the ear senses not only melodic connections, but scalar, rhythmic, and formal structures taken from ancient Russian church melodies. And yet *znamenniy* chant is not presented here as an isolated phenomenon, juxtaposed against musical language of folk content. It is closely allied with the latter. . . just as in the reworking of the opera's narrative various legends were combined and fused.[75]

Rather than focusing on the passages with obvious biblical allusions (the choruses of act IV, scenes 1 and 2) or on the single *znamenniy* chant quotation in the score (the appearance in the orchestra of the Kievan melody "Behold, the Bridegroom Comes" ["Se Zhenikh gryadet"] when Vsevolod's ghost appears), Korablyova centers her discussion on Fevroniya's act I arioso "Day and Night We Observe the Sabbath" ("Den' i noch' u nas sluzhba voskresnaya"). She reports that the melody consists of a sequential repetition of a two-measure pattern whose pitch content and rhythm recall two mode three psalms from the fifteenth century. Though she does not mention it, the date is important: during the fifteenth century, the *znamenniy* chant tradition rooted in the practice of Byzantium was superseded by the *stolpovoy* chant tradition—the name referring to the *stolp*, the eight-week cycle of chants preserved in the liturgical book called the *Oktoikh*. The development of *stolpovoy* chant coincided with a number of major events in Russian history: the conclusion of the Tatar-Mongol occupation, the founding of the Russian state, and the establishment of Moscow as a Church center. The old chant books were edited and brought into accord with contemporary practices, and the first manuals were created to indicate the duration, rhythm, and dynamic of the specific chants.[76]

The source of Korablyova's examples is the second edition of Nikolai Uspensky's study *The Art of Ancient Russian Chant* (*Drevnerusskoye pevcheskoye iskusstvo,* 1968), a taxonomy of the chant from its formative period to the seventeenth century. The study provides examples of the melodic formulae that define each mode of the chant. There are eight such modes, and they were derived in concept from the eight Byzantine *echoi,* a system that grouped chants not by underlying scale but by phrases or tunelets called *popevki.* For example, the first mode was defined by ninety-three *popevki,* each characterized by a festive but reverent affect. The other seven modes also had characteristic affects. *Znamenniy* chant scribes and singers of the late fifteenth century were required to memorize the modes, the melodic formulae that correspond to the modes, and the names of the formulae. Ideologically compromised, Korablyova does not address these issues, which leave unanswered several questions about Rimsky-Korsakov's compositional process and his acquaintance with *znamenniy* chant. The comparisons made by Korablyova between the score and Uspensky's examples are somewhat uncertain. She does not discuss the difference between the "affect" of Fevroniya's arioso and the "affect" of the *popevki* transcribed in her musical examples, nor does she discuss the relationship between the strophic structure of the arioso and that of the psalms from which the *popevki* are extracted. More puzzling, however, is Korablyova's application of "Western" modal terminology to "Eastern" *znamenniy* chant. In her overview of the arioso, for example, she comments that the "Lydian scalar color gives a uniquely bright and cheerful tone to the *popevka.*" [77] The only conceivable explanation for her conflation of "Eastern" and "Western" nomenclature resides in her shaky thesis that certain passages in the score combine "folk" and "liturgical" intonations: she labels "folk" intonations with "Western" modal terminology, and "liturgical" ones with "Eastern" chant terminology.

Korablyova is on firmer ground when discussing the overall structure of the arioso and the manner in which the orchestral accompaniment recalls the sound of bells. She detects the influence of bardic genres on "a whole series of scenes" typified by "threefold repetitions, as in folk tales (questions and answers in Fevroniya's scene with the Princeling in the first act, the performance of the bear trainer, Kuterma's mockery of Fevroniya in the second act, the prayers in the third act, etc)." [78] She notes, too, the influence of antiphonal church psalmody on the form of the opera's final scene. Threefold repetition governs the melody, harmony, and form of the arioso. At rehearsal number 34, for example, Fevroniya sings a two-measure phrase three times, the second time transposed up a minor third from a starting pitch of e^1 to g^1, and the third time transposed up a major third from g^1 to b^1. Korablyova remarks that the subsequent melodic surges, "reflecting Fevroniya's increasing rapture," are marked "by shorter and shorter phrases, these logically resulting in the middle section in the subdivision of the *popevki*. . . . The bell-likeness *[kolokol'nost']* of the orchestral accompaniment acquires strength with the further development of supporting themes derived from the even undulating figures of the accompaniment, these likewise resembling festive bell chimes."[79] At rehearsal number 35, the "undulating figures" comprise iterated sixteenth-note arpeggios (e^1-d^1-b♭-g / e^1-c♯-b-g) above c and A pedal tones. The final section of the arioso is characterized by a rising and falling quarter-note figure that "recalls *znamennïy* chant in intonation, scale, and rhythmic features." Korablyova specifically associates it with a mode five *poglasitsa* or "signature": the cluster of pitches, derived from various sources, which are used to define the principal melodic features of the mode. The five measures preceding rehearsal number 37 become a "solemn march" with a "hymn-like quality." The entire setting, the writer concludes, "expresses a pantheism that stems from folk beliefs and concepts that arise from *popevki* of the *znamennïy* type. This particular poetic relationship to nature, and those features of its personification that reflect a feeling of commonality between people and the surrounding world, is endemic to ancient Russian art—not only folk art, but also professional art."[80]

This comment is both technically and conceptually problematic. Rimsky-Korsakov did not quote "folk" melodies—and only quoted one "liturgical" melody—in the opera. He relied instead on his creative intuition to abstract and stylize their principal attributes. On 23 August 1904, he informed Yastrebtsev that it "makes me laugh, when people become convinced that I studied folk songs. Believe me, dear friend, that this imagined study came about simply because I, owing to talent, easily remembered and mastered what is most typical in the tunes—that's all."[81] By reworking the "songs," distancing them from their original contexts, he arguably rendered them timeless and universal. A similar impulse arguably dictated the ordering of musical and verbal events in the score, a score that, as Korablyova intimates, was cast in the form of an epic. The narrative structure of an epic differs markedly from that of later literary genres. It is rounded; its ending is enclosed in its beginning. Events in an epic are removed from reality: they belong to a realm in which time unfolds in a predetermined sequence, without randomness or chance. In accord with the structure of an epic, the events of act I and act IV, scene 1 of the *Legend of Kitezh* parallel one another, as do those of act II and act III, scene 1. The circular structure is manifest on a smaller level in the entr'actes of acts III and IV, which quote from their respective finales. It is also evident on the level

Example 18.   Fevroniya's act I arioso (complete) *(continues)*

of individual numbers: the melody of the arioso repeats with little essential change as its harmony, tonality, and instrumentation enact a series of transformations around it. The inspiration for Rimsky-Korsakov's dramatic plan was not an ancient, authentic literary epic but a relatively recent musical one: Glinka's *Ruslan and Lyudmila*, a "mock" epic opera based on

Example 18. *(continues)*

Example 18. *(continues)*

Example 18. *(continues)*

Example 18. *(continues)*

Example 18. *(continues)*

Example 18. *(continued)*

Pushkin's 1820 "mock" epic poem of the same name.[82] Together with his musical borrowings, Rimsky-Korsakov's imitation of the formal outline of *Ruslan and Lyudmila* in the *Legend of Kitezh* suggests that he intended his opera as a creative tribute to a cherished component of the national operatic tradition.

The opening tunelet, or *popevka*, of the act I arioso—involving the pitches e^1, c^1, d^1, $f\#^1$, and g—permeates many of the vocal and instrumental lines of act IV. As such, it not only elucidates the rounded structure of the *Legend of Kitezh* as a whole, it completes the dramatic arc between Fevroniya's act I prophecy of transcendence and its act IV actualization. Transposed up by a diminished fifth and presented in four-part harmony, the melody accompanies the appearance of Vsevolod's ghost at rehearsal number 295 of act IV, scene 1. Transposed down by an augmented second and presented in three-part harmony, the melody embellishes an alternating $d\flat^2$ and $d\flat^3$ triplet pattern at rehearsal number 296. It thereafter permeates the vocal lines, recurring (again in transposition) in the opening section of Fevroniya's and Vsevolod's G minor duet "We shall not be parted" ("Mï s toboyu ne rasstanemsya") at rehearsal number 300. It recurs one final time in the F major orchestral entr'acte between act IV scenes 1 and 2: the postmortem procession to the invisible city. The melody is the most prominent attribute of a motivic congeries involving the offstage bells of the Church of the Assumption and the offstage voices of the birds of paradise Alkonost and Sirin, who at rehearsal number 318 confirm the fulfillment of Fevroniya's prophecy: "The Lord promised his people and seekers: 'for you, dear children, all will be new'" ("Obeshchal Gospod' lyudyam ishchushchim: 'budet, detushki, vam vsyo novoye'"). The combination of onstage and offstage sounds expresses the transcendental unity between people and nature, this world and the other, that was central to both Rimsky-Korsakov's pantheistic and Solovyov's ecumenical philosophy.

In contrast to Fevroniya, Vsevolod, and Greater Kitezh, the music assigned to Grishka, the Tatar-Mongols, and Lesser Kitezh has more in common with "folk" than "liturgical" music.[83] Korablyova identifies distant resonances between Grishka's B-flat major dirge, "Ha, thank you, wise drunkenness!" ("Ekh, spasibo khmelyu umnomu!") from rehearsal number 95 of act II, and the penitential verse "What joy to be poor" ("Chego radi nishch est'"), which dates from the second half of the sixteenth century. Rather than a sincere, or genuine, verse, Korablyova comments that "What joy to be poor"—preserved in a late sixteenth-century manuscript that employs hooked notation and in a late seventeenth-century manuscript that employs square notation—has "a sarcastic quality."[84] The major point of correspondence between Grishka's dirge and the penitential verse is their extremely narrow range: the former moves by step within the range of a perfect fourth, the latter within the span of a major third. The psaltery player's song "From beyond the deep waters of Lake Yar" ("Iz-za ozera Yara glubokogo"), sung at rehearsal number 72 of act II, likewise resonates with an ancient source. The text is directly derived from the Kievan epic poem about the prophet of doom Vasiliy Ignatyevich.[85] The selection of this text was clearly programmatic. Separated into three strophic verses with three choral refrains, it encapsulates the principal images and events of the opera. The psaltery player sings about a holy city that rises from the waters, a fair maiden who summons the faithful to prayer, and the maiden's vision of a licentious city's ghastly fate. The events are outlined in reverse chronological order from how they actually transpire in the opera. The psaltery player forecasts events at the end, then those in the middle, and then those at the beginning. His performance less resembles a traditional operatic ballad, which serves to introduce a riddle at the beginning of the plot that requires resolution by the end, than it does Bayan's performance in act I of *Ruslan and Lyudmila:* a prophecy of the hero and heroine's imminent struggles and subsequent bliss. Though moving backward, the psaltery player's song, as a narrative loop, once again highlights the circular, iterative structure of the surrounding drama. The *Legend of Kitezh* assimilates not historical time but ahistorical time, affirming through repetition that faith determines destiny.

To the Tatar-Mongols Rimsky-Korsakov assigned two variations of the melody "On the Tatar Captivity" ("Pro tatarskiy polon"), these being the eighth and ninth entries in his 1877 compilation *One Hundred Russian Folk Songs (Sto russkikh narodnïkh pesen)*, the first of two such volumes

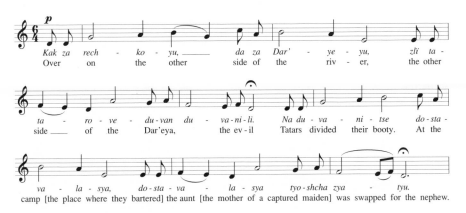

Example 19.   Variation 1 of "On the Tatar Captivity"

that he published. The first variation of the folk song serves as Bedyay and
Burunday's motif. It is initially sung by Burunday at rehearsal number 126
of act II as he instructs his cohorts to take Fevroniya prisoner. His and
Bedyay's speech is ridiculously crude and garish, less a sincere attempt by
Rimsky-Korsakov and his librettist to depict them as fearsome and ominous than a lampoon of the manner in which previous Russian composers
had stereotyped and orientalized Eastern and Southern outsiders.[86] They
are clearly marked as degenerate, predestined to lose to the Russians in
accord with the logic of an epic. The motif recurs in various guises in nine
instrumental passages, the most prominent being the second half of the
act III entr'acte, "The Battle near Kerzhenets" ("Secha pri Kerzhentse"), a
representation of the battle between the Tatar-Mongols and the ill-equipped
soldiers of Lesser Kitezh. (The first half of the entr'acte, predictably enough,
is dominated by the melody of a soldiers' song, and its rhythmic and harmonic content brings to mind Wagner's "Ride of the Valkyries" from *Die
Walküre* [1856].) The second variation of "On the Tatar Captivity," sometimes heard alongside the first, has a reflexive role. It is performed by the
Tatar-Mongols as they prepare to attack Lesser Kitezh and by the Lesser
Kitezh survivors as they grimly recount the siege. At rehearsal number 151
of act III, scene 1, for instance, Poyarok quotes it as he describes to Vsevolod
how the Tatar-Mongols stormed the city and then captured and blinded him.
The allegorical significance of his sightlessness becomes apparent in later
scenes. Despite being blind, Poyarok nonetheless perceives the pathway to
salvation, while those responsible for his injury cannot.

Though defining dramatic registers, the sheer volume of musical and
verbal quotations in the score compels one to speculate that Rimsky-

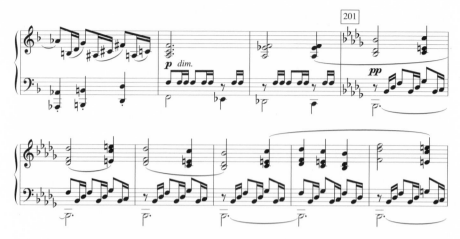

Example 20.   Its appearance in the second half of the act III entr'acte, "The Battle near Kerzhenets"

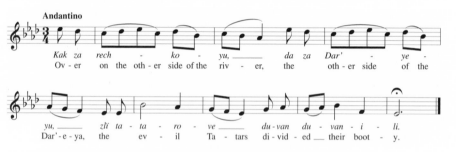

Example 21.   Variation 2 of "On the Tatar Captivity"

Korsakov did not compose his opera so much as compile it. Every melodic line, harmonic progression, and rhythmic gesture is a found object with a plurality of possible meanings. In forging a tribute to the past, he elevated the score to the status of an authorless masterpiece. Ironically, because the music embraces a plethora of styles and genres, the *Legend of Kitezh* connotes the creative attribute that Rimsky-Korsakov most dreaded: form- or shapelessness. At the same time, the compilation of musical and verbal subtexts has metaphoric significance. It becomes on a syntactic level what the composer tried to achieve on a thematic level: the transformation of belief systems, the generation of a universal narrative, the representation of an ideal Russia. Permeable and multivalent, the score is *pantheistic* in the broadest sense of the term. Just as the source legend underwent continual expansion and extension over the centuries, so too did the opera un-

Example 22.   Its appearance in Poyarok's act III, scene 1 narrative

dergo continual recoding and revising. Structurally, the opera resembles the most elaborate of the ten manuscript variants of the legend discussed by V. L. Komarovich in his 1936 study *Kitezh Legend: An Approach to Studying the Local Legends (Kitezhskaya legenda: Opït izucheniya mestnïkh legend)*. This variant, compiled in the seventeenth century by Old Believers, has four parts: "a historical section (recounting the life and death of a great Prince [Georgiy Vsevolodovich]), an apologetic section (describing the miracle that occurs in the city), a short historical section (recounting the death of other Russian princes) and, finally, a meditation about the path to Kitezh (incorporating multiple citations from the Bible and other religious texts)."[87] The four acts of the *Legend of Kitezh* correspond to the four parts of the variant, though, as noted, the librettist, to the composer's chagrin, embellished them with references to Symbolist travel writings about Kitezh. These references altered the historical narrative, rendering it ethereal and illusory. The listening experience, which reflects fluctuations in the physical and psychological aspects of the drama, speaks for the capacity of music to negotiate the barrier between the plausible and implausible, real and unreal.

THE LIGHT WAVE IN THE SOUND WAVE

Four musical devices penetrate this semiotic forest: the tonality of F major (aligned with light and ever-increasing radiance), the muted Greater Kitezh fanfare motif (recalling that of *Tannhäuser*), the recurring forest murmurs *(Siegfried)*, and the Church of the Assumption bells *(Boris Godunov* and *Parsifal)*. These four devices occupy the space between discrete dramatic realms—the material and secular world and the immaterial and sacred world—that the Greater Kitezh citizens are destined to traverse.

To clarify this point, we must turn to a 1922 article by Boris Asafyev, which posits that the entire score gravitates toward light and the pastoral tonality of F major. The action, Asafyev contends, is "drawn to the radiant F major of the last iconically built scene, in which the tonality acquires the character of a motionless repository, fulcrum, or pillar."[88] In essence, the dramatic progress toward the miracle of act III, scene 1 and the apotheosis of act IV, scenes 1 and 2 is marked by increased modulations to this tonality. To Asafyev, F major serves "as a beacon of hope and therefore sounds more stable, obstinate, and even static" as the opera draws to a close.[89] The tonality is virtually absent in act I, appearing at rehearsal number 65 for just two measures in conjunction with the Greater Kitezh fanfare motif. (The F major chord is supplanted by an F minor chord, a functional component of the C minor cadence that concludes the act.) Its appearance is associated with Fevroniya's discovery that the person she fell in love with in the forest is the son of the ruler of Greater Kitezh. The aforementioned act II psaltery player's melody "From beyond the deep waters of Lake Yar" is set in F major, as is Fevroniya's prayer "O God, make the city of Kitezh invisible" ("Bozhe, sotvori nevidimom Kitezh grad"), which commences four measures after rehearsal number 136. In the latter example, the tonality is once again heard in conjunction with the Greater Kitezh fanfare motif. It sounds as a "beacon of hope" amid a falling tone-semitone "octatonic" passage (a-g-f♯-e-e♭-[d♭]-[C]-b♭) that is centered around the pitch *a*. (This is one of several such passages connected in the *Legend of Kitezh* to the Tatar-Mongols. In general, "octatonic" music in Rimsky-Korsakov's operas is aligned with malicious forces, the preternatural, and the exotic.) At rehearsal number 172 of act III, scene 1, F major returns as a page boy reports from a steeple tower that "the hills are barren and deserted, the bright waters of Svetlïy Yar are swathed in a bright mist, like a bridal veil radiating light" ("Pusto sholomya okatisto, shto nad Svetlïm Yarom ozerom, belïm oblakom odeyano, shto fatoyu svetonosnoyu"). From this faint glimmer, the tonality increases in brightness over the scene, becoming the principal tonality as Greater Kitezh is shrouded and vanishes. At rehearsal number 241 of act III, scene 2, F major recurs when Grishka sees the reflection of the invisible city on the lake's surface, and at rehearsal number 245 when the Tatar-Mongols do. Their frightened dispersal is marked by the appearance of another descending tone-semitone "octatonic" passage (f-e♭-d-c-B-[A]-[A♭]-g♭), this one centered around the pitch *f*. The absorbing of "octatonic" music into a diatonic context obviously represents the triumph of the Greater Kitezh citizenry over the Tatar-Mongols. F major sounds momentarily at the beginning of act IV, scene 1, but firmly establishes itself in the entr'acte that depicts the emancipation of Fevroniya's soul as she travels to the invisible city. The wonder is executed after Grishka loses his mind, and after a bird of paradise, Alkonost, appears to inform Fevroniya that she is about to die, but will afterward be reunited with her betrothed, who perished in the battle against the Tatar-Mongols.

The subsequent dominance of F major symbolizes the transformation of the material world, the conclusion of time as measured by the nonbelievers, and the beginning of time as measured by the Old Believers. From his experience creating a performing edition of Musorgsky's inchoate *Khovanshchina*,[90] Rimsky-Korsakov knew that the real Old Believers, the schismatics who had rejected the reforms introduced into the Church by Patriarch Nikon, interpreted the ascension of Peter the Great as a harbinger of apocalypse and Peter the Great himself as the Antichrist. In the *Legend of Kitezh*, the state threat against the Old Believers becomes an enemy threat against ancient Russia, while the potent figure of the Antichrist becomes the hapless figure of Grishka. The "spiritual" crisis is converted into a "national" crisis. This conversion less represents Rimsky-Korsakov's personal beliefs than the widespread nationalism that came to typify studies of the Old Believer traditions in the late nineteenth and early twentieth centuries.[91] These traditions are represented in the score by the F major choruses whose style recalls the *a cappella* Orthodox style that flourished in St. Petersburg in Rimsky-Korsakov's day and that eventually became aligned with the Moscow Synodal Choir. The chorus at rehearsal number 343 of act IV, scene 2, for instance, relies on simple triadic progressions with the roots amplified at the octave—a typical feature of Synodal Choir text settings. The sentiment of the text, which is addressed by the choristers to Fevroniya, is serene and lofty: "Stay with us here forever, settle in our radiant city, where there is neither weeping nor infirmity, where there is sweetness everlasting, joy . . . eternal" ("Budi s nami zdes' voveki, vodvorisya v svetlom grade, gde ni placha, ni bolezni, gde zhe sladost' beskonechna, radost'. . .vechna"). The homophonic declamation of the operatic Old Believers does not resemble the monophonic declamation of the actual Old Believers, the *peniye* rooted in Byzantine tradition. Rather, it recalls the harmonized and accompanied versions of the chant that appeared in Russia in the eighteenth-century, and which Rimsky-Korsakov likely became familiar with through the collections edited by Alexey Lvov (1798–1870) and Nikolai Bakhmetev (1807–91). It is a symbolic reference to a forgotten tradition.

Asafyev, writing from a pseudo-Marxist perspective, makes only an oblique reference to the Old Believers in his article. In a footnote, he observes that the "continuously returning inflections of F major bring to mind an image of the choir of early Christianity, of rapture in the circle dance of our Pentecostal sects." This rapture, he explains, "is stylized; it is motionlessly, rather than emotionally, represented." [92] Asafyev intimates that the establishment of F major represents the cessation of the narrative unfolding of the action and the aforementioned shift to the rituals and customs of the Old Believers. As if to suggest that these rituals and customs are lodged in amber, wholly removed from quotidian reality, Rimsky-Korsakov relies on melodic and harmonic sequences and juxtaposed blocks of sound that neither suppose nor require development. In the final act, choral singing predominates over solo singing; the representation of ecumenical communion (the Old Believers' *sobornost'*) predominates over the representation of individual ecstasy (Fevroniya's *a-oo's*). The collusion of events that makes Greater Kitezh invisible—that enables the positive characters "to perceive the light wave in the sound wave" [93]—arrests the action. Spiritual elevation is expressed through a pastoral tonality that inaugurates and then culminates in a sacred miracle.

Rimsky-Korsakov had to work out a familiar operatic problem: the representation of the unrepresentable journey to heaven. He did this, it seems, by liberating parts of his score from the shackles of notation and the shackles of narrative. In act III, scene 1, the stage music loses its indexical markings: the Old Believers perceive the bell peals not as coming from a church, from a material source, but as radiating from the beyond. Their interpretation of the chiming affirms the Bergsonian notion that there is a reality that is external yet given directly to the mind. It also affirms Asafyev's theory that the perceived meaning of the tolling constantly changes, as if regulated by an indefinable force: "Contemplating in certain instances a single degree of the intensity of the affect, one nonetheless perceives a kind of difference *[raznost']* that is apprehended as if subtracted from the general given perception, removed from the composition as a whole—as if parts of the impression had remained behind the threshold of consciousness. Detached from the mass of impressions, this difference constitutes a strong feature of the noted affect."[94] This remark recalls several by Rimsky-Korsakov, who stressed the need for the tolling to develop on its own over the course of his work. He aimed (no doubt with reference to the Coronation Scene in the Prologue to *Boris Godunov*) at forging a distancing effect with the bells, allowing the decay of the chiming to resonate from the foreground to the background of the stage world, as though the echo was actually composed. To the faithful, the sound takes on objective significance, literally becoming a *Ding an sich*. Concerning the orchestral carillon between act IV, scenes 1 and 2, Rimsky-Korsakov informed his librettist,

> In the entr'acte I want to bring the bell sound to *forte;* this effect is necessary here at least once. The first time, soon after the departure of the Apparition [of Prince Vsevolod] and Fevroniya, the bell sound will come as if from the distance—in *piano*. The singing of the paradisiacal birds from behind the curtain will follow, and then the bell sound in *forte*. When the curtain rises, the *forte* will diminish. . . . The opera will conclude with a *piano tremolo* F major chord in the bells; it will be necessary to try this out beforehand with the bells of the Mariyinsky Theater.[95]

By having the bells beneath the stage play softly and the bells behind the curtain play loudly, the composer eroded the conceptual distinction between natural and supernatural, worldly and otherworldly sound.

These points amply show the extent to which the opera is marked by bells and bell-like sounds. It was typical of eighteenth- and nineteenth-century composers to employ only a small set of tuned bells in their operas, thus limiting the proliferation of overtones. However, the *Legend of Kitezh* calls for a large set of untuned bells, the high and low fundamental pitches being augmented by brass instruments. Audience members at the St. Petersburg premiere commented on the size and peculiarity of their casting. Gnesin, a pupil of Rimsky-Korsakov and fellow traveler of the Russian Symbolists in his early career, recalled that, during the performance, each clang of the Greater Kitezh bells brought to life a plurality of pitches. These "located themselves in the field of our aural perception" and "left only a faint trace in our consciousnesses." [96] To add acoustic breadth and depth to the stage world, Rimsky-Korsakov allowed the singers to explore the color and range of the play of the bells and the instrumentalists to augment the chiming with doubled octaves and tremolos. The incorporation of brass, string, and woodwind representations of bell sounds likewise creates a condition of resonance in the opera. Sensing the coloristic potential of the chiming, the composer transformed the orchestra into a prism of its acoustic ambiance.

The most striking instance of this procedure occurs after rehearsal number 155 of act III, scene 1, when Prince Yuriy sings the lament to misfortune "O, glory, vain wealth!" ("O, slava, bogatstvo suetnoye!") above a triplet pattern of reverberating tonic and dominant (g-d^1) fifths in the cellos and pizzicato harmonics in the basses. As in Fevroniya's act I aria, the accompaniment imitates the chiming of bells. Four measures after rehearsal number 157, following a modulation from G major to C minor, the accompaniment shifts to an oscillating minor third (e^1-g^1) and minor sixth (c^1-a♭^{1}) sextuplet pattern in the violins. Four measures later, after a modulation from C minor to D-flat major, the violas perform alternating triplet thirds (f^1-a♭^{1}) and (d♭^{1}-f^1). As these patterns unfold, both the Greater Kitezh fanfare motif and the ostinato bass motif derived from the "Good Friday Spell" sound. An abbreviated reprise of the lament is heard at rehearsal number 159; it concludes with the entrance of the page boy, who narrates the downfall of Lesser Kitezh, and the chorus, who fall prostrate in prayer. The descent of a golden mist over Greater Kitezh after the prayer marks an aurotic change in the music. The "Good Friday Spell" and Greater Kitezh fanfare motifs are combined and brought into focus as the real and represented bells respond to each other in a dramaturgical *mise-en-abîme*. At rehearsal number 181 the stage bells begin chiming by themselves, their ululations imitated by the harps and cellos. The sound is thereafter gradually displaced into the orchestra, this denoting the passing of cognitive perception into intuitive perception. The chiming, audible long after Greater Kitezh dissolves into the mist and the stage bells are quelled, loses connection to its point of origin—the Church of the Assumption and Orthodox faith. It traverses the boundary between two "semiospheres": "subjective reality" and the "objective reality" located "beyond its limits." [97]

Example 23.   Rehearsal number 181 of act III, scene 1 (the bells begin chiming by themselves) *(continues)*

For the positive characters, of course, the tintinnabulation stands for spiritual salvation, just as for the negative characters it stands for religious retribution. Grishka, unable to see Greater Kitezh on the shore of Lake Svetlïy Yar, hears the ringing in his head. To escape the incessant din, he runs to the water to drown himself but stops short when he sees the light of dawn and the reflection of the invisible city on the surface. The tolling becomes the sound of the Last Judgment. While Fevroniya and the Old Believers intuitively perceive the noumenal realm, Grishka and the Tatar-

Example 23. (continued)

Mongols cognitively perceive only its phenomenal trace. The punishment for their treachery is madness, the eternal eclipse of the sun.

Assessing these events abstractly, one could argue that Grishka, lacking spiritual humility, could never observe the light wave in the sound wave, the essence of natural acoustics. It was not possible for him to become familiar with what Gnesin called the steeple chimes' "aural rainbow," the "'prisms' of the sonic ray."[98] Central to the opera's climax is the concept that, just as hearing is but one of the five senses, cognitive perception is but one aspect of the totality of experience. Rimsky-Korsakov represents intuitive perception, the grouping of universal meaning, through the commingling of the senses. Light does not merely blend with sound: rather, light actually becomes sound as the limit of the visual spectrum (the limit of everyday awareness) is traversed.

In the opera as a whole, the tendency toward naturalness, beginning with the mimetic tracing of the forest murmurs, concludes with the bell ringing. This ringing is not "natural" sound, but it belongs to nature. Act I commences with an innocent portrayal of different aspects of forest life, the bear and the cuckoo, rustling leaves and gentle breezes, but gradually makes these sounds an integral element of the musical fabric, one element of the acoustic spectrum. Musical events of the type described above lose their semantic meaning: beyond the forest murmurs, the steeple chimes, and the prayers of the agitated populace, the listener perceives symbolic harmony. The score gradually, inexorably defines an altered landscape, a landscape beyond time and space. Vladimir Jankélévitch, referring both to the story "The Bell" (1872) by Hans Christian Andersen (1805–75) and to the *Legend of Kitezh*, expands this point:

> A bell rings mysteriously in the forest, and nobody knows where the church is, or the belfry, or where the marvelous ringing of this bell comes from. In truth it is the grand church of nature and poetry; it is the ever-present and ever-absent church that seems to hear the Hallelujah of the holy invisible bell. The country of dreams, the country that belongs to no one, the fatherland of nonexistent things, the mystic Jerusalem of the Requiem, the invisible and otherworldly city of Kitezh also denotes the dubious fatherland that is neither here nor there, but everywhere and nowhere. "Your soul is a chosen landscape. . . ." And just as the soul challenges cerebral locations and God challenges terrestrial locations, so too celestial Kitezh, the absent and ever-present Kitezh, near and far, that which is pure music in itself, is not represented on any map. The site of Utopia, like the φίλη πατρίς [fatherland] of the Neo-Platonists and the self-willed remoteness of the troubadours, defies all topography.[99]

By referring to the bells as "that which is pure music in itself," Jankélévitch unwittingly intimates that Rimsky-Korsakov created an opera that embraces the musical metaphysics of the "mystic" Symbolists. Irrespective of the composer's apparent anti-metaphysical sentiments, he accepted the Symbolist precept that music was the one art that accessed the inner being of the world, the secret of creation. There is thus a double irony to the score: on one hand, it is religious art by a declared atheist; on the other, it is Symbolist art by a declared anti-Symbolist. Rimsky-Korsakov anticipated that the *Legend of Kitezh* would be his ultimate rather than his penultimate stage work (it was succeeded by the Pushkin-based comic opera *The Golden Cockerel* [*Zolotoy petushok*, 1908]). Perhaps for this reason, he used it to make a remarkable statement about musical and spiritual doctrine. To paraphrase Jankélévitch, the opera proves that, in contrast to the days of old, "nobody speaks of music [anymore], and musicians less than others! In the same respect: nobody truly speaks about God, least of all theologians!"[100]

The depiction of the ascent to heaven in the *Legend of Kitezh* differs from that of *Khovanshchina* (the 1913 Stravinsky–Ravel version), in which, as Caryl Emerson suggests, it is military trumpets, rather than church bells, that lose their connection to their physical point of origin, Peter the Great's army, and that, for the Old Believers, come to represent the apocalyptic brass of the Book of Revelation. Upon hearing the fanfare, the Old Believer Marfa, a fictional figure in a historical opera, "sees wholly beyond reality; accordingly, the world of her remembered experience can now be recoded as a dream." The non-Christians, engaged in acts of corruption and violence, hear the brass as such. Confined to "Petrine time," they, like the audience in the theater are "walled out and left behind" as Marfa and the other Old Believers achieve spiritual salvation and entrance to the other world through self-immolation.[101] Thus, it does not matter whether we suspend our disbelief in the sacred event occurring on the stage because we do not share in it, as we are shut out of the other world. For all that we can access it, the miracle on stage could both be depicted and enacted, fiction and reality. Although we are also shut out of the marvel that occurs in the *Legend of Kitezh*, the lasting impact of the score is optimistic rather than pessimistic. Rimsky-Korsakov's overall message is that paradise emerges through extrasensory perception. His music adheres to the principles of Nietzsche's Apollo rather than those of Nietzsche's Dionysus; it opens mental but not physical portals to the beyond. His decision at the end of his career to set a centuries-old tale of spiritual salvation using the music of centuries-old composers attested to his fervent belief that art—especially musical art—was in and of itself a kind of miracle.

SYNAESTHESIA

Such an interpretation of the opera raises difficult questions. Do the F major interruptions, the iterated fanfare motif, the forest murmurs, and the bell patterns merely support the opera's musical narrative, in which the chromatic and "octatonic" threat posed by Grishka and the Tatar-Mongols is gradually eradicated? Or were Rimsky-Korsakov and Belsky attracted to the concept of synaesthesia, itself a form of syncretism? It has been documented that in 1907 Rimsky-Korsakov and Scriabin discussed the notion of "color hearing," the most common form of synaesthesia, and agreed that "E major" corresponded to "deep blue" while "G major" corresponded to "orange."[102] Rimsky-Korsakov did not, however, subscribe to Scriabin's belief that artistic induction into a synaesthetic frame of mind heightens awareness and sensitivity, transporting one into a dream state. The cross-referencing of one sense to another was an integral element of the conception of Scriabin's mature works but does not factor into the *Legend of Kitezh*. The "mystic" Symbolists attempted to create synaesthetic art, but Rimsky-Korsakov was as dismissive of them as of the "decadent" Symbolists and sought to dissuade his librettist from embracing their thinking. He sarcastically described Scriabin's *Poem of Ecstasy* (opus 54, 1907) as "forceful, but all the same it is a kind of musical $\sqrt{-1}$"[103]—a comment as much about the chimerical, synaesthetic elements of the score as about the instability of its structure (loose ternary form) and syntax (chains of suspended dominant ninths and elevenths).

Rimsky-Korsakov forbade the absence or removal of rules. This is borne out by the fact that in his later years he corrected, revised, and edited the operas of Musorgsky, Dargomïzhsky, and Borodin in order to rescue them from the oblivion to which their incorrect voice-leading had likely consigned them. Yet he could not control the multiple meanings that accrued to the *Legend of Kitezh* by virtue of its references to his own earlier works, to Wagner, and to stylized folklore and church chant. The overlaying of allusions in the opera itself suggests a peal of bells: though Rimsky-Korsakov imposed a symmetrical form on his score, its overall effect is of a joyful cacophony. He represents the passage into the other life, but he was primarily concerned with ennobling the voices not of the dead but of the living. His was a secular heaven. Like the "polyphonic" Dostoyevsky, Rimsky-

Korsakov felt that "death can be an act in this world" but that it does not represent the sealing off of the deceased person's consciousness from those that are left living. "Once death occurs, the word that had been embodied returns to the pool of ideas out of which our selves are born. The Kingdom of God is located not within you but among you."[104] Rimsky-Korsakov's concern with the living may help explain why the opera slows down in the postmortem scenes, why to some critics the music becomes more repetitive and less engaging. Act IV is nevertheless a profound statement of faith. Like the "monologic" Tolstoy, Rimsky-Korsakov illustrates that death "closes down and harmonizes the narrative" of life. In this regard, it "accomplishes something; the dying process is bathed in external and internal light."[105]

It would appear that, through the proliferation of quotations, the resurrection and elevation to heaven of the output of deceased composers, Rimsky-Korsakov succeeded in extending creativity into religion, realizing Belïy's theurgic vision. Besides the finished manuscripts, he left behind 114 pages of alternate versions of the most crucial musical passages. They involve variations in orchestration, different harmonizations, adjustments of tempo, and reassignment of instrumental and vocal solos. He wrote "see the [orchestral] arrangement" on several pages of his copy of the printed piano-vocal score, but did not make any alterations to the indicated passages. In his copy of the printed orchestral score, he crossed out a number of measures and phrases and inscribed the word "begone" ("vïyede") above them.[106] Rimsky-Korsakov evidently wavered in his thinking about these excerpts. By far the most intriguing variant concerns the finale of act IV, scene 2. In the original version of the orchestral score (dated 29 January 1905), the "doors of the [Kitezh] cathedral part to reveal indescribable light" as the curtain slowly descends and the strings approach the tonic F major chord. However, in the revised version (dated 27 September 1906), the chord is altogether removed from the string part. The sound is subsumed into light. Rimsky-Korsakov, in representing an unrepresentable ideal, suggests that music, as a "form of art," is only an ephemeral stop on the pathway to an impossible absolute: transcendent drama. The various versions of the score, like the borrowed materials in the score, relate to one another as do overtones to a fundamental. To the faithful, this fundamental tone is the work underlying the work, the reality underlying reality.

In a 1913 monograph, Sergey Durïlin declared that the *Legend of Kitezh* was "internally necessary" for Rimsky-Korsakov, as it resolutely confirmed his pantheistic, rather than atheistic, worldview.[107] The church bells do not chime in Wagner's invisible orchestra but in the Old Believers' invisible city. Likewise addressing the personal significance of the opera to the composer, his friend Ivan Lapshin, a professor at the St. Petersburg Conservatory and liberal nationalist, observed, "there is always religious pathos in Rimsky's art—in the guise of a rapturous relationship to the world as a whole, in the guise of a reverence for the 'eternal feminine'. . . . But he employed Christian religious elements only occasionally, for the sake of color, not from a demand of the heart." Nonetheless, Lapshin adds that, in the composer's late works, there began "to appear the symptoms of the last great period of any creative life." He refers to the *Legend of Kitezh* as "religious art" that "flows from the individual, independent of a [scriptural] source."[108] Marina Rakhmanova clarifies that "this new quality is naturally connected in the perception of listeners with the Christian traits of the musical realization of the Kitezh legend." Beyond expressing personal faith, the opera, in her opinion, constituted a watershed in Russian culture. "The pantheism that Rimsky-Korsakov glorified in his prior operas as an integral folk world view had for a long time been part of the past," she writes. "However, thousands of pilgrims continued to go to the 'invisible city' on Lake Svetlïy Yar in the years when the opera was composed. The legend about the 'city of the devout' lived in the people and attracted the attention of the intelligentsia."[109] The phrase "lived in the people" is too close for comfort to the clichés of Soviet rhetoric, but Rakhmanova correctly intimates that the score's sacred content mirrored that of other apocalyptic works by the Symbolists. In the final act, he represented that which they sought achieved: "the birth of a new world—an invisible, universal cathedral—through a physical and spiritual feat."[110]

For this reason, the opera (and its source texts) captured the imagination of the Symbolists, despite Rimsky-Korsakov's resistance to their causes. (Thus, as in the case of Chaikovsky, it would appear that the only way to create a Symbolist opera is by accident. A Symbolist opera cannot be designed; it can only arise by default out of its reception.) The influence of the *Legend of Kitezh* extended beyond the Silver Age. Following its premiere, it came to embody the hopes of the Revolution. Mstislav Dobuzhinsky's 1906 painting *Conciliation (Umirotvoreniye)* portrays the Moscow Kremlin rising out of the waters, crowned by a rainbow. After 1918, some erstwhile Symbolists associated the Bolshevik establishment with Lesser Kitezh and the religious-philosophical opposition (the Brotherhood of the Radiant City, Knights of the Radiant City, and Northern-Caucasian United States) with Greater Kitezh. The post-Soviet revival of the opera, finally, emblematized the revival of Orthodox religion in Russia: the steeple of St. Basil's Basilica, like that of the fabled *grad*, rose out of the deep. Rimsky-Korsakov

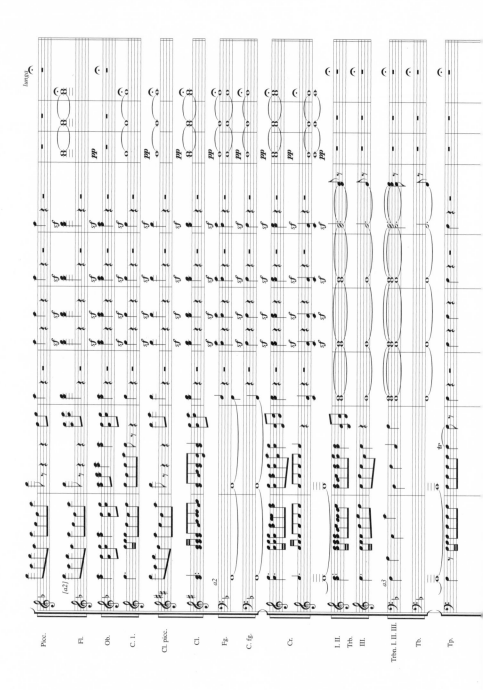

Example 24.   The conclusion of the original version of the orchestral score (dated 29 January 1905)

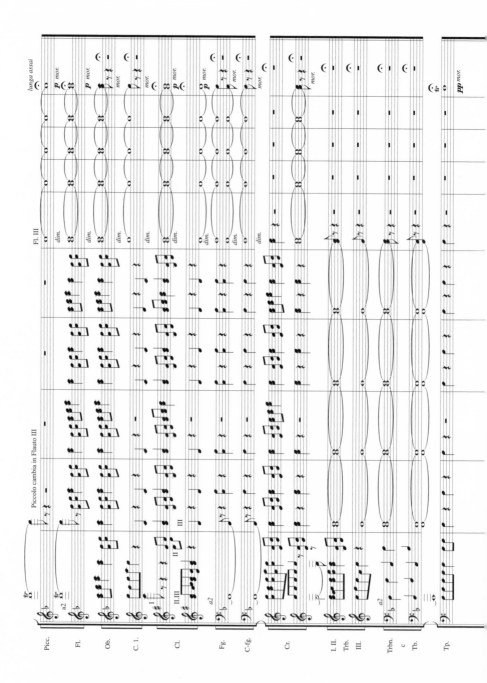

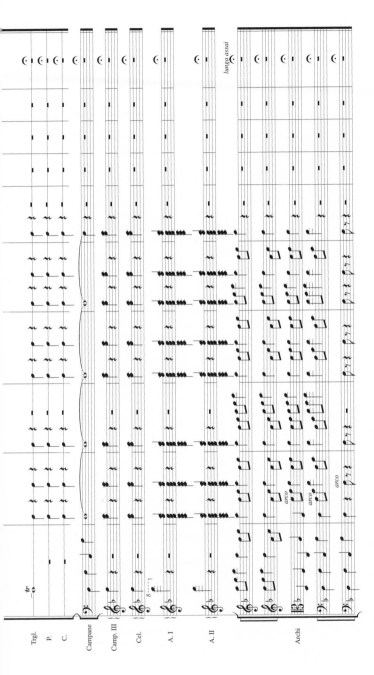

Example 25. The conclusion of the revised version (dated 27 September 1906)

created an opera that, long after his death, symbolized his nation's spiritual rebirth.

NOTES

1. Andrey Belïy, "Formï iskusstva," in *Simvolizm kak miroponimaniye,* ed. L. A. Sugay (Moscow: Respublika, 1994), 93.
2. Ibid. On the same page, Belïy supplements this obscure definition of artistic experience by plumping for the idealist philosophers. "Expressed in Kantian terms," he writes, "each art, arising in the phenomenal, becomes absorbed in the 'noumenal'; or, formulating our concept in Schopenhauer's language, each art leads us to a pure contemplation of the world will; or, speaking in the spirit of Nietzsche, each form of art is defined to the extent that it incarnates the *spirit of music;* or, according to [the British evolutionary scientist Herbert] Spencer [1820–1903], each art aspires to the future." Belïy repeats this formulation on page 101.
3. Ibid., 100.
4. Ibid., 101. The quoted line does not actually appear in the Book of Revelation.
5. Letter of 3 January 1903, in *Aleksandr Blok i Andrey Belïy: Perepiska,* ed. V. N. Orlov (Moscow: Izd. gos. literaturnogo muzeya, 1940), 3. My translation is a slightly expanded version of that offered in Bartlett, *Wagner and Russia,* 151.
6. See the entry for this date in V[asiliy] V[asil'yevich] Yastrebtsev, *Nikolay Andreyevich Rimskiy-Korsakov: Vospominaniya, 1886–1908,* ed. A. V. Ossovskiy, 2 vols. (Leningrad: Gosudarstvennoye muzïkal'noye izdatel'stvo, 1959–60), 2: 10.
7. Nikon, the patriarch from 1652 to 1658, sought to correct the problem of corruptions and errors in the liturgical books. His remedy was to move Russian liturgical practices into exact compliance with contemporary Greek liturgical practices. Nikon was deposed for his opposition to Tsar Alexis, but the Great Council of the Orthodox Church enacted his reforms in 1667. Peter the Great (reigned 1682–1725), the son of Tsar Alexis, subsequently turned away from the Byzantine heritage and reformed the Russian state on the model of Protestant Europe. The Patriarchate was abolished in favor of the Holy Synod, and the capital of the state was moved from Moscow to the newly built city of St. Petersburg.
8. For a much more detailed description of the variants, see Elena B'yashi Motasova, "Drevnerusskaya legenda o nevidimom grade Kitezhe (istoriya, uspekh, bibliografiya)," *Slavica Tergestina* 2 (1994): 161–96.
9. The term *sobornost'* combines the noun *sobor* (council) and the verb *sobirat'* (to unite, or to convene). Before its Symbolist appropriation, it was used by the Slavophile philosopher Alexey Khomyakov (1804–60) to describe qualities of spiritual fellowship and collective faith in the religious practices of pre-Petrine Russians—the Old Believers. For further information, see Andrzej Walicki, *A History of Russian Thought from the Enlightenment to Marxism,* trans. Hilda Andrews-Rusiecka (Stanford: Stanford University Press, 1979), 92–99.
10. The groups are identified by Aleksandr Aseyev, "Okkul'tnoye dvizheniye v Sovetskoy Rossii," *Okkul'tism i ioga* 3 (1934): 90–91; and Anna Kamenskaya, "Russia and Russian Theosophy," *The Theosophist* (Adyar) (November 1931): 204. See also Maria Carlson, *"No Religion Higher than the Truth": A History of the Theosophical Movement in Russia, 1875–1922* (Princeton: Princeton University Press, 1993), 242–43 n. 18.
11. Dorothea Redepenning, *Geschichte der russischen und der sowjetischen Musik,* 2 vols. (Laaber: Laaber, 1994), 1: 372–78; Richard Taruskin, "Legend of the Invisible City of Kitezh and the Maiden Fevroniya, The," in *The New Grove*

Dictionary of Opera, 2: 1124–26. To illustrate the borrowing technique, Taruskin refers to the vocal declamation of Grishka Kuterma, the villain who betrays Greater Kitezh to the Tatar-Mongols, which bears features of the vocal declamation of the Pretender in Modest Musorgsky's *Boris Godunov* (1869/72). The use of irregular meters in the folk choruses similarly recalls Glinka's *A Life for the Tsar* (*Zhizn' za tsarya,* 1836) as well as Alexander Borodin's unfinished *Prince Igor* (*Knyaz' Igor'*). Taruskin also identifies allusions in the *Legend of Kitezh* to Rimsky-Korsakov's own operas: the chromatic harmonies and alternating tone-semitone ("octatonic") scales used in the act III interlude, for example, have their origins in *Sadko* (1897) and *Kashchey the Deathless* (*Kashchey bessmertnïy,* 1902), while the act IV, scene 2 transfiguration replays (in aptly transfigured form) the ending of *The Snow Maiden* (*Snegoruchka,* 1881/98).

12. Bartlett, *Wagner and Russia,* 3.

13. Taruskin, "Legend of the Invisible City of Kitezh and the Maiden Fevroniya, The," 1125.

14. A[bram] A[kimovich] Gozenpud, "Iz nablyudeniy nad tvorcheskim pro-tsessom Rimskogo-Korsakova," in *Muzïkal'noye nasledstvo: Rimskiy-Korsakov,* ed. D[mitriy] B[orisovich] Kabalevskiy et al., 2 vols. (Moscow: Izdatel'stvo Akademii nauk SSSR, 1953–54), 1: 247.

15. Kadja Grönke, "A Deliberately Contradictory Work," in Nicolai Rimsky-Korsakov, *The Legend of the Invisible City of Kitezh and the Maiden Fevroniya,* Kirov Chorus and Orchestra, Valery Gergiev, Philips CD 462–225–2, 10.

16. Aleksey Parin, *Khozhdeniye v nevidimïy grad: Paradigmï russkoy klas-sicheskoy operï* (Moscow: Agraf, 1999), 301–2.

17. Russian National Library (Rossiyskaya natsional'naya biblioteka, henceforth RNB), manuscript division, fund 61, list 1, item 9.

18. Ibid. Rimsky-Korsakov dramatized the Kupala ritual in his 1891 opera-ballet *Mlada.*

19. Yastrebtsev, *Nikolay Andreyevich Rimskiy-Korsakov: Vospominaniya, 1886–1908,* 2: 129.

20. Ibid., 2: 271. Solovyov's dispute with Rozanov began in January 1894 with the publication of Rozanov's essay on ethics, "Freedom and Faith" ("Svoboda i vera"), in *The Russian Herald (Russkiy vestnik),* and the publication of Solovyov's response, "Porfiriy Golovlev on Freedom and Faith (With reference to V. Rozanov's article 'Freedom and Faith')" ("Porfiriy Golovlev o svobode i vere [Po povodu stat'i V. Rozanova 'Svoboda i vera']"), in *The European Herald (Vestnik Yevropï).* It lasted until 1899, when the two writers traded barbs about the Pushkin centenary issue of *The World of Art,* whose content so infuriated Solovyov that he disassociated himself from the journal. Solovyov's reply was published as a "Letter to the Editor" ("Pis'mo v redaktsiyu") in January 1899 in *The European Herald.* At issue in the conflict was less Rozanov's heated rhetoric—although Yastrebtsev reports that Rozanov called Pushkin "empty, obscene, and no longer able to speak for recent generations" (*Nikolay Andreyevich Rimskiy-Korsakov: Vospominaniya, 1886–1908,* 2: 558)—than his spiritual views.

21. Ibid., 2: 340.

22. Pyman, *A History of Russian Symbolism,* 228.

23. The proceedings of the meetings of the Religious-Philosophical Society, initiated by Hippius and occurring between 1901 and 1903, were published as supplements to issues 9–12 (1903) of *New Path.*

24. Solovyov outlines this hypothesis in "Rossiya i vselenskaya tserkov,'" 1889, in *O khristianskom yedinstve* (Moscow: Rudomino, 1994), 181–266.

25. The "decadent" Symbolists chided Solovyov for his belief in spiritual eman-

cipation, particularly his notion, taken from Nietzsche, of *Godmanhood* (*Bogoche-lovechestvo*). Pyman notes that Rozanov, "the Russian Nietzsche," was "out to wrest a blessing for domestic life and procreation" and therefore "could not or would not understand the church's emphasis on the need to overcome the world" (*A History of Russian Symbolism*, 135).

26. Solov'yov, "Obshchiy smïsl iskusstva," in *Sochineniya*, ed. A. V. Gulïga and A. F. Losev, 2 vols. (Moscow: Mïsl', 1990), 2: 392–93.

27. Ibid., 2: 396.

28. Pyman adds, "The Valentinian Gnostics wove a whole mythology about Sophia the Aeon (eternal being) who, for love and pity for the world, became entrapped in matter (where She is known as 'the World Soul') and who yearns to be set free" (*A History of Russian Symbolism*, 229).

29. On the preceding points, see Dimitri Strémooukhoff, *Vladimir Soloviev and His Messianic Work*, trans. Elizabeth Meyendorff (Belmont: Nordland, 1980), 324–34.

30. Pyman, *A History of Russian Symbolism*, 205–6.

31. V[asiliy] P[etrovich] Shkafer, *Sorok let na stsene russkoy operï: vospomi-naniya, 1890–1930 gg.* (Leningrad: Izd. teatra operï i baleta im. S. M. Kirova, 1936), 200.

32. A[ndrey] N[ikolayevich] Rimskiy-Korsakov, *N. A. Rimskiy-Korsakov: zhizn' i tvorchestvo*, 5 vols. (Leningrad: Muzgiz, 1933–46), 5: 74.

33. Yastrebtsev, *Nikolay Andreyevich Rimskiy-Korsakov: Vospominaniya, 1886–1908*, 2: 280.

34. Quoted in Rimskiy-Korsakov, *N. A. Rimskiy-Korsakov: zhizn' i tvorchestvo*, 5: 75.

35. See R. P. Dmitriyeva, *Povest' o Petre i Fevronii* (Leningrad: Nauka, Leningradskoye otdeleniye, 1979), 4.

36. Priscilla Hunt, "The *Tale of Peter and Fevroniia*: The Text and the Icon," *Elementa* 3:4 (1997): 294.

37. *Medieval Russia's Epics, Chronicles, and Tales*, ed. and trans. Serge A. Zenkovsky (New York: Dutton, 1974), 290.

38. RNB, manuscript division, fund 61, list 1, item 8.

39. Ibid. Prutkov was the creation of Alexey Tolstoy (1883–1945) and three brothers, all poets, from the Zhemchuzhnikov family. "His" sayings and verses satirized the tedium and inanities of nineteenth-century Russian life. Many of them became catch phrases.

40. Rimskiy-Korsakov, *N. A. Rimskiy-Korsakov: zhizn' i tvorchestvo*, 5: 78.

41. Quoted in ibid., 5: 76.

42. Letter of 11 May 1904, in V. Simkin, ed., "'. . . Postroyka goroda Kitezha': iz perepiski N. A. Rimskogo-Korsakova s V. I. Bel'skim," *Sovetskaya muzïka* 3 (March 1976): 105.

43. RNB, manuscript division, fund 640, list 1, item 515. The original and revised versions of this passage are quoted in altered form in Rimsky-Korsakov, *N. A. Rimskiy-Korsakov: zhizn' i tvorchestvo*, 5: 76 and 78.

44. Gozenpud, *Russkiy opernïy teatr mezhdu dvukh revolyutsii, 1905–1917* (Leningrad: Muzïka, 1975), 161.

45. RNB, manuscript division, fund 640, list 1, item 515.

46. *Drevniye rossiyskiye stikhotvoreniya: sobrannïye Kirsheyu Danilovïm* (1955), as quoted in Gozenpud, *Russkiy opernïy teatr mezhdu dvukh revolyu-tsii, 1905–1917*, 162. Danilov also collected and edited a different version of the tale, the epic song "Grishka the Unfrocked Monk" ("Grishka rasstriga"); it is

included in the second supplemental edition of *Drevniye rossiyskiye stikhotvo-reniya* (Moscow: Nauka, 1977), 256. This second version is relevant because it in-spired Mel'nikov-Pechersky's "Grisha" (1860), the short story at the heart of the novel *In the Forests*, one of the source texts of the *Legend of Kitezh*. "Grisha" tells the story of an orphaned boy who is taken into the care of an Old Believer family. He earns his keep tending to the needs of visitors to the Trans-Volga re-gion. He eventually falls under the sway of the village elder, who enjoins him to give away the family's wealth, which, according to the elder, is a source of evil. The elder turns out to be entirely self-serving, however, and leads Grisha to self-destruction.

47. Lyubov' Serebryakova, "*Kitezh*: Otkroveniye 'Otkroveniya,'" *Muzïkal'-naya akademiya* 2 (1994): 90.

48. Ibid., 94.

49. Ibid., 104–5.

50. RNB, manuscript division, fund 640, list 1, item 856.

51. Ibid., item 9.

52. Simkin, ed., "'. . . Postroyka goroda Kitezha': iz perepiski N. A. Rimskogo-Korsakova s V. I. Bel'skim," 111.

53. On this point, see Thomas H. Hoisington, "Mel'nikov-Pechersky: Ro-mancer of Provincial and Old Believer Life," *Slavic Review* 33 (1974): 691. Addi-tional information in this paragraph is taken from pages 679–94.

54. Pavel Mel'nikov-Pecherskiy, *V lesakh*, ed. and introd. I. S. Yezhova, 2 vols. (Moscow: Gosudarstvennoye izdatel'stvo khudozhestvennoy literaturï, 1955), 2: 247.

55. Ibid., 2: 54–55.

56. V[ladimir] G[alaktionovich] Korolenko, "V pustïnnïkh mestakh," in *So-braniye sochineniy*, ed. S. V. Korolenko, 10 vols. (Moscow: Gosudarstvennoye izdatel'stvo khudozhestvennoy literaturï, 1953–56), 3: 131.

57. Z[inaída] N[ikolayevna] Gippius, "Svetloye ozero: dnevnik," in *Alïy mech: razskazï (4-aya kniga)* (St. Petersburg: Izdaniye M. V. Pirozhkova, 1906), 379–80.

58. Letter of 29 April 1904, in Simkin, ed., "'. . . Postroyka goroda Kitezha': iz perepiski N. A. Rimskogo-Korsakova s V. I. Bel'skim," 112. Simkin, in his annota-tion to this letter, assures his Soviet readers that "light mockery can be sensed in [Rimsky-Korsakov's] use of the term 'liturgical opera.'"

59. Yevgeny Petrovskiy, "Skazaniye o nevidimom grade Kitezhe i deve Fevro-nii," *Russkaya muzïkal'naya gazeta* 7 (1907): 197. Published between 1894 and 1918, *Russkaya muzïkal'naya gazeta* served as a vehicle for the promotion of Wag-ner's music dramas.

60. Petrovskiy, "Skazaniye o nevidimom grade Kitezhe i deve Fevronii," *Rus-skaya muzïkal'naya gazeta* 8 (1907): 241.

61. Of *Tristan und Isolde*, Petrovsky wrote: "In *Tristan* the creator inseparably merges with his creation. . . . The heroes and the sounds belong to each other, but at the same time they represent the personal, painful experience of their author. . . . To separate the subjective and the objective is impossible, this being the funda-mental character of a work of mysticism" ("Skazaniye o nevidimom grade Kitezhe i deve Fevronii," *Russkaya muzïkal'naya gazeta* 11 [1907]: 306).

62. Vyacheslav Karatïgin, "Peterburgskaya muzïkal'naya khronika," *Zolotoye runo* 3 (1907): 77. The quoted words are from the opera's libretto.

63. Ibid.

64. Ibid., 78.

65. Yastrebtsev notes that on 1 May 1904, he and Rimsky-Korsakov "conversed about V. Belsky's talent and about how the character of *Kitezh* is mystical and even

rather optimistic. To this Nikolai Andreyevich jokingly replied: 'More accurately, the opera is mystical overall'" (*Nikolay Andreyevich Rimskiy-Korsakov: Vospominaniya, 1886–1908,* 2: 308).

66. This last point recurs in other reviews of the St. Petersburg and Moscow premieres of the *Legend of Kitezh.* These include: N[ikolay] Kashkin, "*Skazaniye o grade Kitezhe,*" *Russkoye slovo* (17 February 1908); V. Kolomiytsov, "*Skazaniye N. A. Rimskogo-Korsakova,*" *Rus'* 40 (9 February 1907), 42 (11 February 1907), and 43 (12 February 1907); Mizgir', "Novaya opera—*Skazaniye o nevidimom grade Kitezhe i deve Fevronii,*" *Golos Moskvï* 40 (17 February 1908); and Y[uliy] E[ngel'], "*Skazaniye o nevidimom grade Kitezhe i deve Fevronii,*" *Russkiye vedomosti* 52 (2 March 1908).

67. Quoted by Marina Rakhmanova, "K bïloy polemike vokrug *Kitezha,*" *Sovetskaya muzika* 10 (October 1984): 82.

68. Letter of 5 August 1903, RNB, manuscript division, fund 61, list 1, item 8.

69. Letter of 8 August 1903, RNB, manuscript division, fund 640, list 1, item 856.

70. Indeed, just after embarking on the score, Rimsky-Korsakov began attending rehearsals for a staging of *Siegfried* at the Mariyinsky Theater and reacquainted himself with other Wagner scores. On 22 December 1901, he informed Belsky: "Tomorrow (Sunday) at 12 I'll be at the rehearsal of *Siegfried,* after which, between 3 and 4, I'll drop by to see you" (RNB, manuscript division, fund 61, list 1, item 8). Yastrebtsev adds that on 5 February 1902, Rimsky-Korsakov declared an intention to "acquire the scores of *Walküre, Siegfried,* and *Tristan*" (*Nikolay Andreyevich Rimskiy-Korsakov: Vospominaniya, 1886–1908,* 2: 233).

71. Letter of 6 January 1903, in *Aleksandr Blok i Andrey Belïy: Perepiska,* 9. For the broader context of Belïy's statement, see Bartlett, *Wagner and Russia,* 150–52.

72. Grönka, "A Deliberately Contradictory Work," 12.

73. Gozenpud, "Iz nablyudeniy nad tvorcheskim protsessom Rimskogo-Korsakova," 189.

74. The sketchbooks are housed at RNB, manuscript division, fund 640, list 1, items 457 (the remark "Solovyov bibliography" appears on page 96), 458, and 459. The sketches of the passages in question closely resemble their final versions, which is somewhat surprising given the opera's lengthy gestation and the existence of 114 pages of corrections and emendations to the piano-vocal and orchestral scores.

75. K. Korablyova, "Rol' drevnerusskoy pesennosti v opere N. Rimskogo-Korsakova 'Skazaniye o nevidimom grade Kitezhe i deve Fevronii,'" in *Iz istorii russkoy i sovetskoy muzïki,* ed. M. Pekelis and I. Givental (Moscow: Muzïka, 1978), 76.

76. This is not the place to present an analysis of the *znamenniy* chant corpus, but certain points are worth noting. The history of the corpus is usually divided into three periods: the pre Tatar-Mongol period, which dates from 988 to the mid-thirteenth century, the Tatar-Mongol period, which extends from the mid-thirteenth to the mid-fifteenth centuries, and the late period, which extends from the mid-fifteenth century to the reforms inaugurated by Patriarch Nikon. There are approximately twenty-five extant manuscripts from the pre–Tatar-Mongol period; these witness the departure of the Russian liturgical tradition from its Byzantine origins. The Byzantine notation used in the manuscripts is known as *kondakarian* notation and consists of written symbols above the syllables of the text that indicate (as far as can be determined) musical pitch and duration. The Tatar-Mongol period left behind few manuscripts but witnessed the development of *znammenïy* chant into a distinctive genre with a distinctive notation. The scale used in the chant

consisted of twelve pitches that spanned a minor tenth. Each three-pitch segment of the scale was referred to as an accord, or *soglasiye*, and was aligned with specific vocal timbres: low, somber, bright, and thrice-bright. The principal problem with *znamennïy* chant notation of the period was that it indicated accords but did not indicate which of the three pitches in the accords were to be sung. The problem was alleviated somewhat in the late sixteenth century, when a system of auxiliary red letters began to be included with the *znamennïy* chant notation in the liturgical books. The system was replaced in the early seventeenth century by the square notation found in the official edition of the chant published by the Holy Synod. This edition, if any, would have been Rimsky-Korsakov's source for his "liturgical" opera. On these points, see I[rina] E. Lozovaya, "Tserkovno-pevcheskoye iskusstvo," in *Khudozhestvenno-esteticheskaya kul'tura drevney Rusi: XI–XVII veka*, ed. V. V. Bïchkov (Moscow: Ladomir, 1996), 267–99.

77. Korablyova, "Rol' drevnerusskoy pesennosti v opere N. Rimskogo-Korsakova 'Skazaniye o nevidimom grade Kitezhe i deve Fevronii,'" 79.

78. Ibid., 78. Without citing Korablyova, Rakhmanova expands this point as follows: "The new quality of the *Kitezh* dramaturgy, determined by its plot subject and sources—ancient Russian legends—is not only the epic slowness of the action as a whole, the statue-like and oratorio-like series of scenes (though these aspects of the epic genre have a place in opera), but the lingering or, more precisely, *contemplative* quality of the dramaturgy, the conveying of 'action' in the preferred manner of ancient Russian literature: as a written and oral form of dialogue-interviews (the conversations of Fevroniya with Princeling Vsevolod and Grishka Kuterma, the question-answer structure in various episodes of the scenes in Greater and Lesser Kitezh, in the finale and so on), or in forms of a ritual character" (*Nikolay Andreyevich Rimskiy-Korsakov* [Moscow: RAM im. Gnesinïkh, 1995], 225).

79. Ibid., 80.

80. Ibid., 81–82.

81. Yastrebtsev, *Nikolay Andreyevich Rimskiy-Korsakov: Vospominaniya, 1886–1908*, 2: 424.

82. On this point, Marina Frolova-Walker reports, "The musical structure of [*Ruslan and Lyudmila*] fully corresponds to the cyclical time-structure of an epic: a static form whose end is in its beginning is to be found at the level of a single number, of an act, and indeed of the whole opera. *Ruslan* is, in other words, what we might call a 'late,' or self-conscious epic: the composer reflected on what he was doing" ("On *Ruslan* and Russianness," *Cambridge Opera Journal* 9:1 [1997]: 38).

83. This fact enabled Soviet scholars to classify the *Legend of Kitezh* as a nationalist opera exhibiting *kuchkist* aesthetic principles. Two vastly different essays in this spirit are Igor Glebov's [Boris Asaf'yev's] "Skazaniye o nevidimom grade," *Yezhenedel'nik petrogradskikh gosudarstvennïkh akademicheskikh teatrov*, 14 April 1921, 3–16, and Rakhmanova's "K bïloy polemike vokrug *Kitezha*," 82–90.

84. Korablyova, "Rol' drevnerusskoy pesennosti v opere N. Rimskogo-Korsakova 'Skazaniye o nevidimom grade Kitezhe i deve Fevronii,'" 92 n. 26.

85. Ibid., 91 n. 23. The author also suggests that "in its majestic, mournful character, [the psaltery player's song] recalls the spiritual verse 'The Last Judgement' ['Strashnïy sud']."

86. The same observation could be made about Rimsky-Korsakov's depiction of the Varangian, Indian, and Venetian traders in scene 4 of his opera *Sadko*, except

182 / Russian Opera and the Symbolist Movement

that these outsiders are not invaders but guests of the nation. Whereas the orientalism of the *Legend of Kitezh* is cynical, that in *Sadko* is nostalgic.

87. Motasova, "Drevnerusskaya legenda o nevidimom grade Kitezhe (istoriya, uspekh, bibliografiya)," 166 n. 9.

88. Boris Asaf'yev, "Yeshcho o 'Kitezhe,'" in *Ob opere: Izbrannïye stat'i*, ed. L. Pavlova-Arbenina, 2nd ed. (Leningrad: Muzïka, 1976), 195.

89. Ibid.

90. Musorgsky left behind only a piano-vocal version of the opera, the individual scenes drafted between 1873 and 1880. Some scenes were orchestrated and performed during his lifetime, but the finale was only sketched. For an overview of the compositional process and editions of the score completed by Rimsky-Korsakov, Stravinsky, and Shostakovich, see Caryl Emerson, "Musorgsky's Libretti on Historical Themes: From the two *Borises* to *Khovanshchina*," in *Reading Opera*, ed. Arthur Gross and Roger Parker (Princeton: Princeton University Press, 1988), 240–45, 265–66.

91. Of course, the complete separation of research into the chant from ecclesiastical concerns occurred in the Soviet era. See, for example, N[ikolay] F[yodorovich] Findeyzen, *Ocherki po istorii muzïki v Rossii s drevneyshikh vremen do kontsa XVIII veka*, 2 vols. (Moscow: Muzsektor, 1928–29). For an assessment of chant scholarship in Rimsky-Korsakov's lifetime, see Nicolas Schidlovsky, "Sources of Russian Chant Theory," in *Russian Theoretical Thought in Music*, ed. Gordon D. McQuere (Ann Arbor: UMI Research Press, 1983), 83–108, esp. 93–98.

92. Asaf'yev, "Yeshcho o 'Kitezhe,'" 195.

93. Ibid., 194.

94. Ibid., 192.

95. Letter to Belsky dated 16 August 1903, RNB, manuscript division, fund 61, list 1, item 8.

96. Mikhaíl Gnesin, "Tserkovnïy zvon i muzïkal'noye tvorchestvo v Rossii," *Luchi solntsa* 1–2 (February 1919): 40.

97. Yuriy Lotman, *Kul'tura i vzrïv* (Moscow: Progress, 1992), 9. Lotman uses these terms, which recall the Kantian binary of the phenomenal and noumenal, to demarcate the semiosphere belonging to language and the semiosphere residing beyond its borders.

98. Gnesin, "Tserkovnïy zvon i muzïkal'noye tvorchestvo v Rossii," 42.

99. Jankélévitch, *La musique et l'ineffable*, 130. Jankélévitch does not identify the source of the quoted words.

100. Ibid., 129.

101. Emerson, "Apocalypse Then, Now, and (for Us) Never: Reflections on Musorgsky's Other Historical Opera," in *Khovanshchina: The Khovansky Affair*, ed. Jennifer Batchelor and Nicholas John (New York: Riverrun Press, 1994), 19–20.

102. On this subject, see A[ndrey] I. Bandura, "A. N. Skryabin i N. A. Rimskiy-Korsakov: Muzïkal'naya fantastika russkikh misteriy," in *A. N. Skryabin: Chelovek, khudozhnik. mïslitel'*, 129.

103. Yastrebtsev, *Nikolay Andreyevich Rimskiy-Korsakov: Vospominaniya, 1886–1908*, 2: 424.

104. Emerson, "The Tolstoy Connection in Bakhtin," in *Rethinking Bakhtin: Extensions and Challenges*, ed. Gary Saul Morson and Caryl Emerson (Evanston: Northwestern University Press, 1989), 168.

105. Ibid., 162.

106. See the foreword to *Notes and Additions*, volume 3 of Nicolai Rimsky-Korsakov, *The Legend of the Invisible City of Kitezh and the Maiden Fevronia: Conductor's Score* (Melville, N.Y.: Belwin Mills, 1981), xii. The volume is an English

translation of volume 14B of Rimskiy-Korsakov, *Polnoye sobraniye sochineniy,* ed. A[ndrey] N[ikolayevich] Rimskiy-Korsakov et al. (Moscow: Muzgiz, 1949).

107. Sergey Durïlin, *Rikhard Vagner i Rossiya* (Moscow: Musaget, 1913), 61.

108. Undated letter to Ekaterina Lebedeva, quoted in Rimskiy-Korsakov, *N. A. Rimskiy-Korsakov: zhizn' i tvorchestvo,* 4: 32.

109. Rakhmanova, *Nikolay Andreyevich Rimskiy-Korsakov,* 223–24.

110. Bandura, "A. N. Skryabin i N. A. Rimskiy-Korsakov: Muzïkal'naya fantastika russkikh misteriy," 129.

Chapter 3 Scriabin and Theurgy

Valeriy Bryusov, the virtual founder of the Russian Symbolist movement, made this hierophantic pronouncement in his 1905 essay "The Holy Sacrifice" ("Svyashchennaya zhertva"):

> We demand of the poet that he should constantly offer up his "holy sacrifices," not only in his verses but in every hour of his life, every feeling: in his love, in his hatred, in his achievements, and in his failings. Let the poet create not his books, but his life. Let him keep the altar flame unquenched like the Vestal fire, let him make it burn like a mighty bonfire having no fear that his own life will be consumed within it. On the altar of our divinity we fling—ourselves. Only a magus's knife, even as it cuts open the chest, gives one the right to be called a poet.[1]

The statement's quasi-religious imagery captures the spirit of the Symbolist quest to free art from utilitarian aims and to fuse art and life. Its title comes from the second line of the 1827 poem "Poet" by Pushkin, in which Pushkin decried the "ordinariness" of the poet's life when he is not called upon to make "holy sacrifices" to Apollo. The quotation lent the authority of Russia's most beloved poet to Bryusov's assertion that the Symbolists should become the subjects of their creative works and should actually live them out.

Too conservative to pursue such ideas himself, Bryusov left them to the Russian "mystic" Symbolists—the faction that called for *collective creation,* the collaborative attempt to create a bridge between artistic form and events in the real world. Those with philological inclinations immersed themselves in studies of ancient Slavonic culture, pagan rites, and the dead languages; those of a more daring turn of mind experimented with narcotics, attended séances, and took to bizarre games of make-believe. To this latter group belonged a single composer, Alexander Scriabin, who took the precepts of Symbolism to an extreme and, in the opinion of his poet friends, became a prophet and a martyr to the cause.

Scriabin's involvement with the "mystic" Symbolists manifested itself in his *Mysterium (Misteriya)*, or *Mystery Play*, which he had conceived as a Wagnerian opera but which gradually came to encompass all of the "mystic" Symbolists' philosophical and religious obsessions: the Scriptures, the philosophies of Nietzsche and Schopenhauer, the ecumenical religious thought of Vladimir Solovyov, and the Theosophical doctrine of Helene Blavatsky.[2] The performance was to be held for seven days and nights in India, during which time Scriabin planned to remove the barriers separating audience and performers and to create conditions favorable for spiritual communion *(sobornost')* and all-unity *(vseyedinstvo)*. He imagined that the *Mysterium* would involve all people as votaries in a ritual enacting the miracle of terrestrial and cosmic transformation.

In 1913, however, Scriabin informed his friends that he was unable to acquire and marshal the resources to perform the *Mysterium* and that his uncertainties concerning his dual role as author and participant in the project had led him to a dead end. In its place, he decided to compose a "mystic" Symbolist prelude, a *Preparatory Act (Predvaritel'noye deystviye)*, which would test "the mystic responsiveness of contemporary humanity."[3] Before his bathetic death in April 1915, he completed a draft libretto and fifty-five partially filled pages of musical sketches for it. Though no dramaturgical plan survives to connect them, the material offers clues as to how Scriabin intended to stage the *Preparatory Act*. The libretto describes the birth of the Cosmos and union of its Feminine and Masculine Principles; the extant music expresses the dissolution of the ego and the cessation of time, tasks for which even the well-known "Prometheus," or "mystic" chord proved unsuitable. Scriabin assigned himself the role of Narrator in the drama. In what follows, I will argue that his vision embodied the impossible aspirations of the "mystic" Symbolists, while his crisis of authorship revealed the paradox inherent in creating communal art. The story of the *Mysterium* and *Preparatory Act* relates a specifically "mystic" Symbolist tragedy: how one composer's philosophical speculations led to creative disaster in the real world, a "holy sacrifice" that led to silence.

"I" AND "NOT I"

Boris Shletser (de Schloezer, 1881–1969), Scriabin's brother-in-common-law, documented the long genesis of the *Mysterium* and the *Preparatory*

Act in an essay printed in *Russian Propylaea (Russkiye propilei)* and in a monograph entitled *A. Scriabin: Personality, Mysterium.*[4] These publications provide first-hand accounts of the composer's philosophical self-education and working habits.[5] Shletser also narrates Scriabin's transformation from an artist into an artist-theurgist: a Promethean figure who hoped to unite Heaven and Earth. He observes that the *Mysterium* was conceived in 1902, while Scriabin was writing the libretto for an opera on the Eros and Psyche myth.[6] The unidentified musician-hero—an idealized self-portrait modeled on Ovid's Orpheus, Nietzsche's *Übermensch,* and Wagner's Siegfried—possesses the power to change the Earth. Debased and harassed by his foes, he exhorts and finally forces the masses to succumb to his ideal. He brings together humanity and the gods, individual "fire" and the origin of all "fire." The musician-hero foretells the deed:

> When my star ignites as fire
> And magical light enfolds the earth,
> Then my flame will be reflected in people's hearts
> And the world will grasp its calling.
> With the *powerful charms of celestial harmony*
> I will waft caressing dreams over people,
> And with the infinite and wondrous *force of love*
> I will make their life a likeness of spring.
> I give them long desired peace
> With the *force of my wisdom.*
> Peoples, rejoice! Awaited for ages,
> The end of suffering and sorrow has come.
>
> [Kogda zvezda moya pozharom razgoritsya
> I zemlyu svet volshebnïy oboymyot,
> Togda v serdtsakh lyudey ogon' moy otrazitsya
> I mir svoyo prizvaniye poymyot.
> Ya *siloy char garmonii nebesnoy*
> Naveyu na lyudey laskayushchiye snï,
> A *siloyu lyubvi* bezmernoy i chudesnoy
> Ya sdelayu ikh zhizn' podobiyem vesnï.
> Daruyu im pokoy davno zhelannïy
> Ya *siloy mudrosti* svoyey.
> Narodï, raduytes', ot veka zhdannïy
> Konets nastal stradaniy i skorbey.][7]

Scriabin stopped working on the opera at the end of December 1903, after composing a few vocal motifs (now lost) and drafting the verses of several monologues, vocal duets, and choruses. According to Shletser, Scriabin subsequently labeled them "immature and not self-sufficient," merely the seeds of the *Mysterium*, whose "alluring phantom" gradually "displaced it in his imagination."[8] The text did, however, supply the eschatological theme of the *Mysterium:* the elevation of the spirit from the physical plane to the astral plane. It also provided the prototype for the Christ-like protagonist of the *Preparatory Act*. In his late poetry, Scriabin stated more clearly the significance of Prometheus, who in his view had rejected the world but had sought the will of God to alter it. Promethean imagery thereafter assumed a central place in his creative thinking. Bryusov commented on it in the sonnet that he wrote after the composer's death:

> He dared to melt the metal of melodies
> And wanted to pour them into new forms;
> He constantly sought to live and live,
> In order to create a monument through his accomplishment,
>
> But Fate judges. The work will not be finished!
> The molten metal cools idly;
> No one, no one can set it in motion. . . .
>
> [Metall melodiy on posmel rasplavit'
> I v formï novïye khotel izlit';
> On neustanno zhazhdal zhit' i zhit',
> Shtob zavershennïm pamyatnik postavit',
>
> No sudit Rok. He budet konchen trud!
> Rasplavlennïy metall bestsel'no stïnet:
> Nikto yego, nikto v ruslo ne dvinet. . . .][9]

Long before "Fate" judged the *Mysterium*, Scriabin sought its justification in a wide-ranging study of idealist philosophy and Eastern religion. Nietzsche, Blavatsky, Schopenhauer, Solovyov, and Wagner all figured in his grand conception. The kernel consisted of ideas of subjective consciousness outlined by Schopenhauer in his 1818 treatise *The World as Will and as Representation (Die Welt als Wille und Vorstellung)*, and on ideas of *vseyedinstvo* put forth by Solovyov in his 1889 French-language study *Russia and the Universal Church (La Russie et l'église universelle)*. To achieve a state of synthesis in his artwork between the performers and spectators, Scriabin decreed that both groups see its enactment as advantageous, a means to elevate consciousness to a transcendental nexus. Through spiritual commingling, humanity would gain access to the hidden reality behind matter and experience the Cosmic Will as it is in itself rather than as it is manifested in phenomena. In accord with Nietzschean thought, Scriabin ascertained that he alone was the "higher type" who would lead the "herd" to a higher plane. To achieve his goal, Scriabin speculated that he had to surmount his "ya" ("I") for his "ne-ya" ("not I"), the Ego for the non-Ego, the individual Will for the Cosmic Will. His Swiss diaries contain pronouncements on these subjects ranging from "I am God" to "I am nothing," from "Individuality (multiplicity)" to "Divinity (unity)." The diaries also disclose his aspiration to serve as the catalyst for the ultimate drama of the human race:

> I want to live. I want to create. I want to act and to conquer. I want to know struggle. I want to make struggle. I am struggle (suffering). I am nothing. I am only what I make. Struggle became multitude. Plurality was struggle. I am multitude. I am I and not I. . . . I arouse you to life with the tender, secretive charm of my promises. I summon you to live, hidden yearnings, disappearing in a chaos of sensations. Arise from the secret depths of the creative spirit! [10]

These lines date from 1904. Following his encounter with Theosophy the next year, Scriabin abandoned such megalomaniacal effusions. He came to believe that humans are at one with the Cosmos. The Divine Principle resides in all consciousnesses and all matter, he argued, since all is the emanation of the Divine Principle. Scriabin also determined that the Cosmos evolves in fixed and immutable patterns, and that the life cycles of humanity replicate in miniature those of the stars:

> In cosmic history *there are limits,* behind which newer and newer planes of existence appear. Two evolutions occur: 1) a stratum that evolves into human form; 2) a stratum *as such* that acquires new characteristics in a *new guise.* The stratum developing into man perceives itself and transforms itself into this new guise and new characteristics. Cosmic history is, expressed conventionally, a *"one time evolution"* of all moments in time, all systems of relationships, one pertaining to another. It is the gradual awakening to absolute alertness—which is also—absolute sleep. [11]

Through the *Mysterium,* Scriabin hoped to accelerate the course of Cosmic unfolding. He imagined that his closeted artistic activities could dictate out-of-doors social events, but he reduced his own role in the planned work from creator to facilitator. Success would be predicated on the desire of all to reach another reality. As Blavatsky wrote in *The Secret Doctrine:*

> The Universe . . . manifests, periodically, for purposes of the collective progress of the countless *lives,* the outbreathings of the One Life [the Soul of the Universe, or Brahman of Indian religious doctrine], in order that through the *Ever-Becoming,* every cosmic atom in this infinite Universe, passing from the formless and the intangible, through the

mixed natures of the semi-terrestrial, down to matter in full generation, and then back again, reascending at each new period higher and
nearer the final goal; that each atom, we say, *may reach through individual merits and efforts* that plane where it re-becomes the one un-
conditioned All.[12]

The *Mysterium* was to be a work of art only insofar as its performance
would commence in a theater with an audience and a cast. As events un-
folded, however, it would cease to be a *work* and transform itself into a religious *rite* involving all people and culminating in a higher reality. From
its 1903 conception to its ultimate abandonment, the *Mysterium* did not
and could not exist in this world. Yet Scriabin persisted with it despite
every practical obstacle. His colleagues, interested in how his labors would
turn out, saw the composer as a Titan who had descended from the heavens to the Earth, a pilgrim soul in a cause of renewal, injured in his battle
to stir the masses, yet always prepared to struggle onward.

WAGNERIANA

From December 1909, Scriabin was drawn into the world of the "mystic" Symbolists. The decisive meeting between him and the poets came in
St. Petersburg, after a recital he gave at the editorial offices of *Apollo*, the
last influential Symbolist journal. Enraptured by the performance, the
distinguished poet Vyacheslav Ivanov presented Scriabin with an inscribed
copy of his prose collection *According to the Stars* (*Po zvezdam*, 1909).
It contained reprints of Ivanov's essays on Nietzsche and Wagner and on
his conception of communal art. Ellen von Tideböhl, accompanying Scriabin on a concert tour of the Volga region in the spring of 1910, noted the
strong impact that this book, along with Nietzsche's *Birth of Tragedy*, had
on him:

> I had with me Nietzsche's book *Die Geburt der Tragödie*. Scriabin, see-
> ing it in my hand one day, spoke of the wonders of the book and the
> view on art, especially where the philosopher speaks of Dionysus. He
> confessed he had been much strengthened in his doctrines and work by
> this book, and spoke of another that had had an equal influence on him.
> Next morning he brought me the book to lend me to read—Vyacheslav
> Ivanov's *All Above* [sic] *the Stars*.[13]

When Scriabin met Ivanov again in April 1912 in Moscow, the poet gave
him a copy of his two-volume poetry collection *Heart Burning* (*Cor ardens*,
1911–12).[14] Its symbolism stems from Goethe, Novalis (1772–1801), the

Bible, and the Earth. The epitaphs are taken from Greek and Latin verses, while the actual poems name the deities of the old Slavonic world. Bryusov, among others, warned of the effort required to understand Ivanov's poetry. Scriabin found it too dense and too confusing and complained to his friend and sometime confidant Leonid Sabaneyev (1881–1968) that Ivanov had "a strange style and manner, quite thick and tart. . . . There are so many symbols that it becomes stifling, airless. And I until now have avoided symbolism in my texts." But he immediately added that Ivanov was "terribly interesting" and "very profound. . . . I feel, L[eonid] L[eonidovich], that they [the "mystic" Symbolist poets] will become my closest friends!"[15]

So it came to be. From 1912 on, Scriabin and Ivanov maintained close artistic and personal ties. Ivanov convinced him that the artist's primary task was to use poetic and musical symbols to fix forever moments of insight into other tiers of being. For Ivanov, a symbol was a resonant device, provocative and revelatory in the imprecision of its meaning, which offered unfamiliar perspectives on existence, penetrating the outer cover of reality into its essence. Symbols evolved: they demonstrated a supersensory process of growth and change; they mediated between incarnate and spiritual realms. Ivanov, like the other "mystic" Symbolists, believed that art and humanity had become separated. Symbols aided in the quest for reintegration because they recalled the lost spirit of the people, the origins of language, and the era of festive spectacles and communal rites. The desire to recreate these rites (and the desire to use symbols to mediate between discrete levels of perception in art and also between art and life) became the most important factor in Ivanov and Scriabin's creative alliance. Ivanov located the formula for combining the chorus and rhapsode in Scriabin's late works. He, like Bryusov, described the composer as a Promethean being, a Titan whose fiery music was destined to cleanse the human spirit and the Earth. Ivanov interpreted the *Mysterium* as a spiritual extension of Wagner's *Gesamtkunstwerk* ideal, a means to synthesize the arts and reunite people.

Two of Ivanov's Wagner essays will clarify these points. They embrace a range of philosophical and historical ideas, though their organizing principle comes from Nietzsche. Ivanov believed that the *Gesamtkunstwerk* symbolized the forsaking of Apollonian order in art for Dionysian delirium. Patricia Mueller-Vollmer observes that, to Ivanov, as to Nietzsche, Apollo represented the "last stages of the historical age of individualism," while Dionysus represented "the future organic age and the spiritual harmony that will pervade it."[16] Like his poet colleagues, Ivanov adopted as his own Wagner's *topoi* of death potions, endless nights, and grail pilgrimages. Brünnhilde and Isolde symbolized the "World Soul," the "Primordial Unity." In the two Wagner articles included in *According to the Stars*— "Nietzsche and Dionysus" ("Nitsshe i Dionis," 1904) and "Wagner and the Dionysian Act" ("Vagner i dionisovo deystvo," 1905)—the poet described the leitmotif as a musical symbol, a reflection of the Cosmic Will, and a means to experience reality without the shroud placed on it by human consciousness. Like a poetic symbol, the leitmotif spanned the distance between the external realm of objects and the internal realm of the senses. Ivanov's remarks embraced a basic tenet of Kantian (neo-Platonic) metaphysics, namely, that reality comprises both phenomena and noumena: things that are apprehended by the senses and things that are only thought. Phenomena are the material forms projected by noumena, which are inaccessible transcendental shapes. Ivanov posited that, in Wagner's music dramas, leitmotifs float between the visible (phenomenal) stage and invisible (noumenal) orchestra. For the *dramatis personae* and the audience alike, leitmotifs recalled lost memories and furnished proleptic knowledge.[17]

The basic idea in "Nietzsche and Dionysus"—that Wagner uses leitmotifs symbolically and mnemonically—was challenged by Max Hochschüler (Alexander Bisk). In "A Letter from Bayreuth: the *Ring of the Nibelungen* and *Parsifal*," Hochschüler argued that two types of leitmotifs are found in Wagner's operas: the first type is "allegorical," an illustration of the libretto "based upon [dramatic] characterizations"; the second type is "symbolic," an entity that "penetrates the essence of a phenomenon, accentuating in an image its 'idea,' that is, becoming a symbol." Hochschüler added that, since Wagner used leitmotifs allegorically and symbolically, his music is both "Apollonian" and "Dionysian."[18] Impressed by Hochschüler's argument, on 19 October 1904 Ivanov humbly wrote to Bryusov that Hochschüler "ascribes to me more than I said: so he is polemicizing against that with which I already agree. Of course Wagner is not a pure Dionysian. But that his 'art was devoted to serving Muse and Dionysus' is quite right: his *merit* lies in the fact that he was the first artist to speak about Dionysus in theoretical essays."[19] In "Wagner and the Dionysian Act," Ivanov's formal response to Hochschüler, he further clarified his views, conceding that Wagner had shifted from Dionysus to Apollo in the interregnum between composing *Der Ring des Nibelungen* and *Parsifal*.

Wagner's greatest achievement resided in what Ivanov termed the emancipation of the communal *(soborniy)* component of music drama, both through the relocation of the orchestra out of sight, which brought the crowd closer to the stage performers, and through the revival of ritual myth, which resurrected the inflamed Bacchanalian songs and choric hymns of Classical drama:

> Resurrecting the ancient Tragedy, Wagner had to clarify to himself the meaning of the primordial chorus. He made the orchestra of his musical drama the chorus. Just as heroic sympathy arises theatrically in choral performance, so too does dramatic action emerge from the bosom of the instrumental Symphony. Thus, the chorus was for him no longer an "ideal viewer," but in truth the dithyrambic premise and Dionysian basis of drama. Just as a chorus of Titans bore for Aeschylus the action of *Prometheus Unbound,* so too the multi-voiced yet mute Will, as a wordless chorus of musical instruments, intones for Wagner the primal principles of that which, in the Apollonian vision of the stage, as isolated heroes, has a human face and speaks with a human voice.
>
> The gathered crowd joins mystically to the poetic voices in the Symphony; and just as we near Wagner's sanctuary—to "create," not only to "contemplate"—we become ideal molecules of the orgiastic life of the orchestra. We are already active, but active potentially and latently. The chorus of Wagnerian drama is a secret chorus.[20]

Ivanov here argues that Wagner gave his audience an interpretative and transitional role in the achievement of his aims. Yet he laments that the audience could "contemplate" but not "create" his music dramas. Wagner, in his view, had fallen shy of his own expectations by not removing the barriers (the footlights) between stage and audience. The dream of transforming life with art had faded. "The bridge," Ivanov added (with reference to Aeschylus, Euripides, and Sophocles), had not yet been "thrown across the two 'assemblies' (πάροδος), through the cavity of the unseen orchestra from the kingdom of Apollonian dreams to the realm of Dionysus."[21]

To Ivanov, the "bridge" meant a return, through art and religion, to forgotten unity; without it, theatrical experience would not assume the character of a theurgic rite. It was not enough for him that Wagner had covered his orchestra in an attempt to unite audience and cast, for the footlights and pews remained in place, and space had not been left in front of the stage for mass acts. Ivanov based his expectations of transformation from theater into liturgy on Schopenhauer's belief that the orchestra represented the metaphysical voice of the Cosmic Will. Through the resurrection of the Greek chorus and ancient communal dance, he imagined spectators and singers united in orgiastic fervor. Humanity would thereby overcome the individualism and isolation of contemporary life. The basis of his vision of communal art was not the Bayreuth *Festspielhaus* but the theater of ancient Athens, where Ivanov believed poets had communed with the populace, their perfect integration of poetry and music facilitating spiritual catharsis and rebirth.

All of these ideas found a place in Scriabin's planned *Mysterium*, which was to consume his last five years and make him a martyr to the "mystic" Symbolist cause. Ivanov's artistic theory, mythic vision, and belief in the capacity of art to transform life impelled Scriabin not just to "contemplate" but actually to "create" a synthesis of the spiritual and ideal. For this reason, several historians, notably Malcolm Brown, have detected affinities between Scriabin's and Ivanov's ideas.[22] Yet a close inspection of the source material shows that Ivanov's vision of a *Mysterium*, based on ancient Greek tragedy, was less apocalyptic than Scriabin's frankly Theosophical one. While the two agreed on the theurgic purpose of art, the ideal of *vseyedin-stvo*, and the mutational power of the symbol, Ivanov could not countenance Scriabin's outlandish claim that a single artwork might transform humanity. Ivanov felt that such a plan was best mooted in scholarly forums, as he did with his own artistic plans, since any attempt at actual realization would smack of charlatanism. When Scriabin persisted in his belief that the *Mysterium*, if and when performed, would open up the path to eternity, even Ivanov had to suspect mental aberration. To Nikolai Ulyanov (1875–1949), a painter involved with the *World of Art* circle, he complained:

> Scriabin is unstable! . . . He has now lost his true spirit. But could it be otherwise! You see he has taken upon himself a task exceeding human powers. It would take many years to realize his fiery orchestra. And the *Mysteriums* [sic] for which I am helping him write the text . . . will they ever be finished?! We can never agree, we think differently, divided right from the start. There's something wrong with him, a serious spiritual ailment.[23]

The tone is harsher than usual for Ivanov, who wielded a subtle pen, and who himself had argued for a transformation of drama into liturgy. Like Scriabin, he believed that music and poetry were not ends in themselves, as aestheticist or formalist theory dictates, but an enactment of world creation, a preparation of the mind and soul for the comprehension of God's work. He had tried to form an alliance against the inertia of an unsatisfactory world and to use art in the cause of revival. Yet, unlike Scriabin, he admitted that the goal of transcendental art lay in the future: he did not try to stage his own pair of *Mysteriums*, the tragic dramas *Tantalus* (*Tantal*, 1905) and *Prometheus* (*Prometey*, 1919). The "mystic" Symbolists might prepare the way for the era of organic culture, he reasoned, but they dared not attempt its fruition.

THE ASYMPTOTIC PROCESS

In 1910, Sabaneyev remarked that he had become reconciled to the *Mysterium*. In his view, if the plan was

> insane—then it was fascinating insanity. And in [Scriabin's] presence the insanity intoxicated me like wine. I not only started to "believe" in those irrational parts of his unconscious being, but also became strangely accustomed to the idea of the *Mysterium*, that fantastic dream about the "last celebration of humanity.". . . An intensity, part bliss, part anguish, gleamed in his eyes and communicated to me, a positivist and a "scientist," accustomed to the clear language of experiment and precision of mathematical formulae. I just could not understand how he had "seriously" (not as an artistic creation of his fantastic imagination, not as a literary dream, but as truth, as something indisputable and believable) created and bound up his life with this intangible creation of his genius. "Is he in part just imagining? Or has he really set himself on it?" I thought, losing myself in conjectures.[24]

Sabaneyev supported Scriabin's efforts, but failed to grasp how a new reality could be constituted through a single artistic expression, even if the artist was a theurgist, a "mystic" Symbolist who was in touch with divine or supernatural agents. He doubted that the *Mysterium* would become a "communal creation and communal act" with a "unified, communal, multifaceted personality."[25] The concert pianist Anna Goldenweizer (1881–1929) was equally skeptical. When she asked Scriabin to explain how the *Mysterium* would truly bring about the transformation of humanity, he provided only a vague description of the performing forces:

> In this artistic event there will not be a single spectator. All will be participants. [Wagner's] misfortune lies in the fact that for his reforms he did not acquire the money to construct the theater, to organize the invisible orchestra, and so forth. . . . [The *Mysterium*] requires special people, special artists, a completely different, new culture, which money does not provide. . . . The cast of performers includes, of course, an orchestra, a large mixed choir, an instrument with visual effects, dancers, a procession, incense, rhythmicized textual articulation. . . . The form of the cathedral, in which it will all take place, will not be of one monotonous type of stone, but will continually change, along with the atmosphere and motion of the *Mysterium*. This, of course, [will happen] with the aid of mists and lights, which will modify the architectural contours.[26]

Ideally, Scriabin wanted performers and spectators in the *Mysterium* to interact, to change places, so that, eventually, anarchy reigned, social divisions disappeared and, both inside and outside the theater, humans experienced *vseyedinstvo*. Yet while he characterized the planned work as a communal rite, a liturgy involving a select few and then all people, he gave his colleagues no information about its musical, textual, and choreographic contents. The musically literate "mystic" Symbolist poet Andrey Belïy considered the entire project to be insubstantial, its mysticism a theoretical abstraction. Scriabin, in his estimation, had no clear idea how to transform theater into liturgy; instead, "all that was being achieved was a treacly mixture of socialism and individualism," a "synaesthesia right down to 'smell-effects,' and the 'goat dance,' the *kozlovak*, a barbaric, lascivious capering over the shards of [Russian and Western European] civilization."[27] To succeed, it would appear that Scriabin's plan required a broad shift in social outlook; without the shift, only dark forces, political authoritarianism, or the collective unconscious could allow the *Mysterium* to occur.

The main problem was that the *Mysterium*, to be a freely collective experience, had to be "authorless." From reading Blavatsky, Solovyov, and Nietzsche, Scriabin ascertained that Platonic love, the ideal of sexual love symbolized by Eros, and the World Soul might act as catalysts for transcendental experience and might allow spiritual communion to "author" itself. At the same time, he paradoxically assigned himself the dual roles of author and performer in the drama. He intended to preside over the enormous orchestra, to set the events in motion, and to narrate parts of the text. Scriabin's colleagues viewed the paradox as proof of the *Mysterium*'s impossibility. They advised him that he could not "author" an "authorless" score, since a true *Mysterium* would have no teacher to "create the final accord of the race, uniting it with the [Cosmic] Spirit."[28] It was one thing for Wagner to create a *Gesamtkunstwerk* to assail a passive audience, quite another to activate the world's peoples and incorporate them into an artist's conception of a transcendental score. Shletser affirmed this point, noting that a society focused on the material fulfillment of spiritual needs would not be drawn to the *Mysterium*, thus leaving the composer in a creative cul-de-sac:

> To him, the dream . . . was a precognition of mysterious, obscure, and inchoate cravings of all nature for eventual transfiguration. But at the same time he was forced to acknowledge that the realization of his personal ecstasy amid an indifferent world was impossible and self-contradictory. The specific number of people experiencing the sensation of ecstasy was, of course, immaterial. What does it matter if two mil-

lion people or a thousand million people experience the state of ecstasy, when a single soul remains excluded from universal light? Such a partial consummation cannot be imagined; either all mankind and nature undergo transformation, or none do.[29]

But Scriabin escaped the paradox. His ruminations on the *Mysterium* taught him that the creative process might itself *be* the creative result, and that what he most valued about the work was its openness, its incompleteness and indeterminacy. In this regard, he came to understand that elements of ambiguity and uncertainty were crucial to his objective. To adapt a materialistic society to the grandiose changes he envisioned, his meta-operatic *Mysterium* would have to advocate the "mystic" Symbolist conception of *collective creation* as an antidote to social injustice. Uncertainty, the "infinite, asymptotic process of realizing the moral Ideal," would sustain "the dimension of ethical universality."[30] Like an asymptote, a line that continually approaches a curve but never reaches it, Scriabin's creative act would move ever closer to his creative ideal but never achieve it. The *Mysterium* would never be completed.

The asymptotic process started with the *Preparatory Act*. In 1913, Scriabin reassessed the *Mysterium* and determined that it required an introduction to prepare humanity for contact with the world beyond. His thinking underwent a radical transition: the text fragments of the *Mysterium* were assigned to the *Preparatory Act*, even though, based on the original scheme, they were too broad in scope; the unrealized *Mysterium*, meanwhile, preserved its abstract and indeterminate shape. Shletser described the alteration:

> We see . . . that what should have served as the content of the *Mysterium* becomes the content of the *Preparatory Act*, which for us now takes on the same contours as that united process involving the evolution and involution of worlds, human races, and distinct personality that had been summoned to complete the *Mysterium*. What, then, is the meaning of the metamorphosis? That, without a doubt, the *Preparatory Act* is now no longer just a phase and means for approaching the *Mysterium*, but actually is the *Mysterium*, restricted and abridged by the artist within such limits as to allow it to be realized.[31]

The project was not an admission of defeat, for it would still remind people of the covenant, the promise of spiritual synthesis, no matter how far beyond his scope it might be. Scriabin denied that the *Preparatory Act* would simply be a cantata, an opera, or an oratorio, for these were musical genres in which representation supplanted enactment. He remained convinced that opera—even if the orchestra was concealed, as at the Bayreuth *Fest-*

spielhaus, and the audience reverently hushed—was simply spectacle, a closed art form that did not offer itself up for audience participation. Citing Ivanov, he vowed that his project would not have "symbolizations and allegories. I don't want any kind of theatricality. The footlights—the partition between the spectator and performer—will be destroyed. They are the legacy of the materialization process, when everything became fixed, differentiated, stratified."[32] Though Wagner had approached the grand scale of the *Mysterium* and *Preparatory Act* in his music dramas, he had nonetheless confined himself to the theatrical sphere of material representation. Scriabin promised to do better. He declared that there would be no set pieces, arias, or duets in the *Preparatory Act*; separate scenes, in the theatrical sense, would be minimal and presented in pantomime. He claimed that the lyric poetry of the libretto had to be "epic, [for epic is] necessary to explain the cosmic importance of personal experiences; the history of each emotion, of each aspiration, comprises the history of the universe."[33] The spectators would become participants, performing dances, assisting in the Dionysian rituals, and revealing how the world conflagration of the *Mysterium* was to transpire. The *Preparatory Act* would divulge the end of the human race: it would take the essential leap from what Belïy and Ivanov termed *realia*, the real world, to *realiora*, the "realer" world.[34]

Adopting something like the guise of an impresario, Scriabin devoted the initial months of 1913 to the selection of the *dramatis personae* for the *Preparatory Act*. Theosophists and "mystic" Symbolist adepts would be under his control from the center of the stage; other participants would stand in order of rank from the front to the back. Less spiritually advanced people would sit in the balconies. Scriabin considered founding a training center in London for the dancers and singers. He had conversations on this topic with the theater director M. O. Tereshchenko and the pianist Alexander Ziloti (1863–1945). The plan did not come to fruition. Regarding the performance space, Shletser noted that Scriabin initially wanted to build a half-temple with a dome, the floor partitioned into terraces extending from the proscenium to a body of water. Later, he modestly conceded that any concert hall would do. His most ambitious idea was to fill the hall with fragrances and then open the roof to include the sounds of nature, the light of sunset and dawn, and the movement of the stars. He announced that "it might be necessary, at the last moment, to destroy the temple itself, to demolish its walls in order to emerge into open air, under the skies."[35] With this statement, Scriabin was unwittingly invoking Wagner, who, in a letter to Theodor Uhlig (1822–53), declared that *Siegfried*, when finished, would be performed by amateur singers in "a crude theater of planks and beams"

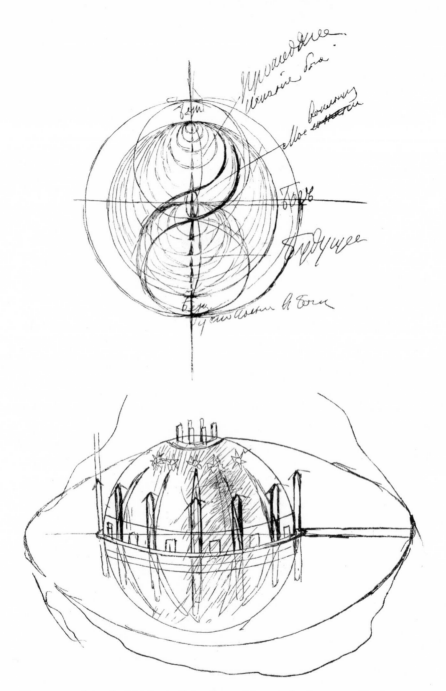

Figures 1 and 2. Scriabin's pencil drawings of the temple. Source: Mikhaíl Gershenzon, ed., "Zapisi A. N. Skryabina: Libretto operï, 1900–1902 gg." *Russkiye propilei: Materiali po istorii russkoy mïsli i literaturï* 6 (1919): between 156 and 157.

in a "beautiful field" near Zurich. Wagner added that, after the third performance, "the theater would be torn down, and [his] score burnt."[36]

A period of intense work on the text and music of the *Preparatory Act* commenced in August 1913. At his dacha in Petrovskoye, Scriabin studied a translation of Asvagosha's poem *Life of the Buddha (Zhizn' Buddi)* by the first-generation Symbolist poet Konstantin Balmont. The poem, along with Blavatsky's arcane writings on Brahmanism in *The Key to Theosophy* and *The Secret Doctrine*, convinced Scriabin that the *Preparatory Act* should be performed in a remote, "oriental" setting: the mountainous north or tropical southern peninsula of India. His interest in India was encouraged by his companion Tatyana Shletser, who was also a Theosophist, and by his colleague Alexander Bryanchaninov, editor and publisher of the journal *The New Link (Novoye zveno)*. Scriabin and Bryanchaninov took a spiritually fulfilling trip to London in February 1914. While there, Scriabin sought out British Theosophists and met with officials who represented India in the British Parliament. He even managed to buy a plot of Indian land in Darjeeling. On returning to Moscow, he and Bryanchaninov began to make plans for a long, exploratory journey to India. To Sabaneyev, he confided his desire to "travel there, to the monasteries, where they already know everything. For the conception of the *Mysterium* arose there and will only be realized there for us all. They [British Theosophists] told me that the monasteries are in Northern India, but that the actual route to them is unknown. It is not revealed to anybody."[37] Scriabin orated at great length about the knowledge and experience he planned to acquire in the East. Sight unseen, he believed that his vision of spiritual commingling, of surmounting the "I" for the "not I," could only be realized in ancient, authentic India.

This delusional plan was postponed by the outbreak of World War I, an event that Scriabin initially viewed as a signal of a coming apotheosis, a first glimpse of a Mystery that would transform humanity. He declared that it is "important that we see how nations rally around their spiritual leaders. A hierarchy that had been forgotten triumphs once again. We come once again to the end of world history and back to the original hierarchy."[38] In his imagination, World War I anticipated the cyclic cataclysm depicted in Brahman and Theosophical doctrine. It also affirmed his view of earthly being as *polemos*, the dialectical struggle between opposites. After this troubling period of enthusiasm, however, the nightmarish quality of World War I became obvious even to Scriabin, and he began to interpret Europe's chaos as a *Mysterium tremendum:* a fearsome Mystery. Far from the expansion of consciousness, it betokened the onset of anarchic darkness.

His gloom was compounded by illness: a boil he had contracted on his upper lip while in London had not healed and, despite a series of treatments and minor operations, became seriously infected. In March 1915, Scriabin was diagnosed with incurable septicemia. His body temperature soared, and he suffered bouts of dementia and severe hallucinations. The newspaper *Russian Morning (Utro Rossii)* commissioned Sabaneyev (who was maintaining vigil over the composer) to write an obituary. The bedridden Scriabin's last hours were marked by feelings of tragic pathos, tempered only by the conviction that his inchoate *Mysterium* and *Preparatory Act* constituted his masterpieces. On the eve of his death, he shouted out, "Who's there?" to a vision of Sister Death, one of the characters in his libretto for the *Preparatory Act*.[39] The arrival of the apparition foreshadowed his transition from one state to another and the conclusion of his heroic struggle to make the impossible possible.

Such, at least, was the view taken by his friends. Ivanov declared that, at the end, Scriabin transformed his life into art by supplanting the embers of the *Mysterium* with a personal sacrifice that left a durable flame in the memories of all uncomprehending mortals. He reiterated this idea in five essays and eight poems about Scriabin, all written shortly after his death.[40] Ivanov reasoned that—due to the unfeasibility of Scriabin's plans—the composer was obligated in April 1915 to depart the Earth in search of another place, a "realer" reality. Ivanov also intimated that Scriabin's theurgic philosophizing had led to calamity in the real world . . . to silence and death:

Did other great innovators, the architects of unbuilt cathedrals, achieve their aims? Was the "Preparatory Act" actually the future *Mysterium*, which Scriabin was creating when Parcae cut the thread of his days, when Destiny severed it, so that all that remained for us were verses of fascinating charm and grandeur, a poetic text of astounding depth and speculative refinement for the holy drama, and numerous incoherent— as though muffled by a jealous god, like the murmurs of dying Pythia— sketches of musical themes for the drama[? And did] everything else that had once floated before the artist, like a misty vision, vanish into oblivion, into that place where, in Pushkin's words, the fragrant shadows of dead flowers bloom above the waves of Lethe? Or is all this only the deception of our perspective and reason, and all of the magical music of the second half of Scriabin's creative work already the "Preparatory Act," leading us to the threshold of the *Mysterium*, which, in the mystic's own conception, would have been neither his personal creation nor even a work of art, but internal events in the soul of the world, bringing about the end of time and the birth of a new human?[41]

Here Ivanov sums up the tragic paradox of Scriabin's creative aspirations: as a transcendental project, the *Mysterium* could only be enacted by its material trace, a symbol by which it might appear to the consciousness, for any genuine attempt to realize it would transform its essence. While he believed that the *Preparatory Act* was such a symbol, the surviving text and music left him with a sense of anticlimax, of deception, because it confirmed that transcendental art could not be achieved within the horizon of phenomenal reality. Ivanov also intimates that there were in fact two asymptotic processes in effect at the end of Scriabin's life: together with the aspiration to represent the uncomposable *Mysterium* by its shadow trace— the *Preparatory Act*—there was a contrary aspiration to abandon music making altogether when he realized that he could not create the necessary conditions for divine communion and for magical music to be made in and of itself. The "text" of the *Mysterium* was replaced by "becoming a text," then "becoming a text" was replaced by total silence. The silence grew louder as Scriabin gave up his role as a composer and instead became a metaphysical philosopher of "mystic" Symbolist art.

THE EXTANT FRAGMENTS OF THE *MYSTERIUM*

The text of the *Preparatory Act* was drafted in four notebooks. Notebooks "A" and "B," dating from the summer of 1914, contain a few text incipits and some musical motives that were eventually incorporated into Scriabin's opus 74 Piano Preludes. Notebook "C," dating from the winter of 1914, contains a rough draft of the entire libretto. Scriabin was confident enough about its quality to decline offers of help with the revisions from his poet friends. He even boasted to Sabaneyev that he understood

> some things about poetry better than they do. . . . For example, they can't possibly appreciate some of the new sensations that I am including [in the libretto]. But besides this, they are not musicians, which means a lot. You see, a musician pays attention to sound, but they only to rhythm. Sound flies away from them. . . . Much remains for them to discover. . . . It's perfectly clear to me that vowels and consonants are different, that instrumentation and color in poetry are analogous to orchestration in music. Moreover, vowels correspond to the string and wind instruments and consonants to percussion. Music opens up so much to the understanding of poetry. I think that at present only musicians understand poetry. We should teach them [the poets], and not them us, because in the hierarchy of arts, music is higher, more spiritual, more mystical, and less tied to the mental plane. It is more magical, and physically more astral, than poetry.[42]

Here Scriabin was in over his head. He borrowed extensively from the styles and techniques of the Symbolist poets in his texts and was in no position to lecture them on the elemental music of "vowels and consonants," or on the enhancement of their works using sound groups and floods of euphony. When he read his draft libretto to Balmont, Jurgis Baltrušaitis (1873–1944), and Ivanov in November 1914, he came in for a storm of ridicule. He discovered that many of the literary symbols and dramatic spondees had to be removed, and he abandoned his plans to publish the libretto ahead of the music. He then undertook a total overhaul of the libretto in Notebook "D," completing half of it before his death.

Both Shletser and, more recently, Valentina Rubtsova point out that textual incipits and performance indications for the *Mysterium* were preserved in Notebook "B" along with the cited *Preparatory Act* material.[43] They affirm that Scriabin intended to perform it over seven days and nights. The events of the first four days (part one) would be *represented;* the events of the final three days (part two) would be *enacted.* In all, the *Mysterium* was to trace the "anthropogenesis" of humanity from the distant past to the future, individual consciousness to communal consciousness, corporeal life to spiritual life.

The text incipits of the *Mysterium* in Notebook "B" read as follows:

Page 1: Plans and ideas for part 1
Page 2: The basic idea is conveyed as a mood.
He did not yet exist, but his poem was
already being created.
Page 3: Our weariness puts the living principle
of the world within us.
The shrine fills with clouds of uncertainties being born.
Greatness is being fulfilled, love awakens!
Love, loving itself, love creates itself with love!
O desire! O life, your divine light
is ignited, the universe arises!
Page 5: Third day
Page 17: Plans for part 2
Second day
Page 33: Fourth day
Page 44: Fifth day
Page 55: Sixth day
Page 60: Sunbeam strings (sunbeam sounds).
Page 64: Seventh day
O, holy secret of dissolution, secret
of the conception of a new universe.

[Skhemï i mïsli 1-y chasti
Osn[ovnaya] ideya dana kak nastroyeniye.
Yego yeshcho ne bïlo, no poema yego uzhe
sozdavalos'.
V nas tomleniyem zhivushcheye mira
nachalo.
Khram napolnyayetsya tumanami
rozhdayushchikhsya neopredelyonnostey.
Velikoye svershayetsya, probuzhdayetsya lyubov'!
Lyubov', sebya lyubyashchaya,
lyubov' lyubov'yu sebya sozdayushchaya!
O zhelaniye! O zhizn', zagorayetsya tvoy
bozhestvennïy svet, voznikayet vselennaya!
Den' tretiy
Skhemï 2-y chasti
Vtoroy den'
Chetvyortïy den'
Pyatïy den'
Shestoy den'
Strunï solntse-lirnïye (zvuki solntse-lirnïye).
Sed'moy den'
O, svyashchennaya tayna rastvoreniya, tayna
zachatiya novoy vselennoy.]

We can begin sorting out these fragments by noting that Scriabin sought to realize the central task of Theosophical doctrine in the *Mysterium:* to enable humanity to recognize that the material world is illusory and to commence the journey back into spirit. Scriabin based the incipits in Notebook "B" almost exclusively on Blavatsky's writings. They reflect her work both because they are inchoate, material illusions of a project that existed in the noumena of reality, and because they embrace her ideas about the origin and destiny of the Cosmos. The seven-day and seven-night length of the *Mysterium* perpetuates Blavatsky's theory (itself derived from Buddhism, Brahmanism, and Hinduism) that humans, the Cosmos, and history are septenary in form. Blavatsky enumerated the seven principles of humanity (the principles that comprise the body, soul, and spirit) as follows:

An Upper Triad:
1. *Atma.* Pure, Universal Spirit. An emanation of the Absolute.
2. *Buddhi.* Spiritual Soul. The vehicle of Universal Spirit.
3. Higher *Manas.* Mind. Intelligence. Human, or Consciousness Soul.

An Intermediate Dyad:

4. *Kama Rupa.* Lower *Manas,* or Animal Soul, the seat of animal desires and passions. Line of demarcation between the mortal and immortal
elements. The agent of Will during the lifetime.

5. *Linga Sharira.* Astral Body (vehicle of life). Sentient soul.

A Lower Dyad:

6. *Prana.* The Etheric Double. Life essence, vital power. Matter as Force.

7. *Rupa.* The Dense Body. Gross, physical matter.

Blavatsky roughly associates the seven principles of humanity with the
seven planes of Cosmic reality:

1. Divine (*Maha-para*-nirvanic) Plane
2. Monadic (*Para*-nirvanic) Plane
3. Spiritual (Nirvanic) Plane
4. Intuitional (Buddhic) Plane
5. Mental (*Manas* or *Devachanic*) Plane
6. Astral Plane
7. Physical Plane

For Blavatsky (and for Scriabin), human evolution is a cyclic journey upward from the seventh to the fifth level of the two septenary groups: the
body and soul journey from *Rupa* to *Prana* to *Linga Sharira* and back. The
Lower and Higher *Manas* represent God in Man, though in most people
the Higher *Manas* is not developed. Passage into the two highest parts of
the tiers, *Buddhi* and *Atma,* lies in the far future, at the end of the seven
times seventh cycle of *Rupa, Prana,* and *Linga Sharira.* Scriabin was impatient: he hoped that the performance of the *Mysterium* would radically
enhance the reincarnation process. He wanted the work to provoke the final apocalypse, a Cosmic conflagration of matter, time, and space, and the
union of the spirit with the *Anima Supra-mundi:* the Cosmic Over-Soul.
The *Mysterium* fragments basically chart the path from the lower to the
upper parts of the tiers. The first day of the *Mysterium* would detail the
"weariness" and placid state of life in *Rupa.* Subsequent days would mark
the conversion of animal desire to spiritual love, Lower *Manas* to Higher
Manas ("love awakens! . . . O life, your divine light is ignited"), and then
to *Buddhi* and *Atma* ("O, holy secret of dissolution, secret of the conception of a new universe"). In this, the drama would also reveal that the microcosm of human evolution replicates the macrocosm of Cosmic evolution.
Based on the Hindu concept of correspondences, the seven-day and seven-
night span of the work would duplicate in the small a cycle of the stars.

Blavatsky claimed that the Cosmos is reborn every seven Cosmic Days, or *Manvantaras,* and seven Nights, or *Pralayas,* a span of 60,480,000,000 years.[44]

The grand scheme of the *Mysterium* was necessarily truncated for the *Preparatory Act,* which Scriabin initially billed as its general rehearsal but which over time took on its grandiose proportions. The first, revised half of the libretto sheds light on the meaning of the *Mysterium* text incipits but also shows the impact of Ivanov, Wagner, and "mystic" Symbolism on his Theosophical views. The libretto also names most of the participants in the drama: a Chorus *(Khor),* a Feminine Principle *(Golos zhenstvennogo),* a Masculine Principle *(Golos muzhestvennogo),* Waves of Life *(Volnï zhizni),* Awakening Emotions *(Probuzhdayushchiyasya chuvstva),* a Light Beam *(Luch),* Mountains *(Gori),* Fields *(Polya),* Forest *(Les),* and Wilderness *(Pustïnya).*

The list is tantalizing, but its parts are unrelated: organic and inorganic materials, visible and invisible beings. Yet here again, the key to making sense of it resides in Theosophy. In *The Secret Doctrine,* Blavatsky distinguished two forms of the human Ego: a mortal, personal Ego; and an immortal, impersonal Ego. The mortal Ego is the seat of everyday human consciousness, the sentient soul or Lower *Manas.* The higher Ego is the immaterial, transcendent Will, or Higher *Manas.* In the *Preparatory Act,* Scriabin names the two parts of the Ego the Masculine Principle and the Feminine Principle, but also refers to them as "I" and "not I." The Masculine Principle is connected to the historical incarnation of humanity in earthly matter; the Feminine Principle is connected to the infinite life of the spirit in the astral planes. *She* represents the end goal of *his* mortal striving.

Blavatsky further proclaimed that the Cosmos passes through multiple incarnations. The Cosmic "round" has seven planetary manifestations, and on each planet there are seven natural spheres:

> By a "Round" is meant the serial evolution of nascent material nature, of the seven globes of our chain, with their mineral, vegetable, and animal kingdoms (man being there included in the latter and standing at the head of it) during the whole period of a life-cycle. The latter would be called by the Brahmans "a Day of Brahma." It is, in short, one revolution of the "Wheel" (our planetary chain), which is composed of seven globes (or seven separate "Wheels," in another sense this time). When evolution has run downward into matter, from planet A to planet G, or Z, as the Western students call it, it is one Round. In the middle of the Fourth revolution, which is our present "Round," "Evolution has reached its acme of physical development, crowned its work

with the perfect physical man, and—from this point—begins its work spirit-ward."[45]

The Mountains, Fields, Forest, and Wilderness of the *Preparatory Act* text symbolize the mineral kingdom and natural kingdoms of the Earth, the first three "Rounds" of the Wheel of Cosmic life. The Waves of Life and Light Beam refer respectively to the spiritualized state of humanity in the sixth and seventh "Rounds." With the Feminine and Masculine Principles, this exotic cast (perhaps the most exotic ever conceived for a stage work) was to depict the cycle of the Blavatskian Cosmos. The Awakening Emotions, moreover, would denote the laughter of the *fin-de-siècle* apocalypse.

PILGRIM SOULS

What, then, is to happen in the *Preparatory Act?* Marina Scriabine, the composer's daughter, notes that the libretto depicts the cycle of humanity, from the primeval era when the "first race" rebelled against the Over-Soul to a future era when the "seventh race" embraces it.[46] Put as simply as possible, it portrays the combining of the Lower *Manas* (or Masculine Principle) and Upper *Manas* (or Feminine Principle) in the fourth "Round." The event is further allegorized as a smelting of "wave and light" in a Cosmic temple. After this, the Chorus asks the Cosmic Over-Soul to explain why humanity fell into disgrace on Earth. There follows a Theosophical parable about the entrapment of humanity in matter and its journey back to spirit. The Narrator introduces us to a biblical hero, a cruel and insatiable warrior. He threatens to annihilate his enemies with his army but leads it into defeat. Badly wounded, he buries his sword and wanders into the desert. There he meets Sister Death, a benevolent figure who instructs him to atone for his deeds. He stills the cries of those who have been martyred by him and calls upon all peoples to seek peace and spiritual harmony. He dies redeemed: his soul ascends into the noumena of all realities.

Scriabin's libretto is Theosophical in plot but Symbolist in content. To read it is not so much to be told a story as to sort through a dense thicket of allusions to Symbolist poetry, idealist philosophy, Wagner, and the Scriptures. Panorama replaces narrative. There is no actual suspense, for the second half of the libretto (the tale of the hero) is but a reflection of the first half (the union of the Feminine and Masculine Principles). Instead, as in the poetic cycles of Balmont, Ivanov, and Solovyov, the libretto has an epic tone. The events of the story, less an artwork than a prophecy, are to be enacted in the distant future.

The *Preparatory Act* begins with a programmatic statement. After a series of *pianissimo* tremolo bell chimes (which, Sabaneyev and Shletser maintained, Scriabin played on the piano but did not write out[47]), the Narrator declaims:

> Once again the Primordial One wills you
> To accept love's grace
> Once again the Infinite One wills
> To recognize itself in the finite.

> [Yeshcho raz volit v vas Predvechnïy
> Prinyat' lyubvi blagodat'
> Yeshcho raz volit Bezkonechnïy
> Sebya v konechnom opoznat'.]

The Chorus continues:

> The heat of the moment sires eternity,
> And illuminates the depths of space;
> Infinity breathes worlds,
> Chimes have enveloped the silence.

> [Mgnoveniya pïl rozhdayet vechnost',
> Luchit prostranstva glubinu;
> Mirami dïshet bezkonechnost',
> Ob'yali zvonï tishinu.[48]]

The circularity implied by the words "once again" originates in Theosophical doctrine, namely Blavatsky's description of the cycle of Cosmic history. The "Primordial One" is the Cosmic Over-Soul, or *Brahman*, from which all matter emanates and to which all matter returns. There are also echoes in the passage of Nietzsche's principle of "eternal recurrence," introduced in part 3 of his 1885 *Thus Spoke Zarathustra*. Scriabin encountered this text at meetings of the Moscow branch of the Religious Philosophical Society in 1902 and 1903. He attended the meetings on the recommendation of Sergey Trubetskoy, a professor of philosophy at Moscow University. The influence of *Zarathustra* is evident in almost all of Scriabin's literary writings, notably his unfinished 1902–03 opera libretto and 1905 Swiss diaries. Compare, for example, Scriabin's declaration

> Oh life, Oh creative surge (wish!)
> All-creating urge,
> from the center eternally from the center
> to freedom
> to knowledge! . . .
> I have already created you many times world (how many living essences), unconsciously

from his 1905 diaries, and Nietzsche's remark from *Zarathustra:* "I myself belong to the causes of eternal recurrence. . . . I come back eternally to this same, self-same life, in what is greatest as in what is smallest, to teach again the eternal recurrence of all things."[49] Nietzsche's impact on Scriabin preceded Blavatsky's. The philosopher's concept of the Cosmos as an interplay of endlessly organizing and reorganizing forces filtered into the libretto of the *Preparatory Act,* as did his view that the forces are regulated by a fundamental disposition labeled "will to power."

There follows the duet between the Masculine Principle (Lower *Manas*) and the Feminine Principle (Higher *Manas*). The two seek union, but the Masculine Principle does not possess the will to leave the Physical Plane, and the Feminine Principle declines to depart the Spiritual (Nirvanic) Plane.[50] Had the passage been set to music, Scriabin intended to use his color organ, or *tastiera per luce,* to splay colored light when the Feminine Principle speaks of the "multicolored spaces" and "colorful worlds" between her and the Masculine Principle. The instrument, built for him by the engineer Alexander Mozer for use in *Prometheus: The Poem of Fire,* serves to represent synaesthesia, or what Scriabin called "color hearing," the commingling of the aural and visual senses. In *Prometheus,* he calibrated the organ to specific tonalities and pitches, using it to project the colors that appeared spontaneously in his mind while hearing the score. For the *Preparatory Act,* he imagined that the stimulation of another sense in addition to the one being directly stimulated by the music would supply a vision of the reality underlying reality.

The depiction in the libretto of Masculine-Feminine synthesis calls to mind a broad range of religious and philosophical texts on androgyny. Ivanov, an authority on German Romanticism, introduced Scriabin to two of them: the *Mysterium Magnum* by the Protestant Theosophist Jakob Böhme (1575–1624), and *Hymn to the Night (Hymnen an die Nacht)* (1800) by Novalis. Böhme's text was translated into Russian by Alexey Petrovsky (1881–1958), a Theosophist as well as an Anthroposophist follower of Rudolf Steiner (1861–1925). Sara Friedrichsmeyer points out that this text is a mystical reinterpretation of the Book of Genesis:

> Postulating the need for self-knowledge as the primary driving-force within the universe, Böhme justified the fallen world as the manifestation of an undifferentiated first principle, the necessary mirror through which the supreme being could attain consciousness. As the first principle, in Böhme's idiom the *Urgrund,* was deemed androgynous, "a masculine virgin, neither woman nor man," so too from the Biblical

account of Eve's creation out of Adam's rib did Böhme deduce Adam's originally dual-sexed condition.[51]

The principal correspondence between the *Mysterium Magnum* and Scriabin's libretto lies in Böhme's contention that the Fall of Man occurred in two phases: a fall into matter on Earth (and splitting of an ideal androgynous being into two), and a subsequent fall into evil in the Garden of Eden. At the end of the *Mysterium Magnum*, Böhme describes a third, future phase in Man's evolution: the return to a spiritual state. Scriabin depicts all three events in modified form in the *Preparatory Act* libretto.

From Novalis, whom Ivanov himself translated, Scriabin derived his symbols of light and dark. The theme of *Hymn to the Night* is the metaphoric union of earthly light and celestial night: "Lost primal harmony, the speaker claims, has resulted in a world of Light which has vanquished the supremacy of the realm of Night. Only the reunion of these antipodal forces can create a harmonious future. The particular attributes of the opposing principles, which are sustained throughout the work and gradually subsume the entire world, are associated from the beginning with sexual dichotomies."[52] Scriabin further defined Novalis's binary world in his libretto, specifying that celestial night is overseen by a feminine ruler, and earthly light by a masculine one.

The other androgynous text that informs the *Preparatory Act* is one that, in different forms, influenced works by Belïy, Ivanov, and other "mystic" Symbolists. It is the text of Wagner's *Tristan und Isolde*, a gloss on Gottfried von Strassburg's Medieval tragedy, in which the ideal of androgynous synthesis is associated with death and the overcoming of the ego. Following the act II love duet in that opera, Tristan and Isolde experience a merging of spirits and unimaginable bliss. The union is depicted in the aural rather than the visual realm, through a transposition of vocal registers, exchanges of instrumental and vocal sounds, and explicit crescendo effects. From Sabaneyev, we know that Scriabin sought to use all of these devices to depict the synthesis of the Masculine and Feminine Principles. He also planned to score the two roles for tenor and contralto, a sonic vesting of their androgynous coupling.

The union of these characters leads to a second such union in the *Preparatory Act* of the Wave (*Volna*, a feminine noun) and the Light Beam (*Luch*, a masculine noun). The Wave declaims:

I fly to you, valiant one
A moment more—I raised myself

And as tender foaminess
Was diffused into the languid-damp crevice.
O, divine moment of creation
A moment blessed, fiery
You revealed to me the reflection
Of white, fateful death.
You awakened in me awareness
Of dual being.
I am from now on a combination
Of "I" and an alien "not I."
[. . .]
O all-powerful desire
You live—and you are not I
Our impassioned caresses are alive
In multicolored being.
You and I and our supplication
Are a world of revealed wonders
Intoxicated by a vision
By the life of slumbering skies.
The miracle of union came to pass
The circle closed and there arose
The fruit of the marriage of wave and light
The starry face of the created world.

[Ya lechu k tebe, otvazhnaya,
Mig yeshcho—ya vozneslas'
I v poniklost' tomno-vlazhnuyu
Nezhnoy vspennost'yu vpilas'.
O, svyashchennïy mig tvoreniya
Mig blazhennïy, ognevoy
Tï yavil mne otrazheniye
Smerti beloy, rokovoy.
Razbudil vo mne soznaniye
Dvuyedinogo bïtiya.
Ya otnïne sochetaniye
"Ya" i chuzhdogo "ne-ya."
[. . .]
O zhelaniye vsevlastnoye
Tï zhivyosh',—i tï—ne ya
Zhivï laski nashi strastnïye
V mnogotsvete bïtiya.
Tï i ya i nashe moleniye
Mir raskrïvshikhsya chudes
Op'yaneniye snovideniyem
Zhizn'yu dremlyushchikh nebes.

Sbïlos' chudo sochetaniya
Krug zamknulsya i voznik
Plod volnï s luchom venchaniya
Mirozdaniya zvyozdnïy lik.[53]]

In Scriabin's hands, the Wagnerian theme of sexual bliss is made heavy and overly ornate—as evidenced by the first stanza of the excerpt. The lines "I am from now on a combination / Of 'I' and an alien 'not I'" refer to those declaimed by Tristan and Isolde in Wagner's act II love duet—"Du Isolde, Tristan ich, nicht mehr Isolde!; Tristan du, ich Isolde, nicht mehr Tristan!"—altered to suit a Theosophical context. The structure of the syntax shows Scriabin's adoption of a characteristic Symbolist poetic device: the uncoupling of language into its constituent phonemes. Scriabin offsets long and short vowels, accented and unaccented syllables. Each word sets others reverberating. As if Scriabin sought to encode the bell chimes that were to open the *Preparatory Act* into the actual language of the libretto, "ya" and "tï" pronouns reverberate with "ya" and "tï" noun endings. The result is a cacophony of verbal references that, taken together, augment the libretto itself with an infinity of associated meanings.

Scriabin did not identify the speakers in the second, unrevised half of the libretto, but he apparently wrote it for the Chorus and Narrator, since the events are described from the third person. Within it, he traces the fall and redemption of his biblical hero, adhering throughout to the alchemical principle that every object contains something of its opposite. Sister Death is both evil and good, a black angel and a "white ghost." The hero evolves from the Antichrist to Christ, Ivan the Terrible to the Good Shepherd, Cain to Abel. A comparison of two excerpts—the first taken from the start of the desert scene, the second from the end—will illustrate this point:

And there lacerated, all covered with abrasions
With a pierced heart, all in rags and dust
He lies, a God, forgotten by himself and others
The terrible potentate of his bloodstained earth.
[. . .]
Renewed in suffering, he strives toward people
To teach them what awaits them on the path;
He goes on wings of love and knowledge
To save them from the force of blind passions.

[I tam rasterzannïy, ves' yazvami pokrïtïy
S pronzyonnïm serdtsem, ves' v lokhmot'yakh i pïli
Lezhit on, Bog, sebya zabïvshiy i zabïtïy
Vlastitel' groznïy obagrennoy im zemli.

[. . .]
Stremitsya k lyudyam on, stradaniyem obnovlennïy
Im prepodat', shto ozhidayet ikh v puti;
Idyot lyubov'yu i znaniyem okrïlennïy
Ikh ot nasiliya strastey slepïkh spasti.[54]]

These contrary portrayals of the hero stem not from Nietzsche and Wagner but from Balmont and Solovyov. The depiction of exile and redemption
recalls Balmont's poetic cycle "Desert Star" ("Zvezda pustïni," 1898), in
which the protagonist journeys into the desert to find solace or enlightenment after rebelling against a cruel deity. The poem's imagery suggests ascension. One scholar notes that the line, "He lies, a God, forgotten by himself and others," is an "inexact" reference to Solovyov's line, "A wingless
spirit, imprisoned by earth, / a god forgotten by himself and others," from
an untitled 1883 poem.[55] Scriabin was doubtless drawn to Solovyov's poem
for its reference to the music of the spheres—the echo of "unearthly song"
and "heavenly harmony"—and the image of aspiring souls. But the symbolism extends further. As mentioned in chapter two, Solovyov was influenced by the Valentinian Gnostics, specifically their writings about the
Greek and Hebrew goddess Sophia, who desires to escape matter.[56] Though
Scriabin did not name his sources, it seems that he, in a manner strangely
akin to Rimsky-Korsakov, modelled the protagonist of his grand drama on
figures like Sophia.

The final scene of the libretto depicts the spiritual emancipation of the
Earth's peoples, who, like the hero, rise up to the stars. It begins with a solemn incantation from the Narrator and ends with an updraft of joy from
the Chorus. Scriabin's language turns impressionistic; the images shift
from dark to light, mobility to stasis. As if faced with the inexpressible, the
lines get shorter, and the concluding words trail off into ellipses:

Ignite, sacred temple from hearts' flame
Ignite and become a sacred fire
Merge blessedly in us, o ravishing father,
Merge with death in a heated dance!
In this final moment of divestment
We will cast off the eternities of our instants
Into this final lyre-consonance
We will all dissolve in the ethereal whirlwind
We will be born in the whirlwind!
We will awaken in heaven!
We will merge emotions in a united wave!
And in the splendid luster

Of the final flourish
Appearing to each other
In the exposed beauty
Of sparkling souls
We will disappear . . .
Dissolve . . .

[Zazhgis', svyashchennïy khram ot plameni serdets
Zazhgis' i stan' svyatïm pozharom
Smesis' blazhenno v nas, o sladostnïy otets,
Smesis' so smert'yu v tantse yarom!
V etot poslednïy mig sovlecheniya
[Za]brosim mï vechnosti nashikh mgnoveniy
V etom poslednom [so]zvuchii lirnom
Vse mï rastayem v vikhre efirnom
Rodimsya v vikhre!
Prosnyomsya v nebo!
Smeshayem chuvstva v volne yedinoy!
I v bleske roskoshnom
Rastsveta poslednego
Yavlyayas' drug drugu
V krase obnazhennoy
Sverkayushchikh dush
Ischeznem . . .
Rastayem . . .[57]]

These lines attest to the transformation of the *Preparatory Act* from a stage play into a quasi-liturgical drama. Scriabin structured them as an antiphonal dialogue between the Narrator and Chorus. (In Notebook "C," Scriabin indented the lines assigned to the Chorus; I have italicized them.) It is possible—though clearly anachronistic—to compare the passage to such Medieval liturgical texts as the *Quem quaeritis* dialogue, believed to have been used in the tenth century as an initiation ceremony, but later occupying the role of preface to the Introit of the Roman Catholic Easter Sunday Mass (and, even later, dislodged from the Mass to the end of Matins before the *Te Deum*).[58] The point is not to establish a connection between such remote texts but to stress that Scriabin conceived the conclusion of the *Preparatory Act* as a liturgy of resurrection—replete with bells, incense, and a smoking altar. The hero's spiritual path from sin to alienation to Dionysian ecstasy ends in solemn piety.

Scriabin's final lines are sincere: let all peoples commune, *will* the divine event to occur. Yet despite the theme, there is no reconciliation between his contradictory roles as Narrator and participant, no comment on the "authorless" state he intended to sustain in the future *Mysterium*. Paradoxically, he was unwilling to foster even a mirage of such a state in the *Preparatory Act* by remaining invisible and omniscient. In assuming the duties of impresario, he confirmed that, as in all rituals, a mastermind has to hold the performance together, lest it dissolve into chaos. The truly communal artwork proved as elusive to him as it had to Wagner.

THE FLOATING STATUS OF THE *PREPARATORY ACT* SKETCHES

At the points in the *Preparatory Act* text when physical sensations become euphoric, incantational, music becomes the arbiter of mystic experience. While Scriabin described the creative search for a better world in terms of the Wagnerian and Ivanovian synthesis of art forms, he contended that music alone could change the inner psyche, that harmony and melody facilitated communal bonding and spiritual uplifting. He wanted his music to be fluid, an outlet or passageway in a process of indoctrination. Marina Scriabine comments that dance and mime were to articulate "the rhythmic phases" of the music; she likewise contends that the composer "spoke of processions, of actors changing places [with spectators], of joint movement, to which the location of the celebration must be inwardly and architectonically adapted."[59] Unlike Nietzsche and Schopenhauer, Scriabin did not believe that music articulated the Cosmic Will in its various grades and provided awareness of symbolic essences rather than their representations. He instead assigned music a facilitating, narcotic role in his drama: his melodies and harmonies are not "pure" noumena but hallucinogens designed to elevate human consciousness to a transcendental locus. In this, Scriabin adopted the "mystic" Symbolist interpretation of the role of music in metaphysical reality, which countered that found in German idealist philosophy. It had tragic results. Since he did not find music to be transcendental art *an sich,* he became disillusioned with it. He did not hear in his music a music yet to come. New thinking set in. When Scriabin fell ill in 1914, he accepted the role of martyr to his own unrealizable artistic cause.

The extant music of the *Preparatory Act*—fifty-four partial pages of sketches in piano score, and a single page in short orchestral score—makes a chaotic impression.[60] Though the score may have been fixed in his mind either as a bounded entity or as a complex set of variations, the vertical sequences, intonational formulae, and melodies that he actually did write down (usually without clefs) provide little indication of the overall relationship between music, text, dance, and gesture in the *Preparatory Act.* It might be argued that the sonic remnants, reflecting the ideal work as it appeared to Scriabin's consciousness, constitute only a semblance of the "complete" *Preparatory Act,* an iconic trace of an unrealizable entity. They would thus illustrate the pattern of creative regression that long characterized his artistic schemes: just as the *Preparatory Act* supplanted the "unknowable" *Mysterium,* the musical sketches supplanted *its* "unknowable" score. At every stage in his creative path, a planned utopian work was replaced by symbolic fragments. Scriabin had sought to mastermind a divine experience, but all he could achieve was its partial representation. He was compelled to give up the actual text for the imaginary act, the asymptotic process that allowed him to sustain his dream of transcendental art, recognizing, perhaps, that the music he wanted to hear could not be heard, much less created, in the real world.

The sketches confirm this basic supposition but also suggest that Scriabin adopted different attitudes toward the compositional process. Despite his frequent, lengthy progress reports, he never provided a key to his musical symbolism because he himself continually shifted his stance toward it. Yet he did not seek to establish a set of stable musical referents in the sketches, an acoustic framework that would project fixed images to the listener. Rather, he evidently allowed the status of the sketches to float, to take on features of what Umberto Eco terms an "open" work.[61] The label is not anachronistic, since "open" work poetics arose during the French Symbolist era, the arcane flowering of *fin-de-siècle* culture that strongly influenced the Russian Symbolist era. Scriabin's sketches are "open" in two ways: in one sense, they *appear* to be the private papers of the composer's workshop, physically incomplete and not intended to impart meaning; yet, in another sense, the sketches offer us interpretative possibilities that suggest they were not in fact private papers but rather an autonomous artwork that imparts meaning in its own right. This paradoxical state of affairs is confirmed by the historical facts. Scriabin conceived the sketches in 1913 as a representation of the *Preparatory Act* libretto, a wobbly support for a Theosophical meditation, but also as the basic outline of an achievable work. In 1914 he re-envisioned them as mnemonic cues to guide him in his improvisations of the *Preparatory Act* at the piano. The sketches now bore an intrinsic mobility, a capacity to assume many different forms in the beholder's imagination. As an "open" work, they were part of the asymptotic process to the ultimate "open" work called the *Mysterium.* Lastly, in 1915, it appears that Scriabin came to see the sketches (and the empty spaces surrounding them) as the iconic traces of an unachievable work, symbols of impossible sound. The music fell off the page.

For an idea of the music of the *Preparatory Act,* we must turn to Sabaneyev, who in the autumn of 1914 heard Scriabin play portions of it.[62] He described his impressions:

> Sitting at the piano, A. N. [Scriabin] began to show the sketches of the *Preparatory Act* to me. Much of it was already somewhat familiar; there were the passages at the start with the "spoken delivery" against a *tremolo* background. Then A. N. began to play something new, "alien," unfamiliar to me. . . .
>
> "Tell me what you think of it!" he said, playing.
>
> It was, I recall, a rather long episode of indescribable charm, in whose music I immediately noticed something in common with the famous op. 74, no. 2 Prelude, which last season left me with such a profound impression. . . . There were secretive, slow harmonies, full of an unusual sweetness and spice, shifting against a backdrop of standing fifths in the bass. . . . I listened with a feeling of paralysis. There were several entirely unanticipated transitions and modulations. . . . The impression of this was, perhaps, the most powerful of all I'd heard from Scriabin, stronger than that of the third Symphony [in C major, opus 43, 1903], the sixth Sonata [in G major, opus 62, 1912], *Prometheus*, and the op. 74 Preludes [1914].
>
> "I'll have this when death appears," A. N. said clearly but quietly. "I think you'll recall that I read these excerpts to you" (these he had never read to me; evidently he had read them to one of his other friends and was confused). "'Death—sister, white ghost,'" he declaimed quietly in the calm, "'My radiant apparition, my sparkling apparition / Your renunciation of earthly life.'"
>
> "Here death will appear. . . . I still haven't finished it all; it will last longer. . . ."
>
> He continued to play the episode. . . . Then he asked me again to hold the bass, this time not the fifth, but some complex combination of sounds, and he continued playing something expansive. . . . It was perhaps greater, in general, than his creative fantasy had produced to date. It was a kind of colossal ascent, radiant, as in the *Poem of Ecstasy*, yet grander and more complex harmonically. There were even grouped trills, recalling the trills at the end of the *Poem of Ecstasy*. . . . What general character did this music have? One might best define its style as being between the first and second op. 74 Preludes, sometimes the fourth (evidently these small fragments arose from the composition of the big sketches). At times it recalled the "Garlands" from op. 73, a tender, fragile sonic fabric, where something mighty, almost painfully heated, sounded. Playing it, Scriabin became more and more animated.
>
> It seemed to me that I'd descended into an ocean of new sounds. . . . Much was similar to the aforementioned pieces, but much was entirely new. . . . The "death harmonies" ["garmonii smerti"] would not leave my head. . . . As though responding to my wishes, A. N. returned to

them and again played through the complete episode with its magical harmonies. . . . The newest [attribute] of this music was its complete transparency and sterility, and even the disappearance of that refined eroticism, which he had had earlier. . . . I felt that I'd descended into an enchanted, holy kingdom, where sounds and colors blended into one fragile and fantastic chord. . . . It all had a hue of illusion, unreality, and dreaminess—as though I'd had a sonic dream. . . .

A. N. broke the resonant silence. "Here I have the waves, remember: 'Waves surging / Surging foaming.'"

Something in the music of the waves, the sluggish and damp figurations, recalled the "waves" in Kashchey's kingdom [in the opera *Kashchey the Deathless*] by Rimsky-Korsakov—only that was simpleminded, while this actually evoked a magical kingdom. "Here the waves part, here the world blossoms. 'We are all united, a current directed,'" he declaimed quietly. . . . Then, as if he had leaped forward in his mind to the end of the outline, he said: "Here is the climax. . . . it will be better than the *Poem of Ecstasy!* . . ."

It was an accumulation of deep and broad harmonies, at the basis of which I recognized two series of standing triads, spaced a semitone apart. Noticing that I was looking at the structure of the harmony, A. N. said to me: "Don't look—you need to hear the effect. I'll show you how it's done later. . . . We're already near the end. . . . There'll be a dance . . . an ultimate dance of Ecstasy."[63]

The enchanting performance lasted several more minutes, but then Tatyana Shletser, roused from her bed by the *fortissimo* chords, entered the room. Upon realizing that her lover was not alone, she retreated, alarmed and unwilling to disturb the séance atmosphere. Sabaneyev imagined her as the "white ghost" of the *Preparatory Act* text, a somnambulist walking in a world of essences under the cover of night. In his view, she was part of the unfolding drama, not only as a prospective actress for the *Preparatory Act*, but also as the witness to the grand "mystic" Symbolist end game that would collapse Scriabin's life into art.

NIHILUM

Mystery: what are the "death harmonies"? They are probably projections of the "Prometheus" or "mystic" chord, which does not appear in the *Preparatory Act* sketches but seems to be the progenitor of the thick harmonies contained therein.[64] The chord is made up of pitches taken from three pitch collections: the periodically centric (but not symmetrical) octatonic scale, the symmetrical (but not centric) whole-tone scale, and the French sixth chord.[65] In measure 595 of *Prometheus*, where the "mystic" chord is spelled Gb-d-ab-c^1-(d^1)-f^1-bb^1, all but bb^1 are contained in a tone-semitone octatonic scale starting on gb, and all but f^1 are contained in a whole-tone scale starting on gb. In addition, the notes shared by the two scales—Gb, d, ab, and c^1—are enharmonically equivalent to a French sixth chord. The importance of the "mystic" chord as a nexus between the collections rests on the fact that each of them retains its pitches when transposed by certain intervals. The French sixth chord is invariant at octave and tritone transpositions, while the octatonic scale is invariant at octave, minor third, tritone, and major sixth transpositions. Like the chromatic scale, the whole-tone scale is maximally invariant, duplicating itself when transposed by any of its constituent intervals. Given that cyclic transpositions of the three collections tend to establish points of stasis in Scriabin's compositions, his use of the "mystic" chord toward the end of *Prometheus* serves to mark a hiatus in time and space.

Scriabin did not use the terms "Prometheus" or "mystic" to describe his famous sonority: they were invented respectively by Sabaneyev and Arthur Eaglefield Hull (in a 1916 article in *The Musical Times*).[66] He had his own name for it: *akkord pleromï*, or "chord of the pleroma." Richard Taruskin explains:

> Pleroma, a Christian gnostic term derived from the Greek for "plenitude," was the all encompassing hierarchy of the divine realm, located entirely outside of the physical universe, at immeasurable distance from man's terrestrial abode, totally alien and essentially "other" to the phenomenal world and whatever belongs to it. What we know as the mystic chord, then, was designed to afford instant apprehension of— that is, to *reveal*—what was in essence beyond the mind of man to conceptualize. Its preternatural stillness was a gnostic intimation of a hidden otherness, a world and its fullness wholly above and beyond rational or emotional cognition.[67]

Thus Scriabin conceived the "chord of the pleroma," or "mystic" chord as a musical symbol. It was to create a parallel, a harmonic correspondence between external reality (what Ivanov termed *realia*) and internal, or higher reality *(realiora)*. It was to establish a relationship between the mobile, temporal world of perceptible phenomena and the immobile, atemporal world of essences.

Andrey Bandura, the resident scholar at the A. N. Scriabin State Memorial Museum, develops this idea in a recent article on Scriabin's musical aesthetics.[68] He argues that Scriabin employed the "mystic" chord to depict a static state that preceded the birth of the Cosmos (the Big Bang), and the vacuum from which creation began. He contends that its "lower tetrachord," spelled G♭-d-a♭-c^1, is an accurate acoustic inversion of its "upper tetrachord," spelled (with duplicate pitches) g♭-c^1-f^1-b♭^{1}. Scriabin, in his view, aspired "to combine the uncombinable" in the "mystic" chord, "fusing in one sonority characteristics of acoustic realms having opposite coordinates in space and time, uniting the world and the 'antiworld.'"[69] Bandura's terminology clearly recalls that of Ivanov, who used it to define certain features of the poetic symbol. In his essay, "The Behests of Symbolism," Ivanov contended that the poetic symbol provides artists with dual vision, showing them that "what is above is also below," the "Macrocosm and the Microcosm." It also "absorbs in its sound echoes of subterranean keys, which resound from unknown places," providing both "a boundary and an exit into a beyond," the "daytime world" of dazzling material displays and the "nighttime world" that "frightens us and attracts us."[70] Unlike Ivanov, Bandura applies this conception of the symbol to Scriabin's music. He also postulates that the composer intended the "mystic" chord (and the chords of the *Preparatory Act* sketches) to be a hallucinogenic sound, a means to elevate human consciousness to a transcendental nexus. The principal problem with his interpretation—one that Scriabin perhaps confronted when composing his late works—is that the "mystic" chord sooner represents than enacts the desired spiritual uplift.

The *Preparatory Act* sketches contain sonorities that expand the qualities of musical stasis found in the "mystic" chord. They also symbolize in sound the implosion of time and space. As Manfred Kelkel and George Perle both note, the sonorities on pages 6, 12, 19(a), and 24 comprised four major seventh chords at minor third transpositions (with the duplicate notes crossed out), yielding vertical statements of all twelve notes of the chromatic scale. Those on page 14 and 19(b), in contrast, each contain two French sixth chords (c-e^1-f♯-b♭/ B♯-e-F♯-a♯ and a^1-c♯^{3}-d♯^{2}-g^2/a^2-c♯^{2}-d♯^{1}-g^3) related by minor third and a diminished seventh chord (g♯^{4}-b^3-d^4-f^3/g♯^{1}-b^3-d^4-f^2) required to complete a chromatic collection.[71] The same principle holds for a sonority on page 25 of the sketches, except that a d^1 supplants the d♯^{1} that would otherwise complete a French sixth chord. (The alteration may be a notational error.) A sonority on page 13, finally, does not arise through harmonic transposition; instead, it comprises hexachords taken from two major keys related by diminished fifth, F♯ and c^2.

From Sabaneyev's account, we know that these are the "death harmonies," inert acoustic structures modeled on traditional harmonies but devoid of functionality. As technical devices, they indicate that Scriabin tried in his last years to replace diatonic scales as the basis of his orchestral scores with octatonic, whole-tone, and semitonal pitch groups. As dramatic de-

Example 26.   Twelve-note sonorities in the *Preparatory Act* sketches; this is an exact transcription from the pages, retaining the vagaries of Scriabin's script

vices, they were likely constructed to express the inert state that follows the transfiguration of the Cosmos in the *Preparatory Act* libretto. They would have been heard at the end of the drama, following the union of the Masculine and Feminine Principles and reconstitution of humanity as a Total Being. As symbolic devices, however, the "death harmonies" impart a great deal more. Taruskin writes:

> Since it is harmonic progression that had always articulated the struc-
> tural rhythm of music, which is to say its sense of directed unfolding
> in time, a music based on universal invariant harmonies becomes quite
> literally timeless, as well as emotionally quiescent. The two qualities,
> invariance and timelessness, insofar as we are equipped to interpret
> musical messages, are in fact aspects of a single quality of quiescence,
> expressed respectively in two musical dimensions, the "vertical" and
> the "horizontal." We seem to experience an eschatological revelation,
> a gnosis that only music may impart: the full collapse of time and space
> and the dissolution of the ego. It was a dissolution at which the com-
> poser deliberately aimed, as we learn from Schloezer.[72]

Taruskin suggests that the "death harmonies," like the "mystic" chord, symbolize the "stripping away of the egoistic tyranny of desire." His read-ing implies that the dissolution of the ego, or "death" in the Symbolist con-cept of experience, involves the dissolution of the knowing consciousness, or "I," and the appearance of a new consciousness, or "not I." In revolving around themselves, recalling themselves to themselves, they act as metaphors for consciousness separating itself from itself. This vision of surmounting consciousness was central to Scriabin's plans. The *Mysterium*, the enactment of events to be depicted in the *Preparatory Act*, was to conclude not in death but in an expansion of life in new guise—a new Mystery of the soul.

Scriabin did not leave behind any details of his envisioned nirvana. We are instead left to evaluate the rest of the sketches for clues as to the broader dramatic shape of the *Preparatory Act*. Here it should first be noted that Scriabin did not notate the bell chords of the planned start. It remains unclear whether they were to be the type of resonant source found in so many Russian operas. (In Rimsky-Korsakov's *Legend of the Invisible City of Kitezh and the Maiden Fevroniya*, of course, church bells peal both on stage and off, therein designating the boundary between the two dramatic tiers of the work: the phenomenal world *[realia]* and the heavenly world *[realiora]*.) On page 1 of the *Preparatory Act* sketches, a blank space marks the place where the bell chimes might have been notated. Scriabin opted not to preserve on paper—or never got around to preserving—what he had played for his colleagues. Sabaneyev offers this remarkable description of the bell chords, which the composer planned to use in both the *Mysterium* and *Preparatory Act:*

> He [Scriabin] played the "bells" from the *Mysterium* for me. It seems the fragment wasn't notated anywhere. Brassy, sinister, and fateful harmony arose, like a "final warning" before the end of humanity, prepared for the terrible and ecstatic hour of ultimate reunion. I thought: what radiant and gloomy fantasy!
>
> My musings were cut short by [Scriabin's] exclamations, pensive and even melancholy: "Ah, why isn't it possible to make the bells ring from the heavens! Yes, they must ring from the heavens!"
>
> Now that was insane.[73]

The next few pages of the sketches contain musical self-quotations: Scriabin jotted down variations of the opening measures of his Poems (opus 71), Dances (opus 73), and Preludes (opus 74).[74] These might be interpreted as the composer's admission that perfect and eternal music can only be conveyed in imperfect and temporal form. They might also be interpreted thematically, however. To Sabaneyev, Scriabin admitted he had recycled older works in the sketches but emphasized that the quoted fragments would "receive extended development." He added that they would be part of a "very big episode of central importance"—an episode depicting both "Ecstasy" and "Death," "universal destruction" and "reconstitution."[75] The remark suggests that Scriabin wanted to vary and then "reconstitute" the quoted fragments in a new guise. They would thus have represented musically the main event in the *Preparatory Act* text: creation of a new world out of the vacuum resulting from a biblical annihilation of the old one.

The excerpts Scriabin extracted from his opus 74 Preludes provide further clues as to his dramatic plans. (It is of course appropriate that Scriabin would use "Preludes" as the basis of a "Preparatory" work.) On page 5 of the sketches, Scriabin cited the opening of his opus 74, no. 3. The original and sketch versions of the Prelude employ a tone-semitone octatonic scale framed by A♯ and A. Scriabin transposes the melodic line of the original by tritone, minor third, and major sixth. Since the octatonic scale is invariant at these transpositions, the pitch content of the melodic line remains unaltered. Scriabin embellishes the first three measures with only two non-octatonic pitches: a passing $g\sharp^1$ and d^2 that fall on the second beats. In the sketch version of these measures, however, Scriabin transposes the melodic line by perfect fourth, thereby enacting a modulation of sorts from the source octatonic collection to a second collection framed by D♯ and D. Beyond adding color to the lines, the irregular transposition appears to enact the start of the thematic dissolution of the Prelude music. In doing so, it vindicates Scriabin's remark that his Preludes were to "receive extended development" in the *Preparatory Act.*

On page 1 of the sketches (below the blank space where the bell chords might have been notated), Scriabin quoted the first three measures of his opus 74, no. 1 Prelude. Both the original and sketch version of the passage employ a seven-note variant of a tone-semitone octatonic scale to which Perle gave the name "derived heptatonic." Perle points out that the new scale (spelled A♯-B♯-C♯-D♯-E-F♯-G) had a particular advantage for Scriabin over the octatonic:

> Since successive t3 transpositions of an octatonic scale are identical in pitch-class content, there are only three independent octatonic collections: no hierarchical structuring is possible, since the intersecting pitch-class content of each with either of the others is always the same; one of the component "diminished 7th" chords is retained, the other one is replaced. The heptatonic scale, however, has twelve independent forms, four for each of the master scales, and each form shares a different collection of six pitch classes with each of the others derived from the same master scale, and a different collection of three pitch classes with each of the forms derived from the other two master scales.[76]

Example 27.   The *Preparatory Act* sketches, p. 5

Example 28.   The opening of the Opus 74, no. 3 prelude

Perle goes on to contend that Scriabin's tonal vocabulary remained "frustratingly restrictive" with the derived heptatonic, since it provided no distinction between vertical and horizontal pitch groups. The scale allowed the composer to compose long stretches of music with some sense of teleological unfolding but little in the way of tonal contrast. It might thus be argued that, like the "death harmonies," the opus 74, no. 1 Prelude evokes a mood of stasis and timelessness. Scriabin varies the flow of events only by occasionally inserting a non-heptatonic passing tone. Perle notes that, in the original version, the substitution of d^1 for $d\sharp^1$ in the second to last measure (not shown in Music Example 30) provides "a whole-tone variant $[a\sharp\text{-}b\sharp\text{-}d^1\text{-}e^1\text{-}f\sharp^1\text{-}g^1]$ of the [source] heptatonic scale." In the sketch version, the substitution of E$\sharp$ for E in the second measure signals the conversion of the source derived heptatonic scale starting on A$\sharp$ to a second such scale starting on B$\sharp$.

On page 15 of the sketches, Scriabin jotted the words "Before the Voice" ("Pered golosom") beside another quotation from the opus 74, no. 1 Prelude, a possible indication that this music was to be played just as the Masculine or Feminine Principle took center stage (as it were). It was not intended for the Chorus or Narrator, since, as Sabaneyev and Shletser attest, those entrances were to be marked by the now-lost tremolo bell chimes. In fact, since the music of Examples 27 and 29 is situated in the first pages of the *Preparatory Act* sketches, it may be that it was intended as an

Example 29. The *Preparatory Act* sketches, p. 1

Example 30. The opening of the Opus 74, no. 1 prelude

introduction, or even accompaniment, to the duet between the Masculine and Feminine Principles. (Scriabin played through the sketches in numerical order for Sabaneyev, so it would appear that they in some way correspond to the sequence of events in the libretto.) In the duet, the Feminine Principle speaks of "the ineffable bliss of dissolution," "abysses of life," and the "multicolored spaces" separating her from the Masculine Principle. The Chorus informs us that the characters arose of a desire to be "incarnated as pure souls," to know "dual being," and to find "contrasts." The recycled Prelude music might have shaped the recycled space that they inhabit; it might also have depicted the moment of struggle that exploded them into heterogeneous materiality. It is even arguable that the Prelude music would have granted the characters a degree of autonomy or consciousness in the work. It was not initially conceived for the *Preparatory Act* and thus was not intended to represent them in conventional drama-

Example 31.   The *Preparatory Act* sketches, p. 8

turgical fashion. Their music was to sound both "inside" and "outside" the score. Their voices were to double Scriabin's own authorial voice but exist alongside it as equally weighty and equally prominent forces in the work. The effect can be compared to Dostoyevsky's "polyphonic" prose, in which different semiautonomous parts of the mind take on the features of personae once they achieve verbal expression.[77] It was perhaps the one way in which Scriabin might have indeed created an "authorless" stage drama.

On page 8 of the *Preparatory Act* sketches, Scriabin quoted the first three measures of his opus 74, no. 2 Prelude, a work that he designated "very slow, contemplative." The Prelude unfolds through a number of chromatic alterations to a derived heptatonic scale starting on A♯. Toward the middle of the piece, these alterations produce a second derived heptatonic scale starting on B♯. (A sixteenth-note motive in measure 3, for example, is based on inflections of the second scale degree.) Sabaneyev reported that the "secretive, slow" harmonies of the Prelude, sounding against alternating F♯-c♯ and c-g fifths in the bass, had "unusual sweetness and spice." He also reported that the music was to accompany the stage entrance of Sister Death in the *Preparatory Act*.

Sister Death has no lines in the first half of the libretto. The Masculine and Feminine Principles refer to her there only as a "reflection," a "pale white and fatal" manifestation in the soul. While playing the excerpt, Scriabin quoted two of her lines from the second, unrevised half of the libretto. The source, a dialogue in quatrains between Sister Death and the unnamed hero, reads as follows:

> *Why did you come to me in the guise*
> *Of a blind monster with a corpse's mouth?*
> Child, you thus perceived the grandeur of death
> Through eyes of fear you saw all as evil.

> *My radiant countenance, my sparkling countenance*
> *Your renunciation of earthly life*
> Only he who flows forth toward me in pure love
> Comprehends me—admires me

Example 32.   The opening of the Opus 74, no. 2 prelude

[*Zachem prikhodila ko mne tï v oblichii*
Slepogo chudovishcha s mertvennïm rtom?
Ditya, tï vosprinyal tak smerti velichiye
Ochami ispuga vse videl tï zlom.

Moy oblik luchistïy, moy oblik sverkayushchiy
Tvoyo otrecheniye ot zhizni zemnoy
Lish′ chistoy lyubov′yu ko mne istekayushchiy
Menya postigayet, lyubuyetsya mnoy[78]]

Sister Death asks the unidentified hero to accept the blessing of "death" as the blessing of "life," to forsake the lap of the Earth for the path to the spirit realm, to the Sun that is good. But what would be the voice of Sister Death? How would she sound? Sabaneyev thought that the *Preparatory Act* would be "sung not with human voices but orchestral colors."[79] He found the music to be more instrumental than vocal. Scriabin told him about the choir and hierophants who would intone the libretto, and about the radiant arias of the characters, but he did not disclose how the sketch music would become stage music. Yet perhaps he did have a plan for Sister Death, a means to depict the dying-out of consciousness, the passage from "I" to "not I." Her sound—illusory and phantasmic, since, in accordance with Theosophical doctrine, "death" is illusory—would decline in volume in the indefinite interspace between onstage and offstage worlds. The erasure of her physical presence would prove liberating, presaging the journey *a realibus ad realiora*. The hero of the *Preparatory Act* first perceives Sis-

Example 33.   The three-voice *fugato* on p. 34 of the *Preparatory Act* sketches

ter Death to be evil but learns as the parable unfolds that "evil" is a "radiant" and "sparkling" light trapped in a material form.

The remaining sketches are motivic groups and agglomerations of octatonic and whole-tone scales *à la* Rimsky-Korsakov. These were to represent the colorful, shimmering Waves of Life, the Light Beam, and Chorus. The final destination of the brass fanfares and the quotation from the *Poem of Ecstasy* cannot be deduced from the shards. Scriabin did declare, however, that he would set the "awakening of the Earth" to dense counterpoint. Accordingly, on page 34 of the sketches, Scriabin included a three-voice *fugato* with a subject containing all twelve notes of the chromatic scale, and (assuming that the clefs are treble and bass) with entries at the diminished fifth and the octave. It provides apt accompaniment to the text it sets, lines in the libretto spoken by the Wilderness:

> Having identified myself in space as wilderness
> A dry and burning kiss of light and earth
> Having banished forest life from my fields
> And loathed the living songs of a stream.

A winged caress, I began to flutter like a bird,
And I, tormenting, returned to life in beastly form.
Twisting-crawling, I awoke as a snake
Wearied, I take kindly to the damp.

[Sebya pustïney ya v prostranstve opoznavshiy
Lucha s zemlyoy sukhoy i znoynïy potseluy
Lesnuyu zhizn' iz oblastey svoikh izgnavshiy
I nenavidyashchiy zhivïye pesni struy.

Ya laska vskrïl'naya, ya ptitsey vstrepenulas',
A ya, terzayushchaya, zverem ozhila.

Izvivno-polznaya, zmeyeyu ya prosnulas'
Stikhii vlazhnoy ya, istomnaya, mila.][80]

These lines come immediately before the biblical tale told by the composer in the guise of Narrator. The words "twisting" and "crawling," an allusion to the sensuous "I" who seduces the Earth, are mirrored in the *fugato*, whose serpentine subject, reminiscent of the b-minor fugue in *Das wohltemperierte Klavier* book 1 (BWV 869), is woven into a texture with further Bachian resonance: the chorale prelude *Through Adam Came Our Fall* (*Durch Adams Fall ist ganz verderbt*, BWV 637). Both of Bach's compositions are parables about original sin; both also decry the cravings of the individual will. The other point of comparison for the *fugato* is the excerpt entitled "On Science" ("Von der Wissenschaft") from Richard Strauss's tone poem *Thus Spoke Zarathustra* (opus 30, 1896), also a *fugato* whose subject contains all twelve notes of the chromatic scale. Perhaps needless to say, both Scriabin's and Strauss's works have a common programmatic basis in Nietzsche's philosophy. Lastly, it must be noted that Scriabin's *fugato* is the most concrete music in the *Preparatory Act* sketches, and it accompanies the most concrete passage in the libretto, the last stanzas the composer managed to revise before his death.[81]

Like the other excerpts discussed so far, the *fugato* was conceived as representation of the text. Yet what Sabaneyev heard Scriabin play marked a further stage in the evolution of the sketches. Scriabin actually engaged his colleague as collaborator in his improvised version of the *Preparatory Act*. After describing the planned performance at the Indian temple, he moved to the piano to demonstrate how he intended to bring together the audience and cast. He played through the sketches, and then, as if "responding to [Sabaneyev's] wishes," "returned to them and played through them again" to heighten the effect. To use Ivanov's expression, Sabaneyev not only

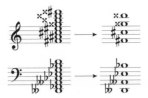

Example 34.   A twelve-note sonority and its eight-note reduction on p. 12 of the *Preparatory Act* sketches

"contemplated" but helped to "create" the *Preparatory Act*. The sketches became part of an "open" work that would let its audience determine its contours and proportions. It would demand *collective creation:* the free flow of thought between the minds of the composer, performer, and the populace—all without altering its plot or impairing its divine intent.

This is a necessarily loose and unavoidably paradoxical interpretation of the sketches. We cannot know that they would have constituted an "open" work by demanding audience participation, as suggested here. For they are ineluctably "open" simply because they are physically incomplete. Sabaneyev's recollection of the séance with Scriabin provides a speculative link between the two scenarios: the sketches are the first "open" stage in the creation of an "open" work, the first mnemonic cues to guide Scriabin in the performance of the score at the Eastern shrine. Both the composing and the performing of the *Preparatory Act* would imply a fusion of separate consciousnesses and a "polyphonic" process of change and growth. To compose and to perform the *Preparatory Act* would be to offer it up to this process.

Scriabin indicated little else in the sketches about the sonic shape of the *Preparatory Act*. To his friend, he remarked only that "the *Mysterium* will have enormous simplification. Everybody thinks that I make everything more and more complex. I do, but in order to surmount complexity, to move away from it. I must attain the summit of complexity in order to become simple. In the *Preparatory Act* I will have two-note harmonies and unisons." [82] The statement shows the extent to which the *Mysterium* and *Preparatory Act* had become one in Scriabin's imagination. It also reveals that he planned to parallel the progression from mystery to revelation in the libretto with a corresponding move from ultrachromatic chords to pristine dyads in the music. To his participants, the readiness to welcome dissonance in this world would be a necessary prelude to consonance in the next. The sketches evidently illuminate the process. On page 7, Scriabin included an example of first species counterpoint; on page 8 and following, he jotted down sequences of open fifths, tritones, and trichords containing major and minor thirds and seconds. Lastly, on page 12, he reduced a twelve-note chord to its basic framework, a stack of perfect and augmented fifths that itself constitutes an octatonic scale.

In between these reduced and simple passages are only erased notes and empty spaces. What do they suggest? They appear to illustrate the pattern of diminishing expectations that for so long dogged Scriabin's theurgic aspirations. But they imply more. To the two interpretations of the sketches advanced so far—the sketches as extant vestiges of a possible but unrealized score, and the sketches as mnemonic cues for improvised performances of the *Preparatory Act*—we must add a third: the sketches as a *work* in the broadest metaphysical sense of the term. In fact, the final pages suggest that Scriabin sought to frame emptiness, to preserve the schism between possible and impossible sound as an integral part of the *Preparatory Act*. For if it was to be the expression of an ideal, he realized that it could not take on material shape. It could retain from the libretto only the impression of void, emptiness, a reduction of experience into silence.

In this scenario, the composer's apocalyptic vision altogether thwarted representation. It led only to the blasting of sight and sound evident on the final, partly orchestrated page of sketches: page 55. The music is largely incomprehensible. On the left side of the page, Scriabin provided a 2/4 time signature for music in 3/4 time; in the margin on the right side, he jotted faint rhythmic patterns (not shown in Music Example 35); on the four systems, he inscribed melodic motives and scale incipits in seemingly random places. The rhythms seem only to impede one another.

Had this page been completed, Scriabin might have filled in the gap separating the chromatic melody containing the pitches b♯, e^1, d♯^{1}, d^1, g♯, d^1, b♭^{1}, f♯^{2}, a^2, f♯^{2}, e^2, d^2, a^1, b♭^{1} on the first system, fifth staff, and the melodic fragments that succeed it on the upper three staffs. He also might have composed a bridge between the octatonic pattern containing the pitches g♯, d, c♯, G, g♯, G, g♯, d, c♯, G, g♯ on the fourth system, third staff, and the whole-tone pentachord that follows. The spaces in between also have an indexing value. The silence offers a hallucination of nothing. What is this "nothing"? It is the anaphora of an ineffable work, a symbol of Scriabin's last rite. He had literally reached that ultimate stage in creativity where, in Ivanov's words, there was no longer a "barrier" between him and an uncovered abyss "that opens up into silence."[83]

In sum: the page could not be completed. The ideal of the *Mysterium* gave way to the *Preparatory Act*, which in turn yielded a partial libretto, some musical sketches, and finally silence. Each phase symbolized the theurgic ideal, the noumenal entity beyond phenomena, but each receded further from it, the whole process amounting tacitly to an acknowledgment that the ideal was unachievable within the realm of human experience. By 1915, the *Preparatory Act* was no longer an "open" work but an empty castle haunted by forsaken *dramatis personae*. Scriabin was not in the end defeated in his plans—he triumphed—but at a fearful cost: creative block and compositional paralysis. He did not fail; no artist could accomplish what he set out to accomplish. Rather, like Mallarmé in his unfinished *Livre*, he transcended artistry.[84] His vision dissolved in the "mighty bonfire" of a "holy sacrifice."

THE UTOPIAN DOMAIN

A final point in conclusion concerning the status of possibility and actuality in the *Preparatory Act*. Earlier it was suggested that in the hypothetical finished versions of the libretto and music the opposition between the Feminine and Masculine Principles would resolve in the utopian figure of a Total Being, a symbol of the spiritual emancipation of humans irrespective of gender, race, creed, or social rank. Through the androgynous joining of the two protagonists, the boundary between worlds would be traversed and made invisible. Like the draft libretto, the incomplete musical sketches for the *Preparatory Act* designate the limit between earthly vice and divine ecstasy. They articulate transcendence (marked by a merging of consciousnesses and *vseyedinstvo*), and establish a homology between the composer's inner world and the outer world. It appears in retrospect, however, that, like the *Mysterium*, Scriabin's effort to attain his artistic goal was more significant to him than its actual attainment. He may have realized that, while the desire for transcendence was an animating force, life in a utopian domain where this desire was actually sated would be unbearable; a "universe of pure fantasy" would be "a universe without surplus enjoyment . . . a perfectly balanced universe where the object-cause of desire cannot be brought into effect."[85] By not completing the *Preparatory Act*, Scriabin was able to retain his "object-cause of desire": the vision of utopia that preoccupied and sustained the "mystic" Symbolists.

In the end, the outlandish subject matter, antique references, and familiar Wagnerian precepts could not hide the fundamental paradoxes and inconsistencies of Scriabin's ideas. For all his claimed benevolence and concern for humanity, the *Mysterium* and *Preparatory Act* were fruits of solipsism, less a plan for communal celebration than for the artist's own

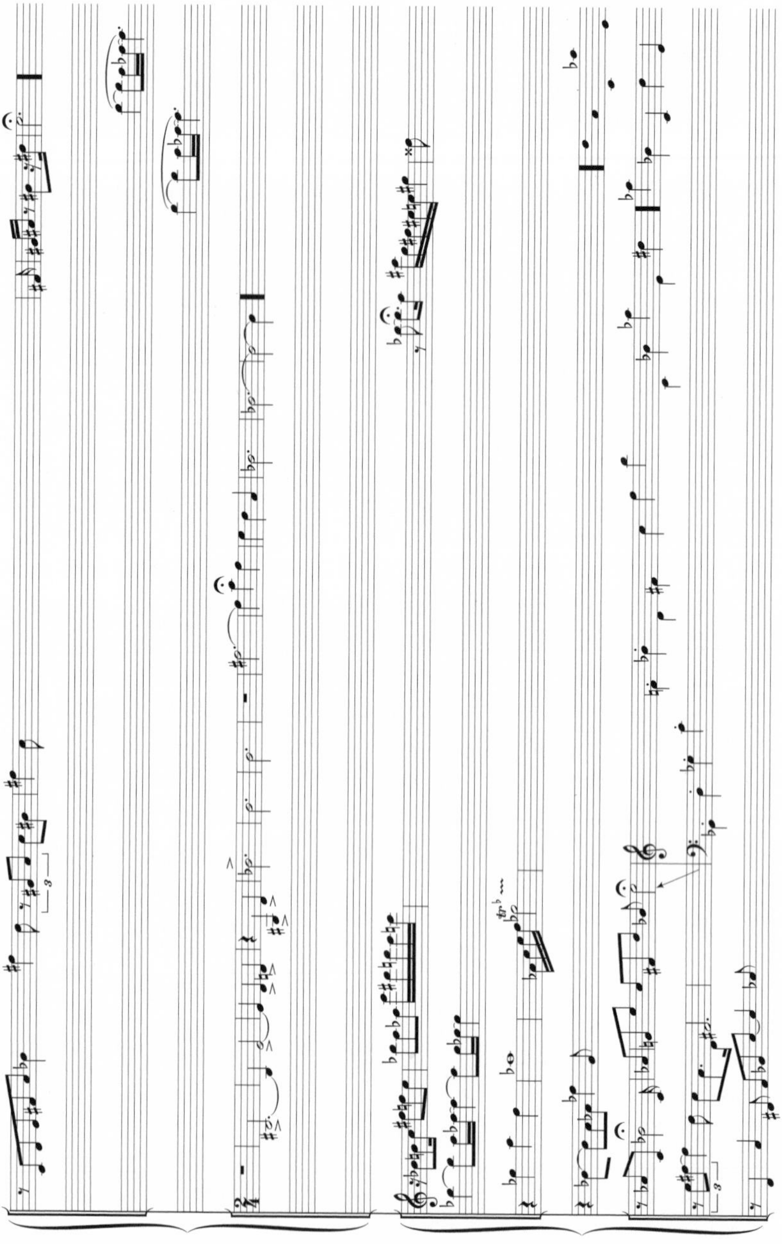

Example 35. The *Preparatory Act* sketches, p. 55

spiritual emancipation. In 1905, he declared, "For every curve in my fantasy another past and future is required."[86] This remarkable statement shows finally that it was less a concern for others that motivated Scriabin in his creative work than the search for his inner self. Christ, with whose suffering he identified, the Theosophists, whom he admired, and humanity at large were reduced in his grand plan to metaphors for his own, purely personal, experience. Scriabin hoped to assume the role of High Priest to the entire "mystic" Symbolist movement but formed in solitude the artistic concept his poet friends sought in vain. Yet, as Ivanov noted, there was no "teacher's role" for Scriabin to take, no way to "author" an "authorless" work. What is both distressing and unsettling in the tale of his final work is that it not only silenced his voice but encouraged him to accept the silencing of his own body. His was an unfortunate end, despite his belief that the path of the soul led to eternity and light. The tragedy was not unique to Scriabin: it was typical of the "mystic" Symbolist era, whose legacy is largely one of broken lives and abandoned ideals. The era ended with the cataclysmic events of 1917, which the "mystic" Symbolists generally supported but which presaged their communal, or collective, demise. For that event, Scriabin's vision of apocalypse was just the Preparatory Act.

NOTES

1. Valeriy Bryusov, "Svyashchennaya zhertva," in *Sobraniye sochineniy*, ed. P. G. Antokol'skiy et al., 7 vols. (Moscow: Khudozhestvennaya literatura, 1973–75), 6: 99. My translation and interpretation of the passage is a modified version of that provided in Pyman, *A History of Russian Symbolism*, 178–79.

2. Helene Blavatsky, a clairvoyant and spiritualist, established the Russian Theosophical Society in 1875. It aimed to found a world religion and "Universal Brotherhood" without distinctions of creed or race. Carlson (*"No Religion Higher than Truth": A History of the Theosophical Movement in Russia, 1875–1922,* 3–14, 198–205) notes that the "mystic" Symbolists defined their world view in Theosophical terms as a synthetic religious and philosophical doctrine informed by ancient occult dogmas. Scriabin encountered Theosophy not in Russia but in France, where he read French editions of Blavatsky's *The Secret Doctrine: The Synthesis of Science, Religion, and Philosophy* (1888) and *The Key to Theosophy* (1895). In a 25 April 1905 letter from Paris to his lover, Tatyana Shletser, he exclaimed: *"La Clef de la théosophie* is a wonderful book. You will be amazed how close it is to me [my thought]" (A. Skryabin, *Pis'ma,* ed. A. V. Kashperov [Moscow: Muzïka, 1965], 369). In 1908, while staying in Brussels, Scriabin enrolled in the Belgian Sect of the Theosophical Society; from 1911 in Moscow he subscribed to three Theosophical journals: *Le revue théosophique belge,* the Italian *Societa theosofica,* and the St. Petersburg publication *Vestnik teosofii.*

3. Scriabin, undated diary entry, as quoted by Andrey Bandura, "O 'Predvaritel'nom deystvii' A. N. Skryabina," in *Ucheniye zapiski,* ed. O. M. Tompakova (Moscow: Kompozitor, 1993), 119.

4. See B[oris] F[yodorovich] Shletser, "Zapiska B. F. Shletsera o 'Pred-varitel'nom deystvii,'" *Russkiye propilei: Materialï po istorii russkoy mïsli i literaturï* 6 (1919): 99–119; see also idem, *A. Skryabin: Lichnost', Misteriya* (Berlin: Grani., 1923). This book was revised and translated by Nicolas Slonimsky as Boris de Schloezer, *Scriabin: Artist and Mystic* (Berkeley: University of California Press, 1987).

5. These accounts are unfortunately colored by Shletser's ideological and personal biases. For instance, Shletser (*Scriabin: Artist and Mystic*, 64–66) downplayed the importance of the Hegelian philosopher Sergey Trubetskoy (1862–1905) in Scriabin's intellectual maturation, claiming instead that Georgiy Plekhanov (1856–1918), a Marxist and—by 1917—Leninist philosopher he himself admired, had a greater influence on the composer. However Bryusov (*Dnevniki: 1891–1910*, ed. I. M. Bryusova, introd. N. S. Ashukin [Moscow: Izdanie M. and S. Sabashnikovïkh, 1927], 111), among others, noted that the opposite was true.

6. This was the third operatic project undertaken by Scriabin. The M. I. Glinka Central State Museum of Musical Culture (Gosudarstvennïy tsentral'nïy muzey muzïkal'noy kul'turï imeni M. I. Glinki) in Moscow holds thirteen pages of piano-vocal sketch materials for a childhood project entitled *Liza* (fund 31, item 143, 1879–80), and four pages of verse lines and melodic motives for *Keystut i Biruta*, a projected opera to a text by M. Lipina (fund 31, item 144, 1890).

7. Mikhaíl Gershenzon, ed., "Zapisi A. N. Skryabina: Libretto operï, 1900–1902 gg.," *Russkiye propilei: Materialï po istorii russkoy mïsli i literaturï* 6 (1919): 129.

8. Schloezer, *Scriabin: Artist and Mystic*, 163–64.

9. Bryusov, "Na smert' A. N. Skryabina," in *Sobraniye sochineniy* 2: 200–201. My thanks to Michael Wachtel for allowing me to quote his translation of these two stanzas.

10. Gershenzon, ed., "Zapisi A. N. Skryabina: Zapis' 1904–1905 gg.," *Russkiye propilei: Materialï po istorii russkoy mïsli i literaturï* 6 (1919): 151.

11. Gershenzon, ed., "Zapisi A. N. Skryabina: Zapis' 1905–1906 gg.," *Russkiye propilei: Materialï po istorii russkoy mïsli i literaturï* 6 (1919): 183.

12. Blavatsky, *The Secret Doctrine: The Synthesis of Science, Religion, and Philosophy*, 2 vols. (1888; reprint, Covina, Calif.: Theosophical University Press, 1925), 1: 268.

13. Ellen von Tidebӧhl, "Memories of Scriabin's Volga Tour (1910)," *The Monthly Musical Record* 6 (1926): 168.

14. The signed copy is housed in Moscow at the A. N. Scriabin State Memorial Museum (Gosudarstvennïy memorial'nïy muzey A. N. Skryabina). Ivanov's inscription reads: "To deeply respected Alexander Nikolayevich Scriabin in memory of a passing acquaintance and in hope of a deeper one." For a detailed summary of the mythological and autobiographical aspects of Ivanov's poetry cycle, see Wachtel, *Russian Symbolism and Literary Tradition: Goethe, Novalis, and the Poetics of Vyacheslav Ivanov* (Madison: University of Wisconsin Press, 1994), 102–5.

15. L[eonid] Sabaneyev, *Vospominaniya o Skryabine* (Moscow: Muzïkal'nïy sektor gosudarstvennogo izdatel'stva, 1925), 162.

16. Patricia Mueller-Vollmer, "Ivanov on Skrjabin," in *Cultura e memoria: atti del terzo Simposio Internazionale dedicato a Vjaceslav Ivanov*, ed. Fausto Malcovati, 2 vols. (Florence: La Nuova Italia, 1988), 1: 191.

17. For an exploration of these ideas as manifest in Wagner's music dramas, see Abbate, *Unsung Voices: Opera and Musical Narrative in the Nineteenth Century*, 156–249.

18. Max Hochschüler, "Pis'mo iz Bayreyta: 'Kol'tso Nibelunga' i 'Parsival,'" *Vesï* 1, no. 9 (September 1904): 43–44. My discussion of this passage, and my discussion of Ivanov and Wagner, is greatly indebted to Bartlett, *Wagner and Russia*, 126–37.

19. V. R. Shcherbina et al., eds., *Literaturnoye nasledstvo 85: Valeriy Bryusov* (Moscow: Nauka, 1976), 463–64.

20. Vyacheslav Ivanov, "Vagner i Dionisovo deystvo," in *Rodnoye i vselenskoye*, 35.

21. Ibid., 36.

22. Malcolm H. Brown, "Skriabin and Russian 'Mystic' Symbolism," *19th-Century Music* 3 (1979–80): 42–51. Brown claims that Ivanov's Symbolism, more than Blavatsky's Theosophy, informed Scriabin's post-1909 compositions. As evidence, Brown notes the similarity between Scriabin's remarks about Wagner to Sabaneyev and Ivanov's remarks about Wagner in "Premonitions and Portents" ("Predchuvstviya i predvestiya," 1906) and "On the Limits of Art" ("O granitsakh iskusstva," 1913).

23. Nikolai Ulyanov, unpublished memoirs, quoted by I. A. Mïl'nikova, "Stat'i Vyach[eslava] Ivanova o Skryabine," in *Pamyatniki kul'turï. Novïye otkrïtiya. Yezhegodnik 1983*, ed. T. V. Nikolayeva (Leningrad: Nauka, 1985), 92. For an eyewitness account of Ivanov and Scriabin's relationship, see Lidiya Ivanova, "Vospominaniya o V. Ivanove," *Novïy zhurnal* 148 (1982): 158–60.

24. Sabaneyev, *Vospominaniya o Skryabine*, 82.

25. Ibid., 150. The comment dates from 1911.

26. Anna Goldenweiser (Gol'denveizer), undated diary entry (1912?), in Skryabin, *Pis'ma*, 612. Scriabin's surprising remark about Wagner is strong evidence of his ignorance about the construction of the Bayreuth *Festspielhaus*, and his reliance on Ivanov, Sabaneyev, and others for details about Wagnerian aesthetics. Though *Lohengrin, Der Ring des Nibelungen,* and *Tristan und Isolde* were frequently performed in St. Petersburg and Moscow, Scriabin knew little about Wagner's *Gesamtkunstwerk* ideal. He instead derived his ideas about synthetic art from Ivanov's writings on Dionysus and Apollo, Solovyov's ideas about spiritual communion, and his own sketchy knowledge of pagan ritual and Eastern religious doctrines. He studied Wagner's scores as Rimsky-Korsakov had: not for their "mystic" insights, but for their musical and literary *topoi*. On this point, see Richard Taruskin, *Stravinsky and the Russian Traditions*, 2 vols. (Berkeley: University of California Press, 1996), 1:487–90.

27. Andrey Belïy, "Oblomki mirov," 1908, as paraphrased in Pyman, *A History of Russian Symbolism*, 300.

28. Scriabin's description of his role in the *Mysterium*, as paraphrased by his biographer Yuliy Engel' in "A. N. Skryabin: Biograficheskiy ocherk," *Muzïkal'nïy sovremennik: Zhurnal muzïkal'nogo iskusstva* 4–5 (1916): 90.

29. Schloezer, *Scriabin: Artist and Mystic*, 183. Scriabin acknowledged this problem in his philosophical writings, yet persisted in his plans to create the *Mysterium*. In his 1905–6 diaries, for example, he mused: "Reality presents itself to me as a multitude of moments in the infinity of space and time; in this my experience is the center of a sphere of infinitely large radius. . . . On the one hand, honestly reasoning, I should deny everything lying outside the sphere of my consciousness. . . . On the other—within me exists the conviction . . . that my individual consciousness is only a drop in the ocean of spheres that are separate and concealed from one another" (Gershenzon, ed., "Zapisi A. N. Skryabina. Zapis' 1905–1906 gg.," 164–65).

30. Slavoj Žižek's definition of "ethical uncertainty," itself derived from Kantian, Hegelian, and Lacanian definitions of subjectivity. See his *Tarrying with the Negative: Kant, Hegel, and the Critique of Ideology* (Durham: Duke University Press, 1993), 70–71. For a clarification, see 69–73.

31. Shletser, "Zapiska B. F. Shletsera o 'Predvaritel'nom deystvii,'" 104–5.

32. Sabaneyev, *Vospominaniya o Skryabine,* 103.

33. Scriabin, 1913 diary entry, cited by Shletser, "Zapiska B. F. Shletsera o 'Predvaritel'nom deystvii,'" 114.

34. The phrase *"a realibus ad realiora"* ("from the real to the realer") is discussed by Belïy in his article "Realiora," *Vesï* 5, no. 5 (May 1908): 59–62.

35. Schloezer, *Scriabin: Artist and Mystic,* 265.

36. Letter of 20 September 1850; Richard Wagner, *Sämtliche Briefe,* ed. Gertrud Strobel et al., 8 vols. (Leipzig: Deutscher Verlag für Musik VEB, 1967–93), 3: 425–26.

37. Sabaneyev, *Vospominaniya o Skryabine,* 265.

38. Ibid., 275.

39. Ibid., 307. Faubion Bowers provides the unpleasant details of Scriabin's illness in *Scriabin: A Biography of the Russian Composer 1871–1915,* 2 vols. (Tokyo: Kodansha International, 1969), 2: 277–82.

40. The essays are titled "Scriabin's View of Art" ("Vzglyad Skryabina na iskusstvo," 1915), "The National and the Universal in Scriabin's Creative Work" ("Natsional'noye i vselenskoye v tvorchestve Skryabina," 1916), "Scriabin and the Spirit of Revolution" ("Skryabin i dukh revolyutsii," 1917), "Skryabin" (1919), and "A Speech in Memoriam of A. N. Scriabin for an Evening at the Grand Hall of the Conservatory" ("Rech', posvyashchennaya pamyati A. N. Skryabina na vechere v Bol'shom zale konservatorii," 1920). Ivanov read his drafts of the first three essays at meetings of the Scriabin memorial society, Scriabin's Wreath (Venok Skryabina), and then rewrote them for publication as a monograph. Financial problems compelled his publisher, Alkonost, to postpone and then cancel the printing. Proofs showing Ivanov's corrections are preserved at RGALI, fund 225, list 1, item 33. Ivanov read the last two articles at Scriabin memorial concerts. Mïl'nikova includes "Skryabin" in "Stat'i Vyach[eslava] Ivanova o Skryabine," 113–15. The fourth essay is preserved at RGALI, fund 225, list 1, item 40.

For a discussion of the poems Ivanov dedicated to Scriabin, see Rolf-Dieter Kluge, "Vjaceslav Ivanovs Beitrag zu einer symbolistischen Theorie der Literatur und Kunst als Schlüssel zum Verständnis seiner Aufsätze über Aleksandr Skrjabin," in *Vjaceslav Ivanov. Russischer Dichter-europäischer Kulturphilosoph. Beiträge des IV. Internationalen Vjacheslav Ivanov Symposiums. Heidelberg, 4.-10. September 1989,* ed. Wilfried Potthoff (Heidelberg: Universitätsverlag C. Winter, 1993), 240–49.

41. Ivanov, "Vzglyad Skryabina na iskusstvo," in *Sobraniye sochineniy,* ed. D. V. Ivanov and Ol'ga Deshart, 4 vols. (Brussels: Foyer Oriental Chrétien, 1971–87), 3: 174 (additional volumes are in the process of publication). In Greek and Roman mythology, Parcae are the three goddesses who decide people's fates, specifically their allotment of misery and misfortune. In Greek mythology, Pythia is a guardian of the oracle of Apollo at Delphi. Lethe, another figure in Greek mythology, is the daughter of Eris (Strife) and the incarnation of oblivion. Lethe is also the name of a river in the infernal regions.

Mark Meychik echoed Ivanov's views about Scriabin on the occasion of the composer's funeral: "He did not die. They took him away from the people when he neared the realization of his conception. The expression 'in the heavens they see to it the trees do not reach the sky' does not exist for nothing. Through music Scriabin beheld much of what is not given to Man to know, and he aspired to convey all of this to the people. Scriabin was not that Prometheus who stole fire from the Gods for the people. No, he wanted to lead people to the very kingdom of the Gods and thus he had to perish!" ("Nad mogiloy A. N. Skryabina," as quoted by Bandura, "O 'Predvaritel'nom deystvii' A. N. Skryabina," 121.)

42. Sabaneyev, *Vospominaniya o Skryabine*, 266.

43. Shletser, "Zapiska B. F. Shletsera o 'Predvaritel'nom deystvii,'" 101; Valentina Rubtsova, *Aleksandr Nikolayevich Skryabin* (Moscow: Muzïka, 1989), 356–57. Notebook "B" is preserved in Moscow at the A. N. Scriabin State Memorial Museum as fund 26098, no. 3.

44. Information in this section is taken from Carlson, *"No Religion Higher than Truth": A History of the Theosophical Movement in Russia, 1875–1922*, 116–28; the two tiers are reproduced, with slight modifications, from 120–21.

45. Blavatsky, *The Secret Doctrine: The Synthesis of Science, Religion, and Philosophy*, 1: 231–32. The quoted phrases are from the Book of Dzyan, the "secret" and possibly spurious Sanskrit text that lies at the heart of her Theosophical paradigms.

46. Marina Scriabine, "Überlegungen zum *Acte préalable*," trans. A. Michaely and H.-K. Metzger (from French), *Musik-Konzepte* 32/33 (September 1983): 14–15.

47. Shletser, *Scriabin: Artist and Mystic*, 296.

48. Gershenzon, ed., "Predvaritel'noye deystviye: Poslednyaya redaktsiya," in *Russkiye propilei: Materialï po istorii russkoy mïsli i literaturï* 6 (1919): 235. Publication of the libretto (Notebooks "C" and "D") in the serial was abetted by Ivanov, who, in addition to participating in the Scriabin memorial society, headed up a committee dedicated to preserving the composer's poetic texts.

49. Bowers, *Scriabin: A Biography of the Russian Composer 1871–1915*, 62, 102; Nietzsche, *Thus Spoke Zarathustra*, in *The Portable Nietzsche*, trans. and ed. Walter Kaufmann (New York: Viking Press, 1984), 333. Ann Lane assesses Nietzsche's impact on Scriabin in "Bal'mont and Scriabin: The Artist as Superman," in *Nietzsche in Russia*, ed. Bernice Rosenthal (Princeton: Princeton University Press, 1986), 209–12.

50. Gershenzon, ed., "Predvaritel'noye deystviye: Poslednyaya redaktsiya," 236.

51. Sara Friedrichsmeyer, *The Androgyne in Early German Romanticism: Friedrich Schlegel, Novalis, and the Metaphysics of Love* (Bern: Peter Lang, 1983), 29–30.

52. Ibid., 93.

53. Gershenzon, ed., "Predvaritel'noye deystviye: Poslednyaya redaktsiya," 245–46. The line "The starry face of the universe" is a reference to Balmont's poem "Star-faced" ("Zvezdolikiy"), the fourth to last poem in his 1909 collection *Zelyonïy vertograd. Slova potseluynnïye (A Green Garden. Kissing Words)*.

54. Gershenzon, ed., "Predvaritel'noye deystviye: Rannyaya redaktsiya," *Russkiye propilei: Materialï po istorii russkoy mïsli i literaturï* 6 (1919), 223, 226.

55. Mïl'nikova, "Stat'i Vyach[eslava] Ivanova o Skryabine," 91, col. 2. In the original Russian, Solovyov's despondent lines read "Beskrïlïy dukh, zemleyu polonennïy, / Sebya zabïvshiy i zabïtïy bog."

56. See p. 124 and p. 178, fn. 28.

57. Gershenzon, ed., "Predvaritel'noye deystviye: Rannyaya redaktsiya," 234–35; emphasis added. The phrase "Ignite, holy temple from hearts' flame" refers to the title and motifs of Ivanov's poetry collection *Cor Ardens*.

58. For a summary of recent arguments about the origins of the *Quem quaeritis* dialogue, see George Klawitter, "Dramatic Elements in Early Monastic Induction Ceremonies," in *Drama in the Middle Ages: Comparative and Critical Essays,* ed. Clifford Davidson and John H. Stroupe (New York: AMS Press, 1991), 43–60.

59. Scriabine, "Überlegungen zum *Acte préalable,*" 24.

60. The sketches for the *Preparatory Act,* dating from 1913 to April 1915, are preserved at the A. N. Scriabin State Memorial Museum as fund 26098, no. 233. Two of the fifty-five pages are blank, a fact that has symbolic significance. The music is notated in black, blue, red, and violet pencil, so as to designate the diatonic, octatonic, and whole-tone systems in use in specific sections. Bowers (*The New Scriabin: Enigma and Answers* [New York: St. Martin's Press, 1973], 94) claims that Scriabin "pasted two pieces of ordinary score paper together in order to have enough staves on which to write the massiveness of the music—seventy lines, not the usual thirty he used in *Prometheus,* which was, indeed, grandiose enough." He is mistaken: the sketches are on twenty– and thirty-two–staff paper.

61. Umberto Eco, *The Open Work,* trans. Anna Cancogni, introd. David Robey (Cambridge: Harvard University Press, 1989).

62. Like Chopin and Liszt, Scriabin was famous for improvising upon his own compositions, and even inscribed alternate versions of his opus 8 Etudes, opus 11 Preludes, and opus 17 Mazurkas on a *Vorsetzer,* a Player (or Reproducing) Piano. See on this topic P. V. Lobanov, *A. N. Skryabin — interpretator svoikh kompositsiy* (Moscow: Iris-press, 1995), 8–22.

63. Sabaneyev, *Vospominaniya o Skryabine,* 281–83. The reference to *Kashchey the Deathless* indicates that Scriabin intended to set the lines of the Waves of Life to octatonic harmonies, which Rimsky-Korsakov, in his opera, used to illustrate Kashchey's wicked sorcery. (For an analysis of the applications of octatonic and whole-tone collections in the music of the New Russian School, or *moguchaya kuchka,* see Taruskin, "Chernomor to Kashchei: Harmonic Sorcery; or Stravinsky's 'Angle,'" *Journal of the American Musicological Society* 38 [1985]: 72–142.) The "standing triads" mentioned at the end of the Sabaneyev quotation might have an octatonic—rather than a diatonic—origin. Scriabin tended to arrange (or rearrange) octatonic collections so that the three lowest pitches formed a major triad. In the *Preparatory Act* sketches, he wrote out the octatonic scale segment E-F♯-G-A-B♭-C-D♭ as C-E-G-B♭-D♭-F♯-A. The pitches C-E-G make up a "standing [major] triad."

64. Bowers (*The New Scriabin: Enigma and Answers,* 135) states, "In Scriabin's sketches for the 'Prefatory Action,' there is one ['mystic'] chord written out experimentally under the caption 'Investigation: Melody, Harmony, Rhythm': C, F♯, B♭, E, A, D, G, and over it is written the overtone numbers, eight through fourteen (the twelfth, G, included)." Bowers is mistaken: the chord on page 12 is spelled C-F♯-B♭-E-A-D-G-B-D♭-F. The cited heading does not exist on that or any other page of the sketches.

65. On this point, see Taruskin, review of James M. Baker, *The Music of Alexander Scriabin,* and Schloezer, *Scriabin: Artist and Mystic,* in *Music Theory Spectrum* 10 (1988): 160. For what follows, see 163–68.

66. See Roy J. Guenther, "Varvara Dernova's System of Analysis of the Music of Scriabin," in *Russian Theoretical Thought in Music,* ed. Gordon D. McQuere (Ann Arbor: UMI Research Press, 1983), 171, 214 n. 15.

67. Taruskin, *Defining Russia Musically,* 341–42. Citing a paper by Igor Boelza, Taruskin notes, "At an early rehearsal of *Prométhée,* Rachmaninoff, stunned at the sound of [the chord], asked Scriabin, 'What are you using here?' Scriabin answered, 'The chord of the pleroma'" (340–41). The chapter in *Defining Russia Musically*

from which this anecdote is taken—"Scriabin and the Superhuman: A Millennial Essay"—amplifies many of the technical points made in this chapter.

68. Bandura, "Skryabin i novaya nauchnaya paradigma XX veka," *Muzïkal'naya akademiya* 4 (1993): 175–80. The essay concerns the possible influence of Max Planck's quantum theory, Albert Einstein's theory of relativity, and Nils Bohr's atomic theory on Scriabin's musical thought.

69. Bandura bases this interpretation on the long discredited notion that Scriabin derived his sonorities from the harmonic series. He states that the "upper tetrachord" of the "mystic" chord "is derived from the 8th, 11th, 15th, and 20th overtones," while the "lower tetrachord corresponds to the 4th, 5th, 7th, 11th, and 16th undertones." The analysis is accurate only when the sonority is spaced out over six octaves.

70. Ivanov, "Zavetï simvolizma," in *Rodnoye i vselenskoye,* 182, 186. Ivanov surveys the Russian Romantics and the historical role of the symbol in art. The end of his essay takes a spiritual turn: Ivanov calls on the Symbolists to be "religious organizers of life," a call that Scriabin heeded.

71. See Manfred Kelkel, *Alexandre Scriabine: Sa vie, l'ésotérisme et le language musical dans son oeuvre,* 3 vols. in 1 (Paris: Editions Honoré Champion, 1978), 3: 77–78; see also George Perle, "Scriabin's Self-Analyses," *Music Analysis* 3 (1984): 120. Perle adds that Scriabin's notation is consistent with the spellings of the three independent octatonic scales. A French sixth chord spelled C-E-F♯-B♭, for example, refers to the octatonic collection E-F♯-G-A-B♭-C-D♭-E♭; if the chord is enharmonically respelled B♯-E-F♯-A♯, it refers to the octatonic collection A♯-B♯-C♯-D♯-E-F♯-G-A.

72. Taruskin, *Defining Russia Musically,* 348–49.

73. Sabaneyev, *Vospominaniya o Skryabine,* 82.

74. Sigfried Schibli (*Alexander Skrjabin und seine Musik* [Munich: R. Piper, 1983], 344) claims that, for Scriabin, "the *Preparatory Act* sketches were a reservoir of musical ideas, from which he was able to create his last piano works," and that Scriabin "saved the sketches from oblivion by deriving his last piano pieces from the 'raw material.'" It must be emphasized, however, that Scriabin composed the Poems, Dances, and Preludes before the sketches for the *Preparatory Act.* The sketches were not a repository of ideas for the piano compositions; rather, they constituted a framework for the *Preparatory Act,* one that Scriabin followed when he improvised it for Sabaneyev.

75. Sabaneyev, *Vospominaniya o Skryabine,* 283.

76. This and other references in the paragraph are taken from Perle, "Scriabin's Self-Analyses," 103–4.

77. On this point, see Mikhail Bakhtin, *Problems of Dostoevsky's Poetics,* ed. and trans. Caryl Emerson (Minneapolis: University of Minnesota Press, 1984), 5–46; see also Ivanov, "Dostoyevsky i roman-tragediya," in *Borozdï i mezhi* (Moscow: Musaget, 1916), 33–34.

78. Gershenzon, ed., "Predvaritel'noye deystviye: Rannyaya redaktsiya," 224–25; emphasis and punctuation added.

79. Sabaneyev, *Vospominaniya o Skryabine,* 283.

80. Gershenzon, ed., "Predvaritel'noye deystviye: Poslednyaya redaktsiya," 247; emphasis added.

81. In the *Preparatory Act* text, the phrase "songs of a stream" refers symbolically to music and water. From these images arise others of the Earth's ancient peoples, their veneration of land, and the windpipes that they used to charm pagan gods. The phrase also alludes to texts by Ivanov and Pushkin, and affirms their view

that the symbol evokes the lost soul of the people. In his 1905 essay, "The Crisis of Individualism" ("Krizis individualizma"), Ivanov calls on man to overcome "differentiation" and "individualism" and to cease being "lost . . . in the wilderness from 'unity'" ("zabluditsya . . . v pustïne svoyego ot 'yedineniya'"). The line is itself a reference to Pushkin's 1826 lyric poem "The Prophet" ("Prorok"), which depicts the conversion of a mortal into an Old Testament prophet. The poem, cast in archaic Biblical style, begins: "Spirit parched in thirst, / In barren wilderness I stumbled forth" ("Dukhovnoy zhazhdoyu tomim, / V pustïne mrachnoy ya vlachilsya"). In the *fugato,* Scriabin perhaps intended the chromatic scale to evoke a desolate landscape, and strict imitation to depict ancient "unity." See John E. Malmstad, "'O, sick children of the world': 'Fio ergo non sum,'" in *Cultura e memoria: Atti del terzo Simposio Internazionale dedicato a Vjaceslav Ivanov,* 1: 182, 184.

82. Sabaneyev, *Vospominaniya o Skryabine,* 269.

83. Ivanov, "Zavetï simvolizma," 181–82.

84. See Jacques Schérer, *Le "Livre" de Mallarmé: Premières recherches sur des documents inédits* (Paris: Gallimard, 1957).

85. See Žižek, *Tarrying with the Negative,* 261, n. 46.

86. Gershenzon, ed, "Zapisi A. N. Skryabina: Zapis' 1905–1906 gg.," 139.

Chapter 4   Prokofiev and Mimesis

Both the French and Russian Symbolists believed that there was an un-graspable realm beyond material reality, a realm that gives us only frag-mentary clues to its fiery existence. Charles Baudelaire called it the *au-delà*, an inaudible, invisible realm of which we are only partially aware. Vyache-slav Ivanov and Andrey Belïy called it *realiora*, the "realer" world. These poets believed that the imagination allows us to perceive vertical connec-tions between events in our world and events in the other world. Moreover, they rejected Platonic and Aristotelian theories of art as mimesis—the imitation of events in everyday life. Since the boundaries that marked off representation from enactment were fragile and unclear to them, osten-sibly fictional events in their works acquired the status of actual events. Everything belonged to both realms. Rather than mimesis, the portrayal of life in art, they practiced *life creation (zhiznetvorchestvo)*, the portrayal of art in life.[1] This doctrine established a more real world behind the shad-ows of the real world, which was merely a repository of images. To the "mystic" Symbolists, life creation proved harrowing. The effort to fuse art and life—whether through participation in games of make-believe, experi-mentation with narcotics, or involvement in the occult—adversely affected their psychologies. Having departed quotidian existence, it was difficult for them to find the path back to it.

In an emotional 1928 testimonial, the modernist poet and critic Vladi-slav Khodasevich (1886–1939) forcefully condemned the practitioners of life creation:

> The Symbolists did not want to separate the writer from the person, literary biography from personal. Symbolism did not want to be just a literary school, a literary trend. It always sought to become a life-creative method, and therein lay its most profound, perhaps unembodi-

able truth. Its entire history was spent as if in constant pursuit of this truth. It was a series of attempts, now and then truly heroic, to find a fusion of life and art, a kind of artistic philosopher's stone. Symbolism stubbornly searched its midst for a genius who would be able to fuse art and life as one. We now know that the genius did not appear, the formula was not revealed. As it happened, the history of the Symbolists turned into a history of broken lives, and their creative work was not entirely embodied: part of their creative energy and part of their internal experience was realized in writings, but the not entirely embodied part leaked into life, as electricity leaks due to inadequate insulation.[2]

The pretext for this statement was the suicide in Paris of Moscow socialite Nina Petrovskaya (1884–1928), the part-time mistress of Belïy and his rival Valeriy Bryusov and a prototype for the heroine Renata in *The Fiery Angel (Ognenniy angel)*, Bryusov's *roman-à-clef*. Khodasevich reported that Petrovskaya delighted in her role in the novel and, heeding the behests of life creation, sought to live out its final chapters. These, however, were based not on the breakup of the love triangle but on the tragic conclusion of Goethe's *Faust* Part I. According to Khodasevich, her suicide elevated her into a "true victim" of "mystic" Symbolism:

> Those sins that grew and developed from *inside* symbolism were decadent. It appears that symbolism was born with this poison in its blood. It affected to the same extent all of the people of symbolism. To a certain degree (or at a certain time) each became a decadent. Nina Petrovskaya (and not only she) took from symbolism only its decadence. She had always hoped to *perform* her life, and in this essentially fraudulent task she retained veracity and honor until the end.[3]

The Symbolists created an untenable situation in life and art, and it became impossible for them to differentiate their fictional activities from their real activities, their nocturnal dreams from their diurnal dramas. Instead of remaining trapped in a world of unrequited love, Petrovskaya chose to sacrifice herself to the ideal image of the *Faust* heroine Gretchen. Khodasevich, seeing that Bryusov and Belïy had toyed with her feelings, attributed her demise to a debased and immoral artistic practice.

Uncannily, while Petrovskaya was living in Paris, the Russian *émigré* composer Sergey Prokofiev was finishing an opera based on Bryusov's *roman-à-clef*. The opera, on which he labored nearly a decade (completing a first version in 1923, a revision in 1927, and planning a second version in 1930), was a creative debacle for the composer, arguably the worst setback of his troubled operatic career. It was deemed old-fashioned by modernist connoisseurs and, despite his efforts to promote it, was not staged in his lifetime. With benefit of hindsight, once could argue that *The Fiery Angel* marked a turning point in Prokofiev's career, having a decisive impact on the subsequent development of his style. My present inquiry, however, has a somewhat narrower, if more provocative focus: namely, how Prokofiev came to create an opera that parodied Symbolist poetics. The score's surface brilliance, in particular the manner in which the elaborate syntax endows stage events with false mystical meaning, bears witness to the falseness of Symbolist ideals. The opera's end, moreover, depicts no spiritual emancipation but rather oblivion, the annulment of theurgic striving. In what follows, I will assess both the parodic and symbolic aspects of the opera, focusing first on the completed 1923 and 1927 scores and then on the extant materials of the unrealized 1930 score.

A TRUE STORY

The opera's source text oscillates between fiction, legend, and reality. Published as a serial in the leading Symbolist journal *Libra* between January 1907 and August 1908, *The Fiery Angel* centers on demonic possession and religious persecution in sixteenth-century Lutheran Cologne. In keeping with the style of an actual Gothic romance, Bryusov summarized the plot in a lengthy subtitle:

> A True Story, in which it is related of the Devil, more than once appearing in the image of a Radiant Spirit to a Maiden, and seducing her to Various Sinful Deeds, of Unholy Practices of Magic, Astrology, Alchemy, and Necromancy, of the Trial of the Maiden under the Presidency of His Eminence the Archbishop of Trier, as well as of Encounters and Discourses with the Knight and thrice Doctor Agrippa of Nettesheim, and with Doctor Faustus, composed by an Eyewitness.[4]

At the novel's outset, the knight Ruprecht encounters the maiden Renata in a dilapidated inn near Cologne, where she tells him about her past, her visitations by demons, and her devotion to the elusive Count Heinrich, whom she believes to be the earthly incarnation of a benevolent fiery angel named Madiel. Smitten, Ruprecht agrees to help Renata locate Heinrich, a task that involves his real-or-imagined attendance at a witches' Sabbath, a meeting with a fortune-teller, indoctrination in the black arts, and encounters with the occult book dealer Jacob Glock and alchemist Agrippa of Nettesheim (a real historical figure who, like Faust and Mephistopheles, figures in the black comic subplot). When Renata eventually finds Heinrich, he claims not to know her. Mortified, she asks Ruprecht to defend her honor by defeating him in a duel. Though the knight vows to do so, he badly loses the fight. More out of guilt than remorse, Renata treats his wounds and then departs to reside at a distant convent, there hoping to atone for her sins and to free herself of her supernatural visions. Meanwhile, Ruprecht considers a liaison with Agnes, the sister of his university crony and roommate Matthew, but finds himself unable to shake his feelings for Renata and resolves to learn her whereabouts. He is escorted to the convent by Mephistopheles and Faust, whom he meets seemingly by chance on the streets of Cologne. Upon witnessing Renata's interrogation and sentencing by the Catholic Inquisition, Ruprecht attempts to rescue her, but she chooses to perish in prison. The knight concludes his narrative by resolving to resume his former life in the newly discovered Americas.

The Fiery Angel makes reference to such diverse texts as the Bible (the parable of the prodigal son), Homer's *Iliad* and *Odyssey*, Virgil's *Aeneid*, Dante's *Divine Comedy* (1320), Cervantes's *Don Quixote* (1605), Goethe's *Faust* and the legend that inspired it. Bryusov also includes historical details in the novel gleaned from his study of the writings of Cornelius Agrippa of Nettesheim (1486–1535), a wandering occultist (except for a period when he was employed as a physician and astrologer at the court of Queen Margaret of Austria and King Francis I of Lyons) who participated in theological disputations that predicted a Christian Apocalypse in the twentieth century.[5] Intrigued by Agrippa, Bryusov devoted as much space to him in *The Fiery Angel* as he did to Faust and Mephistopheles and, as his perturbed colleagues observed, even adopted some of Agrippa's physical features himself.

Bryusov expected that the novel, despite being a compendium of German literary tropes, would become a Russian literary classic. To shore up his intellectual reputation, he polemicized within it against those writers who had exerted the most influence on the early Symbolist movement. In response to the religious philosopher Vladimir Solovyov, who posited in his work that paradise could be revealed and restored to humanity through Platonic and spiritual love, Bryusov contended that love does not have a celestial dimension. Hence Ruprecht, after his futile pursuit of Renata, and Renata, after her futile pursuit of Madiel, find out that love, whether profane or sacred, is merely a "distorted 'echo'" of the "other, fuller 'harmonies.'"[6] Love suggests nirvana but does not enable them to experience it. In response to the "decadent" Symbolist Dmitriy Merezhkovsky, who aspired in his work to reconcile Christian and pagan belief systems, Bryusov insisted on a cold duality. Renata's involvement in the occult contradicts her Catholic upbringing; the Inquisition apprehends and imprisons her for it. Ruprecht's fate, moreover, is predicated not on the outcome of the struggle between the opposing belief systems but on his reason and will. Renata leads him into occult temptation, but he overcomes it and, at novel's end, expresses regret that he had ever entered her inferno:

> But with all sincerity I can here give my vow, before my conscience, that in the future I will never give up so blasphemously my immortal soul, instilled in me by the Creator, into the power of one of His creations, however seductive it may be clothed, and that never, however weary the circumstances of my life, will I turn to the aid of divinations condemned by the Church, or to the forbidden sciences, nor will I attempt to cross the sacred edge separating our world from the dark sphere where spirits and demons float. Our Lord God, seeing all the depth of the heart, knows the purity of my vow. Amen.[7]

In his preface to the expanded 1909 edition, Bryusov claimed that *The Fiery Angel* was a translation of a 1535 German manuscript containing a lansquenet's confessions. He concealed the fact that it was based on a real-life love triangle: Ruprecht (the first-person narrator) is Bryusov's fictional self, the learned Count Heinrich and fiery angel Madiel represent Belïy, and Renata represents Petrovskaya. (Ivanov and his spouse may have been the prototypes for Matthew and Agnes.) Petrovskaya was despondently married to Sergey Sokolov (real surname Krechetov 1879–1936), founder of the short-lived Symbolist publishing firm Gryphon. In 1903, at a gathering at her home, she was introduced to Belïy, who subsequently introduced her to a spiritualist society known as the Argonauts. They developed an innocent relationship in accord with the asexual ideal advanced by Solovyov. "My friendship with N[ina], passing into tender empathy, sustained me with a utopian view of myself as the healer of her soul," Belïy wrote.[8] To his dismay, however, the relationship lost its innocence. Disgruntled with Petrovskaya and increasingly enamored with Lyubov Blok (*née* Mendeleyeva) as the embodiment of the Eternal Feminine, in July 1904 Belïy informed Petrovskaya that he could no longer associate with her. On this occasion Bryusov, attracted to Petrovskaya and realizing that she was vulnerable, began to woo her, engaging her in games of make-believe in such mythical locales as Lake Saima in Finland. "His curiosity, at first an almost scientific curiosity, grew with each passing day," Petrovskaya recalled in her memoirs. "I too now experienced an intense, morbid curiosity about Bryusov, and, completely entangled in mystical cul-de-sacs, came to have strange desires for him. . . . I once said to [him]: 'I want to fall into your darkness—irrevocably and forever.'"[9] Her interaction with the two writers eventually led her to a nervous breakdown. One night, she smuggled a pistol and a flask of poison into a literary society lecture that Belïy was delivering on the Orpheus and Eurydice myth and, "reducing 'symbols' to material reality, insisted that [he] 'lead her from hell.'"[10] Bryusov, who was also in attendance, disarmed her and escorted her home.

Jealous of the emotional bond that had developed between Petrovskaya and his rival, in November 1904 Belïy challenged Bryusov to a poetic contest for her affections. Bryusov responded with "Loki to Baldur" ("Bal'deru Loki"), a poem that casts the two poets as figures from Scandinavian legend. He depicted Belïy as Baldur, "a radiant young god, the son of Odin, whose role is that of passive victim," and himself as Loki, "a primitive, 'demonic,' and multifaceted character who sows division among the gods."[11] In the final stanza of the poem, Loki pledges to destroy Baldur, prophesizing the annihilation of "heavenly forces" and the accession of a "twilight" age.

Belïy interpreted "Loki to Baldur" as an attack on his personal philosophy of love: his advocacy of celibacy, his image of the Eternal Feminine, and his veneration of Eros. His animosity toward Bryusov intensified when the latter spoke ill of Merezhkovsky, whom Belïy esteemed as a mentor. Piqued when Belïy warned him not to do so again, Bryusov challenged him to a duel in a Moscow alley (one of many events that illustrate the degree to which the Symbolists, especially the "mystic" Symbolists, lived in an invented reality, the Renaissance that, historically, Russia never had). Reports of the quarrel prompted Ivanov, who was then living in Paris, to try to make peace. In a 24 February 1905 letter to Bryusov, he wrote:

> I thank the forces by which I am appealing to you that you committed the crime *only* in the potential world. For you wanted to kill Baldur. This I gleaned from your note (don't regret that you added yet another complication to our friendship). Let it "not come to be"; for as you know, all that *was* eternally is. I can't describe the terrible, stifling grief that you sent me into for days and nights. . . . Killing Baldur, "you were wrestling with God in the night." Σκληρου σοι προσ κέντρα λακτιζειν. . . . Just bear in mind one thing: if a poet's entire life is a "holy sacrifice," then all of us, perceiving ourselves and each other as true and "real," are holy priests and theurgic brothers. Let it not occur, so that we don't become Cains. Besides, I'm convinced that in the dispute B[aldur or Belïy] was right. . . . Do as I wish: make peace with Baldur fully and fraternally, for although you don't know it, you too are a *god of light*."[12]

Though the duel was postponed, Belïy sent Bryusov a poem, "To an ancient enemy" ("Starinnomu vragu"), which portrayed their feud as an epic battle between the Magi:

I was in a canyon. A mountain demon
Flapped his wing—eclipsing the light.
He threatened me with sustained battle.
I knew: in battle there is no mercy.

Then I lifted a palm. Then a white cloud
Bore me up to the azure.
Once again in the ether, I grew
Free, bold, cleansed by tenderness!

You rose up alongside me,
Like a wild eagle.
But toppled by heavy hail,
You fell, powerless, onto the rock.

You stood up as dust, but fire will burn
dust, and thunder will cut through soot.
No, do not fly up: it is futile to flap
Your tattered wing.

My armor burns in a bonfire
Lightning is my spear, sun my shield.
Do not approach me: in heated rage
The storm will turn you to ash.

[Ya bïl v ushchel'ye. Demon gornïy
Vzmakhnul krïlom—zatmilsya svet.
On mne grozil bor'boy upornoy.
Ya znal: v bor'be poshchadï net.

I dlan' vozdel. I oblak belïy
V lazur' menya—v lazur' unyos.
Opyat' v efirakh vol'nïy, smelïy,
Omïtïy laskovost'yu ros!

Tï nessya vvïs' so mnoyu ryadom,
Podobnïy dikomu orlu.
No oprokinut tyazhkim gradom,
Tï pal, bessil'nïy, na skalu.

Tï pïl'yu vstal, no pïl', no kopot'
Spalit ogon', rasseyet grom.
Net, ne vzletish': bestsel'no khlopat'
Svoim rastrepannïm krïlom.

Moya bronya gorit pozharom
Kop'yo mne—molniya, Solntse—shchit.
Ne priblizhaysya: v gneve yarom
Tebya groza ispepelit.][13]

Figure 3.   Beliy's caricature of Bryusov, including
two lines from "Loki to Baldur." Source: V. R.
Shcherbina et al., eds., *Literaturnoye nasledstvo 85:
Valeriy Bryusov* (Moscow: Nauka, 1976), 337.

Beliy casts Bryusov as a wizard who laments his inability to subdue the
tempests of life. The older poet had once been an inspiration to the Symbolists but, his influence waning, had turned bitter—like the emasculated
demons in modernist operas. Beliy, in contrast, depicts himself as a wizard
who seeks to vanquish a demonic threat to his moral integrity.

Beliy recalled that the poem had a tremendous impact on his rival:
"Upon receiving it, he dreamed that we were dueling with foils and that I
had stabbed him with my blade; he woke up with pain in his chest (I heard
this from N. I. Petrovskaya)."[14] Interpreting the dream as a symbol of his
ultimate defeat in the poetic contest, in January 1905 Bryusov sent Beliy a
self-humbling and flattering work entitled "To Baldur II" ("Bal'deru II"):

> Which of us won—I don't know!
> It must be you, son of light, you!
> And I, submitting, encounter
> All my hopeless dreams.

And I also marked her, for whom
The battle was staged, with a sign
I fell as darkness into her soul
And dragged her into the abyss after me.

But in the very horror of the fall,
At the nadir of grief and darkness,
Your distant light dispersed the shadows,
And we looked into the heavens!

[Kto pobedil iz nas,—ne znayu!
Dolzhno bïť, tï, sïn sveta, tï!
I ya, pokorstvuya, vstrechayu
Vse beznadezhnïye mechtï.

Svoim i ya otmetil znakom
Tu, za kogo vozdvigsya boy,
Yey na dushu upal ya mrakom
I v bezdnï rinul za soboy.

No v samom uzhase padeniy,
Na dne otchayan'ya i t'mï,
Tvoy dal'niy luch rasseyal teni,
I v nebesa vzglyanuli mï!][15]

Petrovskaya's involvement in the affair prevented Bryusov from publishing his poem.[16] Nevertheless, her material image, like the dream image
of Belïy defeating him in a bloody battle, became an integral part of *The
Fiery Angel*, which transplanted the three of them into the German
Renaissance. Bryusov, to recap, became Ruprecht, the lonely knight who
journeys between the real and more real; his rival became Count Heinrich
(Madiel), detached but radiating Platonic love; his inamorata assumed the
part of Renata, fated to perish at the stake for witchcraft. The story line
articulated Bryusov's literary credo: that artists should be their own creative subjects and should commit themselves fully to their work. Unlike
his "mystic" Symbolist colleagues, however, he separated art from life
and did not endeavor to transcend the real. In *The Fiery Angel*, Bryusov's
(Ruprecht's) love for Petrovskaya (Renata) is not ideal but only potentially
so; Belïy (Madiel) stays silent, unable to express his philosophical views. As
in reality, Bryusov was both a character and narrator in the love triangle
and, as such, could participate in it and parody it at once. In Avril Pyman's
view, "that [he] was here sacrificing life upon the altar of art according to
his own prescription did not serve so much to enrich the plot as to sap the
human content from his relationship with [the other two], perhaps because
the ending is disingenuous and stems from Goethe, not from the dis-

Figure 4. Two figures from sixteenth-century Germany, as copied by
Bryusov from Fr. Hossenroth, *Deutsche Volkstrachten* (1900). Source:
V. R. Shcherbina et al., eds., *Literaturnoye nasledstvo 85: Valeriy Bryusov*
(Moscow: Nauka, 1976), 345.

tressful parting of the real-life lovers, at which, it seems, no rescue was
offered."[17] The strange events that followed the novel's publication confirm
this analysis while also objectifying the tumults of the Symbolist era.

In 1919, after the Russian Symbolist movement had ended, Prokofiev
chanced upon a copy of *The Fiery Angel* in a New York City bookshop. At
the time, he did not know that it was a *roman-à-clef* and read it chiefly for
its descriptions of the Catholic Inquisition and the black arts—subjects
that accorded with his interests in Christian Science and Gothic manuals
like *Le comte de Gabala*.[18] Enthralled, he swiftly developed an opera scenario for it, one that centered not on the knight Ruprecht but on "wildly
passionate" Renata, with scenes involving "wandering Fausts [*sic*] and
fulminating archbishops." Prokofiev realized that his "enthusiasm" for the
subject matter "was not with the times," but he was in search of a new crea-

tive project after the Chicago Lyric Opera postponed staging his *Love for Three Oranges* (*Lyubov' k tryom apel'sinam*, opus 33, 1919). "I had started [that opera] with a commission in my pocket," he explained, "but it ran into trouble. To start on a major work now, without prospects for it, was foolish. Maybe I was being stubborn, unconsciously: one opera didn't work out, so I'd write another."[19] He convinced himself that Bryusov's novel suited the composition of a score with alternating natural and supernatural tableaux in the manner of Giacomo Meyerbeer's *Robert le diable* (1831), a *grand opéra*, and Charles Gounod's *Faust* (1859), a *comédie lyrique*, whose conventions he aspired to resurrect and modernize.

When his friend Nikolai Myaskovsky (1881–1950) cautioned him that the subject matter might be too "theological" for modern opera audiences, Prokofiev quipped: "There's little theology in *The Fiery Angel*, but endless orgies. Only Allah knows when I'll orchestrate it all."[20] Though brusque, this remark proposes that he was more interested in the pyrotechnic than the chivalric scenes in the novel and that he was intent on setting them with maximal orchestral firepower.[21] Prokofiev sought to parody the novel—in the sense of formulating a quintessentially modernist critique of it—without at the time knowing that the novel was itself parodic: a trans-contextualization of the means by which the Symbolists made spectacles of themselves in their endeavor to traverse the boundary between the ideal, immaterial world that they imagined and the real, material world in which they lived. Wittingly or unwittingly, the composer revealed that the Symbolists' attempts, through artistic experimentation, to transcend an oppressive reality could not succeed in a desacralized world.

His opera was not the *succès de scandale* he had hoped for. Petrovskaya's attempt to transform her life into art proved futile, as did Prokofiev's. Despite seven years of labor and one complete and one partial overhaul of the libretto and music, he was unable to secure a single stage performance of the opera, and heard only a concert version of two scenes from act II. Tragically, he rebuffed concrete proposals for productions—from the Cologne Opera in the autumn of 1925 and Frankfurt Opera in the spring of 1926— in hopes of securing more prestigious and lucrative venues. In the spring of 1925, he received an offer to stage the work at the Paris Opéra Comique, but it was rescinded when the director, Albert Wolff, was sacked. Then, in the spring of 1926, Prokofiev signed a contract with Bruno Walter for a 1927 production at the Berlin Städtische Oper, but this too fell through when orchestral parts for the revised score—including a German translation of the libretto—arrived after the stipulated rehearsal deadline.[22] Although he had been alerted in advance by his Berlin agent that Walter was under heavy pressure to reduce the number of performances of foreign operas, Prokofiev complained to Myaskovsky that this second cancellation was merely "a case of swinishness on Bruno Walter's part: if he could not put it on in the fall, then he could have in the spring."[23] His friend attempted to console him: "I am not mistaken in deeming *The Fiery Angel* to be the work in which you have risen to your full height as a musician and an artist. In order to give characters such as Renata and Ruprecht all their depth and unbelievable human complexity, you had to mature to full brilliance. Though your Renata lives only on paper, her music brings to mind a bright visual image."[24] Accolades aside, Myaskovsky had reservations about the score: the enormous stamina (range and volume) required of the soprano (Renata) and baritone (Ruprecht), the thickness and complexity of the harmony, the compressed dramatic structure. Most problematic was the final scene at the convent. The final act's curtain falls only six measures after the Inquisitor sentences Renata to death: we do not hear her or Ruprecht react to her fate. Irrespective of Myaskovsky's claim that the finale would have a lasting impact on audiences, the blunt cessation of the action leaves the spiritual issues raised by the opera unresolved, while the heroine's disappearance into oblivion arguably reduces its intellectual appeal.

In 1928, Prokofiev asked his publisher Serge Koussevitzky (1874–1951) whether at least a concert performance of act I of the opera could be arranged. On 14 June Koussevitzky instead conducted the act II, scene 1 dialogue between Renata and Ruprecht and the act II, scene 2 dialogue between Ruprecht and Agrippa of Nettesheim. A few unidentified members of the Ballets Russes attended. The troupe was hostile toward conventional opera, and those in attendance rebuked Prokofiev for attempting to disinter nineteenth-century styles that, in their view, could not be disinterred. Their remarks struck home. Prokofiev informed Myaskovsky that act II of the opera was

> a big success, though the perception of the local listeners was of course rather superficial—and your opinion is a lot more valuable to me. The Diaghilev group reacted to the opera with hostility, and for some reason [Pyotr] Suvchinsky took their point of view. Evidently, they still hold the opinion that one has to write something contemporary, the latest and the very latest, while *Angel* was conceived in 1920. There was one comic event: [Leonid] Sabaneyev and [Alexander] Grechaninov came up to me and began to praise act II to the skies. I was embarrassed and decided that the piece was perhaps not very good after all.[25]

It was not so much the negative reaction of the music critic (and Stravinsky ghost writer) Suvchinsky as the positive reaction of Grechaninov (1864–

1956) that galled Prokofiev. In 1912, Grechaninov had composed a three-act opera based on Maeterlinck's contemporaneous French Symbolist play *Sister Beatrice (Soeur Béatrice)*. Shortly after its premiere at the Solodov-nikov Theater in Moscow, the opera was banned at the behest of the Orthodox Synod for religious slander.[26] Moreover, Grechaninov was chided for his reliance on a fixed set of leitmotifs to represent his characters. Opera critics denounced the technique as outmoded, for it neither accommodated the subtleties of Maeterlinck's language nor demonstrated the internal development required of symbolism. Yuliy Engel complained that the leitmotifs (derived, strangely enough, from popular melodies by George Bizet and Chaikovsky) usually recurred without alteration, and thus offered little insight into the psychological states of the *dramatis personae*.[27] That Grechaninov praised *The Fiery Angel* suggested to Prokofiev that it too might be outmoded, for he had also represented his characters with recurring leitmotifs. To his chagrin, the intuition was confirmed by Myaskov-sky, who informed him that a student at the Moscow Conservatory found the opera's Wagnerism *passé*. Prokofiev attempted to joke about it:

> Is it possible that in Moscow they see a Wagnerian influence in the opera? The devil take it! I had nothing like that in mind, and to a sufficient degree deviated from that composer. By the way: tell your little modernist that another little modernist who is revered as the dictator of fashion, isn't averse to whistling a bit of *Meistersinger* in his *Apollo* [1928]—just so our Moscow friend hasn't "fallen behind the times"![28]

Stravinsky, the "little modernist," was Prokofiev's principal competition in Paris, and the critical failure of *The Fiery Angel* was a decisive setback in the latter's efforts to surpass the former as a dramatist.[29] With no other prospective performances of the opera in the offing, Prokofiev decided to extract a symphony from it. The result, his Symphony No. 3 in C minor (opus 44), was performed for the first time in Paris on 17 May 1929. Prokofiev cynically labeled it one of his most significant scores. He also stressed that it was a largely autonomous work, since some of the themes had been composed before he conceived the opera, without a causal source.[30] This was almost a declaration of intent, for Prokofiev had in fact included found musical objects—spare parts from previous projects—in the opera, these enhancing the atmosphere of emotional and psychological detachment.

His last chance to bring Renata and the other characters in *The Fiery Angel* to life came in January 1930, when the Metropolitan Opera in New York City expressed interest in staging it. After meeting with the board of directors, Prokofiev wearily embarked on yet another overhaul of the score, supplanting the 1927 scenario of five acts and seven scenes with one of three acts and ten scenes, of which two scenes had entirely new music and text. He reasoned that the 1927 scenario had too many static passages to be successful as a live spectacle: "One of the artists working in the theater gave me the idea of animating these places visually, if not with scenic action. In other words, a slow act, by means of insignificant alterations in the text and music, could be broken into several scenes that give new impressions and eliminate the sense of slowness."[31] This comment suggests that Prokofiev had capitulated and abandoned one of his dramaturgical ideals: to allow the apocalyptic drama to unfold principally in the music, the only artistic medium suitable for representing the unrepresentable conflict between angelic and demonic forces, and to confine the visual component of the score to stylized gestures. To enliven the visual action, and presumably appeal to American audiences, he resolved to collapse the motionless, static *tableaux* into action-packed, dynamic *tableaux*, but to no avail. His proposed revision was turned down by the board of directors on the hard-to-fathom excuse that the opera—one of the noisiest in history—had too many subtleties for a large theater. Prokofiev fell into a deep depression. Lost and confused by the turn things had taken in his life he stopped working on the new version and began to rethink his career choices. The conductor Charles Bruck recalled that performance materials of *The Fiery Angel* "were carefully packed up and consigned to oblivion in the cellars of the Russian music publisher [Koussevitzky's firm Édition Russe de Musique] in Paris."[32] Then silence. *The Fiery Angel* gathered dust until 25 November 1954—more than a year and a half after the composer's death—when Bruck organized a complete concert performance (recorded and issued by the Erato firm) at the Théâtre des Champs-Elysées in Paris, the site of the premiere of Stravinsky's *Le sacre du printemps* (1913). The opera was first staged on 14 September 1955 at the Teatro La Fenice in Venice.

What had gone wrong? In Myaskovsky's view, *The Fiery Angel* was ahead of (rather than behind) its time. On playing through the piano-vocal score, he determined that the music had

> colossal musical and emotional (even this is imprecise, more than emotional, I can't find the word right now) intensity. I fully understand the Diaghilev group and even in a way Suvchinsky. The fact is, it's very hard (in my view) to approach *The Fiery Angel* with any sort of aesthetic criteria, the more so with taste, and so on. It's too grand for this to occur; there's something elemental in it. It is in general not a subject for admiration, for calm appraisals, comparisons, and so on—like some

kind of knick-knack, even one of grand proportions, like Stravinsky's *Oedipus* [*Rex*, 1927]. I don't think that it can be assessed with the standard of measurement applied to a cyclone, an earthquake, and so on. Though the "element" of your opera is only "human," it is expressed with such power, so fully, in such a "global" context, that the sonic forms, becoming almost visible, are overpowering in their significance. For me, *The Fiery Angel* is more than music, and I think that the authentic and unusually pungent "humanity" of the composition will make it eternal.[33]

For Myaskovsky, the opera had the raw force of another pagan ritual like *Le sacre du printemps* (rather than a mythic oration like *Oedipus Rex*). He deemed the orchestral music fantastic, an apparition born of the visions of Renata, who is under threat from both the natural and the supernatural world. Spirits lurk behind the sets, betrayed only by occasional bangs and rustles in the orchestral pit. In stating that *"The Fiery Angel* is more than music," Myaskovsky fancifully and presciently hinted that it had messianic force, the potential to become something more than itself. He imagined Prokofiev as an impassive sorcerer who, resisting the modernist musical temptations that surrounded him, proposed to demonstrate that Romantic opera was viable and destined to find renewal in his own age. He was a musical Belïy wrestling with a musical Bryusov—his Parisian foe, Stravinsky.

IN WHICH IT IS RELATED OF THE DEVIL

Prokofiev conceived *The Fiery Angel* as a summation of his ideas about dramaturgy and, in subsequent years, regarded it as his masterpiece. It reflected a general interest in the occult that developed in his childhood, during his first trip to the opera. In January 1900, when he was only eight years old, his parents decided to inaugurate the new century by taking the train from the estate they managed in Sontsovka, Ukraine, to Moscow. During their stay in the city, they took their son to see a performance of Gounod's *Faust* at the Solodovnikov Theater. Before the act I curtain rose, his mother, Maria Prokofiev (née Zhitkova), offered him this outline of the plot: "You see, there once lived Faust, a scholar. He was already old, and was already reading books. The devil came up to him and said: 'Sell me your soul, and I will make you young again.' Well, Faust sold it, the devil made him young, and then they began having fun."[34] *Faust* left the future composer with a rich store of impressions. He was obviously intrigued by the *Auerbachs Keller* episode (act II), where Mephistopheles shatters the soldier Valentin's sword, the *Walpurgisnacht* episode (act V, scene 1), with its witches, paper skeletons, and chorus of demons, and the following banquet episode, where Faust and Mephistopheles entertain the beautiful women of history. He was bored, however, by the military and pastoral choruses, the orchestral interludes, and the static recitatives—all of which, he felt, detracted from the plot:

> They played the overture, and the curtain rose. There were piles of books, and Faust in a beard. He read from a thick tome and sang something, read again and sang again. So where was the devil? It was all so slow. Ah, finally! But why was he in a red costume with a sword and looking so elegant? For some reason I thought the devil would be black, like a Negro, half-naked and perhaps with hooves. Later, when "they began having fun," I immediately recognized both the waltz and the march that my mother played in Sontsovka. My mother evidently chose *Faust* because she wanted me to hear familiar music. I did not comprehend much of what they were up to in their fun, but the sword fight and the death of Valentin impressed me. . . .
>
> I didn't quite understand why a white spotlight sometimes shone on Marguerite, whereas a rich red one shone on Mephistopheles, especially when he sang for a long time. But perhaps I didn't know all there was to know about devils, and it was appropriate for him to be bathed in a red light.[35]

Because he was too young to have been aware of them, Prokofiev does not mention the novel musical effects in *Faust:* the descent of the act III curtain to Mephistopheles' cacophonous chortles (following Marguerite's lovelorn soliloquy about Faust); the sound of muffled horns beneath tremolo strings when Mephistopheles casts a spell over the flowers in Marguerite's garden; the rising tonal sequences of the act V, scene 3 apotheosis. Yet he likely retained an unconscious record of these devices. Later, in composing *The Fiery Angel,* he actually adopted certain features of *Faust's* plot and staging (notably the paper skeletons). Conceptually, the two works share a deficiency. To paraphrase a remark by Carl Dahlhaus, their shortcoming is not their remoteness from their source texts but their dependence on these texts despite the remoteness. Without literary context, certain characters and events seem to be extraneous to their plots.[36] To project at least the illusion that *The Fiery Angel* was entirely original, Prokofiev added acoustic diablerie to it: choruses of nuns and Indians (the latter a musical reminiscence of Ruprecht's time in the Americas), inexplicable knocking on the walls of Renata's Cologne room, and (for the planned 1930 version) electronic feedback. But even in this regard, it referred back to Gounod, who prided himself on innovative orchestral effects. Prokofiev did not make light of his model but remained true to its spirit and to the central element of its dramaturgy: the focus on the past. Unlike his anti-operatic opera,

The Love for Three Oranges, The Fiery Angel does not eschew nineteenth-century conventions but embraces them. It is a nostalgic work.

To be sure, Prokofiev's nostalgia did not extend to the Symbolist movement, to which he had been exposed during his youth but which had a negligible influence on the formation of his compositional method. He knew only one Symbolist writer: Konstantin Balmont, a polyglot traveler and student of Eastern religion. By 1900, Balmont was considered to be old-fashioned by his colleagues, but the euphony of his poetry made him popular among composers even after the Revolution. Prokofiev's Balmont settings include the bombastic cantata *They Are Seven* (*Semero ikh*, opus 30, 1918/33), the text of which is based on an ancient incantation summoning the spirit of the earth to destroy the evil forces that afflict humanity. Prokofiev's music epitomizes the short-lived "Scythian" trend in composition, which in part concerned the representation of pagan conjugation rituals. (The term "Scythian" refers to the Scyths, a half-mythic people who were supposed to have once occupied land north of the Black Sea and who were lauded by the "mystic" Symbolists as students of the natural sciences.) Though Prokofiev is often labeled apolitical, he claimed in his 1941 autobiography that he had conceived *They Are Seven* as a commentary—albeit disingenuous—on the Revolution:

> The revolutionary events that had jolted Russia subconsciously affected me and demanded expression. I did not know how to do this, but my aspiration, having taken this odd turn, was directed to ancient themes. The fact that the thoughts and feelings of that time had lasted for many millenniums stimulated my imagination. Such was the Chaldean incantation carved in cuneiform characters on the walls of an Akkadian temple, deciphered by [the German archeologist Hugo] Winckler and converted by Balmont into verse.[37]

The music of the cantata—arranged around a diatonic-octatonic axis and replete with iterations of the title phrase—is agitated and overwrought, much like the contemporary events it purports to represent. *They Are Seven* was first performed in 1924 in Paris (the enormous performing forces it requires being unavailable in 1918 in Russia). It fared well in the local press, prompting Balmont to deem Prokofiev the foremost "Scythian" composer. In an unpublished sonnet, the poet declared that, within the composer's soul, "an orchestra yearns for forgotten summer sounds, / and an invincible Scythian beats on the tambourine of the sun."[38]

Aside from his temporary flirtation with "Scythianism," Prokofiev embraced a Symbolist concept that, to varying degrees, influenced all of his mature operas: *theatrum mundi*, the montage of stage worlds. The "mystic" Symbolists adopted the concept from the Baroque Italian *commedia dell'arte* and made it the basis of their theatrical experiments. It involves the juxtaposition of dichotomous events, the staging of plays within plays, and the removal of the barrier between the stage and audience. In the early twentieth century, the poet Alexander Blok and director Vsevolod Meyerhold set out to revive the dramas of Carlo Gozzi (1720–1806), which combined puppet farce, Italian folklore, and social satire. Blok also paraphrased Gozzi in his aptly titled poetry cycle *From the Real to the Realer* (*A realibus ad realiora*, 1908) and in his metatheatrical play *The Puppet Theater Booth*.[39] J. Douglas Clayton observes that, within these two works, "*theatrum mundi* implies not a one-for-one correlation between the composing elements of the different worlds, but a tragic disharmony, a lack of equivalence that boded ill for the future of culture."[40]

In 1914, Meyerhold translated and published Gozzi's most famous play, *The Love for Three Oranges* (*L'amore delle tre melarance*, 1761), in his short-lived theater journal of the same name. Four years later, he recommended it to Prokofiev as a possible subject for an opera. They had known each other since October 1916, when Meyerhold proposed to produce Prokofiev's first completed opera *The Gambler* (*Igrok*, after Dostoyevsky's novel) at the Mariyinsky Theater. The planned production was delayed—due to the cast's resistance to the music—and, after much hand-wringing, cancelled. Ten years later, however, they revised and successfully performed it. Like *The Gambler*, *The Love for Three Oranges* reflects Meyerhold's commitment to supplanting traditional operatic numbers with passages of continuous musical declamation and his intent to incorporate *commedia dell'arte* and *theatrum mundi* devices into his stagings. Prokofiev began writing the libretto while aboard an ocean liner bound for San Francisco. By the time it had docked, he had expanded the role of the commentators on the action that had been added by Meyerhold to the original Gozzi fable. Cranks, Jesters, Pure Tragedians, Everyday Comedians, and Empty Heads appear periodically from twin towers on the stage to interpret or manipulate the action. They function like the Author in *The Puppet Theater Booth*: to frustrate the suspension of disbelief endemic to theater viewing. In a review of the first Soviet staging of *The Love for Three Oranges* in 1926, Boris Asafyev commented that the score "consists of a mosaic-like alternation of sharply-delineated musical moments, distinct in character, force of expression, coloring, and so on. These are not unified by continual mechanical movement, an imprinted rhythm, by the idea of adventure or device of escapade—but by an essential governing principle: life, as a series of transient, closely linked episodes."[41] Asafyev implies here that the discontinuous music and text of the opera recapitulate the discontinuities of life. The world of the stage is an explicit metaphor for the world at large.

Structurally and stylistically, *The Love for Three Oranges* is the antithesis of *The Fiery Angel*. Whereas the earlier opera mocked dramatic conventions by defamiliarizing them—drawing the "real" audience into the action, placing a "fictional" audience on the stage, and determining the outcome of the plot via a game of cards—the later one did not. Yet at least one scene of *The Fiery Angel* appears to have been informed by *The Love for Three Oranges:* the brief tavern scene featuring the itinerant Mephistopheles and Faust. Rather than malevolent and terrifying, Mephistopheles is presented as a buffoon and a trickster, much like Fata Morgana in *The Love for Three Oranges*. Based on his recollection of *Faust*, Prokofiev evidently decided that, like Gounod, he could not convincingly represent the Prince of Darkness and so resorted to slapstick.[42] Dissatisfied by the tardy service at a Cologne tavern (the same one that Ruprecht dines at), Mephistopheles plants the boy waiter on the table and swallows him whole, shocking and repulsing the other patrons. The Innkeeper pleads for his return, and Mephistopheles obligingly conjures the lad out of a refuse bin. The inclusion of such coarse humor in an otherwise tragic opera not only debases Mephistopheles, it renders the opera structurally unstable. The audience cannot ascribe the events in the act to Renata's psychosis, to something seen through her eyes, for she does not appear in it. Instead, the dramatically unmotivated appearance of Mephistopheles and Faust intimates a visitation from another opera.[43]

This and the other structural anomalies in the opera are the consequence of its prolonged gestation and complex history. The 1923 and 1927 scores witness numerous shifts in dramatic perspective, the most obvious ones centering on the portrayal of Renata. In the original score, Prokofiev represents the paranormal events as figments of her rather fertile imagination; in the revised score, he introduces verbal and musical motifs that indicate that the events might in fact be real. These motifs, attesting to an integration of natural and supernatural dramatic spheres, extricate the heroine from a position of extreme isolation and tragic devotion and suggest that she might actually be a visionary.

The 1923 libretto stayed within the bounds of Bryusov's *roman-à-clef*. Prokofiev adopted intact Renata's opening monologue (recalling her childhood, her first encounters with Madiel, and her practice in the black arts) and Ruprecht's calls for salvation. He took pains to preserve the special effects: the mysterious knocking, the extinguishing candelabras, and Mephistopheles' cruel practical jokes. Agrippa of Nettesheim, the bookseller Glock, and the fortuneteller retain their secondary roles, as do Agrippa's occult disciples Aurelius and Hans, who ascribe Renata's hallucinations to an imbalance of the humors. Ruprecht, an uncomprehending skeptic of the occult, accepts their diagnosis. Following Bryusov, Prokofiev portrays Count Heinrich (Madiel) as a scholar, a product of scientific thought who denies involvement in the black arts, fails to recognize Renata, and feels remorse for injuring Ruprecht in the duel. Also preserved intact is the ending of the novel: the knight seeks to free the maiden from the convent, but she elects to die alone. To enhance the sentimental tone, he portrays her death as a religious apotheosis, complete with an organ prelude reminiscent of Dietrich Buxtehude, a chorus of nuns, and a smoking altar.

Of the paranormal events in the novel, only the chapter 4 scene of Ruprecht's attendance at a witches' Sabbath was excised from the 1923 version of the opera. A comment Prokofiev jotted down in the margins of page 85 of his personal copy of the novel's first edition explains his decision. "The scene must be excluded," he wrote. "On stage it will lose all of the mystical horror demanded by the average viewer."[44] Prokofiev resisted creating a scene like Gounod's *Walpurgisnacht*, with its demons straddling broomsticks and tinkling piccolo and cymbal music. He evidently decided that, just as he could not convincingly represent Mephistopheles, he could not convincingly represent a witches' Sabbath. On stage, the picture of debauchery and degradation that he had formed in his imagination would have merely been a mirage. The witches' Sabbath would also have posed a nettlesome dramatic problem, for given that Ruprecht rather than Renata attends it, the audience would not be able to ascribe the otherworldly ceremony to her aberrant psychology and would therefore have to accept it as "actually" happening.

In the 1927 version of the opera, Prokofiev resolved to foreground such conundrums. The distinction between the natural and supernatural dissolves, as does that between the sacred and profane. Rita McAllister notes that the impression of the 1927 score "is of a dim and dark surrealistic world where figures act as in a nightmare. The feeling persists that the characters on the stage do not exist only as their human or subhuman selves but act as part of some deeper plan." Moreover, the cryptic nature of the plot makes it unclear whether the audience should "accept the supernatural as a real and constant presence" or merely as "symptomatic of Renata's unbalanced mental state." Also left undecided are the veracity of Renata's identification of Count Heinrich (Madiel) with the fiery angel and the question of Madiel's good or evil nature, whether or not it is embodied in Count Heinrich.[45] As the drama unfolds, chaos triumphs over order. Renata endeavors with increasing desperation to ascertain whether Count Heinrich (Madiel) is a messenger from heaven or hell. Her destiny, whether she will attain eternal salvation or perdition, depends on the answer, but that answer is withheld both from her and from us.

The uncertainties arose because Prokofiev deliberately supernaturalized the 1927 version of *The Fiery Angel*. The plot remains unaltered but now unfolds in a distant time and place. Agrippa of Nettesheim becomes a necromancer, engaging in unlawful experiments. Jacob Glock and the fortune-teller issue alarming prophecies about Renata's descent into the flames of the Inquisition. Count Heinrich (Madiel) never speaks, much less sings, and appears only at stage rear in a red spotlight—comparable, perhaps, to the one that shone on Mephistopheles in the 1900 staging of Gounod's *Faust*. His duel with Ruprecht occurs off stage. Most notably, Prokofiev re-worked the finale, thereby eliminating a conspicuous resonance between *The Fiery Angel* and *Faust:*

> In the first version I ended *The Fiery Angel* with the death of Renata, but dramatically this seemed very boring, particularly with the presence of Faust and Mephistopheles, which recalled Marguerite's death scene. Despite all my conniving I had not managed to avoid some static moments in the earlier acts. I destroyed the final scene (which, by the way, added nothing new to the music) and decided to end with violent shouting. If somewhere in the middle of the opera the audience dozes off, then at least they will wake up for the final curtain.[46]

In the 1927 version, Ruprecht, led by Mephistopheles (a tenor rather than the baritone called for by Gounod), arrive at the convent not to rescue Renata but to witness her trial by the Inquisitor and Archbishop of Trier. The *auto-da-fé* is based on the witches' Sabbath episode of the novel: the nuns perform a frenzied round dance and invisible demons tear at their habits. Light floods the stage, the nuns accuse the Archbishop of wickedness, armed sentries rush in, and the curtain descends.

The catastrophic denouement is the inevitable outcome of some grandiose occult battle, but the audience is left to ponder whether it has occurred in reality or in Renata's mind. Just as the moral distinction between good and evil evaporates over the course of the drama, so too does the distinction between natural and supernatural events. Renata seems to be the victim of evil spirits with whom Ruprecht also seems to cavort, while the other characters enter and exit like particles in an uncontrolled chemistry experiment. Prokofiev had initially designated the natural and supernatural as polar opposites but eventually relocated them to the same dramatic

plane, suggesting that he composed the opera without a consistent scenario. Each version of the libretto was formed out of a separate close reading of the source novel and shaped according to the composer's changing
assessment of its meaning. He attempted to tease out the underlying order
of the events and consolidate their musical possibilities. Some scenes remained untouched between successive drafts; others betray significant contraction, expansion, and invigoration.

Three brief examples will lend support to this last assertion. In act I of
both libretti, Prokofiev included a brief conversation between Renata, the
innkeeper, and the fortuneteller. He adapted it from chapter 2 of Bryusov's
novel, in which Ruprecht, abetting Renata's search for Count Heinrich
(Madiel), recounts their brief stay in the village of Geerdt:

> It immediately seemed strange to us that everything in the village was
> intended for the comfort of travelers, and that many of those journey-
> ing in the same direction as us also stopped at Geerdt. I asked the peas-
> ant woman in whose house we rested and ate breakfast why this was,
> and she informed us with pride and vainglory that their village was fa-
> mous in the area for its fortuneteller, who could predict the future with
> great mastery. We were told that each day dozens came to learn their
> fate, not only from nearby places, but from distant cities and villages,
> even from Paderborn and Westphalia, since the fame of the Geerdt for-
> tuneteller had spread throughout all the German lands.
> These words were *like the whistle of a snake-charmer to a snake* to
> Renata, because she immediately became extremely excited and, having
> forgotten all our jokes and suppositions, desired to go straightaway to
> the witch.[47]

In the 1923 libretto, Prokofiev abbreviated this passage and transposed
it from Ruprecht's part to those of the fortuneteller and innkeeper. The resulting (declaimed) lines effectively typecast the fortune-teller as a benevolent con artist and the innkeeper as a hoary skeptic of the occult:

FORTUNETELLER: Each day dozens come to me to learn their fate, from
    Paderborn and Westphalia and even from Dalmatia.

INNKEEPER (ironically to Renata): . . . thus the snake-charmer whistles for
    snakes.

   [GADALKA: U menya sobir[a]yut yezh[e]dn[e]vn[o] desyatki lyudey
    uznat' svoyu sud'bu, iz Paderborna i Vestfalii i dazhe
    iz Dalmatsii.

KHOZYAYKA (ir[oni]ch[e]ski R[e]n[a]te): . . . kak svist zaklinatelya dlya
    zmey.[48]]

In the 1927 libretto, Prokofiev expanded this passage to include a brief exchange between Renata and the fortune-teller about psychic divination, thus revealing Renata's impressive knowledge of occult doctrines. For comic effect, he then transferred the snake-charmer reference from the innkeeper to the laborer. He represented the sound of the whistle abstractly via the first violin, which undertakes an upward run of triplet eighth notes in B-flat minor (framed by orchestral cadences in D minor and B major):

INNKEEPER (somewhat ironically): Wouldn't my esteemed guests like to hear their fortunes told? She tells fortunes with great skill. People from Westphalia and even Dalmatia come to her to learn their fate.

RUPRECHT: Never mind!

RENATA (animated): Ah, but of course I've heard about her. (To the fortuneteller) Old woman, are you familiar with chiromancy?

FORTUNE-TELLER: And with geomancy.

RENATA: Perhaps also with crystallomancy?

FORTUNE-TELLER: And with catoptromancy, and likewise with goety. (She gives her a packet of herbs, which Renata looks at with excitement.)

LABORER (to the innkeeper, observing Renata): Thus the snake-charmer whistles for snakes!

[KHOZYAYKA (neskol'ko ironicheski): Ne zakhotyat li pochtennïye postoyal'tsa, shtobï im pogadala vorozheya? Ona gadayet s masterstvom udivitel'nïm. K ney za sud'boy prikhodyat lyudi iz Vestfalii i dazhe iz Dalmatsii.

RUPREKT: Ne nado!

RENATA (ozhivlyonno): Akh, nu, konechno, ya o ney slïkhala. (Gadalke) Tï, babushka, znakoma s khiromantiyey?

GADALKA: I s geomantiyey.

RENATA: Mozhet bït', i s kristallomantiyey?

GADALKA: I s katoptromantiyey, a takzhe s goyetiyey. (Dayot yey puchok koren'yev, kotorïy Renata s volneniyem rassmatrivayet.)

RABOTNIK (Khozyayke, nablyudaya za Renatoy): Kak svist zaklinatelya dlya zmey!]

Prokofiev embellishes his libretto with a euphonious litany of occult folklore: chiromancy, divination using the hand; geomancy, divination using signs taken from the earth; crystallomancy and catoptromancy, divination with crystals and mirrors; and goety, the invocation of spirits. The exchange between Renata and the fortune-teller is comical, but the laborer's remarks add a dark lining to the episode. He is an unfeeling brute who chides Renata and who, at rehearsal number 165 of act I, hums a weird imitation of a snake-charmer's whistle—"La-la-la-la"—to the pitches b and e^1. The string basses accompany him with fs and f#s, articulating the sometimes inaudible division between white key (natural) and black key (supernatural) musical spheres in the opera. The ostinato music of the scene recurs in the act V *auto-da-fé*, where it underscores Renata's degradation and destruction at the hands of the Inquisitor and the Archbishop of Trier. Though perceived by occultists as angelic and glorious, she is perceived by Catholics as demonic and shameless.

The blurring of the natural and supernatural in the 1927 version of *The Fiery Angel* is most evident in those passages where Ruprecht seeks to understand the black arts. One instance is the beginning of act II, scene 1, which depicts Ruprecht and Renata engaged in the study of magic spells. In the source text, Ruprecht reads aloud from the treatise on the subject that he has procured from Glock:

> The first responsibility of the conjurer is always the magic circle, for it serves as a defense against the attack of hostile forces from outside. The use of this circle—in accord with the name of the demon invoked, the distribution of the stars, the place of the experiment, the time of year and the hour—always requires much attention. We first carefully drew the magic circle on paper, and only on the day of the experiment transferred it in charcoal to a corner of the room. It consisted of four concentric circles (the largest with a diameter of nine elbows), enclosing three perfect circles placed one inside the other. The outer, middle, and inner circles were each set a palm apart. The middle ring was separated into nine different sections, and in these houses was inscribed [the following]: in the first, turned straight toward the west, the secret name of the hour chosen for the invocation, that is, midnight on Friday, *Nethos;* in the second, the name of the demon of that hour, *Sachiel;* in the third, the character of that demon; in the fourth, the name of the demon of that day, *Anaël,* and his servants, *Rachiel* and *Sachiel;* in the fifth, the secret name of that time of year, that is, autumn, *Ardarael;* in the sixth, the names of the demons at that time of year, *Tarquam* and *Guadbarel;* in the seventh, the name of the root at that time of year, *Torquaret;* in

the eighth, the name of the earth at that time of year, *Robianara;* in the ninth, the names of the sun and moon at that time of year, *Abragini* and *Matasignais*.⁴⁹

And so on. In the 1923 libretto, Prokofiev necessarily condenses this passage but preserves enough detail to illustrate that Ruprecht has decided to attempt to win Renata's affections by indulging her interest in magic spells:

RUPRECHT (reading from a book): . . . Of the three magic circles, the middle one is separated into nine different sections. In the first is inscribed the secret name of the hour chosen for the conjuration; in the second, the secret names of the sun and moon; in the third . . .

RENATA (bringing Glock in with her): Ruprecht, my friend [indecipherable] to sell us new books.

[RUPREKT: (chitayet v knige): . . . Iz tryokh magicheskikh krugov, sredniy razdelen na devyat' raznïkh chastey. V pervom napisano taynoye nazvaniye chasa, izbrannogo dlya zaklinaniya; vo vtorom—taynïye imena solntsa i lunï; v tret'yem . . .

RENATA (vvodit Gloka): Ruprekt, moy drug [indecipherable] prodat' n[a]m nov[ïye] knigi.⁵⁰]

In the 1927 libretto, black turns to white: Renata, rather than Ruprecht, begins the conjuration. Though the knight affirms his belief in the forces that may or may not be engulfing the maiden, her influence over him has clearly waned, for he curses her for turning them into vagrants, destined to wander the streets of Cologne like unhappy ghosts:

RENATA (reading): . . . Of the three magic circles, the middle one is separated into nine equal sections. In the first is inscribed the secret name of the hour chosen for the conjuration. In the second are inscribed the secret names. . . (Ruprecht enters silently and stands for some time behind Renata, following her recitation) . . . of the sun, stars and moon; in the third, the name of the demon of that hour, and also of his black servants. In the fourth is inscribed . . .

RUPRECHT: We have been in Cologne a week already. Everyone lives normally, but we alone are two outcasts. From morning to night we search for Heinrich, sometimes performing invocations, other times just wandering the city.

[RENATA (chitayet): . . . Iz tryokh magicheskikh krugov, sredniy razdelen
na devyat' ravnïkh chastey. V pervom napisano
taynoye nazvaniye chasa, izbrannogo dlya zaklinaniya. Vo vtorom napisanï taynïye imena . . .
(Ruprekt, neslïshno vkhodit i nekotoroye vremya
ostanetsya pozadi Renatï, sledya za yeyo cht-
eniyem) . . . solntsa, zvezd i lunï, a v tret'yem,
imya demona etogo chasa, a takzhe chornïkh slug
yego. V chetvyortom napisano . . .

RUPREKT: Vot uzhe nedelya, kak mï v Kol'ne. Vse zhivut
polyudski, i tol'ko mï budto dvoye obrechonnïkh.
S utra do nochi ishchem Genrikha, to zaklinayem,
to prosto rïshchem po gorodu.]

Making sense of Prokofiev's reworking of this section of the libretto requires considering the symbolism of the magic circle. In pagan folklore, the
magic circle usually denotes a space devoid of malevolent spirits. Linda
Ivanits notes that the standard Russian term for such spirits is *chert*, "a
term likely connected with the Russian word for 'line' or 'limit' *(cherta)*
and related to a magic line *(chur)*, usually a circle, that the unclean force
cannot cross."[51] Pagan Russians used the circle to create a division between
the chaste space inhabitable by humans and the defiled space conceded to
disease- and misfortune-bearing energies. In the 1923 libretto, Ruprecht
uses it to corral the energies invoked in his séance. The circle's apotropaic
capacity is represented by a gradual decrease in the volume of the strings
and brasses. The surges of sound previously signaling supernatural incursions are suppressed. In the 1927 libretto, Renata draws the circle not to
keep the supernatural in check but to harness and control it. Ominous
thudding infiltrates her room as the strings and brasses increase in volume.
The change in the circle's function assumes great importance in act V. A
group of nuns forms a ring to ward off the demons possessing Renata, but
instead of banishing the demons, the ring actually lures them into the convent to accost her.

By theatricalizing the supernatural, Prokofiev achieved his objective of
replacing the theological element of the text with "orgies." His Renata is
more a Whore of Babylon than an Eternal Feminine. Yet theology does inform the ending of the libretto in both its versions. As the Inquisitor and
the Archbishop of Trier conclude their farcical trial of Renata, Ruprecht
and Mephistopheles appear in a loft high above the stage. Pointing down
toward her, the latter bellows, "Look, isn't that the one who put your viol
out of tune? There she is! There she is!" ("Glyadi, ne eta li rasstroila tvoyu

violu? Vot eta! Vot eta!") In Bryusov's novel, this line is pronounced not by Mephistopheles but by Ruprecht, with regard to his protracted separation from Renata and his trepidation about enlisting Faust and his accomplice to help find her:

> At this time everyone loudly rose from the table and surrounded the Doctor [Faust], expressing their gratitude to him for his decision [to demonstrate his supernatural powers]. I made use of the general movement to depart the room and went for a stroll in the empty gallery, angry that I had not enacted my decision of yesterday [to part company with Mephistopheles and Faust], and, in general, *with my soul feeling like an out of tune viol.*[52]

Why did Prokofiev transpose the line from Ruprecht to Mephistopheles (and from the middle of the novel to the end of the opera)? Possibly to show that the hapless knight has sold his soul to the forces of evil, to the Devil, who now speaks (sings) in his voice. And yet, listeners would have to be intimately familiar with the source novel to detect the exchange of roles: in the opera, the knight alludes neither to the state of his soul (his spiritual health) nor to viols. It is an empty symbolic gesture, a literary allusion without a dramatic context.

Like others, this feature of the libretto is an arcanum that emerges only through a comparison of source materials, and that excludes the audience at a live performance, which can only understand the action through the actual events on stage. It nonetheless casts light on Prokofiev's dramatic intentions, and on the difference between the 1923 and 1927 librettos. In the latter, Ruprecht stumbles from confusion to confusion; the "thrice Doctor" Agrippa of Nettesheim turns out to be a charlatan; Renata hopes in vain for a superhuman entity to liberate her from the constraints of material reality. Indeed, as Mikhaíl Tarakanov has suggested, Renata's earnest desire to learn the truth about her visions impels her to a fateful action. She demands that the fiery angel appear to her in material form, or, in other words, for spiritual bliss to become physical bliss.[53] Prokofiev shows the irreconcilable paradox of this aspiration. By obfuscating the relation between dramatic planes, he suggests that spiritual fulfillment resides not in the transformation of heavenly love into earthly love but in achieving harmony between the body and soul. Moments of spiritual revelation do occur in the opera, but not without their immediate subversion, the outcome being the dissolution rather than the affirmation of the possibility of transcendence. Like Bryusov in the source novel, Prokofiev is aware of his theurgic goal but does not allow his score to achieve it.

Alas, for Prokofiev, the issue of the opera's thematic content and dramatic effect became moot, as he did not live to see it staged. For him—as for Bryusov—Ruprecht, Renata, Count Heinrich (Madiel), Faust, and Mephistopheles existed "only on paper."

OF THE TRIAL OF THE MAIDEN UNDER THE PRESIDENCY
OF HIS EMINENCE THE ARCHBISHOP OF TRIER

Myaskovsky claimed that *The Fiery Angel* provided a "radiant visual image" of Renata (and the other characters as well). But what did he mean? Was he implying, for example, that Prokofiev wanted the score to provide an accurate mimetic reflection of the events in the source novel?

Prokofiev did not. Although the opera is constructed of easily identifiable leitmotifs, the composer ensured that it could not be subjected to a routine semiotic decoding. To be blunt, the listener must contend with noise, increasingly overlaid and increasingly clamorous orchestral ostinati patterns (in the acts II and III entr'actes and in the acts II and V finales) that not only drown out the singers' voices but disrupt and segment the narrative flow. In this regard, the score appears to embrace a Futurist concept, emulating what Luigi Russolo (1885–1947) termed "the chaos of noise in life" and denouncing "sentimental strumming" and "melodic clichés."[54] Renata's visions resist representation; her psychological state is unspecified. Instead, her reminiscences of her amorous encounters with the fiery angel are annotated by "pure" sound values, music that cannot be decoded, music of unrecognizable timbre. Though these coarse chromatic orchestral passages are sometimes associated with stage events, they most often denote the absence of stable meaning, the mysticism of the unknowable, even the nihilism of the death drive. Just as an unbridgeable chasm separates the heroine from the hero in *The Fiery Angel*, an unbridgeable chasm separates the traditional leitmotivic scaffolding of the score from its combustible acoustic background.

Upon examining the musical organization of *The Fiery Angel*, one can largely accept McAllister's claim that the composer extracted much of it from his inchoate adolescent project *Maddalena* (opus 13, 1911/13).[55] The dramatic trajectories of the two operas are almost identical. The source play of the earlier work—based by Magda Gustavovna Liven-Orlova on the theatrical fragment *A Florentine Tragedy* (1908) by Oscar Wilde—relates a tragic love triangle between a painter (Genaro), his alchemist friend (Stenio), and his dissolute spouse (Maddalena). To her complete indifference, the two men kill each other in a duel for her affections. Prokofiev conceived the four scenes as an almost continuous dramatic buildup, each climax and each dissonance raising the tension that leads inexorably to the cataclysmic conclusion. He evidently believed that the plot stemmed from Wilde's poetic system, as he drafted the score along the lines of Richard Strauss's one-act operas *Salome* (1905) and *Elektra* (1909), the former based on Wilde's play of the same name. The entire opera is organized by a conglomerate of leitmotifs that serve to supply the personalities of the three characters and the conflicts between them. Other leitmotifs function to convey the atmosphere and mood of the four intermeshed scenes. Prokofiev also deploys "tonal," "polytonal," and "atonal" sonorities to denote love, loneliness, and emotional breakdown.

Maddalena furnished all but one of the leitmotifs for *The Fiery Angel*. Their transformation shows how Prokofiev shifted the dramaturgical focus of his *émigré* operas from realism to surrealism. Renata is a degradation of Maddalena, but her aberrant behavior and mental anguish establish, *a contrario*, the truth of divine harmony. And whereas Genaro and Stenio expose Maddalena as inhuman, Ruprecht portrays those around him as hostile caricatures.

Genaro's and Ruprecht's leitmotifs are deformed cadential gestures, the first confirming D major (at the end of scene 2 of *Maddalena*), the latter confirming A minor (at the start of act I of *The Fiery Angel*). The two characters do not sing their leitmotifs: they are instead performed in the orchestra over the course of the operas in a manner that reflects the characters' deteriorating psychological states. Following Ruprecht's act III, scene 2 swordfight with Count Heinrich (Madiel), for example, the bassoons intone a distorted (wounded) version of his leitmotif in imitative counterpoint: the constituent intervals are chromatically altered, and the concluding turn figure (c^2-b^1-c^2-a^1 in Music Example 37) is missing. The variation sounds in C-sharp minor, the accompaniment in F-sharp minor. The equivocal sounding of harmonies from disparate tonal realms is a common feature of *The Fiery Angel*. The practice cannot be attributed to what Richard Bass terms Prokofiev's "technique of chromatic displacement," in which a nondiatonic pitch in a given tonality "is neither prepared nor resolved" but becomes a diatonic pitch in a second "shadow" tonality. (Thus the displaced pitch "behaves as though nothing were 'wrong' with it in the first place. Even though it comes as something of a surprise, the listener is obliged to deal with it in a diatonic context, as a representative of its diatonic shadow."[56]) In *The Fiery Angel*, the superabundance of chromaticism precludes its easy rationalization within simple voice-leading assemblages.

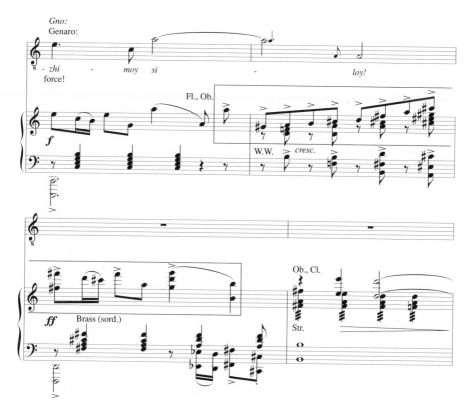

Example 36.   Genaro's leitmotif in scene 2 of *Maddalena*

Example 37.   Ruprecht's leitmotif in act I of *The Fiery Angel*

The cadential flourish that opens the opera, for example, brings together nonfunctional minor triads on B♭ and A, the latter confirmed as the tonic triad through sheer insistence in measures two and three. In its ambiguity, the passage neatly encapsulates the distinguishing features of the opera's musical syntax: reliance on chords related by minor second, major and minor third conflicts, and emphasis on pitch clusters that generate multiple chordal subsets.

McAllister observes that the leitmotif in *Maddalena* linked to Stenio's desire "combines stepwise chromaticism with a major/minor third conflict in its melodic outline." She also observes that the "figure evocative of Stenio's uncontrollable frenzy . . . is in its melody and ostinato rhythm immediately reminiscent of the motif of Renata's agitation in act I." [57] Renata's leitmotif contains rising and falling E and C minor trichords (e^2-$f\sharp^2$-g^2 and $e\flat^2$-d^2-c^2) in compound triple time. It is less audible as a "polytonal" complex than as an embellished and "linearized" major-minor chord (c^2-$e\flat^2$-e^2-g^2) and in this regard bears some resemblance to the Firebird's leitmotif from Stravinsky's 1910 ballet, with which Prokofiev was intimately familiar. When Renata sings the leitmotif, the first pitch of the six-note group usually falls off the beat (as at rehearsal number 14, when she bellows, "Keep away from me!" ["Otoydi ot menya!"] to the invisible [to us] spirits tormenting her), and it is usually embellished with nondiatonic pitches. When Ruprecht sings the leitmotif, it retains its rhythmic and tonal contour (as at rehearsal number 12, when he inquires, "Is anyone in need of my protection?" ["Ne nuzhdayetsya li kto v moyom pokrovitel'stve?"]). In both instances, its syntactic structure is preserved, but the enunciation is not: the phrase expands, becomes displaced, and concatenates other phrases. The leitmotif is also heard in the orchestra, both as an independent line and an accompaniment. Rather than "narrating" Renata's actions or reflecting her moods, the orchestral version remains intact throughout the opera, locking her into a pattern of recurring hallucinations from which—to recall Pyman's comment about the last chapter of the source novel—"no rescue [is] offered." [58]

Ruprecht's and Renata's leitmotifs are complimented in *The Fiery Angel* by several others that are less distinguishable, as they are incorporated into surging, volcanic orchestral passages. As in *Maddalena*, they take the form of rising and falling melodic and harmonic patterns containing conflicted major and minor thirds. The meteoric semitonal phrase aligned with Stenio in scene 3 of *Maddalena*, for example, inspired the bass line allotted to Agrippa of Nettesheim in act II, scene 2 of *The Fiery Angel*. Both have a rising sixteenth-note and dotted eighth-note rhythm and both span a

Example 38.   Stenio's leitmotif in scene 4 of *Maddalena*

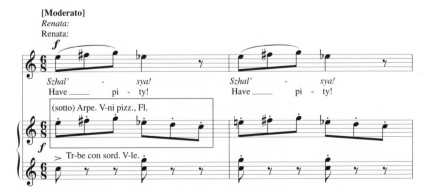

Example 39.   Renata's leitmotif in act I of *The Fiery Angel*

range of a tenth (c^2 to e^3 in the B-flat clarinet line at rehearsal number 261). The tritone figure that heralds the duel in the earlier score likewise became the tritone figure heralding supernatural events in the later score. It is first played by the oboe and English horn at rehearsal number 6 of act I. Prokofiev develops the leitmotifs over the course of the opera and derives secondary leitmotifs from them. In the one episode that could be considered a love duet—the dialogue between Ruprecht and Renata that begins midway through act II, scene 1—Prokofiev introduces a leitmotif comprising three ascending eighth notes that outline a minor third (e^1-f♯^{1}-g^1), these being extracted from Renata's leitmotif, followed by a downward eighth-note leap of a minor sixth (g^1-b). In the next measure, the e^1-f♯^{1}-g^1 pattern is repeated, but this time followed by an ascending upward eighth-note leap of a major sixth (g^1-e^2). The resulting four-note group (e^1-f♯^{1}-g^1-e^2) is a mirror inversion—though at a different pitch level and rhythm—of a gesture (g^1-f^1-e^1-g) heard in the Count Heinrich (Madiel) leitmotif at rehearsal number 195 in the first violins. This subsidiary leitmotif appears as Ruprecht repeatedly pledges to aid Renata in her search for Count Heinrich (Madiel), the implication being that the knight no longer has romantic feelings for the maiden. The leitmotif denies his words by unleashing a cascade of emotion, the boundlessness of his devotion to her denoted by its subsequent extension and variation.

From these and other passages—a rising minor third pattern (f♯^{1}-g♯^{1}-a^1) that typifies the music sung by the nuns at rehearsal number 484 of act V, an ascending diminished third pattern (c♯^{2}-d^2-e♭^{2}) that accompanies the fortuneteller at rehearsal number 148 of act I—one discerns a resemblance between Prokofiev's transformation technique and that found in Strauss's tone poems. To paraphrase McAllister: "The [at times inexplicable] action on the stage merely forms a visual counterpart to what is largely complete [if at times equally inexplicable] in the music."[59] The overall structure of The Fiery Angel, however, suggests less an affinity with modern than with Romantic composition. To establish epic scale—and thus allegorize the confrontation between Renata and Ruprecht as a confrontation between paganism and Christianity—Prokofiev relies on sequencing and transposition in extended passages. The practice recalls Gounod's Faust as well as Robert le diable, a grand opéra that blends medieval legend, superstition, the supernatural, and romance. Indeed, the structure of act V of The Fiery Angel seems to derive from that of the finale of act III of Robert le diable. Both take place in a moonlit cloister and feature debauched nuns participating in a round dance. The choruses are determining factors in the action: their evolving style, progressing from homophonic to

Example 40.   The love duet leitmotif in act II, scene 1 of *The Fiery Angel*

Example 41.   The Count Heinrich (Madiel) leitmotif in act I

nonimitative polyphonic to imitative polyphonic textures, gives shape to the visual events.

A brief comparison of the hallucination scenes in acts I and V will substantiate these remarks. The two episodes are closely related musically, indicating that Prokofiev sought not only to increase the level of tension over the course of the opera, but also to mirror its white key (natural) and black key (supernatural) dramatic planes. The aural symmetries between the scenes do not so much unify the score as supply it with a circular or spiraling form, over the course of which the atmosphere of cataclysm mounts, lending credence to Myaskovsky's claim that the opera has "colossal" intensity and embodies "something elemental." The ostinato writing in these scenes transforms *The Fiery Angel* into a drama of large-scale strophic repetitions that affect the listener less as a series of catharses than as a series of cyclones. From his scattered comments on the opera—notably his declaration that the witches' Sabbath of the source novel would "lose" its "mystical horror" on stage—it appears that Prokofiev intended his music to convey what the stage could not: the battle between angelic and demonic forces for Renata's soul. Whereas several scenes, most notably the duel between Ruprecht and Count Heinrich (Madiel), take place on the threshold between the visible and invisible, the real drama unfolds in the orchestral pit. The composer deploys everything conceivable to manufacture apocalyptic sound: tritone-partitioned chords, unregulated chromaticism, pounding ostinati, deafening dynamics. The superficial modernism of the music affirms that the stage world is also superficial, with the characters unable to calculate or comprehend events, only feel them.

In the act I hallucination scene, Renata recounts her childhood meetings with Madiel and grieves that, once her Platonic love for him became sexual, he abandoned her. She laments that she has long since had horrible visions of demons pursuing her. Between rehearsal numbers 6 and 37, Renata enters a state of panic, imploring the spirits to leave her in peace. Her condition is comparable to what Ivanits labels *klikuchestvo,* "an ailment [first identified by pre-Revolutionary Russian folklorists] characterized by shrieking and howling . . . in the presence of holy objects."[60] At the climax of the scene, extending from rehearsal number 31 to 37, Renata repeats a four-note segment of her leitmotif (e^2-$f\sharp^2$-g^2-$e\flat^2$) thirty-seven times. At the same time, the first violins repeat all six pitches (e^2-$f\sharp^2$-g^2-$e\flat^2$-d^2-c^2) of the leitmotif forty-nine times.[61] In response to Renata's pleas for help, at rehearsal number 32 Ruprecht begins to declaim a four-measure Latin exorcism: "Libera me Domine de morte aeterna." To demonstrate that it has had the desired effect (that it has vanquished the maiden's hallucination), Prokofiev transposes the two trichords of the leitmotif from E and C minor at rehearsal numbers 31 and 32 down to A-sharp and F-sharp minor at rehearsal number 33 ($a\sharp^1$-$b\sharp^1$-$c\sharp^2$-a^1-$g\sharp^1$-$f\sharp^1$) and then down to D-sharp and B minor ($d\sharp$-$e\sharp$-$f\sharp$-d^1-$c\sharp^1$-b) at rehearsal number 34—this last being the tonality of the exorcism. Ruprecht's musical mantra defeats Renata's musical mantra. N. Rzhavinskaya notes that the "vertical conflict" of the two vocal parts cedes to their "vertical contrast" as the modulation to B minor is completed.[62]

This is one of two ways in which Prokofiev signals the defeat of profane music—the leitmotivic cipher of supernatural malevolence—by sacred music. The other lies coarsely in the accordion-like expansion and contraction of instrumental forces. At rehearsal number 31, for example, Prokofiev overlays four rhythmic variants of Renata's leitmotif: she performs the aforementioned four-pitch segment; the first violins repeat all six pitches; the second violins repeat the first and fourth pitches; then the cellos and basses extend the first and fourth pitches from eighth notes to dotted quarter notes. At rehearsal number 34, Prokofiev begins to reduce the instrumental forces: the vertical alignment of the variants cedes to their horizontal stratification. By analogy, one could argue that the music indicates that Renata, on experiencing the revelation of other tiers of reality, has returned to the narrow confines of material existence. More subtly, the music discloses the antipodes of her personality, what John Daverio (writing on Schumann's settings of Goethe's *Faust*, 1844–53) has called "the 'practical' but potentially destructive drive toward self-assertion on the one hand, and the 'theoretical' or 'reflective' but potentially paralyzing drive toward self-examination on the other."[63] The "conflict" between the two drives is reflected in the conflict between Renata's two ariosos in act I, the first describing her suffering at the hands of invisible demons, the second describing her childhood encounters with the fiery angel. Given the stabilization of the orchestral forces, the transition between the two ariosos implies that the drama has traversed a metaphysical barrier of sorts, that

Example 42.   The vertical superimposition of rhythmic variants of Renata's leitmotif in act I

what appeared to be a supernatural event was only a hallucination, and that Prokofiev (or his insistent musical narrator) wants us to perceive Renata as a hysteric rather than a visionary.

The act V hallucination scene replays much of the act I hallucination scene, though it takes place in a tidy cloister rather than a dirty inn, and with a greatly expanded cast: a chorus of nuns, the Inquisitor, the Archbishop of Trier, and Mephistopheles. Whereas in act I Ruprecht restored order when Renata's emotions spun out of control, in act V Renata holds her emotions in check while those of the others rage. As noted, the dramatic frame of act V recalls the finale of *Robert le diable*, though the organ and choral music and Mephistopheles' maledictions were likely also inspired by act IV, scene 3 of Gounod's *Faust*. At rehearsal number 497, the Inquisitor informs the hapless nuns that a demon has assumed the guise of one of them. Turning to Renata, he demands that she "answer: can you offer us evidence that your visions have never been the devil's work?" ("Otvechayte: mozhete li vï predstavit' nam dokazatel'stva, shto nikogda vashi videniya ne bïli delom ruk d'yavola?"). She meekly admits (at rehearsal number 501) that she does not know the source of her visions, but that the angel who came to her in youth spoke the word of God and beseeched her to seek the path of virtue. The ceiling and walls of the convent begin to shudder with dull thuds. In a series of venomous confrontations with the nuns, the Inquisitor demands to know the cause of the din. When Renata answers, "Father, those are spirits knocking" ("Otets, eto dukhi stuchat"), he begins the exorcism and trial that will lead to her martyrdom. In order to confirm that her fate is predetermined (that it has quite literally knocked on the door) and that she has elected to die faithful to her angelic ideal, Prokofiev accompanies her pleas with what might be termed (to borrow a term from film scholarship) "anempathetic" music, music that shows an ostensible indifference to the events on stage, pursuing its own dauntless and mechanical course.[64] It consists of three ostinato patterns that fall into a loosely organized rondo form:

Voice Part	Ostinato Pattern	Duration	Rehearsal Number
Inquisitor	A	08 mm	521
Nuns	C	06 mm	522
Inquisitor	A	06 mm	523
Nuns	C	06 mm	524
Inquisitor	A	11 mm	525
Nuns	C	12 mm	526

Voice Part	Ostinato Pattern	Duration	Rehearsal Number
Inquisitor	B	06 mm	527
Inquisitor	B	06 mm	529
Nuns	C	03 mm	530

Ostinato pattern A comprises a panicked chant-like recitation on the pitches c^1 and a. Ostinato pattern B comprises a panicked chant-like recitation on the pitches c^1, b, a, f, and eb, offset by ostinato pattern A. Ostinato pattern C superimposes four phrases in A minor: a fragmented ascending pentachord performed by the first group of soprano nuns; a descending glissando performed by the second group of soprano nuns; an arching line performed by the third group of soprano nuns; and running eighth notes performed by a group of altos.[65] Of the four phrases, the first three are settings of nonsensical vowel sounds, a reference to the textless outpourings of suffering and ecstasy endemic to Byzantine and Russian Orthodoxy. The jubilation it affords, however, cannot prevent the "anempathetic" music of the scene— the whirling and hammering orchestral metalworks—from laying down its own logic.

The dementia reaches a climax at rehearsal number 545, when the chorus of nuns disintegrates into six parts, each assigned a rhythmic variant of Renata's leitmotif. The top two voices perform four pitches of the leitmotif $(e^2$-f#^{2}-g^2-eb$^2)$ in tandem, the lower two voices perform them down a tritone $(bb^1$-c^2-db^2-a$^1)$ in tandem, and the middle two voice parts complete the consequent tritone-related harmonies: minor seventh chords on A and Eb, the latter in second inversion.

The vertical superimposition of the rhythmic cells in the scene signals none too subtly that the nuns, like Renata, perceive the more real world. The liquidation of these cells does not, however, signal the nuns' return to reality, for they remain possessed until the very end. At rehearsal number 575, as the Inquisitor declaims a Latin incantation reminiscent of that declaimed by Ruprecht in act I ("Spiriti maligni, damnati, interdicti, exterminati!"), the nuns proclaim that he, rather than the much maligned Renata, is black with sin. Momentarily redeemed, she beseeches the nuns to forgive her to the melody of the white key chorus that they sang at the outset of the act. Instead they begin to recite the mocking "la-la-la-la" phrase recited in act I by the laborer. White light floods the stage, and the heroine, having endured the show trial and received her death sentence, embarks on the spiritual path to higher being.

Example 43. The six-part chorus of nuns in act V

But extrasensory perception does not lead Renata to salvation. The ascent to light is thwarted by the final curtain, which descends, as noted, just after the Inquisitor orders her execution. Prokofiev's decision to end the opera at its climax—with a freeze-frame *fortissimo* fermata—leaves his heroine stranded in the material world. By stressing external effect over internal content, his score breaks faith with its subject matter: the occult battle that takes place in outer reality and in each mind. Musically terminating the possibility of liberation from an oppressive existence constitutes the ultimate transgression of the "mystic" Symbolist preoccupation with transcendence. According to Marina Sabinina, Prokofiev's dispassionate conclusion reflects his "sober attitude" toward dramaturgy:

> In the opera, he is able to retain his objectivity; the mystical atmosphere by no means overwhelms it. He truly reconstitutes a gloomy Medieval milieu and depicts Renata's hallucinations and the nuns' hysteria (in the last act) with unusual expressiveness, but he does so as though from the perspective of an outside observer, a psychologist or painter. In this resides the deepest difference between *The Fiery Angel* and the aesthetics of Expressionist "horror opera."[66]

Sabinina here isolates the principal tension in the final act: the mediation between "horror opera" on the one hand and sacred drama on the other. Their convergence foregrounds the paradoxical relationship formulated by the composer between religious persecution and religious revelation.

The oppressive onslaught of dissonance before the curtain descends carries with it the elemental ("Scythian") force of ritual. The sonorities between rehearsal numbers 590 and 591 are derived exclusively from a six-pitch collection—B♭, B, D, F, F♯—whose subsets include B-flat major and B-minor triads, the latter a product of the inversion of the former around its mediant. Though one cannot overlook the volatility of the framing music, the collection can be rationalized as a synthesis of what the Fortean set theorist Neil Minturn has called "third-flip-related triads."[67] Prokofiev concludes *The Fiery Angel* with a rising semitonal sequence from d♭^{1} to d♭^{2} interlaced with ascending and descending trichords redolent of Renata's leitmotif. The common fund of material that links the beginning of the opera with the end reflects on a macrocosmic scale Prokofiev's predilection for conflicting major and minor third patterns. The major third shift from B-flat minor/A minor to D major before rehearsal number 1 complements the minor third turn from B-flat major/B minor to D-flat major after rehearsal number 590. Just as the unfathomable noise of the climactic scene evokes the forces of disintegration surrounding Renata (as they surrounded the Symbolist poets), the inversion of tonal registers upsets the order of things, inverting benevolence and malevolence, heaven and hell.

Although the score concludes on a major third (D♭-F), the consonant interval by no means resolves the preceding musical and dramatic tumult. The dissonance of the final measures is not a prelude to consonance in another world; Renata's pilgrimage through the inferno has served only to expose the moral turmoil of her historical era. Had Prokofiev intended *The Fiery Angel* to be uplifting, he might have established moments of dramatic transparency in the score, moments in which the characters glimpse the heavenly beyond. Instead, to reflect the blurring of the sacred edge between the natural and supernatural, within the panopticons of acts I and V, he exchanged musical ideas between the "good" and "evil" figures, thus calling into question the morality of saints and witches, clergy and cultists alike. The technique has allegorical, rather than symbolic, implications. It enables the viewer to draw moral lessons from the score, to regard mad Renata as a representative of all the visionaries who have been persecuted for their beliefs throughout history. Musically, the 1927 version of the opera does not exhibit the illusory and evolving potentialities that define symbols. Prokofiev's leitmotifs retain the same functions throughout. While he adjusts them to suit the accent and stress patterns of the vocal lines, he locks them into invariant ostinato patterns.[68] In Renata's case, these patterns are evocative less of spiritual rapture than of delirious mania, the obsessive litanies of a hysteric. (Her alternating moods of despondency and exhilaration, moreover, suggest clinical depression.) Though he sympathized with her plight enough to demonize her antagonists, Prokofiev was unwilling to grant his heroine the redemption in the spirit world that she failed to achieve in quotidian reality. Her insistence on the existence of the occult realm and her assistance to nonbelievers does not lead to her spiritual liberation.

There are, however, two properly symbolic passages in the score. These reflect Prokofiev's desire to create a Gothic vagueness of time and space in the opera and to show how the supernatural (or belief in the supernatural) informed Renaissance life. The first—identified by McAllister[69]—takes place in the act III entr'acte, which narrates the offstage duel between Ruprecht and Count Heinrich. After a clamorous chromatic sequence that establishes B minor as the local tonality one measure before rehearsal number 370, we hear two versions of Ruprecht's leitmotif in the lower brass, strings, and woodwinds. The first begins on the pitch F, the second on F♯. (In between these two presentations, a solo trombone sounds the leitmotif on B♭.) The function of the chromatic displacement is unclear until one measure before rehearsal number 371, where D major is established as the local tonality. The modulation is aided by the appearance of a second leitmotif, one that has not been heard before in relation to Ruprecht. To this point in the opera, it has only been heard when Renata refers to Count Heinrich and the fiery angel and, as such, informs us that in her mind the two figures are one and the same. It has not been heard when Ruprecht refers to the fiery angel, for he considers him to be a figment of Renata's imagination. When the leitmotif arises in the duel, however, we are informed that the knight now regards the maiden's visions as true: the connection between Heinrich and Madiel has been solidified in his mind. Heard by us from his perspective, the music offers a fleeting and fragile point of equilibrium between material and immaterial realms.

The Count Heinrich (Madiel) leitmotif is the only one that recurs unaltered in the opera and the only one that does not have a direct dramatic counterpart in *Maddalena* (since it always occurs in the major, it necessarily causes a modulation from B minor to its relative major). Along with the white key music sung in thirds and fifths by the nuns at rehearsal number 484 of act V (a stylization of two-part *organum* suggesting pious serenity and reflection), the leitmotif had been drafted by the composer in 1918 as part of a planned but unfinished String Quartet in C major. This recycled music is not associated with visual images in the opera: Prokofiev specified that the duel should take place offstage and that the nuns should sing behind the stage curtain. In order to imply the interplay of demonic and angelic forces, he created the illusion that this music was unearthly, with no physical grounding or reference. Emanating from nowhere, it was to offer an aural outlet from the dismal reality of the stage world. The leitmotif of the duel ascends through the registers, becoming the orchestral equivalent of what Bryusov, in the poem that concluded his poetic "duel" with Belïy, called the "distant light [that] dispersed the shadows."

The other symbolic moment comes just prior to the conclusion of the opera, when Mephistopheles points to Renata from above the convent floor and asks Ruprecht whether she was "the one who put [his] viol out of tune." Like the Count Heinrich (Madiel) leitmotif, this discordant sound stems from beyond the dramatic frame of reference; unlike it, this sound remains unheard. It is impossible music whose mystery is protected not by silence but by a barrage of discord. We do not hear the real violas when Mephistopheles makes his proclamation at rehearsal number 571: they are drowned out by the cries of the stricken nuns, an orchestral crescendo, a tritonal chromatic descent from f^1 to b in the bass line, tetrachordal grace note figures in the violins, piccolos and flutes generated from tonalities

Example 44. Count Heinrich's (Madiel's) leitmotif in the act III entr'acte
(continues)

Example 44.   *(continues)*

Example 44.   *(continued)*

related by minor second (c^2-d^2-e^2-f^2, $d\flat^2$-$e\flat^2$-f^2-$g\flat^2$, $e\flat^2$-f^2-g^2-$a\flat^2$, e^2-$f\sharp^2$-$g\sharp^2$-a^2), and (after rehearsal number 572), A minor pentachords in the voices offset by G-flat major arpeggios in the harps and trombones. Mephistopheles instead refers to music whose origin is inaudible to our ears and invisible to our eyes: the music of Ruprecht's soul, put out of tune by powers beyond all human control. Prokofiev does not often resort to understatement in this opera, but in the final scene the most potent sound is one we cannot know. Despite succumbing to occult forces in the duel, the knight cannot perceive the *au-delà*. He emerges from his labors with nothing—neither Renata, nor the false reality of the material world. Mephistopheles's appearance in the *auto-da-fé* marks the unleashing of an orchestral cataclysm. As Svyatoslav Richter marveled: "Grandiose masses open up and collapse—it is the end of the universe."[70]

What happens after "the end"? The phrase "Look, isn't that the one who put your viol out of tune?" is a reference to what Bryusov termed "the other, fuller harmonies," a "distorted 'echo'" of the realm of beatitude that only visionaries like Renata can perceive. Though the last act of *The Fiery Angel* points to her death, it is not the cessation of her being but the expression of a Symbolist musical ideal: the transposition out of time and space—out of opera—into another plane of being. This fleeting moment in the score unexpectedly recuperates the notion that reality is false and that the material world is a veil that conceals the immaterial world. The visible stage, as a representation of reality, is no more fictional than life itself. It is a symbol of the fragilities and disharmonies—the "out of tuneness"—of earthly being.

OF ENCOUNTERS WITH THE KNIGHT
AND THRICE DOCTOR AGRIPPA OF NETTESHEIM

This invocation of impossible music and perforated stage sets reflects the Symbolist credo that material reality is transparent. Prokofiev foregrounds music as a medium for exploration beyond the here and now. The opera's purposeful ambivalences are enhanced by the collusion of nineteenth- and twentieth-century dramatic devices. However, the score does not have those features that make the source text, for all its pilfering, ingenious: the attempt to forge a synthesis between different times and places and to strike a balance between literary-technical and spiritual-philosophical issues. The conclusion is anticlimactic, imparting that everything that has occurred on stage was perhaps simply one character's hallucination. It provides few correspondences, few intimations that the conflict between Renata and Ruprecht is part of a broader struggle between forces of dark and light, a struggle that has persisted since antiquity. Prokofiev likely sensed that imbuing the drama with biblical pathos would have constituted an anachronism, affirming religious and spiritual values that no longer applied to modern art.

Three years later, he changed his mind. Evidently frustrated by his inability to solve the dramatic challenge posed by the subject matter—how to enact Renata's supernatural visions, how to make them as much like they are described in the source novel as possible, without settling for something banal—Prokofiev resolved to abandon the "orgies" and to restore "theology" to the opera. He decided, in effect, that *The Fiery Angel* would be less parodic and more symbolic. In 1930, he submitted the 1927 score to the board of directors at the Metropolitan Opera, who informed him that it suffered from insufficient visual action, since crucial scenes contained only extended ariosos and monologues. It became his immediate but unrealized intention to break down the score into short vignettes. He partitioned the two scenes of act II into seven scenes (the first two to words of his own invention, not extracted from the source novel) and interspersed them with brief orchestral interludes. While he continued to center the plot around Renata, Ruprecht, and Count Heinrich (Madiel), he greatly expanded the roles of Agrippa of Nettesheim, Jacob Glock, and the fortuneteller.

The best evidence of Prokofiev's intentions for the 1930 version is a scenario he typed up in English on letterhead of the Great Northern Hotel in New York. On the title page, he commented that the revised second act would be "called the travels of Ruprecht and Renata" and would contain the following "short scenes or miniatures":

Scene 1

A sunny landscape. Renata [is] mounted on a horse which is covered in the medieval fashion with a cloth. Ruprecht leads the horse by the bridle. A crowd of peasants is gathered about a dead cow[,] muttering about a witch who damages the cattle. Renata naïvely asks them "Good people have you not seen Count Heinrich?" The mob grows alarmed[:] this is the witch from whom Count Heinrich fled. The mob becomes threatening to Renata. Ruprecht[,] drawing his sword[,] protects Renata and himself and leads her away.

Scene 2

Night. A destroyed monastery. Renata dismounts, leaves the horse and[,] taking Ruprecht by the hand[,] leads him to the fresco where the image of an angel is painted which is lighted by a moonbeam. Renata says that the Fire Angel looked like the image.

Scene 3

A narrow street. Ruprecht and Renata buy books from a necromancer concerning magic. He warns them to be careful[,] as this very day the inquisitors plan to burn people suspected of heresy. Ruprecht then begs Renata to love him but she replies that she can only love her Fire Angel, Count Heinrich. Heretics pass in a procession to be burned [(]owing to the Inquisition[)],] singing a somber chorus. Windows in all the houses open and the heads of the curious appear.

Scene 4

Abandoned house. Ruprecht and Renata seek a night's lodging. They are met by the fortuneteller (of the first act). Mysterious knockings on the door begin. Ruprecht asks the spirits where Heinrich is. Throu[gh] the knockings they make it known that he will enter the house now. Renata is in indescribable excitement. She sends Ruprecht away, runs to the door[,] and calls Heinrich[,] but no one appears. Renata is desperate. Ruprecht makes up his mind to go to the famous magician Agrippa from [N]ettes[h]eim (historical figure).

Scene 5

At Agrippa's. Agrippa stands on rising ground in a black mantel and a little crimson hat. Ruprecht is at the bottom. At the right [are] three skeletons. Ruprecht questions Agrippa about the mysteries of magic. Agrippa answers in sophisms. His voice is doubled by the chorus with loudspeakers behind the scenes. The skeletons rattle their bones[,] saying to Agrippa "You lie!"

Scene 6

[The f]ront of Count Heinrich's house[,] showing [the] front and balcony. Renata [is] on her knees[,] trying to open the door which someone inside the house holds fast. She cries "Heinrich, Heinrich, why do you close the door?" Ruprecht returns from Agrippa gay and quiet, satisfied that magicians are charlatans. Renata[,] suddenly changing her mood[,] tells Ruprecht that Heinrich has insulted her and begs him to defend her. Ruprecht enters the house to speak with Heinrich. Renata[,] again on her knees[,] prays [to] heaven in a passionate aria to pardon her that she mistook a common mortal for the Fire Angel. The balcony door bursts open and Heinrich appears with Ruprecht at his side. [Ruprecht] accuses him of insulting Renata and challenges him to a duel. Renata[,] seeing Heinrich again so handsome and so like the image of the angel on the fresco of the monastery[,] is troubled that perhaps he really is her angel.

Scene 7
The musical intermission which connects this scene with the one before it represents a duel. [The s]cenery shows the shore of the Rhein. Ruprecht[,] lying unconscious[,] is wounded. He is holding the sword in his hand. At a distance are the vanishing figures of Count Heinrich and his second. Renata is wailing at Ruprecht's side[,] singing to him of love. Ruprecht[,] delirious, thinks she is an Indian girl and thinks he hears the laughter of the Indians.[71]

Example 45.   The 1930 sketchbook of *The Fiery Angel*, p. 1; this is an exact transcription, retaining the vagaries of Prokofiev's script

For act II, scenes 1 and 2—the scenes with dialogues of his own invention—Prokofiev compiled two pages of stage instructions and drafted seven pages of musical motifs and textual incipits in a sketchbook.[72] Scene 1, depicting a hostile meeting between Renata and a throng of superstitious peasants, expands the supernatural aura to include folklore about witchcraft and omens—a feature of the source novel that hitherto had not been reflected in the opera. Prokofiev portrays Renata as an outcast from Lutheran society, not because she believes in the spirit realm but because she belongs to it. The music for the scene—to gradually increase in volume, as evidenced by the block letters c-r-e-s-c-e-n-d-o scrawled down the left side of the first page of stage instructions—indicates that Ruprecht's and Renata's lives have become intertwined and that he, like she, is a practitioner of the occult.

On page 1 of the sketchbook, Prokofiev drafted a G minor melody that combines distorted versions of their leitmotifs. Here, chromatic ascending and descending patterns distantly reminiscent of Renata's leitmotif (b^1-$c\sharp^2$-d^2 and $d\flat^2$-c^2-b^1) combine, in the final measure, with a closing gesture distantly reminiscent of Ruprecht's leitmotif (d^2-$d\flat^2$-c^2-d^2-g^1). Prokofiev commented that the orchestral music of the scene was to shift from *"fortissimo"* to *"suddenly pianissimo"* (*"vdrug pp"*) when the chivalric knight rescues the strident maiden from the mob. As he leads her offstage, the audience would hear a "new crescendo" ("novoye cresc.") and

Example 46.   Agrippa of Nettesheim's leitmotif in act II, scene 2, in the 1927 version of *The Fiery Angel*

Example 47.   From p. 2 (verso) of the 1930 sketchbook

unspecified "music (with voices) from behind the curtain" ("Muz[ï]ka [s g[o]l[o]s[a]mi] z[a] z[a]n[a]v[e]s[o]m"), the latter then serving as the music of the entr'acte. In manufacturing this paranormal sound, Prokofiev endeavored to show that the two characters are disciples of demonic forces and, as such, antagonists of mortal humans. Toward the ending of the scene, he planned to enhance the supernatural aura with a variation of the surging chromatic leitmotif associated with Agrippa of Nettesheim. Included on page 2 (verso) of the sketchbook, the bass and middle lines of the variation outline a C-minor thirteenth chord.

In act II, scene 2, Prokofiev portrays Renata as a religious martyr betrayed by the experience of love and the heavenly utopia promised to her by the fiery angel in her adolescence. Her devotion to Madiel is a reflection of her Catholic rectitude but also, as McAllister comments, of her subservience "to forces of evil and the Devil, a force [*sic*] that tempts Renata in the guise of good, so that she falls wholly under its sway."[73] The source of her despondency is her naïve belief in Madiel's benevolence. Act II, scene 2 commences with Renata leading Ruprecht to a moonlit fresco painted on the walls of a dilapidated monastery. Pointing to the image of a seraph, she proclaims, "Here, Ruprecht [and nothing more]. Look, Ruprecht: it's just like my angel, my gentle, fiery angel [and nothing more]." ("Zd[e]s', Rupr[e]kt [i d(a)l'sh(e) nichego]. Sm[o]tri, Rupr[e]kt, eto t[a]k[o]v moy angel, moy nezhnïy, ognennïy angel [i d(a)l'sh(e) nichego].") The sketches indicate that, as these words are declaimed, two new musical ideas would be heard: a white key melody in C major (page 4 of the sketchbook) and a black key melody in E-flat major (page 5 of the sketchbook). Both in range and intervallic content, they are faintly reminiscent of the Count Heinrich (Madiel) leitmotif. Though tenuous, the connection was confirmed by Prokofiev, who declared that the scene would occupy rehearsal numbers 166 – 81 of the score and, as such, would recycle orchestral music initially composed as an accompaniment to a discussion between Renata and Ruprecht about Count Heinrich (Madiel), during which the Count's leitmotif fittingly predominates.[74] The grotesque alteration of the leitmotif in the sketches appears to have been inspired by Hector Berlioz's *Symphonie fantastique* (opus 14, 1831), which, like the source novel of *The Fiery Angel*, draws from Goethe's *Faust* Part 1 (Berlioz composed the *Symphonie fantastique* two years after his "Oeuvre I," the *Huit scènes de Faust*) and includes an acoustic dream image of a distant lover. Like the E-flat clarinet music of the fifth movement of the *Symphonie fantastique*, the unorchestrated music on pages 4 and 5 of the sketchbook transforms a melancholy leitmotif (or *idée fixe*) into a nightmarish sound object. In this regard, the white key and black key passages can be interpreted as musical symbols, creating echoes and parallels with other compositions. Using them, Prokofiev invokes literary images of Faust, Gretchen, and Mephistopheles and their new musical avatars, Count Heinrich, Renata, and Ruprecht. From this relation arise real-life personae—Berlioz and the Shakespearean actress Harriet Smithson, the models for the characters in the program of the *Symphonie fantastique*. They in turn bring Belïy, Bryusov, and Petrovskaya to mind. Thus, within the 1930 sketches for *The Fiery Angel*, the white key and black key passages suggest unintended correspondences between disparate times and places. If act II, scene 2, had been realized, only the material presence of the stage would bring the audience back to the present, but what the audience would see on stage would prove to be no more than a veil, a visual fragment projected from another sphere.

The other prominent symbolic effect in the 1930 sketches occurs in act II, scene 5: the séance with Agrippa of Nettesheim, Ruprecht, and a trio of skeletons (an addition to the cast inspired by the *Walpurgisnacht* episode in Gounod's *Faust*). Prokofiev intended to include amplification in the

Example 48. From p. 4 of the 1930 sketchbook

Example 49. From p. 5 of the 1930 sketchbook

scene, to double Agrippa's vitriolic outbursts with an offstage "chorus and loudspeakers." The electronic treatment of his voice would convert it into what the film theorist Michel Chion might term a "phantom" sound, an acoustic data stream oscillating between the world of the stage and the world beyond.[75] Prokofiev not only sought to amplify a macabre sound object, Agrippa's voice, but to amplify macabre ex-objects, the eerie and comic emanations of disembodied sound. Cued by the skeletons—who would bellow "You lie!" ("Tï lzhosh'!") when Agrippa denies his study of the black arts—Ruprecht would accept for real what is merely an electronic echo. The séance scene would provide the aural equivalent of a hall of mirrors effect, where multiple sonic reflections spread out, moving from the material to the ideal, the real to the more real. The effect would not be superficial, but would function to articulate what Friedrich Kittler calls the "theory of positive feedback" in opera: the typically Wagnerian reliance on acoustic distortions to supplant the "symbolic (i.e. written) structure" of a score.[76] It is tempting to speculate that Prokofiev's "media technology" was informed by the Symbolists, who were interested in paranormal phenomena. Upon attending a séance in 1905 in Moscow, for example, Bryusov declared, "In time, spirit powers will be subjected to thorough study and may even find some technical application, like steam and electricity."[77]

Prokofiev planned to revise only one other passage in the score: the entr'acte depicting the duel between Ruprecht and Count Heinrich (Madiel). On pages 6 and 2 (recto) of the sketchbook, he composed a new melody for it, an E/G-minor theme marked by dotted rhythms, alternating tonic and dominant harmonies, and meteoric arpeggios. The neoteric melody, expanding intervallic and rhythmic features of the music shown on page 4 of the sketchbook, abstractly imparts something of the thrusts and parries of a duel and thus portrays the stage figures as actual people engaged in actual battle. In another regard, however, they appear as if in a dream. The melody is heard nowhere else in the opera and, as such, situates the duel in a mysterious and remote landscape: Bryusov's Gothic Germany, or perhaps the Dantean setting of Belïy's "To an ancient enemy." The concluding crescendo, representing Ruprecht's collapse and surrender, confirms that he is merely a pawn in a diabolical game. Summoning all of the orchestral brimstone at his reserve, Prokofiev portrays Count Heinrich (Madiel) as an archetypal demon—a fallen, if not fiery, angel.

This was the last melody Prokofiev composed for *The Fiery Angel* before he stopped work on it and stored the score materials at Édition Russe de Musique in Paris. In 1936, he included the melody in the "Dance of the Knights" ("Tanets rïtsarey") scene of *Romeo and Juliet* (opus 64), a neoclassical ballet set in Shakespeare's, not Bryusov's, Renaissance. There it articulates one feature of the love affair between the Verona teenagers but also recalls images of Ruprecht (Bryusov) and Renata (Petrovskaya), who are also ideal, impossible lovers. The transformation of the theme shows that Prokofiev was committed to preserving at least part of *The Fiery Angel* in a symbolic guise. His ballet retained the balance between dream and reality that his opera did not and, after a shaky start, enjoyed widespread popular and critical success.[78] Such reverberations and resonances—indicative of Prokofiev's economical habit of recycling his music—typified his compositions throughout his career. Instead of aligning his art with that of the Symbolists, they reflect a quintessentially modernist musical principle: em-

Example 50.   From p. 6 of the 1930 sketchbook

Example 51.   From p. 2 (recto) of the 1930 sketchbook

Example 52.   The "Dance of the Knights" melody

phasis on form over content, the auditory experience of the arrangement of diverse musical materials over that of the materials themselves.

COMPOSED BY AN EYEWITNESS

This enumeration of the most important features of the three versions of *The Fiery Angel* reveals that Prokofiev's vision of the opera fluctuated in accordance with the expectations of his prospective benefactors. He envisioned not a Symbolist but a Romantic opera, a work with a *tableau* structure, aural and visual shock effects, and abrupt shifts between coloratura lyric scenes and coloratura mad scenes. To his dismay, his reversion to old-fashioned genres did not result in their revitalization in the present and did not advance his operatic career. The 1927 score nevertheless succeeds as a parody of Symbolist aesthetics: the final scene connotes the spiritual beyond, but, as mentioned, Renata is thwarted in her attempt to cross into it. The 1930 sketches enhance the symbolic content of the opera: Prokofiev intended to use electronics to suggest that his characters perceive the mystical substratum. Renata does not confine herself to otherworldly conjectures but hears and sees things that for Ruprecht do not exist. Through Ruprecht, Prokofiev depicts Renata as degenerate and hysterical. His was a "classical" modernist reaction against the outlandish behavior of some *fin-de-siècle* Russian artists. Unfortunately, his attempted reinterpretation of the source text succeeded only in bemusing those it was intended to impress. Like many authentic Symbolist dramas, his inauthentic Symbolist drama was consigned to oblivion in an archive. Meyerhold vowed to stage *The Fiery Angel* in Moscow, but Socialist Realist doctrine could not accept its mysticism and neurosis. His advocacy of the score was a futile attempt to rekindle a flame from a dying ember.[79]

Left to collect dust in the cellar of Koussevitzky's publishing house, *The Fiery Angel* could not represent the events in Bryusov's *roman-à-clef*. But the necropolis awoke: over the next few years, the opera was performed not on stage but in the lives of its makers. Prokofiev (like Bryusov before him) adopted the role of Ruprecht; Belïy adopted the role of Count Heinrich (Madiel); Petrovskaya (as well as Prokofiev's then-fiancé Lina Codina) adopted the role of Renata. They all became participants in the same story, which was not simply a cautionary tale about life creation but, allegorically, another cautionary tale about "mystic" Symbolism—specifically, the real-world outcome of its misguided utopianism.

It began with Prokofiev and Bryusov's chance meeting in Berlin in 1922. According to Codina, Prokofiev told Bryusov about his intention to compose an opera based on *The Fiery Angel*. Bryusov suggested that he do so in the Renaissance Bavarian village of Ettal, a setting comparable to that of the novel. He did not inform him that it was based on actual events, but allowed him to believe that it was a translation of a 1535 manuscript containing references to the cabala, the black arts, and (unbelievably) the Faust legend. Codina recalled that, once in Ettal, she and Prokofiev went on the long walk to Oberammergau to see a Medieval passion play; on the way, Prokofiev pointed to the hillside castles and abandoned monasteries (the true-life setting of act II, scene 2 of the inchoate 1930 version of the opera) and imagined that there "the witches had their meetings" and "Renata had her visions."[80] It was a romantic period in his life. While composing the opera that summer, he adopted a role, assuming the persona of Ruprecht and engaging Codina in the kind of domestic charades characteristic of the Symbolists. In his foppish daydreaming, she became the Eternal Feminine, a material incarnation of the operatic heroine that captured his imagination.

In the fall of 1926, while laboring on the revision to *The Fiery Angel*, Prokofiev received a letter from Anna Ostroumova-Lebedeva, a family friend in Leningrad, who finally revealed to him the autobiographical backdrop to Bryusov's novel. She summarized the relationships between the participants in the love triangle and the scandal of the aborted duel but admitted that she did not know what had happened to the participants after the novel's publication. In his tardy reply, Prokofiev enthused, "This information is not only interesting, but frankly exciting, for it arrives while work on *The Fiery Angel* is in full swing."[81] While it is unclear how the information informed his opera, knowledge of Bryusov's parodic intentions could only have enhanced his own.

In the meantime, Bryusov had ended his relationship with Petrovskaya. Their correspondence is filled with mutual accusations and reprimands. Unable to accept the dissolution of the affair, Petrovskaya decided to become what Bryusov had imagined her to be in his novel. While living in Venice, she told him that she wished "to die . . . so that you will have copied Renata's death from me, so as to be the model of the wonderful final chapter." She then traveled to Cologne in order to live out the disingenuous conclusion of the novel. There she informed Bryusov that she felt "entirely alone in the world—a forgotten, abandoned Renata. I lay on the floor of the church like that Renata whom you created, but later forgot and stopped loving. . . . On the tiles of the Cologne church I experienced all of our life minute by minute. . . . The notes of the organ shook the dark arches, like a real funeral lament for Renata."[82] During World War I, Petrovskaya lived in dire poverty in Rome. In a 1922 note to Khodasevich, she reported that she had converted to Catholicism and that her "new and secret name, written somewhere in the unerasable scrolls in San Pietro, is Renata."[83] In the last phase of her life, she resided in Paris, where she became ill, began drinking and taking narcotics. No angel rescued her: on 23 February 1928, in a Salvation Army hostel on Boulevard St-Michel, she asphyxiated herself with oven gas.

Prokofiev was also in Paris that year, putting the final touches on the opera based in part on Petrovskaya's (Renata's) life. They did not meet and only one knew of the other's existence. Four months later the opera had its partial performance. The negative reviews ensured that it would not be heard again, in whole or in part, for nearly three decades. Taruskin comments: "For one as addicted as Prokofiev to prestige, it was an intolerable situation, one that would lead him inexorably back to Russia and, eventually, to the tragic Stalinist finale of his career." [84]

Here it is worth recalling another morbid twist in the saga of *The Fiery Angel*. Though Bryusov remained in Russia long after the Revolution, he balked at rendering bureaucratic service to the Soviet government. However, his younger sister Nadezhda, a musicologist, worked long and hard to secure a high rank in the cultural establishment. On behalf of the State Academic Council (Gosudarstvennïy Uchonïy Sovet), she played an active role in luring Prokofiev and other Russian *émigré* composers back to the Soviet Union. In an unsolicited letter dated 3 August 1925, she outlined the conditions under which he eventually agreed to return: "The Government consents to your return to Russia. It consents to give you full amnesty for all prior committed misdeeds, if any such occurred. It stands to reason that the Government cannot guarantee amnesty in the event of any such counterrevolutionary activity in the future. The Government likewise guarantees your ability to enter and depart the RSFSR as you wish." [85] Prokofiev did not detect duplicity in the stiff phrasing of this letter, nor did he heed the advice of his friends Asafyev and Myaskovsky not to return. In 1928, he began bit by bit to move to Moscow, establishing new artistic contacts, transferring belongings, and destroying incriminating letters and documents. It is not necessary to summarize in detail the events of Prokofiev's final years. He suffered numerous indignities at the hands of Soviet ideologues, bore mute witness to the government show trials, and lost family members and friends in the purges. He sought to weather the storm by accepting commissions to write official works on bland populist themes but was unable to avoid political censure.

In a memorial essay, Belïy remarked that Petrovskaya's life was shrouded in "an atmosphere of danger, ruin, and fate." [86] His description could also be applied to *The Fiery Angel*—both Bryusov's *roman-à-clef* and Prokofiev's opera. Though facetious in content, the two works encapsulate the contradictions and paradoxes of the Symbolist era. The paranormal events surrounding their creation cannot be rationalized according to patterns of cause and effect. They establish beguiling connections between chance and fate, the past and the present, the living and the dead.

NOTES

1. Irina Paperno assesses the origins of life creation in her introduction to *Creating Life: The Aesthetic Utopia of Russian Modernism*, ed. Irina Paperno and Joan Delaney Grossman (Stanford: Stanford University Press, 1994), 1–11. My summary derives in part from hers.

2. Vladislav Khodasevich, "Konets Renatï," in *Nekropol': Vospominaniya* (1939; reprint, Moscow: Olimpa, 1991), 7–8.

3. Ibid., 11.

4. Valeriy Bryusov, *Ognennïy angel* (1909; reprint, with supplementary materials and an introductory essay by S. P. Il'yev, Moscow: Vïsshaya shkola, 1993), 27. For what follows on the novel and the events that informed it, see Pyman, *A History of Russian Symbolism*, 246–50.

5. Bryusov wrote three articles about Agrippa: "Slandered Scientist" ("Oklevetannïy uchonïy"), "The Legend of Agrippa" ("Legenda o Agrippe"), and "Agrippa's Writings and the Sources of His Biography" ("Sochineniya Agrippï i istochniki yego biografii"). These were published in *Agrippa Nettesgeymskiy: Znamenitïy avantyurist XVI v.*, ed. Zh. Ors'e (Moscow: Musaget, 1913).

6. This quotation is taken from Bryusov's review of Solovyov's 1900 poetry collection, "Vladimir Solov'yov: Smïsl yego poezii," in *Dalyokiye i blizkiye: Stat'i i zametki o russkikh poetov ot Tyutcheva do nashikh dney* (Moscow: Skorpion, 1912), 37. The words "echo" and "harmonies" come from Solovyov's poem "Gentle friend, I believe you not in the least" ("Milïy drug, ne veryu ya niskol'ko").

7. Bryusov, *Ognennïy angel*, 327–28.

8. Andrey Belïy, *Nachalo veka* (Moscow: Gosudarstvennoye izdatel'stvo khudozhestvennoy literaturï, 1933), 277.

9. N[ina] I. Petrovskaya [Sokolova], *Vospominaniya N. I. Petrovskoy o V. Ya. Bryusove i simvolistakh nachala 20 veka*, RGALI, fund 376, list 1, item 3, 23–25. Petrovskaya wrote her memoirs in 1924 and submitted them to P. Kryuchkov for publication in *Beseda* and *Russkiy sovremennik*. These two journals ceased publication in 1925, before the memoirs were edited. Extracts are included in *Literaturnoye nasledstvo 85: Valeriy Bryusov*, 773–98. For additional context on the relationship between Belïy, Bryusov, and Petrovskaya, see Joan Delaney Grossman, "Valery Briusov and Nina Petrovskaia: Clashing Models of Life in Art," in *Creating Life: The Aesthetic Utopia of Russian Modernism*, 122–50.

10. Belïy, *Nachalo veka*, 282.

11. S. S. Grechishkin, N. V. Kotrelev, and A. V. Lavrov's introduction to Belïy's correspondence with Bryusov, in *Literaturnoye nasledstvo 85: Valeriy Bryusov*, 347 n. 44. See pages 336–39 for an account of the poetic contest.

12. "Perepiska s Vyacheslavom Ivanovïm," in *Literaturnoye nasledstvo 85: Valeriy Bryusov*, 473. The line "you were wrestling with god in the night" is taken from Bryusov's 1901 poem "And you again, and you again" ("I snova tï, i snova tï"). The Greek phrase is a quotation from Acts 26:14: "It is hard for thee to kick against the pricks" (Jesus speaking to Saul).

13. Belïy, "Starinnomu vragu," in *Literaturnoye nasledstvo 85: Valeriy Bryusov*, 337–38.

14. Belïy, "Material k biografii," unpublished 1923 manuscript, quoted in ibid., 338.

15. Bryusov, "Bal'deru II," in ibid., 338. My translation of the first stanza is a slightly modified version of that provided by Pyman in *A History of Russian Symbolism*, 248.

16. It appeared long after his death in *Stikhotvoreniya i poemï*, ed. D. E. Maksimov, introd. M. I. Dikman (Leningrad: Sovetskiy pisatel', 1961), 502–3.

17. Pyman, *A History of Russian Symbolism*, 288.

18. The best evidence of Prokofiev's interest in Christian Science is a statement of faith he wrote in English in the 1920s, which he perhaps intended to submit for publication in the *Christian Science Monitor* or to read at the Paris Christian Science Society. The autograph manuscript was unearthed at Boosey & Hawkes in London by Claude Samuel, who published it without commentary in his 1961 monograph on the composer. Among the surviving books from the composer's personal library housed in Moscow at the M. I. Glinka Central State Museum of Musical Culture is a 1921 volume of lectures and essays on Christian Science by Edward Kimball. The volume contains marginalia and notes in Prokofiev's hand.

Though Christian Science rejects mystical for rationalist values, Prokofiev adhered to a mystical belief in the domination of the spirit over the flesh. His statement of faith recalls certain components of Scriabin's philosophical thought, which stems not from a rationalist but from a Theosophical perspective. Prokofiev variously describes himself as "an expression of Life, that is, of the Divine Activity," "an expression of the Spirit," and "a visible manifestation of the thought of the Immortal Reason." On these points, see M[arina] Rakhmanova, "Prokof'yev i Christian Science," *Mir iskusstva / al'manakh*, ed. L. N. Pazhitnov (Moscow: RIK Rusanova, 1997), 380–87.

19. S. Shlifshteyn, ed., *S. S. Prokof'yev: Materialï, dokumentï, vospominaniya*, 2nd ed. (Moscow: Gosudarstvennoye muzïkal'noye izdatel'stvo, 1961), 165–66. The Chicago Lyric Opera premiere of *The Love for Three Oranges* was delayed from December 1919 to 30 December 1921 due to the death of the director Cleofonte Campanini.

20. Nikolai Myaskovsky, letter of 23 December 1923, and Sergei Prokofiev, letter of 3 January 1924, in *S. S. Prokof'yev i N. Ya. Myaskovskiy: Perepiska*, ed. and introd. D. B. Kabalevskiy (Moscow: Sovetskiy kompozitor, 1977), 180, 183.

21. For what follows on Prokofiev's attempts to have the opera staged, the reception of the partial concert version of the opera, and the composer's reluctant abandonment of the opera, I am indebted to Richard Taruskin's "To Cross That Sacred Edge: Notes on a Fiery Angel," in Serge Prokofiev, *The Fiery Angel*, Gothenburg Symphony Orchestra, Neeme Järvi, Deutsche Grammophon CD 431 669–2, 14–17.

22. Prokofiev blamed the delay in part on his copyist, Georgiy Gorchakov, whose duty it was to write out the orchestral score of the opera from a short score that indicated the instrumentation.

23. Letter of 25 January 1928, in *S. S. Prokof'yev i N. Ya. Myaskovskiy: Perepiska*, 268.

24. Letter of 30 May 1928, in ibid., 279.

25. Letter of 9 July 1928, in ibid., 281. This was one of several troubled experiences he had with the Ballets Russes. In 1915, Diaghilev commissioned and rejected Prokofiev's *Rite of Spring*–based ballet *Ala et Lolly* as derivative and uninspired. Prokofiev restructured it as the *Scythian Suite* (opus 20, 1915). His next Diaghilev commission, *A Tale of a Buffoon* (*Skazka pro shuta*, or *Chout*, opus 21, 1920) fared better, but the initial production was delayed for six years because he was not in Paris to undertake revisions to the score. After a long hiatus, Diaghilev commissioned *The Steel Gallop* (*Stal'noy skok*, opus 42, 1925), a reductive depiction of the conversion of Russian peasants into industrial workers. It successfully premiered in Paris and London but later, as one might expect, gave Prokofiev problems with

Soviet cultural authorities, who objected to its sardonic features. His last Diaghilev ballet, *The Prodigal Son* (*Bludnïy sïn,* opus 46, 1929), was also successful, but he and the choreographer George Balanchine quarreled over the rights and refused to work together again.

26. The opera tells the story of the martyrdom of a nun (Sister Beatrice) who abandons her convent to wed a prince but whose acts of charity miraculously continue to be performed by a statue of the Madonna that has come to life and assumed the nun's likeness. The opera was denounced by the Orthodox Synod for degrading the ideal of the Holy Flesh.

27. Yuliy Engel', "Opernïye novinki v Moskve (sezon 1912–1913 g.)," *Yezhegodnik imperatorskikh teatrov* 5 (1913): 96.

28. Letter of 3 August 1928, in *S. S. Prokof'yev i N. Ya. Myaskovskiy: Perepiska,* 284.

29. See Malcolm Hamrick Brown, "Stravinsky and Prokofiev: Sizing up the Competition," in *Confronting Stravinsky: Man, Musician, and Modernist,* ed. Jann Pasler (Berkeley: University of California Press, 1986), 39–50.

30. Prokofiev discussed the creation of the symphony in his 1941 autobiography: "It was a shame that the opera was unperformed and, thus, that all the material laid on a shelf. Make a suite? Here I recalled that one of the entr'actes served to develop the themes presented in the preceding scene. It could be the basis for a symphony. Having noticed this, I saw that these themes rather neatly packed themselves into a sonata allegro. Having an exposition and development, I found the same themes in the other acts, set out differently but suitable for a recapitulation. From this a plan for the first movement of the symphony swiftly arose. The material for the scherzo and andante was also found without trouble. I took more time with the finale" (*S. S. Prokof'yev: Materialï, dokumentï, vospominaniya,* 181–82). For an evaluation of the thematic differences between the opera and symphony, see Natal'ya Zeyfas, "Simfoniya 'Ognennogo angela'" *Sovetskaya muzïka* 4 (1991): 35–41. Zeyfas contends that the music of the symphony enacts an epic struggle between the forces of heaven and hell and ends (altogether unlike the opera) with a sense of spiritual uplift, a hymn to human striving.

31. *S. S. Prokof'yev: Materialï, dokumentï, vospominaniya,* 186.

32. Charles Bruck, "'Ognennïy angel' v Parizhe," *Sovetskaya muzïka* 7 (1955): 128.

33. Letter of 18 July 1928, in *S. S. Prokof'yev i N. Ya. Myaskovskiy: Perepiska,* 283.

34. S[ergey] Prokof'yev, *Detstvo,* 4th ed. (Moscow: Muzïka, 1980), 46.

35. Ibid., 49.

36. Carl Dahlhaus, *Nineteenth Century Music,* trans. J. Bradford Robinson (Berkeley: University of California Press, 1989), 277. This point also pertains to Prokofiev's *War and Peace* (*Voyna i mir,* opus 91, 1952).

37. *S. S. Prokof'yev: Materialï, dokumentï, vospominaniya,* 159. The "verse" in question is included in Balmont's 1909 collection *Calls of Antiquity* (*Zovi drevnosti*), which purports to transcribe the incantations and spells of non-Slavic Eastern peoples. The collection was lauded by some for its rendering of pagan antiquity but deemed an artistic failure by Blok and Bryusov.

38. "V tebe vostoskoval orkestr o zvonkom lete, / I v buben solntsa b'yot nepobedimïy Skif!" (Mstislav [Bal'mont], "O Sergeye Prokof'yeve. Pis'mo iz Frantsii," unpublished essay housed in The Prokofiev Archive, Goldsmiths College, University of London, page 4).

39. Like *The Fiery Angel, The Puppet Theater Booth* is based on actual events. It describes Blok's obsession with the Eternal Feminine and uses the most famous

characters of the *commedia dell'arte* to satirize his and Belïy's rivalry for Lyubov Blok. For an overview of the multiple layers of meaning in the play, see Lucy Vogel, "Illusions Unmasked in Blok's Puppet Motifs," *Canadian-American Slavic Studies* 24:2 (Summer 1990): 169–80.

40. Clayton, *Pierrot in Petrograd: Commedia dell'Arte / Balagan in Twentieth-Century Russian Theatre and Drama*, 11–12.

41. B[oris] Asaf'yev, "S. Prokof'yev: 'Lyubov' k tryom apel'sinam,'" in *Ob opere*, 2nd ed. (Leningrad: Muzïka, 1985), 303. For a survey of Prokofiev and Meyerhold's theatrical collaborations, see Friedbert Streller, "Prokofjew und das vorrevolutionäre russische Theater: Opernästhetische Positionen des jungen Prokofjew," in *Bericht über das Internationale Symposion "Sergej Prokofjew — Aspekte seines Werkes und der Biographie. Köln 1991,"* ed. Klaus Wolfgang Niemöller (Regensburg: Gustav Bosse, 1992), 269–80.

42. The difficulties involved in representing the Devil in opera are summarized in a pseudonymous "mystic" Symbolist article, "Satan in Music" ("Satana v muzïke," *Zolotoye runo* 1 [1907]: 65–67). After commenting on the ubiquity of demonic figures in Classical drama, the author proclaims:

> Satan has ceased to exist in music. Is this not because God has also ceased to exist in the lackluster, comatose force of epic and aesthetic perception in art? . . .
>
> The illustration of Satan has recently drawn the attention of opera composers, but the "representation" of the devil in his philosophical significance clearly lies outside the sphere of musical competence. For illustrations embrace only the external side, and in most cases are reduced to providing the impression made on gentle philistines when Satan appears in flames or when he falls through the earth. . . .The operas that most clearly depict Satan — Gounod's *Faust*, [Anton] Rubinstein's *Demon* [1875], [Arrigo] Boito's *Mefistofele* [1867], and Chaikovsky's *Cherevichki* [*The Little Boots*, 1885]—are not without very subtle features in the characterization of the restless, petty demon, swindling and putting his foot in it. The operatic Satan is totally free-and-easy on stage and is often bestowed with the blessing of the dead. In general, everything is fine as long as he does not start to speak, for he never attains the poisonous mirth of Goethe's Mephistopheles.

The author observes that Gounod, in setting a text based not on Goethe's *Faust* but on Michel Carré's 1850 play *Faust et Marguerite*, sentimentalized the subject matter. The love affair between Faust and Marguerite, for example, replaced the scene of Faust attaining solidarity with nature. Moreover, Gounod employed shopworn *Effektmalerei* (diminished seventh and augmented sixth harmonies, low string tremolos, bass clarinet and muted French horn duos) to betoken unnatural events.

43. Several critics contend that the scene is dramatically flawed. Hans Swarsenski writes that "as an entertainment this scene comes off extremely well but fails somehow to attain the serious character indispensable to its philosophical implications. This familiar, sarcastic Prokofiev, so different from the composer of the rest of the opera, has been taken for a parody [*sic*] by some critics, but the appearance of Mephistopheles in the last act leaves no doubt that he wants to be taken seriously also in the fourth. Dramatically weak though it is, it remains a link" ("Sergei Prokofieff: 'The Flaming Angel,'" *Tempo* 39 [1956]: 23). Given the macabre atmosphere of the rest of the opera, one could argue that Prokofiev perpetrates an artistic hoax in the scene, subverting the supernatural events that he has otherwise asked the audience to interpret seriously. In this regard, the scene fulfills the crite-

ria of kitsch. See Hermann Broch, "Notes on the Problem of Kitsch," in *Kitsch: The World of Bad Taste,* ed. Gillo Dorfles (New York: Universe Books, 1969), 49–67.

44. RGALI, fund 1929, list 1, item 8, page 85.

45. Rita McAllister, "Natural and Supernatural in 'The Fiery Angel,'" *Musical Times* 111 (1970): 785.

46. Letter of 1 May 1928, in *S. S. Prokof'yev i N. Ya. Myaskovskiy: Perepiska,* 276.

47. Bryusov, *Ognennïy angel,* 55. The emphasis was added by Prokofiev on page 31 of his copy of the novel (RGALI, fund 1929, list 1, item 8).

48. Sketch of the 1923 opera libretto, M. I. Glinka Central State Museum of Musical Culture, fund 33, item 972, page 3. Prokofiev habitually omitted vowels in his handwriting, a reflection, on some level, of his predilection for form over content. He signed most of his letters to Myaskovsky "P-R-K-F-V."

49. Bryusov, *Ognennïy angel,* 119–20.

50. Sketch of the 1923 opera libretto, M. I. Glinka Central State Museum of Musical Culture, fund 33, item 972, page 2.

51. Linda J. Ivanits, *Russian Folk Belief* (Armonk, N.Y.: M. E. Sharpe, 1989), 39.

52. Bryusov, *Ognennïy angel,* 248. The emphasis was added by Prokofiev on page 241 of his copy of the novel, RGALI, fund 1929, list 1, item 8.

53. Mikhaíl Tarakanov, *Ranniye operï Prokof'yeva: Issledovaniye* (Magnitogorsk: Gos. In-t iskusstvoznaniya, Magnitogorskiy muz.-ped. In-t, 1996), 114.

54. Luigi Russolo, "The Art of Noise," 1913, in *Classic Essays on Twentieth Century Music: A Continuing Symposium,* ed. Richard Kostelanetz and Joseph Darby (New York: Schirmer Books, 1996), 42–43.

55. Information in this paragraph is taken from McAllister, "Prokofiev's Early Opera 'Maddalena,'" *Proceedings of the Royal Musical Association* 96 (1969–70): 138–39. The author reports that Prokofiev composed *Maddalena* while a student at the St. Petersburg Conservatory. The piano-vocal score of the four scenes was finished on 13 September 1911. He orchestrated the first scene the following summer but set aside the rest of the opera when he learned that it would not be performed at the conservatory. He played through the piano-vocal score for a small gathering at the Moscow Free Theater in the summer of 1913, and a premiere was tentatively arranged. To this end, he decided to revise the last three scenes, completing the task on 15 October 1915. By this time, however, the Free Theater had closed down, and the premiere was cancelled.

56. Richard Bass, "Prokofiev's Technique of Chromatic Displacement," *Music Analysis* 7:2 (1988): 199–200.

57. McAllister, "Prokofiev's Early Opera 'Maddalena,'" 146.

58. To illustrate this point, we might briefly compare Prokofiev's vocal writing to Francis Poulenc's vocal writing in his 1957 *Dialogues des Carmélites,* an opera with several narrative and structural points of correspondence with *The Fiery Angel.* It features an eighteenth-century heroine, Blanche de la Force, who enters a Carmelite convent to escape from the outer world, a show trial of the nuns by French revolutionaries, and a climactic execution scene in which the heroine and her childlike alter ego Constance attain spiritual salvation. The conclusion of Poulenc's score, reflecting his interest in mystical codes of honor, is a positive inversion of the negative circumstances that conclude Prokofiev's score. Unlike Prokofiev, who confined his vocal writing to a single dramatic register consisting of interlocking ostinati patterns, Poulenc separated his into three registers. First, there is a "narrative" register, the declamatory passages that offer plot information and relate the emotional states of the characters. Second, there is a "liturgical" register, the vocal lines that are taken from stylized chant and thus embody religious senti-

ments. Third, there is a register in between, a nonverbal register that conveys spiritual ecstasy and transport. *Dialogues des Carmélites* unfolds in part based on the semantic clash between the three tiers. The "narrative" register symbolizes the nuns' impending demise at the hands of the French revolutionaries; the "liturgical" register symbolizes their martyrdom. Overriding these two registers is the rhapsodic vocal music assigned to Blanche and Constance in the final scene. Expressing indescribable bliss, it symbolizes their overcoming of the fear of death and attainment of grace. See Vincent Vivès, "Du livret à l'aventure prosodique: *Dialogues des Carmélites* ou le transfert de la grâce," in *Le Livret Malgré Lui: Actes du Colloque du Groupe de Recherche sur les Rapports Musique-Texte (G.R.M.T.)* (Paris: Publimuses, 1992), 106–20, esp. 115–20.

59. McAllister, "Prokofiev's Early Opera 'Maddalena,'" 144.

60. Ivanits, *Russian Folk Belief*, 49.

61. For what follows on the act I and act V hallucination scenes, see N. Rzhavinskaya, "O roli ostinato i nekotorïkh priyomakh formoobrazovaniya v opere 'Ognennïy angel,'" in *S. S. Prokof'yev: Stat'i i issledovaniya*, ed. V. Blok and Yu. Rags (Moscow: Muzïka, 1972), 96–130.

62. Ibid., 100.

63. John Daverio, *Robert Schumann: Herald of a "New Poetic Age"* (Oxford: Oxford University Press, 1997), 386. Daverio quotes from Hans Eichner's "The Eternal Feminine: An Aspect of Goethe's Ethics" (1976).

64. See Claudia Gorbman, *Unheard Melodies: Narrative Film Music* (Bloomington: Indiana University Press, 1987), 24, 159–61.

65. The preceding chart is a corrected and modified version of that provided by Rzhavinskaya, "O roli ostinato i nekotorïkh priyomakh formoobrazovaniya v opere 'Ognennïy angel,'" 109–10.

66. M[arina] Sabinina, *"Semyon Kotko" i problemï opernoy dramaturgii Prokof'yeva* (Moscow: Sovetskiy kompozitor, 1963), 52–53.

67. Neil Minturn, *The Music of Sergei Prokofiev* (New Haven: Yale University Press, 1997), 57–58, 209.

68. On Prokofiev's method of text-setting, see Taruskin, "Prokofiev, Sergey," in *The New Grove Dictionary of Opera*, 3: 1136; idem, "Tone, Style, and Form in Prokofiev's Soviet Operas: Some Preliminary Observations," in *Studies in the History of Music, volume 2: Music and Drama* (New York: Broude Brothers, 1988), 215–39.

69. McAllister, "Natural and Supernatural in 'The Fiery Angel,'" 787–89.

70. As quoted by Michail Tarakanow [Tarakanov], "Der feurige Engel," in *Sergej Prokofjew 11. April 1891 — 5. März 1953. Beiträge, Dokumente, Interpretationen. Duisburg 1990/91*, ed. Hermann Danuser, Juri Cholopow, and Michail Tarakanow (Duisburg: Laaber, 1991), 165.

71. RGALI, fund 1929, list 1, item 9, pages 2–3.

72. Ibid., pages 5–6, and item 7.

73. McAllister, "Natural and Supernatural in 'The Fiery Angel,'" 789.

74. He also remarked that the ensuing "entr'acte" was to be based "on the music of Glock" ("antr[a]k[t] na muz[ï]ku Gloka").

75. See Michel Chion, *Audio-Vision: Sound on Screen*, ed. and trans. Claudia Gorbman (New York: Columbia University Press, 1994), 123–37.

76. See Friedrich Kittler, "World Breath: On Wagner's Media Technology," in *Opera Through Other Eyes*, ed. David J. Levin (Stanford: Stanford University Press, 1994), 224, 226.

77. Cited in Khodasevich, "Bryusov," in *Nekropol': Vospominaniya*, 21. On this subject, Carolyn Abbate observes that the French and Russian Symbolists ad-

vanced theories about disembodied sound (sound from the "not-here") that are now common to electro-acoustic music and sound cinema. See "Debussy's Phantom Sounds," *Cambridge Opera Journal* 10:1 (1988): 69–74.

78. *Romeo and Juliet* was conceived in 1934 for the State Academic Theater in Leningrad. The premiere production was postponed when the scenarist, Sergey Radlov, ran afoul of Stalinist authorities and lost his post. The Bolshoy Theater in Moscow took over the project a year later. Prokofiev consulted Radlov while composing the score, but also the choreographer Leonid Lavrovsky and the dramatist Adrian Piotrovsky. The ballet was fully rehearsed at the Bolshoy Theater on 4 October 1935, at which time complaints were raised about the music and the scenario, which had an optimistic rather than a tragic ending. Prokofiev overhauled the score, but the planned performance was cancelled nonetheless. After additional cuts and alterations, the ballet was finally staged in Brno, Czechoslovakia, on 30 December 1938.

79. On 20 June 1939, while working on a production of *Semyon Kotko*, Prokofiev's first Soviet opera, Meyerhold was arrested for a lecture he gave at the Soviet Congress of Directors in which he defended experimentalism in theater and in which he called Socialist Realist theater a "pitiful and wretched thing" (Juri Jegalin's stenographic record of the speech, cited by James Symons in *Meyerhold's Theater of the Grotesque* [Coral Gables: University of Miami Press, 1971], 192). Meyerhold was replaced on the production by the novice actress and director Serafima Birman.

Besides a truncated performance in the industrial city of Perm in 1962, *The Fiery Angel* was not staged in Russia until 1991, as part of a joint venture between the Mariyinsky Theater of St. Petersburg and Royal Opera House of London. David Freeman, the stage director, and Valery Gergiev, the artistic director, sought to enhance and rehabilitate the Symbolist features of the 1927 score. The rafters and thin partitions of the set reflected the transparency of the material world. Demons in white and red makeup slid through walls, assaulted nuns, and metamorphosed into beasts. They allowed the audience to see (if not hear) as the visionary Renata did.

80. Lina Codina, undated taped interview housed in The Prokofiev Archive. Prokofiev said little about Bryusov in his two sets of memoirs. However, a 1927 diary of his two-month concert tour of Soviet Russia contains the following anecdote about the poet: "Apparently when Bryusov died his wife was asked if there were any unpublished manuscripts. There weren't any to speak of, or hardly any, but she did mention the diary that he had recently been writing in ancient Greek, showing off how learned he was. They were extremely glad to get hold of this diary and immediately started work on a translation. But then it transpired that in this diary this most revered of Communists was tearing the Soviet system to shreds. What happened to the diary we don't know" (*Soviet Diary 1927 and Other Writings*, trans. Oleg Prokofiev [Boston: Northeastern University Press, 1992], 101).

81. Letters of 27 September and 6 December 1926, The Prokofiev Archive.

82. Letters of 20 March and 21 October 1908, cited by Grechishkin and Lavrov in "Biograficheskiye istochniki romana Bryusova 'Ognennïy angel,'" *Wiener Slawistischer Almanach* 1 (1978): pt. 2, 83–84.

83. Khodasevich, "Konets Renati," 17.

84. Taruskin, "To Cross That Sacred Edge: Notes on a Fiery Angel," 17. Tarakanov takes this point in another direction, somewhat hyperbolically suggesting that the disaster that befell the composer and his country was actually encoded into the opera's music. *The Fiery Angel*, he states, "bore those traits that made [Prokofiev] a product of an unstable contemporaneity, including that which erupted in the

composer's homeland, falling at the moment of the opera's completion (1928) under the cruelest and bloodiest regime which humanity had ever known. . . . *The Fiery Angel* became one of the artistic creations of the twentieth century that disclosed ('indirectly' of course) the apocalyptic idea of humanity existing in a society moving to a catastrophic conclusion" (*Ranniye operï Prokof'yeva: Issledovaniye,* 112–13).

85. RGALI, fund 2009, list 2, item 4.

86. Belïy, *Nachalo veka,* 278.

Conclusion

However broadly the genre is defined, one can identify only a few Russian Symbolist operas, only a few composers keen to test aesthetic boundaries or commit aesthetic transgressions. The genre is as apparitional as the symbol itself. In each example, Symbolist composers and *littérateurs* served each other as guiding lights or—to translate literally the title of Vyacheslav Ivanov's first collection of poetry—"pilot stars" (*Kormchiye zvyozdï*, 1903). The phrase refers in part to the *Kormchaya kniga*, a collection of devotional readings issued by the Holy Synod. This volume defines sacred and secular laws and addresses ancient and timeless spiritual truths. In various ways, so too do Chaikovsky's *Queen of Spades*, Rimsky-Korsakov's *Legend of the Invisible City of Kitezh and the Maiden Fevroniya*, Scriabin's *Mysterium* and *Preparatory Act*, and Prokofiev's *Fiery Angel*.

The first and last of these works, composed thirty-seven years apart, frame the Russian Symbolist movement. The second and third reflect its "decadent" and "mystic" phases. The composers, despite their differing relationships to the movement, shared a conception of the musical symbol as a motion-filled, mediating device. Chaikovsky, a clairvoyant proto-Symbolist, relied upon the symbol to provide illusory ambiance in his opera. Despite the references to eighteenth-century music, *The Queen of Spades* does more to stir premonition than to stimulate memory, more to anticipate the future than to restore the past. Rimsky-Korsakov, an avowed anti-Symbolist, used the symbol to express religious ecstasy. In the *Legend of Kitezh*, the chiming of the bells of the invisible city marks a transposition from real time to ecclesiastical time, the chronotope of the *au-delà*. Scriabin, a maximalist meta-Symbolist, relied upon the symbol to illustrate, if not precipitate, the dematerialization of the world. His *Mysterium* and *Preparatory Act* represent different phases of his endeavor to create truly communal, truly universal drama. Prokofiev, a capricious post-Symbolist, used the symbol to represent the incursion of the supernatural into human affairs. The novelty of *The Fiery Angel* lies in its absence of novelty. By treating the symbol as a symbol—as a device for artistic evocation rather than a device for physical incarnation—Prokofiev knowingly or unknowingly laid bare the presuppositions of "mystic" Symbolism. Together, these four composers explored the chief tenets of Symbolist poetics: the desire to liberate poetic and musical language from formal constraints, the attempt to extend operatic dramaturgy beyond logical limits, and the contention that artistic activity could somehow influence out-of-doors social events. To varying degrees, their compositions achieve in dramatic form what could not be achieved in dramatic content. Like the literary and musical form known as the fragment, they are at once "complete [in themselves] and torn away from a larger [metaphysical] whole."[1]

The Symbolist movement ended in sorrow and fatigue. The spiritual aspirations of those "decadent" and "mystic" Symbolists who experienced the Revolution clashed with the material aspirations of the Bolsheviks. The demise of their creative purpose prompted them either to leave Russia or to adapt to a new reality. Outside Russia, Symbolism continued in some of the Ballets Russes creations, notably the Stravinsky-Benois *Petrushka*, a ballet in which octatonic and diatonic sonorities, natural and supernatural activities, and human and marionette gestures commingle. (One of the literary sources for Benois's scenario was Alexander Blok's *Puppet Theater Booth*.) Inside Russia, Symbolism metamorphosed into Acmeism and Futurism. It has even been alleged that the artistic policies that musicians and writers were obliged to adopt during the Soviet years had their origins in Symbolist poetics, that the grandiose cultural mythology of the *fin de siècle* informed that of the 1930s. Katerina Clark, for one, observes that Socialist Realism may have been "an attempt, however jejunely realized, at translating intelligentsia ideals into actuality."[2] By "intelligentsia" she refers to the pre- and post-revolutionary avant-garde, the "perceptual millenarians" who advocated the cultural and spiritual revival of Russia. In the first two decades of Soviet power, the "intelligentsia" was mandated to uphold diluted and distilled versions of the ideals it had earlier authored. Several Symbolists welcomed the Revolution, even though they sensed that it would lead to the eradication of their artistic movement. Clark concludes:

As the Russian intelligentsia went into the Revolution, they hoped to function as Hermes figures who might mediate between the language of higher truth and that of the imperfect world around them. Many were particularly attracted by the possibility that they might act as the great demystifiers. Now, however, their role was closer to that of the comprador. . . . By the 1930s, the typical Soviet intellectual had become a comprador in that his task was to mediate between the language of high culture, which he spoke "natively," and that of his masters, the language of ideology and power.[3]

This statement finds support in the memoirs of the Marxist-Leninist propagandist Nikolai Valentinov (1879–1964), which contain a striking comment about the adoption of Andrey Belïy's poetic platform by Soviet cultural bureaucrats:

It may seem strange, but the views of Belïy at the time [1907] and the views of the people in the Kremlin had much in common. They, like him, reject art for art's sake. Art for them is just a means to "transform life" in accord with that absolutely true philosophy (or, if you like, materialistic religion) that they, the Kremlin theurgists, claim to have. Artists are "engineers of souls." Stalin was a hierophant over the theurgists and his every word required incarnation in works of art and life.[4]

Valentinov suggests that the Symbolist doctrine of life creation inspired the Soviet doctrine of Socialist Realism. Needless to say, the situation is more complex, but it is worth noting that the Futurists, the most prominent of the artistic groups that succeeded the Symbolists, also subscribed to a vision of utopia. They claimed that quotidian reality was static and contingent on mechanical modes of behavior; metaphysical reality, in contrast, was reality in motion, reality in a constant state of becoming. Soviet aestheticists adopted this idea but deprived it of its mysticism. In essence, they reconceived the concept of a spiritual progression toward a higher level of being as a dialectical progression toward Communism. Under Joseph Stalin, Soviet artists—both those who habitually acquiesced to the authorities and those who did not—took on the task of representing a radiant Communist future for humanity, despite the fact that such depiction underscored the drabness of the socialist present. Their works were positive rhetorical devices. They did not depict life as it was but life in transformation, life as it would one day be. Socialist Realism was a bowdlerized version of life creation. Both doctrines were utopian on the surface, dystopian beneath. Both doctrines were also apocalyptic, although the later one envisioned a godless apocalypse.

After the Revolution, Valeriy Bryusov, the mastermind of the Symbol-ist movement, became a cultural bureaucrat in Moscow; Belïy continued to write, more often enraging than placating the authorities; Ivanov took up university posts in Baku, Azerbaidzhan, and, later, Padua, Italy. Chaikov-sky, Rimsky-Korsakov, and Scriabin did not live to see the transformation of their homeland; Prokofiev, who as a young composer in Russia had only a tangential and temporary connection to the Symbolist movement, expe-rienced it (literally and figuratively) from afar. Gnesin, the recipient of the commission to compose incidental music for Blok's *Rose and the Cross*, lectured in music theory and composition at the Moscow Conservatory from 1925 to 1936 and the Leningrad Conservatory from 1935 to 1944. He then became the director of the Gnesin State Institute for Musical Educa-tion, which had been founded by his sisters Elena, Yevgeniya, and Mariya. Blok died from a mysterious mental illness; in his last months, he dumb-founded his colleagues by affirming his confidence in the Revolution. One compassionate eyewitness interpreted his passing as the symbolic end of the Silver Age: "Blok died. Friends carried his coffin to the Smolensk ceme-tery in their arms. There were a few people. All who had remained. Blok's death was an epoch in the life of the Russian intelligentsia. The last faith was lost."[5]

NOTES

1. Charles Rosen, *The Romantic Generation* (Cambridge: Harvard University Press, 1995), 48.
2. Katerina Clark, *Petersburg, Crucible of Cultural Revolution* (Cambridge: Harvard University Press, 1995), 296.
3. Ibid., 304–5.
4. N[ikolay] Valentinov, *Dva goda s simvolistami*, ed. Gleb Struve (Stanford: Hoover Institution on War, Revolution and Peace, 1969), 127 n. Information in this paragraph is taken from Irina Gutkin, "The Legacy of the Symbolist Aesthetic Utopia: From Futurism to Socialist Realism," in *Creating Life: The Aesthetic Utopia of Russian Modernism*, 167–96.
5. Victor Shklovsky, *A Sentimental Journey: Memoirs, 1917–22*, as quoted in Victor Erlich, *Modernism and Revolution: Russian Literature in Transition* (Cam-bridge: Harvard University Press, 1994), 27.

Appendix: The Libretto of the *Preparatory Act*

(As Published in *Russkiye Propilei: Materialï po Istorii Russkoy Mïsli i Literaturï* 9 [1916])

Once again the Primordial One wills you
To accept love's grace
Once again the Infinite One wills
To recognize itself in the finite.

Yeshcho raz volit v vas Predvechnïy
Prinyat' lyubvi blagodat'
Yeshcho raz volit Bezkonechnïy
Sebya v konechnom opoznat'.

Chorus

Khor

In lightning flight, in awesome explosion,
In loving creative impulse,
In its divine breathing
Is the hidden face of the created world.

V molniynom vzlyote, groznom vzrïve,
V lyubovnom tvorcheskom porïve,
V yego bozhestvennom dïkhanii
Lik sokrovennïy mirozdaniya.

The heat of the moment sires eternity,
And illuminates the depths of space;
Infinity breathes worlds,
Chimes have enveloped the silence.

Mgnoveniya pïl rozhdayet vechnost',
Luchit prostranstva glubinu;
Mirami dïshet bezkonechnost',
Ob'yali zvonï tishinu.

Greatness is being fulfilled
And, sweet anew,
Love is being born!

Velikoye svershayetsya
I sladostnaya vnov'
Rozhdayetsya lyubov'!

In burning hearts
Our Primordial Father
Is wedding death!

So smertiyu venchayetsya
V gorenii serdets
Predvechnïy nash Otets!

Feminine Principle

To you, dawning one, u u, to you,
impetuous one
My responding moan, u u, my
beckoning cry

Masculine Principle

Who are you, arising in the sacred
silence,
Summoning me with white light
beams?

Feminine Principle

I am the radiant joy of the ultimate
achievement
I am the burning diamond in white
flame
I am the ineffable bliss of
dissolution
I am the joy of death, I am freedom,
I am ecstasy!

Masculine Principle

Impart to me, how to take wing
to you, desired one
Infatuating me with the glitter of
your light beams
Where is your chamber, illuminated
with magical light[?]
Hear my plea and reveal to me
death's secret.

Feminine Principle

Heed, dawning one, the abysses of
life between us,
With its [life's] deceiving, agonizing
visions;
Multicolored spaces separated us

Golos zhenstvennogo

Tebe rassvetnïy, u u, tebe
porïvnïy
Moy ston otvetnïy, u u, moy krik
prizïvnïy

Golos muzhestvennogo

Kto tï, voznikshaya v svyashchennoy tishine,
Luchami belïmi vozzvavshaya ko
mne?

Golos zhenstvennogo

Ya radost' svetlaya poslednego
soversheniya
Ya v belom plameni sgorayushchiy
almaz
Ya neskazannoye blazhenstvo
rastvoreniya
Ya radost' smerti, ya svoboda, ya
ekstaz!

Golos muzhestvennogo

Tï mne poveday, kak vzletit' k tebe
zhelannoy
Menya bezumyashchey luchey
svoikh igroy
Gde tvoy chertog, volshebnïm
svetom osiyannïy[?]
Uslïsh' mol'bu i taynu smerti mne
otkroy.

Golos zhenstvennogo

Vnimay rassvetnïy, bezdnï zhizni
mezhdu nami,
S yeyo obmannïmi, tomitel'nïmi
snami;
Nas razdelili mnogotsvetnïye
prostranstva

In the glorious radiance of colorfully
  starred attire.
In order to capture me, you must
  pass through them
Overcome them and be exhausted
  at journey's end.

Masculine Principle

But I do not see my path in the
  starred attire,
I do not see, gracious one, where
  those spaces and abysses are.

Feminine Principle

They, like I, are in your dream, in
  your willing.
Illume yourself, hear your prophetic
  voice,
And you will make out, you will
  behold in your languor
The colorful worlds separating us.

You fill everything with yourself
I do not exist, only you transpire
When in the light beams of your
  dream
I, glittering, arise
As an image of new beauty
Thus condemning to life
Swarms of fancies, choirs of visions
Assemblies of shimmering worlds.

Only you transpire, not me, not me,
You fill everything with yourself!

(Solemnly)

Speaking within you, I summon you
From the radiant heights of divine
  flights
And appealing to the creative will
  in you,

V siyanii divnom tsvetno-
  zvyozdnogo ubrantstva.
Dabï plenit' menya, tï dolzhen ikh
  proyti
Ikh odolet' i iznemoch' v kontse
  puti.

Golos muzhestvennogo

No ya ne zryu svoyey stezi v
  ubranstve zvyozdnom,
Ne zryu, blagaya, gde prostranstva
  te, gde bezdnï.

Golos zhenstvennogo

Oni, kak ya, v tvoyey mechte, v
  tvoyom volenii.
Tï ozari sebya, uslïsh' svoy veshchiy
  glas,
I tï poznayesh', tï uzrish' v svoyom
  tomlenii
Mirï tsvetnïye, razdelyayushchiye
  nas.
Tï vse soboyu napolnyayesh'
Ne yest' ya, lish' tï bïvayesh'
Kogda v luchakh tvoyey mechtï

Kak obraz novoy krasotï
Ya, igraya, voznikayu
Tem na zhizni obrekaya
Roi gryoz, khorï snov
Sonmï bleshchushchikh mirov.

Net, net menya, lish' tï bïvayesh',
Tï vse soboyu napolnyayesh'!

(Torzhestvenno)

V tebe govorya, prizïvayu tebya ya
S vïsot luchezarnïkh pareniy
  bozhestvennïkh
I k vole tvoryashchey v tebe
  vozzïvaya,

I demand sacrifices and solemn
vows

So that you can taste the bliss of
another timelessness
In your infinite aspiration

Primordial One, you must complete
three feats,
Three sacrifices in intoxicating
transience.

And the initial sacrifice is the dream
about me;
You must forget the caressing vision

And plunge into the abysses that
separated us
And that inspired us to the feat of
love.

Masculine and Feminine Principles

O divine feat, galactic dance,

In you we will attain victory over
the abyss,
In you we, mutually rejoicing, will
find ourselves,
In you we will blissfully expire in
each other

Feminine Principle

You have begun your dance. From
the summit of flight
I now see you in motion, Lord;

I discern the colors of the surrounding spheres—
Of the wedding fabrics adorning you

You now live and, drawing nearer
to me

Ya trebuyu zhertv i obetov
torzhestvennïkh

Shtob mog tï v stremlenii svoyom
bezkonechnom
Izvedat' blazhenstvo inoy
vnevremennosti

Tri podviga dolzhen sovershit' tï,
Predvechnïy,
Tri zhertvï prinest' v
op'yanyayushchey smennosti.

I pervaya zhertva—mechta obo
mne;
Tï dolzhen zabït' o laskayushchem
sne

I rinut'sya v bezdnï, shto nas
razdelili
I tem nas na podvig lyubvi okrïlili.

*Golosa muzhestvennogo i
zhenstvennogo*

O podvig bozhestvennïy, tanets
vsezvyozdnïy,
V tebe mï oderzhim pobedu nad
bezdnoy,
V tebe mï soradno sebya obretyom,

V tebe mï blazhenno drug v druga
umryom

Golos zhenstvennogo

Tï nachal svoy tanets. S vershinï
pareniya
Tebya ya, Gospod', uzhe vizhu v
dvizhenii;

Tsveta razlichayu ya sfer
okruzhayushchikh,—
Tkaney venchal'nïkh, tebya
ukrashayushchikh

Uzhe tï zhivyosh' i, ko mne
priblizhaya

Lives [vital forces] bear you away
  from me
Surrounding you with intoxicating
  visions
Glittering and frothing, shining and
  twanging.

Masculine Principle

Constrained in my motion
By the heavy fabrics of my apparel
I still fly to you, bound to you
By the full force of my fiery hopes.

Feminine Principle

If my cry of joyful summons
Had not sounded in your soul,
You would not have created, o sweet
Lord, the beginning of all beginnings.

You are all longing for me
This is why to overcome everything
In this creative striving
The night of the abyss will aid you.

Behold: seven angels in ethereal
  vestments,
Most pure heralds of your imperish-
  able glories,
Ascendant fiery columns, the radiant
  cupolas
Of your blindingly sparkling
  empires
Advance to serve you in sacred
  vestments!

These are the heaven-dwellers
Fire-bearers
Overseers of destinies
World builders
Border guards
God's warriors
Wall destroyers

They are yours, the progeny pulling
  you apart

Zhizni unosyat tebya ot menya

P'yanyashchimi snami tebya
  okruzhaya
Igraya i penyas', svetya i zvenya.

Golos muzhestvennogo

Ya v svoyom dvizhenii svyazannïy
Tyazhelotkannost'yu odezhd
Vse-zh lechu, tebe obyazannïy
Vsey siloy ognennïkh nadezhd.

Golos zhenstvennogo

Yesli-b krik moy zova radostnogo
V tvoyey dushe ne prozvuchal,
Ne tvoril-bï tï, o sladostnïy
Gospod', nachalo vsekh nachal.

Tï-zhe ves' o mne tomleniye
A potomu vse prevozmoch'
V etom tvorcheskom stremlenii
Tebe pomozhet bezdnï noch'.

Vozzri: sem' angelov v efirnïkh
  oblacheniyakh,
Prechistïkh vestnikov tvoikh
  netlennïkh slav,
Vozletno-ognennïkh stolpov,
  luchistïkh glav
Tvoikh slepitel'no sverkayushchikh
  derzhav
Gryadut sluzhit' tebe v svyashchen-
  nïkh oblacheniyakh!

To nebozhiteli
Ogne-nositeli
Sudeb vershiteli
Mira stroiteli
Graney khraniteli
S Bogom voiteli
Sten razrushiteli

Oni tvoi, tebya terzayushchiye
  deti

Sired by you in your agitated
bosom
Your path to me lies in their
negating flourishing
Advance to your heroic deed in their
likeness!

They are the builders of the
sparkling temple,
Where the drama of world creation
must occur,
Where in delightful dance, in
marriage to me
You will find the other world that
you desire.

I am your will, I am the awesome
instrument
Of your great achievements
With my strength you bring dreamy
intoxications
Down to the crystals [lapidescences]
of creations

And I am your dream about the
future universe
One of the bonds of dual being

I captivated you, but soon will be the
captive
I will be a wondrous star in your
crown.

Lightning flashes of the will, we
crave manifestation
We will be incarnated in strokes of
decisions
In the din of explosions and the
roars of collapses
We will dwell in dreams with
audacity,
Equally serving dark and light
[forces].

We are the radiant offspring of a
divine dream,
We will be incarnated in pure souls
as contemplation

Toboy rozhdyonnïye v vzvolnovan-
noy grudi
Tvoy put' ko mne v ikh
otritsayushchem rastsvete
Tï v ikh oblichii na podvig svoy
gryadi!

Oni stroiteli sverkayushchogo
khrama,
Gde mirotvorchestva dolzhna
sovershit'sya drama,
Gde v tantse sladostnom, v
venchanii so mnoy
Tï obretyosh' toboy zhelannïy mir
inoy.

Ya volya tvoya, ya orudiye
groznoye
Velikikh tvoikh dostizheniy
Tï siloy moyey op'yaneniya
gryoznïye
Nizvodish' v kristallï tvoreniy

A ya mechta tvoya o budushchey
vselennoy
Odno iz zven'yev dvuyedinogo
bïtiya

Tebya plenila ya, no vskore budu
plennoy
V tvoyom ventse zvyozdoyu divnoy
budu ya.

Molnii voli, mï zhazhdem
soversheniy
Mï voplotimsya v udarakh
resheniy
V grokhote vzrïvov i v gromakh
krusheniy
V snakh derznoveniyem budem mï
zhit',
Ravno i tyomnïm i svetlïm sluzhit'.

Mï chada svetlïye bozhestvennoy
mechtï,
Mï v dushakh chistïkh voplotimsya
sozertsaniyem

Through us you will captivate the
spirits of darkness and negation
And you will piece together frac-
tured dreams anew.

We are a radiant assembly of
thought-flames
And of pure lights, light omens
Of you—a world of pining dreams
The earth—of a feast of exultant
stars.

We are born through your desire for
contrasts,
Reflections of celestial fire rouse us

We are waves of passion, a world
of deceptions and apparitions,
We charm everything, twanging
with sunbeam strings.

We are the waves of life

Waves
First
Waves
Timid
First
Rumbles
Timid
Whispers
First
Trembles
Timid
Murmurs

Waves
Gentle
Waves
Swelling
Gentle
Transiences
Swelling
Froths
Gentle
Wingbeats
Swelling
Flares.

Cherez nas plenish' tï dukhov t'mï
otritsaniya
I snï razdroblyonnïye snova
svyazhesh' tï.

Mï sonm luchistïy mïsley-
plameniy
I svetov chistïkh, svetov-znameniy
Tebe—o mire snov toskuyushchikh
Zemle—o pire zvyozd
likuyushchikh.

Mï rozhdyonï tvoim khoteniyem
razlichiy,
Nas budyat otbleski nebesnogo
ognya
Mï volnï chuvstva, mir obmanov
oblichiy,
Mï vsekh plenyayem, luchestrunami
zvenya.

Mï volnï zhizni

Volnï
Pervïye
Volnï
Robkiye
Pervïye
Rokotï
Robkiye
Shopotï
Pervïye
Trepetï
Robkiye
Lepetï

Volnï
Nezhnïye
Volnï
Vsbezhnïye
Nezhnïye
Smennosti
Vsbezhnïye
Vspennosti
Nezhnïye
Vskrïl'nosti
Vsbezhnïye
Vspïl'nosti.

We are all united	Vse mï—yedinïy
A current, directed	Tok, ustremlyonnïy
From eternity to an instant	K migu ot vechnosti
On the path to humanity	V put' k chelovechnosti
Down from transparency	Vniz ot prozrachnosti
To stony gloom	K kamennoy mrachnosti
So as to engrave upon stone	Shtobï na kamennom
In ardent creation	V tvorchestve plamennom
Your Divine face.	Lik tvoy Bozhestvennïy zapechatlet'.

Waves,	Volnï,
Waves,	Volnï,
First	Pervïye
Waves.	Volnï.
Waves	Volnï
With waves	Volnami
Waves	Volnï
Rippling	Volnuyushchiye
Waves	Volnï
With waves	Volnami
Waves	Volnï
Kissing	Tseluyushchiye

And what is this rapture	Shto-zhe za nega
That seethed in the waves	V volnakh vzïgrala
By flares of sleet	Vspïkhami snega
From a foaming billow?	Vspennogo vala?

And what is this secret	Shto-zhe za tayna
That draws us down	Manit nas k dolu
From limitless heights	S vïsi bezkraynoy
To the schism of life?	K zhizni raskolu?

Awakening Emotions	*Probuzhdayushchiyasya chuvstva*

The tender joy	Nezhnaya radost'
Of first contacts	Pervïkh kasaniy
The secret sweetness	Taynaya sladost'
Of moist kisses	Vlazhnïkh lobzaniy

The tender moans	Nezhnïye stonï
Of first longings,	Pervïkh tomleniy,
The secret chimes—	Taynïye zvonï—
Calls of craving.	Zovï vlecheniy.

The tender caresses	Nezhnïye laski
Of first reflections—	Pervïkh otsvetov—

The secret tales
Of loving lights.

Taynïye skazki
Lyubyashchikh svetov.

Waves

Volnï

Weighed down
By deluges of stupefaction
We are swept away
By the stream of life

Livami mleniya
Otyazhelivshiyasya
Zhizni techeniyem
Mï uvleklisya

Having flowed as waves
Into valleys of languor,
We turned into
Storm clouds of desire

V dolï tomleniya
Volnï izlivshiyasya,
V tuchi khoteniya
Mï obleklisya

In the captivity of clouds
Closer to decay [materiality]
Pour—frothing ones—
Farther and farther down

V oblak-plenakh
K tlennomu blizhe
Leytesya vspennïye
Nizhe i nizhe

Decay is delightful
For in decay
You can be
Imprinted

Sladostno tlennoye
Ibo na tlennom
Zapechatlennïm
Mozhesh' tï bït'

Decay is delightful
Since only in decay
In the manifested world
Can you live.

Sladostno tlennoye
Ibo lish' v tlennom
V mire yavlennom
Mozhesh' tï zhit'.

Ever more palpable
Waves u frothing
Ever more distinct
Tender captivities

Vsyo oblechonney
Volnï u penyashchiyasya
Vsyo yavlenney
Nezhnïye plenï

Ever more amorous, ever more
delightful,
Ever more wearying, ever more
gratifying,
Ever more excruciating, fascinating,
Sensual, corporeal;

Vsyo lyubovney, vsyo usladney,

Vsyo istomney, vsyo otradney,

Vsyo muchitel'ney, prelestney,
Oshchutitel'ney, telesney;

O our captivity
Sweet captivity
Ever-present to us,
Unavoidable,
Having enveloped us on all sides,
Having become our apparel and body

O nash plen
Sladkiy plen
Nam povsyudnïy,
Neizbezhnïy,
Nas so vsekh storon ob'yavshiy,
Nam odezhdoy telom stavshiy

Wave

You gleamed, and the sweetness of
    stupefaction
Poured into the moist body
And full of desire
I ascended to you in your dreams.

Born out of an obscure primal state,
A wave united with waves,
I am now parted from my sisters
By languid reverie.

And in your delightful agitation
I am the most inspired of all the
    waves
In bold flight I am your joyful
Divine laughter.

I am the love that sparkled within
    you,
You are the light that sparkled
    within me
I am the wave who identified myself
As a response to your glittering.

Into the over-world realms of the
    spirit,
Where the filament of life originated,
Where your ethereal palaces are
I fly to beseech you:

Awake in me as consciousness,
Awake, o golden beam!
Heed the incantations
And blend with me—as a wave!

Hear the gentle whisper
    of foaminess
About our common destiny
And about our immutability
In our striving to you.

Immortal beam, your reflections
Have long since sparkled in me
And with your lights
You have beckoned and summoned
    me.

I would have remained indistinct
And would not have become a wave

Volna

Tï blesnul, i sladost' mleniya

V tele vlazhnom razlilas'
I k tebe polna tomleniya
Ya mechtami vozneslas'.

Rozhdyona stikhiey tyomnoyu,
Slita s volnami volna,
Nïne gryozoy ya istomnoyu
Ot sestyor otluchena.

I v tvoyom volnenii sladostnom
Ya iz voln okrïl'ney vsekh

V smelom vzlyote ya tvoy radostnïy
Tvoy bozhestvennïy vossmekh.

Ya lyubov', v tebe vzïgravshaya,

Tï vo mne vzïgravshiy svet

Ya volna, sebya poznavshaya,
Kak igre tvoyey otvet.

V dukha oblasti nadmirnïye,

Gde voznikla zhizni nit',
Gde dvortsï tvoi efirnïye
Ya lechu tebya molit':

Probudis' vo mne soznaniyem,
Probudis', o luch zolotoy!
Bud' poslushen zaklinaniyam
I smesis' so mnoy—volnoy!

Slushay shopot nezhnïy vspennosti

Ob odnoy dlya nas sud'be
I o nashey neizmennosti
V ustremlenii k tebe.

Tï davno vo mne otsvetami
Luch bessmertnïy voz'igral
I menya svoimi svetami
Tï manil i prizïval.

Ya ostalas'-bï bezlichnoyu
I volnoy ne stala-b ya

If those unique lusters
Had not given me being

O, fall, disperse as caresses,
Shed your grace,
You will recognize yourself in the
  tales
Told by scattered light beams!

Yesli-b bleski neobïchnïye
Mne ne dali bïtiya

O, padi, razveysya laskami,
Blagodat' svoyu izley,
Tï sebya poznayesh' skazkami

Raskolovshikhsya luchey!

Light Beam

Luch

Only in the solemn guise
Of an awesome, fateful storm cloud
Could I, having abandoned the
  divine assembly,
Meet with you!

Lish' v oblichii torzhestvennom
Tuchi groznoy, rokovoy
Ya, pokinuv sonm bozhestvennïy,

Mog-bï vstretit'sya s toboy!

Wave

Volna

Clothe yourself in our reveries,
Which as intoxicants soar to the
  heights
Shrouded in their mists
You will descend closer to the
  valley.

V nashi gryozï, shto durmanami
V vïs' nesutsya, oblekis'

Ikh okutannïy tumanami
K dolu blizhe tï spustis'.

Chorus

Khor

All covered in the breath
Of a languid reverie about the wave
And, intoxicated by its fragrance,
In sweet sleep

Emanating burning love,
Captured by a single thought,
The light beam hung as a lightning
  cloud
Over the enamored wave.

Ves' oveyannïy dïkhaniyem
Gryozï tomnoy o volne
I yeyo blagoukhaniyem
Upoyennïy, v sladkom sne

Iskhodya lyubov'yu zhgucheyu,
Vzyatïy mïsliyu odnoy,
Luch ponik molniynoy tucheyu

Nad vlyublyonnoyu volnoy.

Wave

Volna

I fly to you, valiant one
A moment more—I raised myself
And as tender foaminess
Was diffused into the languid-damp
  crevice.

Ya lechu k tebe, otvazhnaya,
Mig yeshcho—ya vozneslas'
I v poniklost' tomno-vlazhnuyu
Nezhnoy vspennost'yu vpilas'.

O, divine moment of creation
A moment blessed, fiery
You revealed to me the reflection
Of white, fateful death.

You awakened in me awareness
Of dual being.
I am from now on a combination
Of "I" and an alien "not I."

Tender tissues come to life
The tissues of emotions—my
    apparel
And, restless, rush into the distance
From rising eyelids.

The smoky walls of the purgatories
Melt, sink, and break apart
And assemblies of life-bearers
Stream into the depths.

I became a regal couple
In a world of sacrificial love.
I project the power of giving,
I came to know blood's heat.

O all-powerful desire
You live—and you are not I
Our impassioned caresses are alive
In multicolored being.

You and I and our supplication
Are a world of revealed wonders
Intoxicated by a vision
By the life of slumbering skies.

The miracle of union came to pass
The circle closed and there arose
The fruit of the marriage of wave
    and light
The starry face of the created world.

Ignited by the lightning of the
    sacred moment
The visions of creation blaze, and
    the wave,
Captivating inspiration with spells
    of consciousness,

O, svyashchennïy mig tvoreniya
Mig blazhennïy, ognevoy
Tï yavil mne otrazheniye
Smerti beloy, rokovoy.

Razbudil vo mne soznaniye
Dvuyedinogo bïtiya.
Ya otnïne sochetaniye
"Ya" i chuzhdogo "ne-ya."

Ozhivayut tkani nezhnïye
Tkani chuvstv—moikh odezhd

I nesutsya v dal', myatezhnïye,
Ot vzdïmayushchikhsya vezhd.

Tayut, tonut, razdvigayutsya
Stenï dïmnïye temnits
I v glubinï ustremlyayutsya
Sonmï zhizhney—kolesnits.

Stala ya chetoyu tsarstvennoy
V mire zhertvennoy lyubvi.
Iskhozhu ya siloy darstvennoy,
Ya poznala yar krovi.

O zhelaniye vsevlastnoye
Tï zhivyosh',—i tï—ne ya
Zhivï laski nashi strastnïye
V mnogotsvete bïtiya.

Tï i ya i nashe moleniye
Mir raskrïvshikhsya chudes
Op'yaneniye snovideniyem
Zhizn'yu dremlyushchikh nebes.

Sbïlos' chudo sochetaniya
Krug zamknulsya i voznik
Plod volnï s luchom venchaniya

Mirozdaniya zvyozdnïy lik.

Zazhglis' ot molnii
    svyashchennogo mgnoveniya
I plameneyut snï tvoreniya, a
    volna,
Soznaniya charami plenyaya
    vdokhnoveniya,

Is all given to the contemplation of contrasts.
He shines in the sun, the God of the ruling light
And glitters in the stars in the boundlessness of night
She [the wave] hovers in space as a regal planet
Covered in a veil of pearl [colored] cloud.

And the light beam caresses of the first-chosen couple
Coming to consciousness as a mirage of blinding wonders
Became recognized in the multi-coloredness, multifacetedness
As the adornments of the couple, the brocades of its veils.

(Mountains)

We are the frozen impulses of amorous wraths
We are the petrified surfs of wild caresses
Cooled explosions overtaken by charms
Snowy peaks, valleys, and cliffs.

(Fields)

We are the warm breathing of lips that have not touched
Concealing in itself all the delights of the toxins
We have awakened here with the fragrance of flowers,
We rustle with the rustles of grass

(Forest)

We are soaring pillars in a cathedral of twilights

Vsya sozertsaniyu razlichiy otdana.

Siyayet solntsem, Bog vlastitel'nogo sveta
I bleshchet zvyozdami v bezdonnosti nochnoy
Ona v prostranstve reyet tsarstven-noy planetoy
Ovitoy oblachno-zhemchuzhnoy pelenoy.

A luche-laski u chetï pervoizbrannoy
Ochnuvshis' marevom slepitel'nïkh chudes
Opoznayutsya v mnogotsvetnom, mnogogrannom
Chetï ukrasami, parchey yeyo zaves.

(Gori)

Lyubovnïkh gnevov mï zastïvshiye porïvï
Mï burnïkh lask okamenevshiye valï
Okhladï charami zastignutïye vzrïvï
Vershinï snezhnïye, dolinï i skalï.

(Polya)

Ust nekosnuvshikhsya mï— tyoploye dïkhaniye
V sebe tayashcheye vse prelesti otrav
Syuda prosnulis' mï tsvetov blagoukhaniyem,
Vozshelestilisya mï shelestami trav

(Les)

Mï v khrame sumrakov vozlyotnïye stolpï

We are magnificently clothed in
verdant murmurs
We conceal hordes of mysterious
creatures
Languid, secret lights pour into us.

Mï pïshno shumami zelyonïmi
odetï
Sushchestv zagadochnïkh skrïvayem
mï tolpï
K nam l'yutsya tomnïye, taynstven-
nïye svetï.

(Wilderness)

(Pustïnya)

Having identified myself in space as
wilderness [desert]
A dry and burning kiss of light and
earth
Having banished forest life from my
fields
And loathed the living songs of a
stream.

A winged caress, I began to flutter
like a bird,

And I, tormenting, returned to life
in beastly form.

Twisting-crawling, I awoke as a
snake

Wearied, I take kindly to the damp.

Sebya pustïney ya v prostranstve
opoznavshiy
Lucha s zemlyoy sukhoy i znoynïy
potseluy
Lesnuyu zhizn' iz oblastey svoikh
izgnavshiy
I nenavidyashchiy zhivïye pesni
struy.

Ya laska vskrïl'naya, ya ptitsey
vstrepenulas',

A ya, terzayushchaya, zverem
ozhila.

Izvivno-polznaya, zmeyeyu ya
prosnulas'

Stikhii vlazhnoy ya, istomnaya,
mila.

SECTION B: THE UNREVISED SECOND HALF
OF THE LIBRETTO FROM NOTEBOOK "c"

Awaking in the waters, I swim like
a fish
He blazes, the regal one, as a shining
tenet
This cathedral is like a bright hymn,
this world is like a starry cathedral
The ether reverberates with a golden
summons
That takes souls into the inaccessible
heavens.
The ascent of the Hero-Wave has
concluded

V vodakh prosnuvshayasya,—rïboy
ya plïvu
Gorit on, tsarstvennïy,
siyayushchim zakonom
Sey khram—kak svetlïy gimn, sey
mir—kak zvyozdnïy khram
Efir napolnen zolotïm zazïvnom
zvonom
Shto dushi emlet k nedostupnïm
nebesam.
Volnï-Geroya zavershilos'
voskhozhdeniye

She [the Hero-Wave] is fully illuminated by heavenly light	Nebesnïm svetom vsya ona ozarena
And in her pangs the depth of the delight of the eternal feminine	I vechno-zhenstvennogo v bolyakh naslazhdeniya
Is now revealed to her for the first time	Teper' vpervïye yey otkrïlas' glubina
And from the abyss of the past the curtains wondrously fell	I s bezdnï proshlogo zavesï chudno spali
And in the illumination worlds opened to her	I v ozarenii tom otkrïlis' yey mirï
And before her inquisitive eyes appeared	I pered vzorami pïtlivïmi predstali
The sacred feasts of the chosen peoples,	Narodov izbrannïkh svyashchennïye pirï,
The magnificent enactment of holy rites	Svyatïkh obryadov blagolepnoye soversheniye
And the choral offering of great sacrifices	I zhertv velikikh khorovoye prinosheniye
And the exquisite features of the white face	I lika belogo prekrasnïye chertï
Which revealed itself in the guise of beauty.	Sebya yavivshogo v oblich'ye krasotï.
The wave rested her blissful gaze on it.	Na nem blazhennïy vzglyad volna ostanovila.
She proclaimed in devout rapture	Ona v molitvennom vostorge vozglasila
To the father shining with love within her:	V ney vozsiyavshemu lyubov'yu ottsu:
What sacrifice shall I make to the Creator?	Kakuyu zhertvu prinesti mogu Tvortsu?
Turn	Tï obrati
Your radiant face	Svoy svetlïy lik
To your wearied primal state	K svoyey stikhii istomlyonnoy
You will behold	Svoi puti
Your paths in an instant	Poymyosh' tï v mige
And you will descend into the unquenched	I nizoydyosh' k neutolyonnoy
Your feat is ours!	Tvoy podvig nash!
You are the very living incarnation	Tï nashikh sil
Of our powers	Samo zhivoye voploshcheniye
You will give us life!	Tï zhizn' nam dash'!
You, who revealed	Tï, shto yavil

The face of death, baptize us!	Lik smerti, daruy nam kreshcheniye!
You as a wave	Tï kak volna
Having ascended, must	Vzletiv, dolzhna
Return to your obscure primal state	Sebya vernut' stikhii tyomnoy
You as a wave	Tï kak volna
Having regained sight, must	Prozrev, dolzhna
Give us your borrowed light!	Nam podarit' tvoy svet zayomnïy!
And the fire-bearer, heeding their call,	I ognenosnaya, ikh zovu ustupaya,
Willingly returned to her own primal state	K rodnoy stikhii blagosklonno nizoshla
Thus teaching the waves sacrificial love.	Lyubovi zhertvennoy tem volnï pouchaya.
She gave them the words of holy prayer.	Ona slova svyatoy molitvï im dala.
Herald of the hidden secret	Vestnik taynï sokrovennoy
Torch of the audacious thought	Svetoch mïsli derznovennoy
Answer!	Otzovis'!
Fiery one, radiant one	Ognestvimïy, luchestvennïy
Awaken!	V nas molitvoy vdokhnovennoy
As inspired prayer within us	Probudis'!
Illuminate!	Nashi bezdnï tyomnïye
Our dark abysses	Osveti!
Visit	Nas v temnitse v dni zlostnïye
Us in purgatory on wicked days	Poseti
Bright angel, awake	Svetlïy angel, probudis'
In sweet awakening	Probuzhdeniyem sladostnïm
Answer our call	Na prizïv nash otzovis'
Answer us with a joyful smile!	Nam ulïbkoy radostnoy!
Let us illuminate	Day nam svetom ozarit'
Our suffering life with light	Zhizn' svoyu stradal'nuyu
Let us love, let us create	Day lyubit' nam, day tvorit'
Arise, you who fell asleep within us!	Tï, usnuvshiy v nas, vosstan'!
Let us pass through, surmount	Day postavlennuyu gran'
The set border!	Nam proyti, prevozmoch'!
Let us dispel this night!	Day rasseyat' etu noch'!
In the cathedral of love in dazzling splendor on a blazing throne	V khrame lyubvi v osleplyayu- shchey slave na trone goryashchem

The radiant one preached to those
heeding him:
who dares to violate
My sole law of eternal love and
eternal humility
Will be cast into the great sorrow
and anguish of excommunication.

Mortals, I will reveal to you the
secret of celestial harmonies
May hymns and praises sound
on the sun lyre!

The people, searching for consonant
sonorities, touch the strings that
are alien to them.

What are these lights that flicker
And, enchanting, dazzle?
What are these sounds that emit
The toxin that infatuates us?

What with a flash of lightning,
What in a conjuror's act
In the smoke of our purgatories
Has prostrated us?

It is the beam, the white beam
Dissipated within us, the beam
Is melodious in its languor—
Powerful in its caress.

Fragile, it scattered itself
As lights and sounds
The abysses reverberated
With delighted moans

Rainbows sparkled
Dreams bloomed
With the alluring flowers
Of sensual spring

Everywhere reflections
Everywhere wonders
Secret calls are heard
Voices are heard

Whirlpools in the radiance
Of opalescent beams
Shine with the distrustfulness
Of virgin eyes.

Svetlïy vnimavshikh emu pouchal:

kto zakon moy yedinïy
Vechnoy lyubvi i smireniya
vechnogo derzko prestupit'
Budet povergnut' v velikuyu skorb'
i tosku otlucheniya.

Smertnïye, vam ya povedayu taynï
nebesnïkh garmoniy
Da razdayutsya gimnï i slavï na
solnechnoy lire!

Lyudi, ishcha razreshennïkh
sozvuchiy im chuzhdïkh
kasayutsya strun.

Shto za svetï drozhat
I, charuya, slepyat?
Shto za zvuki struyat
Nas bezumyashchiy yad?

Shto sverkaniyem zarnits,
Shto igroy charovnits
V dïme nashikh temnits
Nas povergnulo nits?

Eto luch, belïy luch
V nas raspalsya, pevuch
Svoyey negoyu luch
Svoyey laskoy—moguch.

Khrupkiy, on rassïpalsya
Svetami i zvonami
Bezdnï oglasilisya
Sladostnïmi stonami

Zaigrali radugi
Rastsvetilis' snï
Tsvetami manyashchimi
Chuvstvennoy vesnï

Vsyudu otrazheniya
Vsyudu chudesa
Slïshnï zovï taynïye
Slïshnï golosa

Omutï v siyanii
Raduzhnïkh luchey
Svetyatsya nevernost'yu
Devich'ikh ochey.

Surfaces of viscous mires
Twinkle like diamonds
Nets of opaline cobwebs
Sparkle.

Strewn with pearls
The gentle wave
With emerald eyes
Calls to the bottom.

Luxuriant flowers
Open up everywhere
The fragrances
Of sweet dream are everywhere

Everything around is saturated
With the scents of herbs
Fraught with languor
The horrors of the toxins.

A new, unintelligible trembling
Embraces the world
In the reflections
Gods disperse their dreams.

Enduring passions
Await gratification.
Their fragrances
Tempt and call.

We, fragrances of the earth, sing
We call you, radiant pilgrim!

Come, o come, lord
Of the dismal, damp depths here

Here, in the guise of strange
   shadows,
Are many wondrous will-o'-the-
   wisps.

A whole assembly of unborn dreams
Exists here in the guise of strange
   flowers

We, the fragrances of the earth, sing
Harken, o pilgrim, to our songs

We sing of the delights of the
   betrayals
Of the joyous collapse of the walls

Iskryatsya almazami
Lona vyazkikh tin
V raduzhnom sverkanii
Seti pautin.

Zhemchugom osïpana
Nezhnaya volna
Vzorami smaragdnïmi
K dnu zovyot ona.

Vsyudu raskrïvayutsya
Pïshnïye tsvetï
Vsyudu blagovoniya
Sladostnoy mechtï

Vsyo krugom nasïshcheno
Zapakhami trav
V tomnosti tayashchimi
Uzhasï otrav.

Novoy, neponyatnoyu
Drozh'yu mir ob'yat
Bogi v otrazheniyakh
Snï svoi drobyat.

Strasti neizzhitïye
Utoleniya zhdut.
Ikh blagoukhaniya
Manyat i zovut.

Mï, zemli aromatï, poyom
Mï, tebya, strannik svetlïy, zovyom!

Tï pridi, o pridi, gospodin
Zdes' toskuyushchikh, vlazhnïkh
   glubin

Zdes', v oblichii strannïkh teney

Mnogo divnïkh bluzhdayet ogney.

Tselïy sonm nerodivshikhsya snov
Zdes' v oblichii strannïkh tsvetov

Mï poyom, aromatï zemli
Nashim pesnyam, o strannik,
   vnemli

Mï poyom o vostorgakh izmen

O krushenii radostnom sten

Of the bliss of corporeal pleasures
We conceal a treasure of wondrous
    songs.

Fragrant songs
Of the damp depth
Longing for you
Full of passion

Pilgrim, heed
The calls of the gentle fragrances
Give the burning thirsts
The joy of gratification!

The iridescent hour—
The sound, whatever you are,
That sires within us so many sweet
    torments—
Has struck

We gave ourselves up to you
As to a secret destiny
We float down
Into the fragrant mist.

Dance-Song of the Fallen

A bewitched choir, we whirl
In two combined tornados
Over the paths, over the pitted
Paths, covered by corpses

We inhale the stench of black blood
It lusts for loathsome delights
We whirl in a fiery dance
In a dance-caress, a dance-fantasy.

To build houses of ill-repute
There to erect our thrones
There to submit to our passion
Which opened its cavernous jaws
    to us.

We whirl swiftly over the precipices
Over the canyons and crevices
Where the flowers of madness grow
To submit to them without pause

So in godforsaken places the pilgrim
    spirit,

O blazhenstve telesnïkh uslad
Pesney divnïkh skrïvayem mï klad.

Pesni blagovonnïye
Vlazhnoy glubinï
O tebe toskuyushchey
Strastnosti polnï

Zovï nezhnïkh zapakhov
Strannik, tï vnimay
Radost' utoleniya
Zhazhdam znoynïm day!

Chem-bï ne bïl tï zvuk
Stol'ko sladostnïkh muk
Porozhdayushchiy v nas—

Probil raduzhnïy chas

Mï otdalis' tebe
Kak zavetnoy sud'be
Mï nesyomsya dolu
V blagovonnuyu mglu.

Pesnya — Plyaska padshikh

Mï po tropam, po izrïtïm
Tropam, trupami pokrïtïm
Po dva vikhrya sopryazhennïkh
Mchimsya khor obvorozhennïy

Chornoy krovi dïshem smradom
Rvyotsya k merzostnïm usladam
Mchimsya v plamennoy mï plyaske
Plyaske-laske, plyaske-skazke.

Stroit' skvernïye pritonï
Tam vozdvignut' nashi tronï
Tam otdat'sya nashey strasti
Nam otkrïvshey zherla-pasti.

Mchimsya bïstro po obrïvam
Po ushchel'yam i po srïvam
Gde rastut tsvetï bezumiya
Im otdat'sya bez razdum'ya

Tak dukh-strannik po trushchobam

Frenzied, wildly celebrates
His sacred breach with heaven
Heeding dark summons

Be thrice damned
You, the repulsive face of horrid
  death
These black holes [vacant eyes] to
  eternity
Our carelessness disdains

After brief contacts with it [eternity]
The passions draw us toward
  embodiment
Our songs are not consonant
With the songs of heaven, which are
  tedious to us

Blind to the revelation of heaven
Only corpses gladden us
Only the splashes of black blood
Of our abhorrent love
We whirl swiftly over the ridges
Over corpses, over corpses
Closer to filth, closer to shame
Soon the walls of the cathedral will
  collapse.

————

Why did the primordial one will to
  allow
His beloved progeny to fall so far[?]

Why, why, did gracious providence
  take
The filament leading to the gateway
  from them?

So that the one tortured by the
  burning thirst of possession
Having drained the phial of seething
  passion
Having experienced all the horrors
  of ultimate suffering
Will extract from its base a sparkling
  crystal

So that later from such multicolored
  crystals

Svoy razrïv svyashchennïy s nebom
Diko prazdnuyet, besnuyas'
Chornïm zovam povinuyas'

Bud' tï proklyat troyekratno
Smerti strashnoy lik otvratnïy

Temi prorubyami v vechnost'

Nasha brezguyet bezpechnost'

Posle kratkikh s ney obshcheniy
Manyat strasti k voploshcheniyam

Pesnyam neba, nam dokuchnïm
Nashi pesni ne sozvuchnï

K otkroveniyu neba tupï
Nam otradnï tol'ko trupï
Tol'ko brïzgi chornoy krovi
Nashey merzostnoy lyubovi
Mï po trupam, mï po trupam
Mchimsya bïstro po ustupam
Blizhe k skverne, blizhe k sramu
Skoro rukhnut grani khrama.

————

Zachem predvechnïy stol'
  glubokoye padeniye
Lyubimïkh chad svoikh povolil
  dopustit'[?]

Zachem, zachem u nikh blagoye
  provideniye
Otnyalo dveri ukazuyushchuyu
  nit'?

Dabï muchimïy znoynoy zhazhdoy
  obladaniya
Ispiv do dna kipyashchiy strastiyu
  fial
Poznav vse uzhasï poslednego
  stradaniya
Dostal so dna yego sverkayushchiy
  kristall

Dabï potom iz tekh kristallov
  mnogotsvetnïkh

[He will] erect the cathedral of
   immortal beauty anew
Where in the solemn burning of
   sacred souls
The sacram⌐⌐⌐ of the capture of the
   dream will be enacted.

One can only penetrate through the
   froth of sweet suffering
Into the secret region, where the
   treasures of the soul are
Where, having ceased to love the
   agitated soul of the passion
The holy one achieves bliss in the
   glorious stillness.

———

Having lost contact with the heavens
We scattered ourselves.
We rise up against each other
We conduct terrible wars

Each awaits a bloody encounter
Each craves a scarlet battle
And strikes with an able hand
So the cowardly enemy will perish!

Woe to those born weak!
Woe, woe to the defeated!
Those debilitated in shackles
Will not escape new torments.

One can hear the clank of iron chains
And the futile pleas
Piercing cries
Drown out our calls.

Call to whom? Pray to whom?
How long, how long,
Will our terrible suffering last
Who will hear the voice of sobbing?

To die. . . But the blissful face
Of death, misconstrued by us
Has turned away from the sufferers
From the wanderers of the dark
   valley.

I am more victorious than everyone,
   more enraptured than everyone

Vozdvignut' snova khram
   bessmertnoy krasotï
Gde pri torzhestvennom goreniye
   dush zavetnïkh
Sovershitsya taynstvo pleneniya
   mechtï.

Proniknut' mozhno lish' skvoz'
   penu stradoslastiya
V tu oblast' taynï, gde sokrovishcha
   dushi
Gde, razlyubiv dushi vzvolnovan-
   noy pristrastiya
Svyatoy blazhenstvuyet v
   siyayushchey tishi.

———

Svyaz' utrativ s nebesami
Mï rasseyalis' i sami.
Drug na druga vosstayem mï
Voynï groznïye vedyom mï

Kazhdïy zhdyot krovavoy vstrechi
Kazhdïy alchet aloy sechi
I razit rukoy umeloy
Da pogibnet vrag nesmelïy!

Gore slabïm rozhdyonnïm!
Gore, gore pobezhdyonnïm!
Im izmuchennïm v okovakh
Ne izbegnut' pïtok novïkh.

Slïshen lyazg tsepey zheleznïkh
I moleniy bezpoleznïkh
Razdirayushchiye kriki
Zaglushayut nashi kliki.

Zvat' kogo? Komu molit'sya?
Dolgo-l, dolgo-l budut dlit'sya
Nashi strashnïye stradaniya
Kto uslïshit glas rïdaniya?

Umeret'. . . . No lik blazhennïy
Smerti, nami izvrashchonnoy
Otvratilsya ot stradal'tsev
Dola tyomnogo skital'tsev.

Ya vsekh pobedney, vsekh
   upoyonney

Bolder than everyone and stronger
than everyone
More intoxicated by the stench of
blood than everyone
I am more lethal than a snake's
poisons!

I hurl the arrows of blind rage
I lay out a challenge to
everything and everyone
And only virgins while still chaste
Will allay the horror of my verses

Horror in defeat is pleasure to me
And the last gasp of dying
I am the God of greed and
destruction
I am the scourge of the peoples, I am
the God of blood!

The insane one charged and in a
wild frenzy
Pierced the hearts of people with a
poisoned sword
And sewing grief and bitterness
everywhere
Threatens humanity with
annihilation.

And he battles a long time, but then
exhausted
All covered in blood, wounded, and
feverish
He drops his sword, defeated in
mismatched battle
And seized with horror, he flees, as
in a delirium.

He flees into the wilderness, where
under cover of silence
In the shelter of peace and all-
prophetic stillness
His soul will grasp all the horror of
the contemplation
Of his deep, unexpiated guilt

And there lacerated, all covered with
abrasions

Vsekh derznovenney i vsekh sil'ney

Dïkhaniyem krovi vsekh
op'yanyonney
Ya smertonosney, chem yadï zmey!

Slepogo gneva brosayu strelï
Brosayu vïzov vsemu i vsem

I tol'ko devï poka ne zreli
Smyagchayut uzhas moikh poem

Mne milï uzhas pri porazhenii
I umiraniya poslednïy vzdokh
Ya Bog alkaniya i razrusheniya

Ya bich narodov, ya krovi Bog!

Bezumnïy rinulsya i v dikom
isstuplenii
Serdtsa lyudey mechem otravlen-
nïm razit
I nasazhdaya vsyudu skorb' i
ozlobleniye
Unishtozheniyem chelovechestvu
grozit.

I b'yotsya dolgo on, no vot
iznemozhennïy
Oblitïy kroviyu, ves' v ranakh, ves'
v ogne
Ronyayet mech', v boyu neravnom
porazhennïy
I, vzyatïy uzhasom bezhit on, kak
vo sne.

Bezhit v pustïnyu, gde pod seniyu
molchaniya
V priyute mira i vseveshchey tishinï

Dusha izvedayet ves' uzhas
sozertsaniya
Svoyey glubokoy neiskuplennoy
vinï

I tam rasterzannïy, ves' yazvami
pokrïtïy

With a pierced heart, all in rags and
dust
He lies, a God, forgotten by himself
and others
The terrible potentate of his bloodstained earth.

And one by one before his eyes pass

Visions of the victims of his un-
bridled passions
He hears the cries that emanate
from the depths of the souls
Of the children orphaned and tormented by him.

Their terrible wailing, their discon-
solate sobbing
Came to life as moans in his sick soul
Having woken as apparitions of the
coming suffering
They sound as an alarm in the
hidden silence

And each wound of his debilitated
brother
Gapes as a fiery wound in his soul

His long-suffering soul is enveloped

By a wave of world despair and
sorrow.

And long, long last the torments and
tortures
Their raging fire is still not
extinguished
And even betrothal to her, to terrible
death
Seemed desirable to him in that
hour.

He grows faint and perishes under
an awesome wave
In an ocean of ardent passions

Then everything became confused
and disappeared in a mist

S pronzyonnïm serdtsem, ves' v
lokhmot'yakh i pïli
Lezhit on, Bog, sebya zabïvshiy i
zabïtïy
Vlastitel' groznïy obagrennoy im
zemli.

I pered vzorom verenitseyu
prokhodyat
Videniya zhertv yego raznuzdan-
nïkh strastey
On slïshit kriki, shto iz glubey dush
iskhodyat
Osirotevshikh, im zamuchennïkh
detey.

Ikh strashnïy vopl', ikh neuteshnïye
rïdaniya
Ozhili stonami bol'noy yego dushi
Prosnulis' likami gryadushchego
stradaniya
Zvuchat nabatom v pritaívsheysya
tishi

I rana kazhdaya izmuchennogo
brata
V yego dushe ziyayet ranoy
ognevoy
Mnogostradal'naya, dusha yego
ob'yata
Volnoy otchayaniya i skorbi
mirovoy.

I dolgo, dolgo dlyatsya pïtki i
mucheniya
Yeshcho ogon' ikh voznosyashchiy
ne ugas
I dazhe s ney, so smert'yu strashnoy
obrucheniye
Emu predstavilos' zhelannïm v etot
chas.

Iznemogayet on i gibnet v
okeane
Strastey pïlayushchikh, pod
groznoyu volnoy
Vot vsyo smeshalos' i ischezlo vsyo
v tumane

That shrouded him with a heavy
veil.

He yielded to someone's secret
suggestion
The link is missing. . . Isolated from
the dreams
And taken by the whirlwinds of
primal perfection
He strives to the light following
someone's gentle call.

———

Don't be afraid, child, I am the one
you desired!
Blinded by me, you did not recognize me!
More than once I followed you
unexpectedly
You feared death, fled death.

Then passions for the valley
separated us
Your gaze was completely absorbed
by the earth
You were not prepared for holy
communion
You could not be enraptured by
me then

Are you indeed the one who with
covetous pricks
Pierced those suffering in the
dungeon of time[?]
My caresses seemed like daggers to
you
And the fear in your eyes distorted
my face.—

Why did you come to me in the
guise
Of a blind monster with a corpse's
mouth[?]
Child, you thus perceived the
grandeur of death
Through eyes of fear you saw all
as evil.

Yego okutavshem tyazheloy
pelenoy.

On ustupil chemu-to taynomu
vnusheniyu
Zveno upushcheno. . . Otorvannïy
ot snov
I vzyatïy vikhryami stikhiynogo
soversheniya
Stremitsya k svetu on na chey-to
nezhnïy zov.

———

Ne boysya, ditya, ya toboyu
zhelannaya!
Tï, mnoy osleplennïy, menya ne
uznal!
Ne raz za toboy ya khodila
nezhdannaya
Tï smerti boyalsya, ot smerti bezhal.

Togda razdelyali nas k dolu
pristrastiya
Tvoy vzor bïl vsetselo zemley
pogloshchen
Tï ne bïl gotov dlya svyatogo
prichastiya
Tï mnoyu ne mog bït' togda
voskhishchen

Uzheli tï takzhe, shto zhadnïmi
zhalami
Pronzala stradavshikh v temnitse
vremen[?]
Tebe moi laski kazalis' kinzhalami

I v strakha glazakh bïl moy lik
izmenen.—

Zachem prikhodila ko mne tï v
oblichii
Slepogo chudovishcha s
mertvennïm rtom[?]
Ditya, tï vosprinyal tak smerti
velichiye
Ochami ispuga vse videl tï zlom.

My radiant countenance, my
sparkling countenance
Your renunciation of earthly life

Only he who flows forth toward
me in pure love
Comprehends me—admires me

In the cathedral of your soul I am
the sweetness of consonance
Of dreams that sing of heaven on
wings
I am the sweetness of unity, I am the
melodious caress
In the blissful merger of all voices.

Your abdication of the crimson
world
Awakened in you a bride—me
Come to know all the joys of
azure heaven
I will reveal all the secrets of the fire
to you!

———

O most pure Virgin, sweetness of
reverie
Allow me to coalesce with you in
perfect love
Sweetest one, the process of the trial
is not completed,
Your sin has not been atoned, your
apparel is bloodied.

You must journey to your dying
brothers
And dedicate your soul to their
service
[You must] prepare people to accept
suffering
[You must] be sacrificed and thus
attain grace
Heed the secret calls of the soul
and hasten
To bring the tidings of heaven

Moy oblik luchistïy, moy oblik
sverkayushchiy
Tvoyo otrecheniye ot zhizni
zemnoy
Lish' chistoy lyubov'yu ko mne
istekayushchiy
Menya postigayet, lyubuyetsya
mnoy

Ya v khrame dushi tvoyey sladost'
sozvuchiya
O nebe poyushchikh voskrïl'yami
snov
Ya sladost' yedinstva, ya laska
pevuchaya
V blazhennom sliyanii vsekh
golosov.

Tvoyo otrecheniye ot mira
purpurnogo
V tebe razbudilo nevestu—menya
Poznay zhe vse radosti neba
lazurnogo
Tebe ya otkroyu vse taynï ognya!

———

O Deva prechistaya, sladost'
mechtaniya
Day slit'sya s toboy v sovershennoy
lyubvi
Sladchayshiy, ne proyden ves' put'
ispïtaniya,
Tvoy grekh ne iskuplen, odezhdï v
krovi.

Tï dolzhen idti k pogibayushchey
bratii
I dushu svoyu na sluzheniye otdat'

Lyudey prigotovit' k stradaniya
priyatiyu
Past' zhertvoy i tem obresti
blagodat'
Taynïm zovam dushi tï
vnimay i speshi
Pogibayushchim vest'

To the dying.

Teach them
What dispelled the darkness,
What you learned from me
About the beginning of beginnings
That in suffering is the light
And that in the light is the answer
That I am this answer
The flower of another being
Announce that we are all
In the dawn glow
That crystals already burn
In the pearl white distance!
So that all would taste
From the chalice of fire, cursing
The blind power of passions
Their dangerous snares
So that everyone would obtain a
  crystal
From the base of this chalice
So that he would wash it with tears
So that he would be prepared
To receive grace
To reconstruct the temple to me
Where you and I
In the dance of judgment day
In the hour of loving wonders
In the dance of the stars that fall
From heaven to us in the palace,
Could be accommodated!

———

The gentle vision dissolved in the
  mist
That had embraced him. The shroud
  again dissolves
He lies alone in the wilderness as
  before
But he is not the same: spring reigns
  in his soul

Renewed in suffering, he strives
  toward people
To teach them what awaits them on
  the path;
He goes on wings of love and
  knowledge

O nebesnom prinest'.

Nauchi ikh tomu
Shto rasseyalo t'mu,
Shto so mnoy izuchal
O nachale nachal
Shto v stradanii svet
I shto v svete otvet
Shto otvet etot ya
Tsvet inogo bïtiya
Tï skazhi, shto mï vse
V zarevoy polose
Shto v zhemchuzhnoy dali
Uzh goryat khristollï!
Shtobï k chashe ognya
Vse pripali, klyanya
Vlast' slepuyu strastey
Ikh opasnïkh setey
Shtobï kazhdïy kristall

S dna toy chashi dostal
Shtob slyozami omïl
Shtob gotovïm on bïl
Obresti blagodat'
I mne khram vossozdat'
Gde tebya i menya
V tantse sudnogo dnya
V chas lyubviynïkh chudes
V tantse zvyozd, shto s nebes
Nizoydut k nam v chertoge,
Nas vmestit'-bï on mog!

———

Videniye nezhnoye istayalo v
  tumane
Yego ob'yavshem. Snova tayet
  pelena
Opyat' v pustïne on odin lezhit kak
  rano
No on ne tot: v yego dushi tsarit
  vesna

Stremitsya k lyudyam on,
  stradaniyem obnovlennïy
Im prepodat', shto ozhidayet ikh v
  puti;
Idyot lyubov'yu i znaniyem
  okrïlennïy

To save them from the force of blind passions.

And he says to those who do not suffer: be tormented!
But to those who have suffered: come to love the bitterness of toils!
In the depths of torment is the disavowal of desires,
And in the disavowal is the light of untold joys!

For us, living in the world of crimson and resonant secrets
The living fire of earthly desires is not extinguished!
We do not understand your tedious speeches!
Vainly, pilgrim, you came to pester us!

How delightful it is for us to be lost in the forest of consonances
And to languish and roam in the cathedral of twilights
How pleasant uncertainty is for us, how sweet chance
And how unfamiliar is the grace of the distant heavens.

The prophet glanced around and saw

The world that he had summoned to life
In all its living, manifold beauty

Breathing with seduction, as vice flourishing with full color.

And he hears the voices of the nocturnal calls
- Come, wonders live everywhere here!

Come, we will guide you to expiration!
Intoxicating love, melodious caresses!

Ikh ot nasiliya strastey slepïkh spasti.

I govorit on nestradavshim: vam mucheniye!
A postradavshim: polyubite gorech' strad!
V glubinakh pïtok—ot zhelaniy otrecheniye,
I v otrechenii svet nevedomïkh otrad!

U nas, zhivushchikh v mire tayn purpurno-zvuchnïkh
Ogon' zhivoy zemnïkh zhelaniy ne ugas!
Ne ponimayem mï rechey tvoikh dokuchnïkh!
Naprasno, strannik tï prishol trevozhit' nas!

Kak zateryat'sya sladko nam v lesu sozvuchiy
I v khrame sumrakov tomit'sya i bluzhdat'
Kak neizvestnost' nam mila, kak sladok sluchay
I kak chuzhda nebes dalyokikh blagodat'.

Okinul vzorami i dïshashchiy soblaznom
Kak vsemi kraskami rastsvechennïy porok
Vo vsey krase yego zhivoy, mnogoobraznoy
Uvidel mir, im k zhizni vïzvannïy, prorok.

I slïshit on zovov nochnïkh golosa

- Pridi, zdes' povsyudu zhivut chudesa!

Pridi, mï tebya ugasaniyu nauchim!

Lyubvi op'yanyayushchey, laskam pevuchim!

You will be like the twilight, enveloped in slumber
And soon, extinguished, you will become darkness.

It is in the darkness that, as a splendid fire,
Infatuating with sweet fumes, a carbuncle will ignite

You will come to know the secrets of earthly beauty
You will pick the flowers of sensations

O the sweetness
Of meandering caresses
O the amorousness
Of flowing streams!

Pilgrim, come to know the truth of the feeling
Mortals find paradise in conjugal happiness
Here is my indivisible one, chosen by me
Awaited in misery by me for ages

Only within me, one of all
Does he see the source of the pleasures of the heart.

Through me, in gracious union

By his own strength he comes to know ecstasy.

Faithfulness in matrimony, means, and comfort
Jointly forge happiness for mortals.

All illuminated with sapphire luster
Our palace breathes with peaceful happiness

Pilgrim, acknowledge the truth of the feeling
Mortals find paradise only in matrimony

Receive, instead of your dream,
The simple truth of reason

Tï budesh' kak sumrak, ob'yatïy dremoy
A vskore, izgasnuv tï stanesh' i t'moy.

Vo t'me-zhe zazhzhotsya roskoshnïm pozharom
Karbunkul, bezumyashchiy slastnïm ugarom

Tï taynï poznayesh' zemnoy krasotï
Tï budesh' srïvat' oshchushcheniy tsvetï

O sladosti
Lask izvivnïkh
O lyubovi
Struy izlivnïkh!

Strannik, tï istinu chuvstva poznay

V schast'ye supruzheskom smertnomu ray
Vot moy yedinïy, mnoyu izbrannïy

Mnoyu ot veka tomitel'no zhdannïy

On lish' vo mne, odnoy iz vsekh
Vidit istochnik serdtsa utekh.

On cherez menya, v blagom yedinenii
Siloy svoyey poznayet upoyeniye.

Vernost' v supruzhestve, den'gi, uyut
Smertnomu schast'ye kupno kuyut.

Ves' osiyannïy bleskom sapfirnïm
Dïshet dvorets nash schast'yem mirnïm

Strannik tï istine chuvstva vozday

Tol'ko v supruzhestve smertnomu ray

Primi vzamen tvoyey mechtï
Rassudka istinu prostuyu

Cast from the steel of experience	Iz stali opïta lituyu
Receive it and you will be exultant	Primi—i schastliv budesh' tï
The sweet deceit of religions	Religiy sladostnïy obman
No longer captivates me	Menya davno uzh ne plenyayet
And my reason is not obscured	I razum moy ne zatemnyayet
By their gently shimmering mist	Ikh nezhno-bleshchushchiy tuman
My mind, always free	Rassudok moy, vsegda svobodnïy
Assures me: I am alone!	Mne utverzhdayet: ya odin!
I am the ruler of the entire universe!	Ya vsey vselennoy vlastelin!
I am the indifferent god of	Ya nablyudeniya bog kholodnïy.
observation.	
My world is not a godly creation	Moy mir—ne bozhiye tvoreniye
My world is motion and dust	Moy mir—dvizheniye i prakh
I defeated the ludicrous fear	Pered Bogom nashikh izmïshleniy
Of the God of our invention!	Ya pobedil nelepïy strakh!
He is the contemplation of harmony	On—sozertsaniye garmonii
And of the all-unity of the world of	I vseyedinstva mira snov
dreams	
And the world is a splendid	A mir—roskoshnaya simfoniya
symphony	
Of his various voices	Yego razlichnïkh golosov
Earthly consonant truths	Zemnïye istinï sozvuchnïye
And heavenly truths	A s nimi istinï nebes
Combined in sonorous chords	Slilis' v akkordï polnozvuchnïye
Of wonders emanating from strings	Iz strun istorgnutïkh chudes
The coming moments	Emu gryadushchiye mgnoveniya
Bring a new order of consonance to	Nesut sozvuchiy novïy stroy
him	
He is engulfed in holy ecstasy	On ves'—svyatoye upoyeniye
By his divine playing	Svoyey bozhestvennoy igroy
And each dutiful string	I pod desnitseyu bozhestvennoy
Is under his divine right hand	Poslushna kazhdaya struna
A flaming wave performs	Na solntse-lire gimn torzhestvennïy
A solemn hymn on the sun lyre.	Igrayet plameni volna.
Ever tighter the lyre strings	Vsyo napryazhenney strunï lirnïye
Ever deeper the glance into the soul	Vsyo glubzhe smotrit v dushu vzor
Empty the ceremonial chalices	Do dna ispeyte chashi pirnïye
Sound, shine, starry chorus.	Zvuchi, svetisya, zvyozdnïy khor.
He repeats to those who do not	On povtoryayet nestradavshim: vam
suffer: be tormented!	mucheniye!
But to those who have suffered: come	A postradavshim: polyubite gorech'
to love the bitterness of toils	strad

In the depths of torment is the disavowal of desires
And in the disavowal is the light of untold joys!

There he is, setting forth, having incurred anger and vengeance
They persecute him and lead him to be tortured
He, however, is blissful, with a smile of forgiveness

I pray for you, brothers who have gone astray,
I bless you who abhor me,

I bless your terrible curses

Through them I am a participant in the celestial fire!

And you—come to know, o come to know the sweetness of torment!
Seek to love the suffering of the heart
To experience sorrow, to experience the thorns of separation;
And grasp the lifeline [Ariadne's thread]!

Unconsciously, you seek death,

And you love life only because
The reflections of death, glittering in [life's] moments,
Tempt you toward them [the reflections] through the darkness of life.

When you unwillingly appeal to death,
And delight becomes fiery pain

And she [death] reveals her face, then you, in your flight,
Will again be held back by fateful prophecy!

Venture, mortals, to drink up the phials

V glubinakh pïtok ot zhelaniy otrecheniye
I v otrechenii svet nevedomïkh otrad!

Vot on, nastaívaya, gnev navlek i mshcheniye
Yego presleduyut, vedut yego pïtat'

A on, blazhenstvuya, s ulïbkoyu proshcheniya

Za vas molyus' ya, zabludivshiyesya brat'ya,
Blagoslovlyayu nenavidyashchikh menya,

Blagoslovlyayu vashi strashnïye proklyatiya
Cherez nikh prichastnik ya nebesnogo ognya!

I vï poznayte, o poznayte sladost' muki!
Ishchete serdtsa vï stradaniye polyubit'
Izvedat' skorb', izvedat' terniye razluki;
I vï obryashchete spasitel'nuyu nit'!

Vï smerti ishchete, togo ne soznavaya,

I zhizn'-to lyubite vï tol'ko potomu,
Shto smerti otbleski, v mgnoveniyakh igraya,
K nim manyat vas cherez zhiznennuyu t'mu.

Kogda-zh nevol'no vï ko smerti vozzovyote,
I naslazhdeniye stanet bol'yu ognevoy
I yavit lik ona, to vï v svoyom polyote
Opyat' zaderzhanï boyan'yu rokovoy!

Derzayte, smertnïye, do dna ispit' fialï

Prepared for you by the father's
willing
Let the multicolored crystals of your
lives
Reflect the hidden face in full.

They marveled at him. But the
people, being disconcerted by him
(He disturbed their peace with his
teaching),
Killed him, and from the heights,
disembodied,
He observed the seeds of his teaching take root

Why does the barely blossomed
flower wilt so easily?!

Why is the enemy coming to destroy
Our newly built house?!

Why does reason remove
The light of truth from those
craving it?

In our best moments
We see the luster of splendid stones.
But how brief is the trance!
One flight, one splash!

We fall swiftly from the heights,
And again gloom. . . and again
decay. . .
And again we all wearily wait,
To be rid of the captivity of the
earth.

How can we possess you, cherished
one,
How can we capture you, o dream
Respond to us, o sweet-lighted one
Send the lifeline [Ariadne's thread]

As dank dungeons
The former cathedrals of wonders
entrapped us
And the light of the heavens only
Illuminates them with a pale glow

Vam ugotovannïye voleyu ottsa

Pust' zhizney vashikh mnogotsvetnïye kristallï
Otobrazyat lik sokrovennïy do
kontsa.

Emu divilis'. No narod im
vozmushchennïy
(Svoim ucheniyem on pokoy ikh
narushal)
Yego ubil, i s vïsotï,
razvoploshchennïy,
On vskhodï semeni ucheniya
nablyudal

Zachem tak legko uvyadayet
Edva raspustivshiysya tsvet?!

Zachem vrag idyot na pogrom
V nash tol'ko otstroyennïy dom?!

Rassudok zachem udalyayet
Ot zhazhdushchikh istinï svet?

Mï v nashi luchshiye mgnoveniya
Kamney roskoshnïkh vidim blesk.
No skol' nedlitel'no zabveniye!
Yedinïy vzlyot, yedinïy vsplesk!

S vïsot mï padayem stremitel'no,
I snova mrak . . . i snova tlen . . .

I snova zhdyom mï vse tomitel'no,
Kogda mï prakha sbrosim plen.

Kak ovladet' toboy, zavetnaya,

Kak, o mechta, tebya plenit'
Day nam otvet, o sladosvetnaya
Poshli spasitel'nuyu nit'

Ob'yali dushnïmi temnitsami
Nas khramï prezhniye chudes

I tol'ko blednïmi zarnitsami
Ikh ozaryayet svet nebes

How we wearied of separation	Kak istomilis' mï razlukoyu
How we suffered in bondage	Kak isstradalis' v uzakh mï
Hearts burn in ultimate torment	Serdtsa goryat posledney mukoyu
And in the desire to overthrow the kingdom of darkness.	I zhazhdoy svergnut' tsarstvo t'mï.
The very same path that, in its descent,	Vsyo tot-zhe put', shto v niskhozhdenii
Led you here to the dungeons	Syuda v temnitsï vas privyol
Will carry you to freedom	Vas povedyot k osvobozhdeniyu
When the valley has ceased to exist	Kogda izzhitïm stanet dol
And the same perpetual motion,	I to dvizheniye izvechnoye,
Which begat this world,	Shto porodilo etot mir,
Will destroy borders, and the finite	Razrushit grani, i konechnoye
Will dissolve delightfully in the ether.	Istayet sladostno v efir.
The dance will destroy all the abodes	Razrushit tanets vse obiteli
Of soulful torments, heartfelt dramas	Dushevnïkh muk, serdechnïkh dram
And you, guardians of the colored stones	I vï, kamney tsvetnïkh khraniteli
Create from them another cathedral.	Iz nikh inoy sozdayte khram.
So that in the blissful intoxication	Dabï v blazhennom op'yanenii
Of its immortal beauty	Yego bessmertnoy krasotoy
In the ultimate, sweet fulfillment	V poslednem, sladostnom sovershenii
You will seize your dream.	Vam ovladet' svoyey mechtoy.
Carry the precious stones	Nesite kamni dragotsennïye
From the fragrant depth,	Iz blagovonnoy glubinï,
The sacred moment has arrived	Prishlo mgnoveniye svyashchennoye
To mend fractured dreams!	Svyazat' razdroblyonnïye snï!
The delightful hour has struck	Probil sladostnïy chas
You awoke in us	Probudilsya tï v nas
We float up	Mï nesyomsya gore
Into the blazing dawn.	K vospïlavshey zare.
And it became clear to us	I prozrelosya nam
That in the motion is the cathedral	Shto v dvizhenii—khram
And that the sacrifice and priest	I shto zhervta i zhrets
Is our creating father	Nash tvoryashchiy otets
Who has decided to subjugate	Voz'igravshuyu plot'
Impassioned flesh.	Voskhotevshiy borot'.
The walls of the cathedral burn as hymns to freedom	Stenï khrama kak gimnï svobode goryat

And the dazzling row of columns sparkle.	I sverkayet stolpov oslepitel'nïy ryad.
Each stone, as a magical singing star,	Kazhdïy kamen' volshebno-poyushchey zvyozdoy
Fell from a burning string of the sun lyre.	So strunï solntse-lirnoy upal ognevoy.
It blissfully fell	On blazhenno upal
Like chiming crystal	Kak zvenyashchiy kristall
Like sparkling sound	Kak sverkayushchiy zvuk
Full of sweet torments	Polnïy sladostnïkh muk
And they glitter like topaz,	I blestyat kak topaz,
Hyasinth, chrysoprase	Giatsint, khrizopraz
Like carbuncle, opal,	Kak karbunkul, opal,
Crystal of sardonyx	Sardoniksa kristall
Like emerald, margarite	Kak smaragd, margarit
Chalcedony, chrysolite	Khalkedon, khrizolit
Like heavenly sapphire	Kak nebesnïy sapfir
Like the caressing world	Kak laskayushchiy mir
It burns, like a single multicolored diamond	On gorit, kak yedinïy vsetsvetnïy almaz
This cathedral—our life, our blooming, our ecstasy.	Etot khram—nasha zhizn', nash rastsvet, nash ekstaz.
On the sacrificial altar—burning hearts!	Na zhertvennik, goryashchiya serdtsa!
On the sacrificial altar—flowers of emotional experiences!	Na zhertvennik, tsvetï perezhivaniy!
Prepare to receive the father!	Gotov'tes' ko priyatiyu ottsa!
To meet the moment of your hopes	Ko vstreche miga vashikh upovaniy
I am descended from the heavens	Ya sletevshiy s nebes
The god of loving wonders.	Bog lyubviynïkh chudes.
Not to teach, but to caress	Ne uchit', a laskat'
The winged army of souls	Dush voskrïl'nuyu rat'
Having invited them to the feast	Ikh pozvavshiy na pir
I came to this world!	Ya prishol v etot mir!
In answer to each craving	Kazhdoy zhazhde v otvet
I offer blooming.	Prinoshu ya rastsvet.
Not the oppression of truth,	To ne istinï gnyot,
Freedom will come to you!	K vam svoboda gryadyot!
I am the all-reviving confirmation,	Ya utverzhdeniye vseozhivlyayushcheye,
I am the all-creating negation	Ya otritsaniye vsesozdayushcheye
Divide, bloom,	Razdelyaytes', rastsvetayte,
Soar to the heights,	Na vïsotï vozletayte,

Celebrate in sacred dance
In the beauty of the heirarchy
[angelic orders]
In unspeakable beauty
The victory over the primal state

The dance is the first order
And the righteous executor of
judgement
Will transform everything into a
united
And sparkling kingdom!

He who is brighter is closer to the
heart
The dimmer, that much lower
He who dares to look
Into the hidden, divine face
Then take wing, blessed one
For you the path is open!

I am the final achievement
I am the bliss of dissolution
I am the diamond of the galaxy

I am freedom, I am ecstasy!

Here he is, here, in the accelerated
beating of hearts
In our living dance the father comes
down to us

Here she is, the firmament in sweet
dissolution
In our living dance death comes to us

Judgment hour has struck
You awoke in us
We float up
Into the blazing dawn.

We are all in love
A current, directed
From an instant to eternity on the
path to infinity
From stony gloom to radiant
transparency
Since upon stone
In ardent creation

I pobedu nad stikhiey
V plyaske prazdnuyte
svyashchennoy
V krasote ierarkhii
V krasote neizrechennoy

Plyaska—pervaya prichina
I suda vershitel' pravïy

Vse sodelayet yedinoy

I sverkayushchey derzhavoy!

Kto svetleye, k serdtsu blizhe

Chem tuskleye, tem vse nizhe
Kto derzayet v sokrovennïy
Lik bozhestvennïy vzglyanut'
Tot vzletay, blagoslovennïy
Dlya togo otkrïtïy put'!

Ya posledneye soversheniye
Ya blazhenstvo rastvoreniya
Ya vsezvyozdnosti almaz

Ya svodoba, ya ekstaz!

Vot on, vot, v uchashchennom
biyenii serdets
V nashey plyaske zhivoy k nam
skhodyashchiy otets

Vot ona, v rastvorenii sladostnom
tverd'
V nashey plyaske zhivoy k nam
gryadushchaya smert'

Probil sudnïy chas
Probudilsya tï v nas
Mï nesyomsya gore
K vospïlavshey zare.

Vse mï—vlyublyonnïy
Tok, ustremlyonnïy
Ot miga k vechnosti v put' k
bezkonechnosti
Ot kamennoy mrachnosti k svetloy
prozrachnosti
Tak kak na kamennom
Tvorchestvom plamennïm

We engraved	Lik tvoy Bozhestvennïy
Your Divine face	Zapechatleli
We are carried away	Mï, uvlechennïye
By the vision of death	Smerti videniyem
We are calmed	Mï, ulegchennïye
In our motion	V nashem dvizhenii
Ignite, sacred temple from hearts'	Zazhgis', svyashchennïy khram ot
flame	plameni serdets
Ignite and become a sacred fire	Zazhgis' i stan' svyatïm pozharom
Merge blessedly in us, o ravishing	Smesis' blazhenno v nas, o
father,	sladostnïy otets,
Merge with death in a heated dance!	Smesis' so smert'yu v tantse
	yarom!
In this final moment of divestment	V etot poslednïy mig sovlecheniya
We will cast off the eternities of our	[Za]brosim mï vechnosti nashikh
instants	mgnoveniy
Into this final lyre-consonance	V etom poslednom [so]zvuchii
	lirnom
We will all dissolve in the ethereal	Vse mï rastayem v vikhre efirnom
whirlwind	
We will be born in the whirlwind!	Rodimsya v vikhre!
We will awaken in heaven!	Prosnyomsya v nebo!
We will merge emotions in a united	Smeshayem chuvstva v volne
wave!	yedinoy!
And in the splendid luster	I v bleske roskoshnom
Of the final flourish	Rastsveta poslednego
Appearing to each other	Yavlyayas' drug drugu
In the exposed beauty	V krase obnazhennoy
Of sparkling souls	Sverkayushchikh dush
We will disappear . . .	Ischeznem . . .
Dissolve . . .	Rastayem . . .

Index

Page references in italics refer to musical examples

Schopenhauer, Arthur, 8, 101, 176n2, 192; *The World as Will*, 187
Schumann, Robert, 111n81; *Dichter-liebe*, 85, 86, 87; settings of Goethe, 277
Scriabin, Alexander, 1, 42; belief in reincarnation, 204; compositional system of, 15–16; "death harmonies" of, 217, 219–20, 223; death of, 200, 237n41; depiction of Cosmos, 218–19; diaries of, 138, 208; illness of, 200, 237n39; improvisations of, 239n62; and Ivanov, 11, 42n20, 189–90, 200–201, 208, 236n22; on musical symbols, 15–16; "mystic" chord of, 217–19, 240n69; "mystic" Symbolism of, 10–12, 185, 308; and "mystic" Symbolists, 189, 234; octatonic music of, 218, 222, 230, 239n63, 240n71; operatic projects of, 235n6; orchestra of, 196–97; on poetry, 201; and Rachmaninoff, 24, 239n67; scientific influences on, 240n68; synaesthesia of, 11, 195, 208; theosophy of, 138, 185, 199, 203, 206, 215, 234n2, 301n18; as theurgist, 186, 194, 200; use of Bach, 228; use of Nietzsche, 187, 189, 207–8, 228, 238n49; use of Solovyov, 185, 187, 212, 236n26; view of consciousness, 187; Wagner's influence on, 15, 187, 231, 236n26; on World War I, 199. Works: Dances, 221; *Mysterium*, 11, 185; —, abandonment of, 15; —, chimes in, 221; —, as communal ritual, 194, 195–96, 231, 308; —, composer's role in, 195, 236n28; —, conception of, 186; —, Cosmos in, 138; —, indeterminacy of, 196; —, motifs of, 186; —, as "open" work, 215; —, performance of, 189, 195–96, 202; —, symbolism of, 190; —, text of, 186–87, 201–6; Piano Preludes, 201; *Poem of Ecstasy*, 169, 227; Poems, 221; Preludes: no. 1,

223, 224; —, no. 2, 225, 226; —, no. 3, 221, 222; *Preparatory Act*, 15; —, androgyny in, 208–9; —, Antichrist in, 211; —, as asymptotic process, 196, 201, 215; —, chimes in, 221, 223; —, as communal ritual, 214, 231, 308; —, composition of, 199, 215; —, Cosmos in, 220; —, *dramatis personae* of, 197; —, harmonies of, 229; —, libretto of, 205–6, 208; —, light and dark in, 209; —, Masculine/Feminine Principle in, 205, 206, 208, 209–11, 220, 223, 224, 231; —, Narrator of, 185, 206, 211, 212, 213; —, nature sounds in, 240n71; —, as "open" work, 229, 231; —, performance of, 197, 199; —, "polyphonic" process of, 229; —, protagonist of, 187; —, publication of, 238n48; —, as quasi-liturgical drama, 185, 187, 212; —, rhythms of, 230; —, self-quotations in, 221; —, silence in, 230, 231; —, Sister Death in, 206, 211, 225–27; —, sketches, 207, 214–31, 233, 239n60; —, staging of, 185; —, symbolism of, 206; —, temple of, 197, *198*; —, theosophy in, 206; —, three-voice fugato, 227, 227–28, 241n81; —, tonalities of, 219–20, 222–23; —, transcendence in, 230; —, twelve-note sonorities of, 219, 220, 229, 230; *Prometheus*, 11, 208, 217–19; Symphony No. 1, 11
Scriabine, Marina, 206, 214
Scriabin's Wreath (memorial society), 237n40, 238n48
Scribe, Eugéne: *La dame de pique*, 58–59, 60
"Scythian" composition, 258, 282
Séances, 184; Scriabin's, 229
Serapion, Saint: *Logos*, 126
Serebryakova, Lyubov, 134, 135
Shakhovskoy, Prince Alexander: *Chrysomania*, 58
Shkafer, Vasiliy, 125–26

Compositor: G & S Typesetters, Inc.
Text: Aldus
Display: Aldus
Printer and binder: Thomson-Shore